PIMLICO

494

GLOBALIZATION IN WORLD HISTORY

A.G. Hopkins, formerly the Smuts Professor of Commonwealth History at Cambridge University and now an Emeritus Fellow of Pembroke College, is currently the Walter Prescott Webb Professor of History at the University of Texas in Austin. He has published widely in the field of African and imperial history, beginning with a pioneering study, *An Economic History of West Africa* (1973), and continuing with two prize-winning volumes, written jointly with P.J. Cain, *British Imperialism: Innovation and Expansion, 1688–1914* (1993) and *British Imperialism, 1914–1990* (1993), which are now available in a second edition in one volume entitled *British Imperialism, 1688–2000* (2001).

GLOBALIZATION
IN WORLD HISTORY

Edited by

A.G. HOPKINS

PIMLICO

Published by Pimlico 2002

3 4 6 8 10 9 7 5 3 1

Selection copyright © A.G. Hopkins 2002
Individual essays copyright © each author 2002

First published in Great Britain by
Pimlico 2002

Pimlico
Random House, 20 Vauxhall Bridge Road,
London SW1V 2SA

Random House Australia (Pty) Limited
20 Alfred Street, Milsons Point, Sydney,
New South Wales 2061, Australia

Random House New Zealand Limited
18 Poland Road, Glenfield,
Auckland 10, New Zealand

Random House (Pty) Limited
Endulini, 5A Jubilee Road, Parktown 2193, South Africa

The Random House Group Limited Reg. No. 954009
www.randomhouse.co.uk

A CIP catalogue record for this book
is available from the British Library

ISBN 0–7126–7740–2

Papers used by Random House are natural,
recyclable products made from wood grown in sustainable forests;
the manufacturing processes conform to the environmental
regulations of the country of origin

Typeset by Deltatype Limited, Birkenhead, Merseyside
Printed and bound in Great Britain by
William Clowes Ltd, Beccles, Suffolk

Contents

Foreword

This path-breaking volume has its origins in the series of Millennium Lectures and one-day conferences organized by the Faculty of History at Cambridge University during the academic year 1999–2000. All were devoted to looking at major contemporary issues in long-term historical perspective. Such an approach is, of course, straightforward common sense. But this sort of common sense, as Mark Twain once remarked, is nowadays uncommon. Among the distinguishing (though not, of course, universal) vices of the late twentieth century were its short-termism and short attention span, as manifested, for example, in the increasing substitution of the sound-bite and the instant opinion for reasoned argument and considered judgement. No previous period in recorded history has been so persuaded of the irrelevance of the past experience of the human race. Because the strange new short-term world has no historical perspective, it has no sense of how bizarre it would have seemed to previous – and will seem to future – generations. In the long term its sheer absurdity will condemn it to oblivion. Sound-bite culture will go the way of Ninja Turtles, hoola hoops and other ephemeral nonsense. The dialectic of historical development will see to that. But, in the meantime, there is a price to pay for the Historical Attention Span Deficit Disorder (to use the correct medical term) which currently dominates the political, and even some of the intellectual, culture of our time.

Our understanding of globalization (a complex concept crudely reduced in sound-bite culture to the status of a slogan) has been distorted by lack of a rigorous historical perspective. There is nowadays a widespread illusion that globalization is simply a Western creation. That illusion will not survive a reading of this book. A further volume for publication in 2002, also based on the History Faculty's Millennium Lectures and conferences, will seek to challenge other ahistorical misconceptions of contemporary issues.

The lack of long-term historical perspective distorts our view of the future as well as our understanding of the present. Most historians are too conscious of the failings of past prophets to wish themselves to prophesy. A merciful Providence allows us, even with the advantage of long-term historical perspective, to foresee the future only as Saint Paul glimpsed heaven – 'through a glass, darkly'. Were it otherwise, we might lack the courage to confront all the trials which await us. But though the past record of the human race, like our own personal experience, gives us no off-the-peg solutions, it provides insights which we ignore at our peril. Without these insights we have little prospect of distinguishing short-term deviations from long-term trends. We cannot hope either to understand the twentieth century or to glimpse what awaits us in the twenty-first unless we view both in long-term historical perspective. As Sir Winston Churchill put it, 'The further backwards you look, the further forward you can see.'

Christopher Andrew
Professor of Modern and Contemporary History
Chair of the Faculty of History
University of Cambridge

Preface

The provenance of this volume is explained in the Foreword. It remains for me, as the editor, to express my appreciation of those who have helped to realize this particular product of Cambridge synergy. Colleagues in the Faculty of History, beginning with the Chair, Professor Christopher Andrew, have encouraged the venture from the outset and have helped in various ways to smooth the path to publication. We owe a considerable debt of gratitude to Emma Rothschild and the Centre for History and Economics at King's College, which provided generous financial, institutional and secretarial support for a workshop in May 2000 that enabled the contributors to come together to discuss preliminary drafts of the chapters in this volume. Emma herself contributed valuably to the proceedings; Amy Price took on additional administrative responsibilities with cheerful efficiency. The Centre's assistance also enabled us to invite four notable discussants, David Held, Charles Jones, Michael Kitson and David Washbrook, who gave willingly of their time and ideas. Additional hospitality was provided, most generously, by St Catharine's College. The contributors themselves have responded to an above average degree of editorial pressure and persuasion with fortitude and tolerance; the editorial team at Pimlico Press has been unfailingly supportive.

A.G. Hopkins
July 2001

A.G. HOPKINS

Introduction: Globalization – An Agenda for Historians

Globalization is the catch-word of the day. It emerged in the 1990s as the preferred term for encompassing the multiplicity of supra-national forces that have imprinted themselves on the contemporary world, and it seems likely to remain in use, and probably in over-use, in the foreseeable future. Examples of globalization – from the mountainous waves generated by sudden financial flows to the less tumultuous but no less striking spread of a universal popular culture – compete for attention and are reported in the media almost daily. The issues thrown up by these and associated developments have also begun to revive the ideological debate, which has been dormant for a decade, about the merits of capitalism. The advocates of globalization, who swept all before them after the fall of the Berlin Wall in 1989, have now to take note of an opposition that is beginning to stir. Free trade is challenged by fair trade.[1] Capitalist triumphalism is confronted by an emerging civic conscience that makes global claims of its own on behalf of the poor and oppressed. Trans-national corporations strive to attach consumers to the brand and the logo; popular demonstrations in Seattle (1999), Prague (2000), London (2000), Quebec (2001), and Genoa (2001) provide evidence of a growing concern with the adverse consequences of globalization and an allied disillusion with representative government.[2] The defending champion has advantages of weight, height and reach, but at least there is now the making of a contest. The workers of the world, whether or not they are thought to be born free and everywhere in chains, are again beginning to attract attention.

These developments present historians with an exceptional opportunity to enter what is currently the most important single debate in the social sciences: the analysis of the origins, nature and consequences of globalization. A large and illuminating literature on the economics, politics and sociology of the phenomenon now lies readily to hand. With few exceptions, however, historians have still to participate in the discussion or even to recognize the subject. The dominant tradition of writing history within national boundaries has contributed to this omission by limiting the number of historians who engage with supra-national issues. National (and regional) specialists leave global concerns to others, but the others are too few to be in a position to alter the direction of the subject.[3] Postmodernism has also helped to narrow the range of enquiry, though in different ways. Its scepticism of 'structural' history and the 'totalizing project' associated with it has not been supportive of spacious enquiries about the material world; its emphasis on the construction of texts and the images they convey has produced work that is strong on cultural issues in general and on representations in particular, but weak on the economic and political questions that stand at the centre of any discussion of globalization.

The main purpose of this book is to suggest that it is time to reorder these priorities by giving the study of globalization a prominent place on the agenda of historical research. The possibilities are as large as the concept itself and cannot be explored fully in a single volume. Nevertheless, the present study, the first on the subject to be written entirely by historians, aims at being sufficiently comprehensive to mark the arrival of globalization as a theme deserving serious historical analysis. The detailed contributions that follow provide abundant evidence of the historical diversity of globalizing forces and the unevenness of the process of globalization. But they also draw out two general themes that bring coherence to the book as a whole: one emphasizes the non-Western dimensions of globalization; the other explores its historical forms and sequences.

In seeking to decentre the analysis, the studies that follow run counter to the dominant assumption of the existing literature, which holds that globalization is the product of the West and, in its current form, of the United States in particular. Of course, the Western world features prominently in the story and is well represented in nearly every essay – and exclusively so in the contribution by David Reynolds on the United States. But the aim throughout the book has been to prevent the history of globalization from becoming simply the story of the rise of the West – and the fall of the rest – under another name. Consequently, the essays underline the antiquity and importance of non-Western forms of globalization and demonstrate that encounters with the West produced a world order that was jointly, if also unequally, created. This approach is especially evident in the chapters by Amira Bennison on Islam and Hans van de Ven on China, but is given prominence by nearly all the other contributors too. By re-mapping the geography of the subject, we hope to point the way towards a truly global history of globalization. In doing so, we also aim to provide a means of drawing separate regional specialists into a much wider historical debate – without at the same time committing them to a particular view of the causes or consequences of globalization.

The question of whether globalization is a product of the contemporary world or has origins that stretch into the distant past is fully recognized by the current literature, even though it has been put by social scientists other than.

historians. Part of the answer depends on the definition of terms, which can trap or misdirect unwary newcomers, and part relies on the use of historical evidence, which is the obvious point for historians to enter the debate. The concept and its uses are introduced in my first essay in this volume, which shows how different definitions of globalization fit different assessments of its causes and consequences, and constructs a guide to the still fragmentary historiography of the subject. It will be apparent from this survey that the existing literature rests on a number of very generalized statements about the past. If these are amplified and repeated, future studies will present the history of globalization as a linear trajectory that will amount to little more than the 'stages of growth' revisited and renamed.[4]

The essays that follow anticipate this danger and try to avert it by showing that, historically, globalization has taken different forms, which we have categorized as archaic, proto, modern, and post-colonial.[5] Since no serious attempt has yet been made to consider whether various types or sequences of globalization can be derived from the detailed historical evidence, these categories must be regarded as being first rather than last thoughts on the subject, and accordingly are put forward to stimulate debate. The main purpose of this essay is to introduce the four categories and relate them to the essays that follow.[6] If subsequent discussion leads to an improved and more refined understanding of globalization in world history, the tentative taxonomy offered here will have served its purpose.

For purposes of exposition, each category will be dealt with separately and in turn. It is important to emphasize, however, that they are best viewed as a series of overlapping and interacting sequences rather than as a succession of neat stages. Typically, one form co-existed with another or others which it may have nurtured, absorbed, or simply complemented. The relationship, whether symbiotic or competitive, does not therefore foreclose on the future. There are interactions and tendencies but there is no inexorable dialectic. Proto-globalization contained elements that were realized by its modern successor, but could itself be steadily stunted or aborted. Today, as in the past, globalization remains an incomplete process: it promotes fragmentation as well as uniformity; it may recede as well as advance; its geographical scope may exhibit a strong regional bias; its future direction and speed cannot be predicted with confidence – and certainly not by presuming that it has an 'inner logic' of its own.

The first of our categories, archaic globalization, refers to a form that was present before industrialization and the nation state made their appearance, and thus covers a very broad swathe of history. The concept and its exemplars are explored in C.A. Bayly's essay, are taken up in Amira Bennison's analysis of Islam, and resurface in John Lonsdale's treatment of Africa. They are given prominence, too, by Hans van de Ven and Tim Harper, whose complementary studies of China and Southeast Asia both emphasize the role of the Chinese diaspora in promoting a form of globalization that was wholly non-Western in origin.

Before the modern era, as C.A. Bayly shows, globalizing networks were created by great kings and warriors searching for wealth and honour in fabulous lands, by religious wanderers and pilgrims seeking traces of God in distant realms, and by merchant princes and venturers pursuing profit amidst risk across borders and continents. At a more mundane level, consumers prized exotic medicinal herbs and precious goods and tokens that they hoped would bring them health and fortune. All this powered archaic globalization. It was sea-borne as well as land-based; and it was promoted particularly by the great pre-modern empires – from Byzantium and Tang to the renewed expansionism of the Islamic and Christian powers after 1500. This was a world in which territorial-state systems were far more fluid than they were to become. The strongest affiliations were both universal and local; the junction between them was found most notably in the development of cities; connections between far-flung cities were made by mobile diasporic networks and migrants of all kinds. The limits to the effective authority of the state, combined with the powerful presence of universal belief systems, notably Hinduism, Buddhism, Islam and Christianity, encouraged the movement of ideas, and with them people and goods, across regions and continents. These developments fostered, in turn, a global division of labour, spanning lower manual and upper distributive occupations, that was superimposed on the local economies with which it was intermittently connected. The strategy of expansion was to co-ordinate rather than to assimilate; distinctive origins were retained not homogenized. Before mass production imposed standardization, difference was an important precondition of trade. This feature is apparent in Bayly's description of Java in the eighteenth century; it emerges even more strongly from Amira Bennison's account of the world of Islam (*dār al-islām*), where the universal Muslim community (*umma*) and Arabic – the lingua franca – provided a common framework for forms of interaction that flourished on diversity.

Archaic globalization thus exhibited some strikingly 'modern' features. The importance of cities, the key part played by migrants and diasporas, and the specialization of labour all point towards themes that figure prominently in the discussion of contemporary globalization, while the presence of systems of belief that made universal claims and extended across continents provides a direct link with the aspirations of the present, when prospects for creating a global civil society are again being canvassed. At the same time, the archaic form of globalization was a circumscribed one. The technical and institutional limits that both restrained the power of the state and permitted mobility beyond its borders also placed checks on the spread of cosmopolitan influences. Archaic globalization did not extend to the Americas or Australasia. Within its spatial compass, ideas percolated down the social scale more easily than goods, which could be traded over long distances only if they had a high value-to-weight ratio. The size of the market, as Adam Smith was famously to observe, was limited by the extent of the division of labour and was in turn limited by it.

We use the term proto-globalization to refer two interacting political and economic developments that became especially prominent between about 1600 and 1800 in Europe, Asia and parts of Africa: the reconfiguration of state systems, and the growth of finance, services and pre-industrial manufacturing. The political and the economic came together most visibly in complementary but ultimately competing systems of military fiscalism. Uneven though the process was, a number of states – Muslim as well as Christian – strengthened the links between territory, taxation and sovereignty during this period, though they had still to claim, or at least to make effective, a monopoly of the loyalties of their subjects. Although Bennison has space only to touch on the proto-globalization generated within the world of Islam, she demonstrates, nevertheless, that periodic renewals (*tajdīds*) ensured that Islam remained innovative and dynamic, while her summary of state-building and commercial expansion suggests parallels with developments in Europe. The African element in this story, as John Lonsdale shows, extended south of the Sahara and beyond the reach even of Islam. Hans van de Ven hints at similar trends in China during the Ming and Qing periods. He, too, stresses the importance of indigenous sources of change, and emphasizes (with Bayly) the role of consumption in preserving and enlarging difference and hence trade in pre-industrial manufactures. These contributions make it clear that the 'rise of the West' was complemented by developments in other parts of the world. The fact that these have yet to receive appropriate recognition points enticingly to prospects for future comparative work in the field of global history.

As for the West itself, Tony Ballantyne describes how Europe, headed by Britain, extended its connections with the wider world in the second half of the eighteenth century. The 1760s were a 'globalizing decade' that not only witnessed the start of renewed commercial expansion and a fresh wave of imperial acquisitions, but also inaugurated a knowledge revolution that mapped, surveyed and classified the world of contact and conquest. Ballantyne's welcome emphasis on the cultural history of globalization is complemented by Richard Drayton's reaffirmation of the importance of the material world and of labour in particular. Improved efficiency in the transactions sector generated flows of goods, bullion and labour that were far more extensive than those achieved under any previous form of globalization. Sugar, tobacco, tea, coffee and opium entered circuits of exchange that created a complex pattern of multilateral trade across the world and encouraged a degree of convergence among consumers who otherwise inhabited different cultural spheres: coffee-drinking, for example, spread to parts of the Muslim world, as well as to Europe, in the seventeenth century. These trends were underpinned by the improved economic management of sea-borne commerce, which expanded the connections between West and East, and made possible the 'green revolution' in the Americas based on the plantation system and on large exports of slave labour from Africa.

In structure, scale and geographical reach, proto-globalization was a departure from its archaic precursor. But it had limits that caused it to fall short of the requirements of its modern successor. Our third category, modern globalization, is defined, conventionally, by the appearance of two key elements after about 1800: the rise of the nation state and the spread of industrialization. The sovereign state based on territorial boundaries was filled in by developing a wider and deeper sense of national consciousness and filled out, variously, by population growth, free trade, imperialism and war. In the course of the nineteenth century, as Tony Ballantyne demonstrates, the cosmopolitanism that was such a marked feature of archaic and proto-globalization was corralled, domesticated and harnessed to new national interests. Political management made growing use of national identity to secure internal cohesion and control with the result that differences between states became sharper. Political developments fitted new economic needs based on industrialization. The labour force gradually shifted from farms to towns, occupational specialization increased, wage-labour became the norm, the link between owning and managing capital was weakened and eventually severed.

These developments brought global influences into the more confined sphere of international relocations. Overseas expansion nationalized the new internationalism by exporting national constitutions and religions and by extending national economies to distant parts of the world. Reciprocally, these exports played an important part in consolidating the nation states that promoted them, as I show in my second essay, which deals with The Netherlands and Britain, and as Reynolds demonstrates in the case of the United States. The new international order was created partly by persuasion and partly by command: free trade delivered one; empire the other. New states, independent and colonial, sprang up in the nineteenth and twentieth centuries. Land was everywhere converted to property; property became the foundation of sovereignty. Sovereignty in turn defined the basis of security both by determining the extent of the monopoly of coercive power and the reach of tax-gatherers, and by guaranteeing international credit, which was essential to the new global division of labour. As the nineteenth century advanced, regions producing raw materials were integrated with the manufacturing centres of Europe, and international trade, finance, and migration experienced an unprecedented, if also irregular, expansion.

The imperial expression of modern globalization gave rise to two main strategies of control: assimilation and association. My second essay shows how Greater Britons settling in Canada tried to eliminate difference by applying assimilationist policies to the First Nations who fell under their sway, while on the other side of the world the Dutch, having tamed Bali's rajahs, then consolidated tradition to produce indirect rule by association. John Lonsdale's complementary analysis of colonial Africa adds the important point that traditions and tribes were imagined from below as well as invented from above, and demonstrates that colonial subjects continued to pursue their own goals while also making unavoidable adjustments to alien rule. The continuities were striking everywhere because the European empires were built on the archaic foundations and proto-globalizing tendencies of the societies they subordinated. As Tim Harper argues with respect to the diasporas of Southeast Asia, the structure and evolution of colonialism itself were heavily influenced by the resilience and continuing dynamism of indigenous institutions. Hans van de Ven makes the same observation about China, which was influenced but not ruled by foreign powers. Moreover, Chinese investors and merchants continued to play a vital part in trade with the West, in promoting a renewed form of regional globalization in the South Seas, and in the sub-globalization launched by Japan in the second half of the nineteenth century.

The agents of modern globalization greatly extended their reach, but they never completed their control, even in the colonial world. The imprint of the universal empires endured, even where their political authority had been dismantled. The concept of a global Muslim community remained unbounded by geography, as it does today. Indeed, one profound reaction to the encroachment of the West, as Amira Bennison and John Lonsdale note, was the renewal of supra-national loyalties expressed in the movements for Pan-Islamic and Pan-African unity that so alarmed the European colonial powers.[7] A second reaction, which Tim Harper and Hans van de Ven comment on too, saw the rise of various 'self-strengthening' movements that sought to turn Western knowledge to local advantage. Long before the end of empire, the subject peoples were adapting the language and ideals as well as the institutions and technology that accompanied the imperial mission. In this way, the extension of nationalism that reached the rest of the world as imperial rule or imperial influence was itself domesticated, thus helping to bring one phase of globalization to an end and pointing the way, albeit uncertainly, to another.[8]

We use the term post-colonial globalization to refer to the contemporary form that can be dated, approximately, from the 1950s. There are other possibilities. But the term 'postmodern' suggests misleading connections, and 'post-imperial' would imply that all types of imperialism, in addition to formal empires, have been eliminated – a claim that offers too many hostages to fortune. By the mid twentieth century, the modern and modernizing empires that had taken over or taken apart their archaic predecessors had themselves fallen. New types of supra-territorial organization and new forms of regional integration had begun to make their appearance. By the close of the century, the nation state had ceased to be the unquestioned vehicle of progress and in some cases had begun to unravel – at times spectacularly. Ex-colonial states were under pressure to make concessions to ethnic and provincial claimants; internal disorder was common, even where formal boundaries remained in place. The world economy had experienced a profound realignment: the exchange of manufactures for raw materials that had underpinned the modern phase of globalization was replaced by a pattern of integration based on inter-industry trade. The geographical ties established in the nineteenth century became relatively less important; links between advanced economies, notably the triad of United States, Europe and Japan, became stronger. The new economy gave increasing prominence to trans-national corporations in general, and to finance, and commercial and information services in particular. As the century drew to a close, there were clear signs that the world economy produced by nation states was again becoming global rather than, in the literal sense, international.

These developments, as is well known, bear the strong imprint of the United States. The concise overview of the 'American century' provided by David Reynolds first traces the pre-history of globalization within the United States, and then explains why the process has achieved such unprecedented reach and depth. Running through his essay is the paradox that the latest and most extensive form of globalization is to a large extent the product of one country – albeit a superpower. This theme connects directly with the lively debate in the current social science literature on whether globalization strengthens or weakens the nation state. The essays dealing with the non-Western world, where typically the nation state is a less formidable force (and is sometimes no more than a quasi-state), place greater emphasis on infranational and supra-national influences that can be traced back to earlier forms of globalization. John Lonsdale's revisionist assessment of tribalism in Africa first sets it in a comparative context and then shows that it can provide the basis of democratic, multi-cultural politics and a means of negotiating globalization. The separate studies by Amira Bennison, Tim Harper and Hans van de Ven all stress the continuing importance of indigenous globalizing forces, whether manifested in the dynamism of the Chinese diaspora, the revival of Buddhism (now assisted by the Internet), or the debate about reconciling the *dār-al-islām* with modern, imported institutions. My second essay looks at the local consequences of globalization, contrasting the success of the Balinese in promoting tourism – one of the principal industries of post-colonial globalization – with the desperate plight of the Innu, who have very nearly been destroyed by other, less benign globalizing forces.

The shape of the world order is more than usually in transition. The boundaries of the 'global village' are fluid; its inhabitants are highly mobile. Each street has its own problems, but each problem impinges increasingly on the population as a whole. The 'tyranny of distance' has been overcome; isolation has been eliminated. Once obscure events now receive intense scrutiny from the international media; local knowledge has become universal information.[9] With the appearance of globalization as a major subject of debate, historians can again join their expertise to the discussion of contemporary issues. The classic subjects of historical research invite renewed attention: political structures are everywhere in doubt; poverty endures. New themes can be added to emphasize the long-standing importance of the supranational, borderless world, where frontiers are mapped by systems of belief, circuits of trade, financial flows, zones of famine and disease, and patterns of migration, and to underline the antiquity and continuing relevance of infranational forces, such as ethnicity.

Neither history nor ideology has come to an end. The advocates of capitalism and free trade see globalization as a positive, progressive force generating employment and ultimately raising living standards throughout the world. The critics see it as a means of expropriating the resources of poor countries by drawing them into debt, encouraging the use of sweated labour, and accelerating environmental degradation. The protagonists will turn increasingly to history for support. The obligation now falls on historians to ensure that the history cited is based on evidence rather than on honorary facts, and to consider how they can apply arguments about the present to improve our understanding of the past.

Notes and References

1 Some varied examples include Diane Coyle (ed.), 'Globalization: A Report to Accompany the New White Paper on Eliminating World Poverty', in the *Independent*, 12 December 2000, Naomi Klein, *No Logo: Taking on the Brand Bullies* (London, 2000), and Noreena Hertz, *The Silent Takeover: Global Capitalism and the Death of Democracy* (London, 2001). The last two are significant for the popularity of their polemic rather than for the strength or novelty of their analyses. A recent academic discussion, focusing on the protectionist implications of fair trade, is Jagdish Bhagwati, 'After Seattle', *International Affairs*, 77 (2002), pp. 15–29.

2 In some quarters government is held to have become, once more, the tool of big business. See Mark Seddon (the editor of *Tribune*) in the *Independent*, 23 April 2001. Elsewhere, it is seen to have failed the national interest by opening the door to globalizing forces. This was evident in the protests in Paris in December 2000. See the *Independent*, 8 December 2000.

3 The paradox that, as globalization proceeds, the study of history remains confined largely within national boundaries is discussed in A.G. Hopkins, 'Back to the Future: From National History to Imperial History', *Past and Present*, 164 (1999), pp. 198–243.

4 Frederick Cooper, 'What is the Concept of Globalization Good For? An African Historian's Perspective', *African Affairs*, 100 (2001), pp. 189–213. We agree with Cooper's view that current studies of the history of globalization have a strong teleological bias that reads the present back into the past. Our purpose here is precisely to counter this tendency by encouraging historians to produce superior accounts of previous (and in some cases still continuing) forms of globalization.

5 I am most grateful to my colleague, C.A. Bayly, for contributing ideas on this issue so freely.

6 Readers are reminded that other themes, touched on earlier, are expanded in my first essay in this volume, 'The History of Globalization – and the Globalization of History?'

7 These are just two of many examples. Others, noted in the essays that follow, are Pan-Turanism, Pan-Arabism and Pan-Buddhism.

8 The theme is developed further in the 'Afterword' to P.J. Cain and A.G. Hopkins, *British Imperialism, 1688–2000* (London, 2001).

9 The attempted suicide of Innu children, discussed in my second essay in this volume, is just one of many striking examples.

A.G. HOPKINS

The History of Globalization – and the Globalization of History?

Early in January 2000, Bruce Beach admitted that he had made a mistake in burying forty-two dilapidated school buses north of Toronto to serve as shelters from Armageddon. His enterprise was impressive but misplaced: his forecast that the Y2K bug would cause widespread power failures followed by riots in cities throughout the United States turned out to be wrong. Next time, however, he would definitely be proved correct. 'Watch out,' he advised reporters, for the moment when 'the trans-Siberian pipeline fails and fuel shortages cause civil war in Russia.'[1]

Mr Beach's failed prophecy, coupled with his continuing hope for doom to come, qualify him to be added to the long list of those who, over the centuries, have prepared for an apocalypse that has yet to occur.[2] In an age of 'high-tech' and material achievement, it is salutary to be reminded that the black arts of the pseudo-sciences are still widely practised:[3] the quixotic battle against the non-existent millennium bug cost approximately $400 billion – a figure so enormous that it can be comprehended only after it has been converted into material equivalents of staggering proportions.[4] From a historical perspective, however, what is so arresting about Mr Beach's eccentricity is that it was derived from the fear that new technology, invented to master the world, would be the cause of its undoing.[5] It was a fear that was widely shared.[6] By the 1990s ideas and anxieties could be transmitted across borders and continents to an extent that was unprecedented because new information systems based on computers had cut the cost and increased the speed of communications.[7] National frontiers could be spanned without physical movement; space could be discounted to the point where, it seemed, geography was about to be abolished. The novelty of Mr Beach's anxiety was that it was a reaction to forces that we have come to refer to as globalization.

Globalization and 'Universal History'

Although globalization is a relatively new term,[8] it has already been designated as the key concept of the 1990s, 'by which we understand the transition of human society into the third millennium';[9] 'an idea', in short, 'whose time has come'.[10] The idea itself has undoubtedly arrived in the form of rapidly expanding libraries of books on the subject, even if the claims it has inspired are, inevitably, much disputed. Guides to what is already a huge literature have now been called into being to rescue stranded students;[11] the sentinels needed to watch over the extensive and changing frontiers of the subject are on permanent alert.[12] Amidst much controversy, contributors to the literature are united in agreeing on the importance of understanding the historical dimensions of globalization. The central question of whether or not globalization is a new phenomenon, and therefore merits its distinctive name, cannot be answered without investigating its historical roots and making judgements about turning points in the past. However, while assessments of this kind abound, they have so far been made almost exclusively by social scientists other than historians.[13] The resulting analysis is often illuminating, but has yet to engage with the historical literature in any depth or detail. Consequently, there is now a sizeable opportunity for historians to make a systematic and effective contribution to this wide-ranging and highly topical debate. The main purpose of this book is to ensure that this happens.

There is, of course, a long tradition of grand historical enquiry stretching from the meta-history of Ibn Khaldun to the mega-history of Arnold Toynbee – and beyond. In the case of the Western world, the impulse to produce a universal history gained distinction and influence in the eighteenth century, when the *philosophes* promoted a new, cosmopolitan ideology.[14] This development, and its broader links to the Enlightenment, though well known to historians of political thought, deserve wider appraisal in the light of the current discussion of globalization. When Voltaire surveyed the history and customs of the world in his *Essai sur l'histoire générale et sur les moeurs et l'esprit des nations* (1756), he began, deliberately, not in Europe but in China.[15] In 1774, Herder asked a set of rhetorical questions that can scarcely be distinguished from those discussed so frequently today: 'When has the entire earth ever been so closely joined together, by so few threads? Who has ever had more power and more machines, such that with a single impulse, with a single movement of a finger, entire nations are shaken?'[16] Shortly afterwards, Kant's *Ideas for a Universal History with a Cosmopolitan Intent* (1784), though devoid of empirical content, developed the idea that moral imperatives allied to reason were universally applicable and could therefore be harnessed to progressive purposes.[17] His lucid, and until recently long-neglected, sequel, *Perpetual Peace* (1795), advanced a speculative plan for spreading a cosmopolitan liberal order that would underpin a state of permanent peace.

The universalism of the eighteenth century marked the emergence, in a recognizably modern form, of the concept of what today would be called a global civil society. It echoes, too, in the current debate over the convergence thesis, which holds that, with the end of the Cold War, there is now only one truly global ideology. At the same time, cosmopolitan aspirations promoted an interest in types of regionalism that fell short of embracing the world but were nevertheless larger than individual states. It was in the late eighteenth century that the idea of European unity, based on what Gibbon called a 'great republic', was refashioned to reflect the increasing emphasis placed on the benign effects of commerce and on the potential for extending the boundaries of a civil society beyond the confines of a single regnum to others that might be drawn together on the basis of shared interests and values.[18] Although the cosmopolitan ideal made its way into and through the nineteenth century, it had to be reformulated *en route* to take account of technological innovation and industrialization. It re-emerged in the shape of complementary and competing programmes of internationalism. Missionaries and humanitarians used the notion to fashion concepts of a civilizing mission; Saint-Simonians envisaged an international order managed by technocrats for the common good. Cobden made practical politics out of the conviction that free trade would bring economic development and universal peace;[19] Marx based his alternative socialist programme on cosmopolitan principles.[20] Both assumed that progress, or improvement, as the Victorians called it, was a universal right that could be realized.

Nevertheless, the cosmopolitan ideal lost ground to the nation state in the nineteenth century and for the greater part of the twentieth century too, and was to a large degree captured by it. This development was reflected in intellectual trends that are exemplified, appropriately and weightily, in the way in which the study of history itself became a professional discipline. Leopold von Ranke founded historical research on the systematic use of documentary evidence, on reconstructing the past 'as it was', and on the ideal of objectivity. These were universal precepts. In practice, however, they were applied almost exclusively to the history of states and nation states in Europe, notably those that were being either formed or refurbished in the second half of the nineteenth century. Virtually all of Ranke's own work, including his *Universal History*, published in nine volumes between 1881 and 1888, was devoted to these themes.[21] Similarly, the *Histoire générale*, edited by Ernest Lavisse and Alfred Rambaud, and published between 1892 and 1901, allotted only about ten per cent of the text to the non-Western world, despite appearing in twelve capacious volumes.[22] The tradition of writing national histories was further entrenched in the twentieth century through the development of national curricula in schools and the production of prestigious series, typically described as being 'monumental' and 'authoritative', that told the 'national story' in an insular style and often in a justificatory manner. This approach was adopted enthusiastically by the new states that came into being following the upheavals brought about by two world wars and decolonization. New flags required new histories.

The paradox that national histories should proliferate at a time when international connections of all kinds were expanding has never been fully reconciled and has often been pushed to one side by the weight of convention that continues to endorse the paramountcy of the national tradition.[23] Where international themes are recognized, they are often treated as spare parts that have to be bolted on to the national story. Where they play a larger role, it is typically as extensions of the national story abroad principally through war, exploration and empire. In these ways historians of the nation state have played their part both in nationalizing internationalism, by treating the wider world as an extension of narrower national interests, and in internationalizing nationalism by exporting the blueprint of the nation state and its attendant historiography to newly independent countries in outer Europe and the non-Western world.

Events in the second half of the twentieth century have inspired renewed efforts to design a form of history that is capable of overcoming these limitations. The foundation of the United Nations, the onset of the Cold War, the post-war reconstruction of Japan, the upheaval caused by decolonization, the subsequent recognition of a non-Western entity called the Third World, and, most recently, the growing participation of China in international affairs, have captured the interest of increasing numbers of historians and generated a remarkable new historiography. Yet the huge difficulty of devising ways of writing a 'universal history' that can both encompass and span nation states has yet to be overcome. The rise of what is known, generically, as Area Studies, has been highly successful in giving prominence to large and previously largely neglected parts of the world, but it has also adopted the approved Western format of writing the history of the nation state. The admirably ambitious movement dedicated to promoting world history has run into formidable obstacles.[24] Everyone approves of the aim; few have been able to make it operational. Attempts to give the endeavour coherence can easily become proxies, witting or unwitting, for a story that is already well known: the rise of the West – with or without the fall of the rest.[25] Alternatively, practitioners find that substantial material, when stretched, tears into fragments that can cover a region or even a continent but not the whole world. Recognition of these problems has led to the appearance of a small reform group writing under the banner of global history and exploring thematic and comparative approaches to the subject. This line of enquiry appears to be the most promising way forward, but it has yet to make much impression on the profession at large and it has still to address the issue of globalization.[26]

The argument put here is not that the study of globalization will produce a miraculous cure for these disabilities. New terms can readily promote spurious originality by disguising old problems: snake oil is rebranded for each new, unwary generation. However, it will be claimed that globalization is a theme that provides a powerful means of moving the study of world history forward. It offers historians two substantial opportunities. The first provides them with a chance to employ their knowledge of the past to comment on the claims made for and against the novelty of globalization. The second invites them to use current preoccupations with the changing shape of the world order to frame new questions about history. Whatever view is eventually taken of the outcome of these investigations, of the merits of globalization, or even of its existence, the research possibilities are so considerable that it is surprising that historians have been slow to recognize them. If it is true, as has been argued,[27] that there has been a tendency to marginalize some of the central questions of historical research in recent years in favour of studying representations of cultural forms, then globalization is a theme that offers the prospect of redressing the balance because it places economic development and the role of the state at the centre of the analysis. Moreover, the discussion of globalization has been concerned as much with realities as with representations, and much more with generalizing about structures and long-run historical developments than with deconstructing texts. Current formulations of the subject therefore offer methodological approval for styles of history that have been regarded with considerable scepticism in some quarters in recent years.[28]

At the same time, most commentators acknowledge the importance of cultural expressions of globalization, whether they appear in the debate over the emergence of a 'global civil society'[29] or at a popular level with reference to what has been called 'Coca-colonization'.[30] At present, however, cultural (and, even more so, environmental) features of globalization tend to be tacked on to more extensive discussions of other issues.[31] This order of priorities arises less from a conscious bias than from the fact that most of the literature on globalization has been produced by specialists whose interests lie in economic development and in the politics of international relations, and is rooted, accordingly, in established concerns with the role of markets, the nature of states, and the function of governments. The result is an element of unevenness in the treatment of the subject that offers a chance for newcomers, including historians, who wish to look at globalization from a different angle, and in particular to pursue interests in cultural history that have helped to advance the frontier of historiography in recent years. In short, globalization is a theme that promises to resurrect some old lines of historical enquiry, to open up new ones, and to stimulate revisions to established interpretations. Each of these prospects is inviting: put together, they ought to guarantee the keen attention of the next generation of historians.

Terminology, Trappings and Traps

To begin with, the term itself requires some consideration.[32] Since globalization is a portmanteau concept employed by several disciplines, and the phenomena it describes are in a state of continuous evolution, it is not surprising to find that different authors have used it in different ways. Some writers have even disowned the term on the ground that it is too vague to be meaningful;[33] others, seemingly proving the point, have used it to refer very generally to cross-border exchanges;[34] the majority, in between, have struggled to provide concrete definitions that fit their particular needs.[35] Historians who recall the frustration expressed by Hancock over the use and abuse of the word imperialism will be familiar with the dilemma, but aware of its resolution too.[36] Large, holistic concepts can indeed be the source of confusion, especially since they invariably carry conflicting ideological messages. Abolishing them, however, even if it were possible, would not remove the difficulty. No one has yet devised a means of avoiding the use of general terms to describe broad issues. The only useful recommendation is that definitions ought to be explicitly stated and framed to match the purpose in hand. This strategy cannot resolve an insoluble problem, but it does have the merits of aligning conclusions with their starting points and of alerting others to the scope and limits of the chosen terminology.

The importance of taking this preliminary step can be seen in debates that have already become entrenched in the social-science literature. Judgements about the novelty of the phenomenon, for example, depend heavily on how the terms of the discussion are drawn: a very general definition allows globalization to be traced beyond the mists of time;[37] a very narrow one ensures that novelty rather than continuity catches the eye. The literature on globalization, like that on imperialism, also shows how easy it is to slip into the error of redescribing what is already known, while supposing that what is being said is new.[38] Unless sufficient thought is given to the language used, whatever case is being argued, historians entering the discussion of globalization may find themselves tempted into adopting a new set of terms to portray developments that are not only familiar but also described in words that are already available and are entirely adequate for the purpose – apart from lacking the frisson that accompanies novelty.

Virtually all accounts of globalization recognize its quantitative significance and multi-dimensional character. It is widely agreed to be a process that transforms economic, political, social and cultural relationships across countries, regions and continents by spreading them more broadly, making them more intense and increasing their velocity.[39] This definition is uncontroversial not least because it includes all the familiar components of globalization – ranging from the role of trans-national corporations to the emergence of a global civil society and the universal dissemination of popular culture, and covering in between a host of other issues, such as the environment and migration. Globalization is also generally regarded as being a process that stems from both national and international roots, though there is considerable discussion of where the emphasis should be placed.[40] This position suggests the possibility of drawing a distinction between international relations, which are the product of ties between nation states, and globalizing processes that are neither explained nor contained by these relations but instead transcend them. Unsurprisingly, the line between the two is not easily drawn, and the distinction itself is much disputed.[41] One prominent argument holds that globalization has eroded the importance of territorial boundaries, which have long been considered to be a fundamental component of national sovereignty and consequently of international relations too.[42] The counter-claim, argued with equal vigour, is that globalization is the product of nation states and can maintain its momentum only if the nation state remains strong.[43]

A second aspect of globalization, regarded by some commentators as being an essential part of the definition, deals with the qualitative changes it is said to represent. Acceptance of this element raises the stakes: the definition becomes tighter and the term can be demarcated more readily from preceding forms of international exchange, but the test is more demanding. It is necessary to show, not just that existing cross-border movements have become markedly more important, but also that they differ in kind from those that went before. On this view, the Internet is not just a faster telegraph, and Microsoft is not simply the most recent example of a long line of transnational corporations that can be traced back to the East India Company. In practice, and in recognition of the difficulty of applying this test to every important constituent of globalization, those who emphasize the qualitative novelty of globalization have been obliged to be selective and to underline the special significance of the specific developments they have identified. One argument, from economics, uses the test of price convergence;[44] another, from sociology, emphasizes institutional innovation at the supra-national level.[45]

Identifying the quantitative and qualitative dimensions of globalization, and exploring the links between them,[46] is a starting point that should appeal to historians who are properly sceptical of definitions that commit them to a particular bias, whether economic, political, social or cultural. In moving beyond this position, however, historians should now be alive to the dangers of using the term without also being aware that different claims about its longevity, novelty and significance are frequently founded on variations in the way it is defined. These issues cannot easily be resolved, and it would be unwise for historians to attempt to pronounce upon them with any confidence at a moment when they have scarcely entered the debate. But they can avoid misjudgements based upon an unreflective use of key words; in doing so, they can also begin to bring their expertise to bear on the considerable segment of the literature on globalization that makes large claims about the past.

The analysis of globalization derived from different definitions of the concept and varying weights attached to its component parts has produced three main schools of thought, each of which could readily be divided into further sub-categories. The most assertive position is held by those who argue that globalization is a recent, dramatic development, is transforming society in a multiplicity of ways, and is bringing about the decline of the nation state. The boldest and least qualified presentations of this view tended to appear at the outset of the debate in the early 1990s, and some of the best known contributions were greatly influenced by the collapse of the Soviet empire.[47]

These claims provoked a reaction that brought out the sceptics, who are less convinced of the novelty of globalization, who argue that it is a myth that conceals the reality of an international order divided into three blocs (the so-called triad of the United States, Europe and Japan), and who hold that national governments remain the most powerful actors on the world stage.[48] In between stand the moderates, who see the strengths and weaknesses of the two extreme positions and try to synthesize them.[49] From this vantage point, globalization may or may not be new in the sense of being qualitatively distinctive, but it is now proceeding so fast that it is transforming societies across the world, even though the direction of change and the final outcome remain uncertain. Indeed, for the third school of thought much of the interest of the process lies in the ways in which, paradoxically, globalization produces diversity as well as promoting lines of convergence. Centrifugal tendencies can be found within the nation state, in the growth of regionalism and ethnic affiliations, for example, and beyond it, in the widening gap between newly developing countries and those still languishing or, in some cases, lost from sight.

These schools of thought are associated with various ideological affiliations, though they cannot be assigned neatly to right, left and centre. Nevertheless, newcomers to the debate on globalization ought to be aware that many of the arguments, and some of the participants, have been attached to what can broadly be called political positions. Among commentators who take an assertive view of globalization, for example, can be found those who espouse the values of the free market, who regard the fall of the Berlin Wall as vindicating the capitalist system, and who believe that the spread of Western values will produce a benign convergence of societies across the world.[50] An influential annex to this position links free markets to democracy and democracy, in turn, to peace and economic progress through the greater responsiveness and accountability it is said to bring.[51] At the same time, the debate has recharged radical critiques of capitalism, which tended either to wither or to be diverted into Gramscian channels following the collapse of the Soviet system and the conversion of China to free-market values. Radical views remain united by hostility towards capitalism, and emphasize the disruptive processes and exploitative consequences of the operation of the free market. Beyond this point, however, radical interpretations of globalization can be both assertive and sceptical. Some writers stress the novelty and penetrative power of globalization and its cataclysmic consequences. Others view it as a further phase in the long evolution of capitalism and one, moreover, that has brought mixed results: the rise of newly industrialized countries outside the triad, for instance, contrasts with the marginalization of large parts of the world that have failed to climb the development ladder.[52]

These views remain a long way apart. To the extent that it is possible to see signs of convergence in the literature, if not on the ground, they are to be found largely in the middle position taken by the third school of thought, the moderates, with respect to two key issues. One centres on the diversity of contemporary capitalism, whether in its Rhenish or Anglo-Saxon guises[53] or whether wearing one of its several oriental masks, and accordingly recognizes the importance of deriving the analysis of structures (and hence predictions about the future) from specific and localized realities. The other reflects a growing awareness of the need, in an age of globalization, to rethink the role of the state not only in promoting appropriate economic policies but also in maintaining security while trying to uphold civil liberties. At this point, the radical critique of the free market shows signs of converging with revisionist thinking undertaken by the World Bank. Having spent the 1980s 'getting prices right', the Bank is now concerned with 'bringing the state back in' – not least in recognition of the criticisms made of policies of structural adjustment and of the part played by the governments of the Asian 'tiger' economies in fostering development.[54]

The main difference between the current ideological debate and that conducted at the time of the Cold War is that, today, the radical critique of capitalism is no longer accompanied by an alternative set of prescriptions centred on state planning and autarky. For the moment at least, the agenda is one of reform rather than revolution, and it is this adjustment more than any other that has made a degree of intellectual convergence possible. On the ground, however, the militant demonstrations in Seattle and Prague suggest that bridges across the great divide are more likely to be burned than built. At present, the opposition is, as Marxists used to say, under-theorized. It rests on a very generalized hostility to capitalism that harks back to the arguments put by advocates of the dependency thesis in the 1960s and 1970s, though few of the present generation of protesters seem to be aware of the connection.[55] Observers with long memories will be reminded of the sound of wheels being reinvented. Yet the protests are highly significant popular expressions of a civic conscience that has universal aspirations. The rapidity with which they spread from Seattle in 1999 to other centres of protest across the world is itself startling evidence of the power of globalizing forces to generate and transmit new supra-national forms of political expression. The analysis of the international role of capitalism advanced by the leaders of the movement may be less than robust, but it has the merits of proclaiming an interest that rises above the concerns of individual nation states, of bringing fresh publicity to the massive problem of world poverty, and of reminding all but the most satisfied of free-marketeers that sweated labour and environmental degradation are issues that too readily escape the grasp of the unseen hand.[56]

The foregoing references to Asian tigers and world poverty serve as reminders that, though globalization is by definition a process that affects the whole planet, the debate remains almost exclusively Western in conception and indeed in orientation too.[57] This paradox, where it has been recognized, has caused some unease among commentators along all points of the ideological spectrum, not least because the concept of the West is itself an invention that owes a great deal to interaction with the non-European world. Yet the well-known bias symbolized by Mercator's projection of the world in 1569 has continued to have a profound influence on perceptions of ourselves and of others by greatly exaggerating the size and, by implication, the importance of regions furthest from the equator. To the extent that the literature on globalization has attempted to deal with this long-standing distortion, it has done so partly through reassessing the history of capitalism, as we shall see, but mainly through the need to rethink the concept of the Third World to take account of its increasing diversity.

The term 'Third World' had its origins in the era of the Cold War, but had already begun to lose its utility in the 1970s, long before the demise of the Soviet empire.[58] The heterogeneity of the Third World manifested itself dramatically following the oil crisis of 1973, which prompted some commentators to propose a fourth category of resource-rich but still underdeveloped countries.[59] Subsequent developments, especially the growth of manufacturing in parts of Southeast and East Asia, further complicated the picture by creating a class of newly industrializing countries, now known in the literature as NICs. While these and parallel developments, such as the alleged marginalization of Africa,[60] have been well studied by regional specialists, it is only recently that they have begun to be placed in the context of globalization. The chief exception is the interest shown in the NICs, whose initial development as manufacturing centres was seen to be linked to the extension of the activities of trans-national corporations based in the triad of the United States, Europe and Japan.[61] A rather different line of investigation regards Third World countries as centres, not so much of manufacturing, but of resistance to processes of globalization imposed by external agencies.[62]

These are valuable contributions, but they display a pronounced bias in treating globalization as the expansion of Western influences (albeit extended to incorporate Japan), and thus parallel the widespread assumption in the historical literature that globalization is essentially the product of one part of the world, and in the first instance of north-west Europe specifically.[63] Whether or not the assumption is justified, it is one that needs first to be tested by being viewed from alternative starting points. It ought to be self-evident, for example, that Christianity (itself an import from the Near East) is not the only system of belief to have made universal claims and to have had a profound influence on regions well beyond its centre of origin: similar cases can be made for Islam, Hinduism and Buddhism. Perhaps the most striking reaction so far has come from specialists on China, whose starting point has been located in indigenous institutions and values, and whose conclusions cast doubt on many of the conventional expectations found in the literature.[64] Edward Friedman's prediction for the new century draws on long lines of continuity with the past: 'parochial analysts elsewhere do not comprehend the growing Asian consensus that, after a short European interregnum, the great civilizations of Asia, as throughout recorded history, once again are to be the decisive factors in the world market'.[65]

Viewing the world from non-European perspectives is an important corrective to the pronounced Western bias that is found in the existing literature. However, it fails to capture all of the processes that enter into globalization and it still runs the risk of reproducing, albeit under a different set of proper names, the conventional preoccupation with national entities. Given this starting point, it is easy to assume that all societies can be encompassed by a teleology that is fundamentally Western in conception. If the history of globalization is to become a recognized subject, it will have to give prominence to alternative ways of assessing the past. These include non-national boundaries of the kind formed, for example, by religious and ethnic diaspora spanning territorial frontiers, and the history of the borderless world, which encompasses the even freer flow of ideas and migrants.[66] One implication of this approach is that the history of the nation state itself needs to be considered from the position of non-national and sometimes centrifugal forces rather than from that of embryonic and ultimately predominant centres. The history of passports and letters of transit – to suggest just one possibility – is rarely mentioned in the general texts, even though it provides an opportunity to chart the classification not only of citizenship, as certified by central authorities, but also of its antonyms – stateless persons and refugees – and to place them, in turn, in the context of currently emerging conceptions of human rights that transcend nationality.[67]

Historiographical Signposts

The preceding discussion has had the modest aim of identifying some of the central issues in the study of globalization in the hope that they will provide compass bearings for the remainder of the discussion, which can now return to the two questions posed at the outset: what can historians contribute to the debate on globalization, and what can the debate on globalization contribute to the study of history? There are several ways of organizing an examination of these issues, but the easiest point of access for historians is over the claims lodged for and against the novelty of globalization. The purpose of the survey that follows is to construct a brief historiography of what is still an uneven and disconnected literature. The discussion fits with that in the Introduction but should also be distinguished from it: there we set out our own suggested typology to assist new work on the history of globalization; here we refer to existing studies that treat the history of the subject but deploy the term in a generalized and often unrefined way. By putting the two parts together, historians should be able to see more clearly both where the main contours of the subject lie and how they might be redrawn in future.

The earliest sighting has resulted from a reappraisal of the history of capitalism undertaken by a handful of writers occupying positions at the radical end of the political spectrum. In essence, they have recycled and to a degree updated the dependency thesis that first sprang to prominence in the 1970s before being overtaken in turn by Marxism, the Annales school, and postmodernism. The most striking claim to date is that made by one of the founders of the dependency thesis, Andre Gunder Frank, who now argues that a migratory capitalist core has existed for 5,000 years.[68] The claim has been disputed by two other noted dependency theorists, Samir Amin and Immanuel Wallerstein, who stand by the more conventional view that 'capitalism is a qualitatively new age in universal history which started around 1500'.[69] Discussion of these issues has caused contributors to revisit the question of whether western Europe was unique and, if so, in what respects. This has led, on the one hand, to an attack on the idea that there was a European 'miracle',[70] and on the other to an exploration (albeit still of a limited kind) of the economic achievements of non-European societies in the period before Western dominance.[71] The argument, broadly speaking, is that capitalism was emerging in many parts of the world by 1500, and that the rise of the West stemmed primarily from the ability of military-fiscal states to create colonies overseas. This conclusion repeats a view that is already well known from conventional radical critiques of imperialism, which hold that the development of Europe was made possible by expropriating wealth from the rest of the world.

The basic argument is a familiar one and it suffers from familiar criticisms that have yet to be rebutted. Indeed, in arguing that capitalism can be traced back 5,000 years and not merely 500, Frank has now stretched even further what many critics thought was a fundamental flaw in the original argument, namely that if capitalism is equated with exchange it can indeed be found, more or less, in all societies and in all periods of history.[72] The corollary, it would seem, is that applying the concept of globalization in this way stretches its meaning well beyond the point where it has any operational definition.[73] All the same, the attempt to revitalize the dependency thesis by connecting it to the latest development in modern capitalism, globalization, has brought a number of interesting contributions in its train. For example, in challenging Frank's claims regarding the universality and longevity of capitalism, Amin offers a restatement of the characteristics of pre-capitalist economies that recognizes the 'brilliant civilization' of the Arab-Islamic world (and by extension of India and China too) but denies that what he calls 'proto-capitalist' elements in these societies were able to escape the 'logic of the dominant tributary system' of power.[74] Amin's argument is pitched at a level of generality that is typical of exchanges between historical structuralists, who remain undeterred by criticisms of what postmodernists refer to as the 'totalizing project'. It nevertheless reopens a major highway into the economic history of the non-Western world, and one, therefore, that is well worth exploring.

The contribution that engages most closely with the historical evidence is that made by Janet Abu-Lughod, a noted specialist on the Arab world in the thirteenth and fourteenth centuries, who has used her detailed research to test the interpretations of world-systems theorists, such as Wallerstein. She suggests that an incipient 'world system' consisting of eight overlapping 'circuits of trade' connecting three to four 'core regions' came into being at the end of the twelfth century and reached its peak at the beginning of the fourteenth century.[75] This system not only predates the rise of the West, which according to Amin, Wallerstein and others began around 1500, but displaces it geographically too by locating its core regions in 'a vast area stretching between north-west Europe and China'. Moreover, though Europe was part of this system, it was not a central part. Indeed, in Abu-Lughod's arresting phrase, 'the fall of the East precedes the rise of the West'[76] – a formula that challenges historians to explore non-Western perspectives on the 'world system' of the period.

This argument deserves more consideration than space allows on this occasion. On the one hand, it would be possible to extend Abu-Lughod's circuits of trade: it is curious, for example, that she has not included sub-Saharan Africa, which was linked to north Africa by trans-Saharan routes during this period in ways that fit comfortably into her analysis.[77] Moreover, her notion of 'non-hegemonic trade' indicates a degree of openness that has affinities with modern ideas of globalization, while her discussion of the 'fall of the East', with its emphasis on China's decision to withdraw from the seas, points to a comparison with the protectionist pressures that stand against globalizing tendencies today. On the other hand, an awareness of the definitional issues that have emerged from the current debate on globalization suggests that the quantitative and qualitative differences between Abu-Lughod's incipient 'world system' and that of the late twentieth century are so vast that they can be overcome only by adopting an excessively generous interpretation of the terms used to describe them. She herself concedes that the connections she identifies, geographically extensive though they were, excluded the New World and Australasia. It could be pointed out, too, that the degree to which trans-state influences penetrated society was also limited, notwithstanding the important exception of the spread of belief systems, such as Islam. Furthermore, institutional differences between the world of the fourteenth century and that of the twentieth century, which was populated by nation states, trans-national corporations and advanced information systems, were even more pronounced.

Historically, too, the notion of the 'fall of the East' is open to the criticism that it fails to take account of developments after 1500.[78] The fact that China withdrew from the oceans in the middle of the fifteenth century did not mean that expansion came to an end.[79] It took place, instead, by land rather than by sea and was accompanied by an increase in both population and living standards in the seventeenth and eighteenth centuries.[80] Japan expanded under

Hideyoshi Toyotomi in the 1580s and 1590s, Persia under the Safavid dynasty (1502–1736), and Mughal India under Akbar (1556–1605). South-east Asia enjoyed a period of 'exceptional prosperity' between 1570 and 1630;[81] the Ottoman Turks stood at the gates of Vienna in 1683. If T.A. Goldstone is right, a Eurasian system of political economy based on the interaction between population change and scarce resources continued to function in the early modern period.[82] The 'fall of the East' may thus have been followed by its revival and not just by the rise of the West. Nevertheless, Janet Abu-Lughod's achievement is to have drawn attention away from Europe, and to have pushed back the dating of Wallerstein's 'world system', even if, in doing so, she has also succeeded in casting doubt on the value of using the term to describe the cosmopolitan connections of the time – unless it is hedged with many more qualifications than its progenitors are prepared to accept or refined in ways that we have suggested in the Introduction and explored further elsewhere in this volume.

The interest in the period before 1600, limited though it is, is still exceptional: contributors to the debate on contemporary globalization often look back through the twentieth century and a few extend their interest into the nineteenth century, but none has given serious thought to the centuries between 1600 and 1800. Of course, some possible connections are already in place: specialists in international relations have long regarded the Treaty of Westphalia in 1648 as marking the start of the modern regime of sovereign states; world-system theorists have extended their analysis of the rise of capitalism into the nineteenth century. Influential though these contributions have been, they fall far short of encompassing the issues thrown up by the new debate on globalization, and they have rarely engaged the historical literature at close quarters. The idea of a 'Westphalian state system' that extended from 1648 to a point in the late twentieth century, when it came under pressure from countervailing forces thrown up by globalization, is too generalized to appeal to historians, which probably explains why they have made so little use of it. Similarly, the argument that the Treaty of Paris in 1763 symbolized the 'victory of certain segments of the world bourgeoisie, who were rooted in England, with the aid of the British state',[83] is too ill-tuned to receive the signals needed to convey important revisions to our understanding of the processes of modernization in what was still becoming the United Kingdom.

It is not the purpose of this essay to try to fill this gap. However, since an omission of several centuries is embarrassingly large, some attempt should be made to suggest how the period, or at least a large segment of it, relates to the history of globalization.[84] Seen from this perspective, the chief characteristic of the period was the developing symbiosis between emerging state systems and growing cosmopolitanism. Today, the claims of the nation state are being challenged by supra-national and infra-national affiliations; between 1600 and 1800, the appeal of non-national loyalties co-existed with a sense of nationality that was only slowly evolving. At the same time, international connections were growing in extent and intensity – from Europe's discovery of the existence of a wider world to Britain's struggle with France to master it – and the cosmopolitan ideal was developed in conjunction with, rather than in opposition to, the growth of the state. The fact that state borders were far more porous than they were to become in the nineteenth and twentieth centuries suggests that the period was marked by a degree of fluidity that, so it has been argued, is also characteristic of the present day. The analogy with the early twenty-first century, though far from exact, has the merit of underlining the point that historical sequences do not necessarily unfold in a linear, evolutionary fashion.

The British case, which has been exceptionally well studied, is worth citing here because it shows how a developing sense of nationality was spurred on both by conflict with the great continental Other – France – and by the extension of international and imperial ties.[85] At the same time, recent work has given prominence to the continuing significance of a range of different loyalties. Colin Kidd has shown how an embryonic sense of nationality and its accompanist, insularity, were balanced by flows of goods, ideas and people that ignored ethnic, religious and racial boundaries.[86] A detailed account of London's expanding overseas trade has revealed how the leading City merchants developed a cosmopolitan view of the world based on their extensive connections with the Atlantic and the East Indies.[87] Even Protestantism, though central to the process of nation-building, may have been a less clearly integrative force than was once thought.[88] In short, eighteenth-century England, which was still emerging into a state of Britishness, was a kingdom in which multiple identities co-existed.[89] Place, family, religion and the polity all exerted claims that were advertised or suppressed according to time and circumstance. In principle, this picture is rather closer to that of the present than to that of the nineteenth and twentieth centuries, when nation states attempted to assert exclusive claims on the loyalties of its subjects.

Ideological cosmopolitanism both reflected and endorsed the global expansion of European influences that so impressed Herder and his contemporaries. Whether measured by trade or by territory, by settlers or by slaves, there was a distinct jump in the importance of links between the West and the non-European world in the second half of the eighteenth century. Non-state actors, as they would be called today, appeared on distant frontiers as migrants and private traders; the trans-national corporations of the day, such as the East India Company, linked producers and consumers across continents in ways that demonstrated the efficiency of new forms of commercial capitalism.[90] The expanding empires of Britain and France were multi-ethnic conglomerates that projected the globalization of the age, even if they only partly contained the expansionist forces they represented.[91] The making of empire and the construction of nationality are, as we now know, closely related themes.[92] However, though European empires were designed to serve the state, they were not, in the eighteenth century, yet servants of the nation state. The term 'British empire' did not come into general use until the close of the century, and even then it did not replace other labels.[93] The continuing fluidity of the empire was also expressed in the intense debate that took place over its organization, purpose and direction.[94] One of the central issues, the question of whether destiny required the empire to be transmuted into a federation, drew upon cosmopolitan notions that have come to the fore again in recent years in discussions of contemporary globalization.

None of these developments is captured by a view of modernization that is predicated on the victory of a 'world bourgeoisie' or even more generally on the triumph of industry, at least as far as the eighteenth century is concerned and even in the case of Britain. Recent thinking has given prominence instead to forces gathered together under the label 'military fiscalism' and to the rise, in the case of Britain, of the financial and service sector.[95] Military fiscalism, essentially the use of state power to command the revenues needed to meet war expenditures, gave impetus to imperial expansion; it also added a predatory, and to that extent non-modern, element to the cosmopolitan ethos of the era. A parallel development, if also an exceptional one, was the impressive growth of the City of London and associated financial and commercial institutions in the eighteenth century, within and beyond the empire. This trend pointed to a stage of development that is regarded as being one of the hall-marks of post-industrial society in the modern age of globalization: the growth of the tertiary sector.[96] These predatory and developmental tendencies were never entirely reconciled, but they achieved an effective accommodation in the nineteenth century under the protection of the nation state, which they both served and commanded.[97] Whether or not the Battle of Waterloo was won on the playing fields of Eton, victory was undoubtedly made possible by Britain's superior expertise in funding the war effort.[98]

The intimations of globalization that emerged in the eighteenth century can be seen far more clearly than those identified by long-sighted observers of the fourteenth century. Whether judged by the scale of activities, their geographical reach, the institutional developments of the period or, perhaps most impressive of all, the conscious creation of a cosmopolitan ideology, the late eighteenth century has some readily identifiable connections with the globalizing processes of the present day. Yet the scale of activities remained tiny compared to what was to come, and institutional innovations were still half-formed, even in finance and commercial services, where, arguably, they were most advanced. Industrialization, though a visible part of the landscape, had yet to 'show the face of the future' to any but a very small minority of proponents and seers, and price convergence was still limited, despite the growth of domestic and international trade. The state was governed in a manner that was still largely patrimonial: patronage held crucial networks in place; cronyism was endemic; the very limits to central authority allowed private forms of cosmopolitanism to flourish while simultaneously encouraging the state to cling, as far as possible, to a combination of protectionism and predation. In these and other ways, the political mechanisms of the age fell far short of Max Weber's criterion of modernity: the emergence of a rational bureaucracy. Rationality was the aim of the Enlightenment thinkers; the bureaucracy of the day was one of the major obstacles to achieving it.

The main weakness of this incipiently Western view of what we have earlier termed proto-globalization[99] is its failure to take account of non-European perspectives on the world order. In the present state of historical knowledge it is difficult to do more than register the existence of a problem that needs much further thought. The continued isolation of China, the closure of Japan after 1639, the 'general' crisis of the seventeenth century in Europe (which has been extended to parts of Asia), and the fall of the Mughals shortly afterwards – all these are consistent with the conventional view that the rise of the West was complemented (finally) by the decline of the East. Yet revisionist research hints at a different story. The Chinese state and economy continued to expand in the eighteenth century, and China's foreign trade made a significant contribution to the process, not least through its links with other parts of Asia as well as with Europe.[100] Japan's policy of closure has been reassessed and substantially reinterpreted.[101] There were also signs of renewed population growth, revived economic prosperity and redesigned state-building in mainland south Asia and central Java in the eighteenth century.[102] The dissolution of the Mughal empire in this period was not the prelude to widespread anarchy but the occasion for the reconfiguration of state systems that, it has been suggested, were better fitted to the expanding commercial needs of the time.[103]

These remarks suggest the need to keep in view the probability that revitalized and competing state systems in Asia contributed to the shape of the world order and therefore should not be edited out of the text or treated as passive recipients of European forces. This hypothesis is reinforced by the need to bring non-state actors into the story too. The eighteenth century saw the continued spread of universal religions, such as Islam and Buddhism, across state frontiers, further into Asia and (in the case of Islam) into sub-Saharan Africa too.[104] This trend towards what today would be called cultural convergence was a manifestation of the part-reality of a *Pax Islamica* which reached from Morocco to Mataram. As a globalizing force, Islam was also challenged from within in the eighteenth century by reformist movements that culminated in the assault mounted by the Wahhabist sect in Arabia – a 'tribal breakout' that is reproduced today in the new manifestations of ethnic and provincial resistance to globalizing forces. Partly because these frontiers were less formidable than they were to become after Weber's bureaucrats took charge of them, the period witnessed, too, the dynamic extension of the great cultural and trading diasporas that ought to have a central place in any discussion of the history of globalization: the Chinese in Southeast Asia are one prominent example at this time; Arab merchants and missionaries in the

Indian Ocean and sub-Saharan Africa provide another.[105] The East had still not fallen: the proto-globalization of the eighteenth century was a joint product of diverse expansionist forces and not simply the story of the inexorable advance of the West.

The third stage that can be discerned in the historiography of globalization begins in the nineteenth century and continues into the second half of the twentieth century. The exact starting point is generally left undefined, though, at the risk of trying to solidify fluidity, it can be said that 1850 is a date that commands a degree of assent, and thus yields a neat, century-long span. The terminal point, however, is not precisely fixed. As we shall see, some scholars treat the period from 1850 down to the present day as forming a coherent, self-contained era of globalization; others judge that the years after 1950 or, in some interpretations, after 1970 mark the start of a new, fourth phase of contemporary globalization.

The third phase has been called into being primarily by those who question the novelty of globalization.[106] In their view, the claim that globalization is new is simply the product of intellectual short-termism; a longer perspective shows that many of the defining features were already in place in the second half of the nineteenth century. These continuities have been obscured, so it is said, by a number of exceptional features, especially the state-led policies of protection and planning that came to the fore between 1930 and 1950. From this perspective, the sub-period 1930–50 is a deviation from trend; the period after 1950 represents a return to normality as projected from developments that were already apparent in the late nineteenth century. This argument, like those applied to earlier periods, has been put chiefly by social scientists looking backwards while simultaneously trying to see the shape of things to come.

Exceptionally, however, the case has also been made by a handful of historians whose explicit purpose has been to use detailed evidence of nineteenth-century developments to test current hypotheses about globalization.[107] The two key changes, in this view, were the shift from state mercantilism to open, free-trading policies, and the development of far-reaching improvements in technology. Structural adjustment, as it would be called today, opened up economic potential on a world scale; technological innovation enabled it to be realized.[108] Improved communications cut the cost and increased the speed of transactions; there was a large and unprecedented increase in inter-continental migration; a well-organized international capital market, based on London, made its appearance; world trade in goods and services underwent a massive expansion.[109] Imperialism made a significant contribution to the process by integrating the non-Western world both by diplomacy, as in Japan and to some extent the Middle East, and by force, as in India, Southeast Asia and Africa.[110]

Although the detailed studies generated by this line of enquiry can only be sampled here, it is worth noting that they have a distinctive place in the historiography of globalization because they bring a fresh analysis to bear on some familiar issues in the history of modern economic development. It is now apparent that the rate of growth of commodity exports and of direct investments from Western developed countries reached levels shortly before 1914 that were not matched until the 1980s.[111] Moreover, there were clear signs of economic convergence in sizeable segments of the international economy in the late nineteenth century as prices became equalized across large areas of what was becoming the developed world.[112] Transport improvements were more dramatic in the late nineteenth century than in the late twentieth century; mass migration encountered fewer barriers and was also on a larger scale than it is today. Between them, the transport revolution and the increasing flow of people within Europe and to new areas of settlement outside it raised the level of integration in the international economy and brought about a marked trend towards the harmonization of labour productivity and real wages in the OECD countries (as they were later to become).[113] A detailed analysis has revealed a similar trend in economic relations between Britain and the United States between 1870 and 1914; separate studies have generalized the argument to cover the Atlantic economy and the underdeveloped world in the nineteenth century.[114]

Recent research would therefore seem to bear out Norman Angell's contemporary assessment that the international order had become integrated to an unprecedented degree: the 'economically civilized world' was now tied together by 'credit and commercial contract'; the 'modern state' was 'losing its homogeneity' and 'classifying itself by interests' instead.[115] Unfortunately, Angell's Cobdenite argument that economic integration made war unlikely as well as undesirable was proved dramatically wrong very shortly after he had given it wide publicity. Not for the last time, he made the mistake of seeing international problems from a British perspective: in the event, the City got the war it did not want.[116] Thereafter, so the current argument runs, the process of integration was interrupted by a phase of 'deglobalization' and divergence between 1914 and 1950 that was not decisively reversed until the last quarter of the twentieth century.[117] It is worth noting that this categorization of the years between 1930 and 1950 is heavily weighted towards policy considerations. The picture might look rather different if other developments, such as the growth of import-substituting industries and joint ventures in a range of countries in the non-Western world, were taken into account.[118] The period might then appear to be less like an interlude and more like the progenitor of changes that were to become more visible after 1950. However, if this speculative qualification is put to one side, the merit of the case for 'de-globalization' is that it provides a reminder, to enthusiasts and doomsters alike, that globalization is not governed by an iron law of linear progress. This is one 'lesson of history' that ought to be learned by prophets who base their predictions on simple extrapolations from current trends.

The main feature of the work undertaken so far on the period between 1850 and 1950 is also its main limitation: it has focused on the economic dimension of globalization, and especially on its measurable features, and has looked at it from a predominantly Western standpoint.[119] Political, social and cultural aspects have still to be explored, though they enter into virtually every definition of globalization; non-Western perspectives have yet to be incorporated fully into the debate. The brief discussion that follows is intended to suggest some of the ways in which historians might begin to reassess features of the period that, traditionally, have been placed in a different context.

In the first place, a consideration of globalization ought to sharpen historical perspectives on the emergence of the nation state. If it is argued that the nation state is now in decline, it is important to be clear about when it was in the ascendant and indeed precisely when it made its presence felt. If it is held, conversely, that this view is flawed because it compares the present against an ideal instead of against the reality of states whose power was conditional, relative and, typically, compromised, then some improved measures of imperfect sovereignty are called for.[120] Either way, the nation state, and not just the Westphalian state, needs to be placed at the centre of the history of globalization, and this means, minimally, taking a fresh look at the nineteenth century.

As we have noted, Enlightenment cosmopolitanism was corralled by the state and harnessed to a growing sense of nationality as the nineteenth century progressed. The multiple identities that characterized the eighteenth century were not eliminated; some became more firmly entrenched.[121] But, in the case of the newly United Kingdom, a concept of Britishness was laid over them and became more visible as the century progressed, legitimizing among other things a form of racism that stood in opposition to the idealism of the Enlightenment. The domestic causes of this burgeoning sense of nationality lie beyond the scope of this essay; what does require comment is the relationship between nationality and internationality, a question that, perhaps surprisingly, has only recently begun to attract serious attention from historians. An argument has been put, though with reference only to Britain, that overseas expansion, imperialism and empire were part cause and part consequence of the growth of the nation state.[122] If it is accepted that expansion (through free trade), imperialism (which could be informal), and empire (which was a constitutional entity), between them comprised a process of globalization, then the globalization of the nineteenth century was not only consistent with the existence of the nation state but reinforced it too.

Moreover, globalization expanded by creating new states as well as by upholding established ones: some were fashioned from existing peoples; others were thrown up as a result of moving settlers into new lands. This process accelerated in the twentieth century, first when the antique empires were broken up and then when their modern successors were taken down after World War II, producing a clutch of hastily arranged legal entities known as quasi-states.[123] It does not follow, of course, that the same relationship holds today: circumstances in 2001 are very different from those in 1900, or even

1950, and may or may not favour the continued paramountcy of the nation state. The point is that the nation state needs to be brought into the equation before firm judgements can be made about the nineteenth-century origins of contemporary globalization. It may well be, as has been suggested,[124] that the economic data point strongly towards continuities with the past. However, the political dimension may reveal more contrasts than similarities if, on further inspection, it turns out that the nation state was much more supportive of globalization before 1950 than it is today. Exploring this issue opens a wide route for fresh historical research; in doing so, it also underlines the importance of distinguishing between different definitions of globalization and aligning evidence and conclusions accordingly to ensure that like is compared with like.

An expanding sense of nationality also helped to shape the character of the global links forged between 1850 and 1950. In 1841 Chateaubriand had already foreseen that distances would shortly disappear, and that 'it will not only be commodities which travel, but also ideas which will have wings'.[125] Many of the commodities were moved between empires as well as around the world in the spaces created by free trade. Multi-lateral links were effected by multi-national enterprise: British shipping carried the freight of other nations; British finance assisted the distribution of manufactured goods produced by other industrial powers. This activity created a need for new international organizations, beginning with the International Telegraph Union in 1865, which can reasonably be seen to be precursors of the International Non-Governmental Organizations (INGOs) that are prominent features of globalization today.[126] The ideas with wings included Christianity, liberalism and racism, all of which fell in readily behind the banner of imperialism. Christianity was capable of drawing different denominations and rival states together in a crusading alliance against Islam; the liberal ideal could produce co-operative as well as competitive solutions to the problems of managing the expanding world order; notions of racial superiority injected a dose of unity into Europe's dealings with 'less civilized' nations.

Yet, when these allowances have been made, the 'global civil society'[127] that emerged during this period carried the imprint of the nationality that propelled it. Links across space and cultures could be sustained only by generating common core values and a lingua franca, and these were put in place by a few dominant nations with the power to spread their own diasporas while also inspiring imitation and instilling deference in other societies. Admittedly, the equivalent of 'Coca-colonization' was still far more limited than it was to become in the second half of the twentieth century, but the non-European world saw the emergence of networks of elites which modelled their aspirations on those prevailing in what could still be called, without irony, the mother country, whose task it was to nurture them. From constitutions to consumer tastes, from weights to measures, and from the creation of postal services to the colonization of time, it was the national stamp that sealed global connections.[128] The Weights and Measures Acts of 1824 and 1878 established the British imperial system of standardized units of weight, capacity and length; Britain's imperial postal service carried the head of the monarch around the world; British standard time became the point of reference when global time zones were agreed in 1884; the British Broadcasting Corporation became the authoritative source of news about international and current affairs within the empire and in parts of the wider English-speaking world after World War I.[129]

The English language became the indispensable common currency of what might be called national globalization, whether for commercial or for cultural exchanges.[130] Samuel Johnson observed that languages are 'the pedigree of nations', and his famous dictionary helped others to create, in the nineteenth century, the national and imperial measure known as 'standard' English. Roget's *Thesaurus* was first published in 1852; Murray's long labour of love in overseeing the production of the monumental *Oxford English Dictionary* (which appeared in 10 weighty volumes between 1884 and 1928), began in 1879. Both were classifying in the approved manner of the Enlightenment. But they were also standardizing and extending the national language and, in Murray's case, consciously linking it to a programme of imperial expansion.[131] As the French (among others) are acutely aware today, language and identity go together: if one is subverted the other will be diluted. In commenting on the issue recently, the writer, Claude Duneton, produced a fine Napoleonic flourish: 'the symbolic unity of France is represented . . . by the sacrosanct, correctly spelled language of the State'.[132] If, as has been claimed, globalization is now a free-floating process without strong national roots, it has indeed become a very different force from what it was in the period 1850–1950.

If historians who have looked at globalization in the years between 1850 and 1950 have given only limited consideration to the political and cultural dimensions of the process, they have also viewed the period from a predominantly Western perspective. Once again, a conscious effort needs to be made to decentre the analysis. In the nineteenth century, as before, not all globalizing forces came from the West and those that did were mediated and adapted by the recipients in ways that produced new institutions and instruments. The research on this period undertaken by Area Studies specialists is now so voluminous that it ought to be possible to locate a number of points at which it can be attached to the debate on globalization, though on this occasion it is again impossible to do more than list a few of many examples.

By asserting the paramountcy of states defined by territoriality, Europe's imperial expansion established a concept of sovereignty that was at variance with Islam's more spacious vision of how the world should be organized. Even so, Islam continued to spread across political boundaries, and often under the protection of Christian empires. Similarly, the great diasporas of the non-Western world extended their reach under the regime of free trade and security provided by the imperial defence system. The numbers of Chinese in Southeast Asia reached unprecedented levels, and new branches of the diaspora were established in the United States, the Caribbean and south Africa. In parallel, the Indian diaspora strengthened its presence in Southeast Asia and opened up a sizeable new frontier in east and south Africa. Asia was distinctive, too, in developing a huge intra-regional trade which linked India, China and Japan and nearly all points in between.[133] Aside from being evidence of the rise of a form of Asian economic globalization, this trade was crucial to the success of Europe's own, much-studied commerce with the region. As is well known, by the late nineteenth century Britain's ability to earn a surplus on her trade with India played a crucial part in settling her balance of payments. What is far less well known is that India's ability to settle her debts with Britain rested to a large extent on her exports of rice and cotton yarn to the Far East.[134] In this way, and however distantly, British power and British incomes were related to China's ability to import rice. By a further twist, in default of valuable exports of her own, China's import-purchasing power in turn depended significantly on remittances from overseas Chinese. The continuing vitality of the borderless world of diasporas was thus of key importance in maintaining the global economic system that is usually thought of as being the product of the West.

These examples are indicative of the independent contribution made to the globalization of the period by non-Western agencies. Better known, though not necessarily more important, are the ways in which a global presence was jointly produced, notwithstanding Western dominance. The study of the European empires that were created or expanded after 1850 has revealed the long lines of continuity that survived the take-over and were often consolidated by it, assisting the new rulers to become Asian autocrats and, in Africa, white chiefs. As a corollary, it is also clear that much of the initiative and capital as well as the labour needed to generate colonial exports came from indigenous sources, and that interventions by the new colonial rulers were often misjudged, even where they were designed to speed the process of integration. In the political field, nationalism, though infused with Western ideas, was not simply another Western export but drew on indigenous affiliations that pre-dated the colonial presence. In the process, Western cultural forms were refashioned to suit local needs: the language of liberty was turned against colonial masters; print capitalism recorded and spread vernaculars; English, fraying at the edges, fell from the standards set by Murray and gained a cosmopolitan *patois* instead;[135] Christianity was to a degree indigenized. The pervasive interaction of local and introduced influences makes it hard to speak of a colonial legacy as if it were solely the product of the rulers. In considering globalization today, the historical record suggests that it is important to avoid slipping into formulations that assume that there are actors and reactors, and that the challenges come from the West and the responses from the rest.[136]

Contemporary Globalization

The possibility of identifying a fourth stage of globalization dealing with the period after 1950, or perhaps after 1970, returns us to the starting point of this essay: the present day. Since some of the substantive issues in the discussion of contemporary globalization have been touched on at the outset, the commentary here will be confined to a consideration of the way in which the periodization of the era has been determined. Many contemporary observers, it will be recalled, consider that globalization began in the second half of the twentieth century. Exactly when and why, however, remain disputed. Those who take a long view are content with an approximate starting point of 1950, which fits with post-war recovery and, more importantly, with the beginnings of structural change in the world economy centred on the growth of inter-industry trade, the rising importance of the triad, and the relative decline of the colonial ties that had characterized the period 1850–1950.[137] A majority of commentators, however, prefer to date the start of the era of globalization from 1970 or, even more precisely, from 1973, which has been seen, variously, as initiating a period of crisis for 'global liberalism' and as marking its ultimate triumph.[138]

Both parties underline the distinctiveness in this period of a number of key economic indicators:[139] the increase in the proportion of world exports to world trade, which rose from seven per cent in 1950 to 17 per cent in 1995; the transition to a post-industrial society signalled by occupational shifts in the advanced economies and the doubling of world trade in services between 1980 and 1995; the rapid rise in the size and velocity of the world's capital markets; the associated growth of foreign direct investment (FDI) and of supra-national financial instruments such as Euro-currencies; the expanding role of trans-national corporations, not only in controlling world trade, but in manufacturing too; and the continuing fall in the cost of communications, from ocean freight rates to air and telephone connections. Less readily measurable but equally impressive developments range from the massive growth of remittances from expatriate communities around the world[140] to the rise of global regulatory structures affecting the civil and criminal law, commercial arbitration, debt-rating and accounting standards.[141] Deregulation, greatly increased capital flows, and the sharp reduction in transactions costs, it is said, have placed the world economy on a more competitive basis. In doing so, they have also challenged the territorial basis of national sovereignty, even though the most powerful states were instrumental in setting change in motion by promoting deregulation and free trade in the first place. The shape of future conflict, on this view, will not be between nation states but between globalizing forces and infra-national resistance movements seeking to preserve their identities.

Analysts on the Left have endeavoured to set these developments in the context of the successive crises that are held to drive the evolution of capitalism. Robert Brenner's assessment, the most thorough to date, treats 1973 as being a watershed between post-war reconstruction based on national economies and a period of crisis ushered in by the revival of competition from Germany and Japan. This development drove down profits and pushed the United States into a series of innovations that ended by changing the shape of the world economy.[142] The influential political scientist, Robert Cox, argues similarly that 'there was a significant breaking point in the mid-1970s', when the international economy became global: 'the Fordist mode of production' backed by 'redistributive state policies acting as an economic stabilizer' came under attack; production and finance became organized in cross-border networks that could 'largely escape national and international regulatory powers'.[143] Immanuel Wallerstein offers a variation on this argument: he accepts that there was a turning point in the early 1970s but denies that it represents a fundamental transformation of the world economy. It was rather that the 1970s marked the beginning of 'the loss of hope by the popular masses' in policies of reform and an increasing shift towards privatization. Between them, these trends have damaged the sovereignty of states and caused them to lose legitimacy. On this view, the vital link between the state and capitalism has been either severed or at least seriously weakened for the first time in 500 years. The contemporary world faces a crisis of major proportions, but it arises because, if the state falls, 'capitalism is untenable as a system'.[144]

Neo-liberals, including some triumphalists, place these developments in a more benign, progressive context. The capitalist system has now conclusively demonstrated its superiority: successive economic and institutional innovations have delivered prosperity on a scale hitherto unknown; political changes, centred on deregulation and the spread of democracy, have promoted free choice and increased the quality of life. Moreover, these economic and political trends interact in positive ways: economic development requires liberated consumers and a freely mobile labour force; democratic processes ensure that governments are accountable and hence efficient. On this view the world is set on a path that is leading economic development, political systems and ideologies to converge. Of course there are problems: economic development in Asia appears to be consistent with authoritarian governments, which is not what the blueprint suggests; much of Africa seems to have dropped out of the world system; there are multiple 'black holes' of social exclusion, as Manuel Castells has called them, throughout the world, including the United States.[145] But problems are not terminal crises: they are matters either of transition, which time will solve, or of faulty policies, which appropriate advice will put right. Neither Chicago nor San Francisco was built in a day.

This analysis, irrespective of the ideological perspective adopted, is strong on the economic and political issues that have attracted the attention of most of those involved in the debate. As we have seen, however, it is weak on the historical dimension of globalization, without which no judgement on the novelty of the present era can stand, it is inclined to treat social and cultural issues as an annex to the main debate, and it is almost entirely Western-centred. Commentators can easily slip into the habit of regarding other influences, such as the inflow of non-Western migrants and the beliefs they bring with them, as 'problems' to be overcome rather than as phenomena to be understood. More specifically, the whole discussion bears the imprint, with its many merits and occasional defects, of the view of the world projected by its most powerful country: the United States. Given the huge influence exercised by the United States on academic disciplines across the sciences and humanities, there is a danger that independent and non-Western voices will not be given the attention they deserve. If this happens, the term globalization will become a euphemism for the perceptions, aspirations and anxieties solely of one country, and the super-state of the planet will be allowed to apply a provincialism of the mind to the problems of the world.

Cautionary notes, though predictably judicious, are not always the right ones to finish on. In this case, a positive conclusion is surely justified. The study of globalization promises to reinvigorate the appraisal of large slices of the past and to link history to the present in ways that ought to inform the discussion of contemporary issues. It is true that the history of globalization has yet to become a major research theme, and that large gaps and numerous uncertainties abound. But the current state of the art offers a prospect and a challenge: this is the moment when the architecture can be designed; the bricks can be laid later. In a globalized world, ideas flow across boundaries even more easily than capital. Historians now have an opportunity to cross disciplinary frontiers by engaging in this debate, and those – the vast majority – who live outside the triad have the chance, if they have the resources to take it, to put across their points of view. Bruce Beach was wrong, but there are bunkers of the mind that those of us who would not wish to climb into one of his sunken buses can still inhabit if we fail to look beyond the confines of our academic specializations – whatever they may be.

Notes and References

1 *The Times*, 6 January 2000, p. 15.
2 The list includes many distinguished names: Newton and Bossuet were among those who believed that the world would come to an end, and both spent a good deal of time trying to calculate the date.
3 And might be thought to be further proof, if it were needed, of Arthur C. Clarke's Third Law, which states that 'any sufficiently advanced technology is indistinguishable from magic'.
4 Anatol Kaletsky offers some stunning conversion figures: $400 billion is 'five times the amount needed to write off completely the debts crushing all the world's developing countries'; alternatively, it is 'roughly ten times the amount spent on cancer research by governments and charities the world over'. *The Times*, 6 January 2000, p. 18.

5 Contrast this novel concern with the traditional preoccupations recorded by David S. Katz and Richard H. Popkin, *Messianic Revolution* (London, 1999) and, even more distantly, with those at the turn of the first millennium surveyed by Robert Lacey and Danny Danziger, *The Year 1000* (London, 1999).

6 Indications of the extent of the alarm in the United States were reported by the *Independent*, 1 December 1999. Members of Weight Watchers may or may not be reassured to know that the company achieved Y2K compliance by dumping its computer systems and reconverting to paper.

7 The major text on this subject is Manuel Castells, *The Information Age* (3 vols., Oxford, 1996, 1997, 1998).

8 Robert W. Cox dates it from the 1970s: 'A Perspective on Globalization', in James H. Mittelman (ed.), *Globalization: Critical Reflections* (London, 1996), pp. 21–2. However, it was not until the late 1980s that the term began to sprout in the literature on international relations and development.

9 M. Waters, *Globalization* (London, 1995), p. 1. For similar statements see Ian Clarke, *Globalization and International Relations Theory* (Oxford, 1999), p. 35.

10 David Held, Anthony McGrew, David Goldblatt and Jonathan Perraton, *Global Transformations* (Oxford, 1999), p. 1.

11 The most comprehensive survey is Held *et al.*, *Global Transformations*. Richard Stubbs and Geoffrey R.D. Underhill (eds.), *Political Economy and the Changing Global Order*, 2nd edn. (Oxford, 2000) provide an accessible set of essays.

12 For example, Ian Clarke, *Globalization and Fragmentation: International Relations in the Twentieth Century* (Oxford, 1997); *idem*, *Globalization and International Relations Theory*.

13 The most sustained attempt to date is by two political scientists, Barry Buzan and Richard Little, *International Systems in World History* (Oxford, 2000).

14 The intellectual origins and legacy are of course much broader than I have indicated here. On the eighteenth century see specifically Karen O'Brien, *Narratives of Enlightenment: Cosmopolitan History from Voltaire to Gibbon* (Cambridge, 1997), which builds on earlier work by, among others, Thomas J. Schlereth, *The Cosmopolitan Ideal in Enlightenment Thought* (London, 1977).

15 And moved on (in ch.1) to Persia, Arabia and Islam before dealing with Europe.

16 Quoted in Emma Rothschild, 'Globalization and the Return of History', *Foreign Policy* (Summer 1999), p. 110.

17 Specifically to establish 'a universal civic society'. A convenient collection of Kant's writings on history and allied subjects is Immanuel Kant, *On History*, ed. Lewis White Beck (New York, 1963).

18 On Gibbon's place in the (late) Enlightenment and his stance with respect to republican virtue see J.G.A. Pocock, *Virtue, Commerce, and History* (Cambridge, 1985), ch. 8.

19 P.J. Cain, 'Capitalism, Internationalism and Imperialism in the Thought of Richard Cobden', *British Journal of International Studies*, 5 (1979), pp. 229–47.

20 Manfred Kossock, 'From Universal History to Global History', in Bruce Mazlish and Ralph Buultjens (eds.), *Conceptualising Global History* (Boulder, Co., 1993), p. 96.

21 Ernst Schulin, 'Universal History and National History in the Lectures of Leopold von Ranke', in Georg G. Iggers and James A. Powell (eds.), *Leopold von Ranke and the Shaping of the Historical Discipline* (Syracuse, NY, 1990), pp. 70–81.

22 Ralph Buultjens, 'Global History and the Third World', in Mazlish and Buultjens, *Conceptualising Global History*, p. 83

23 This theme is explored in A.G. Hopkins, 'Back to the Future: From National History to Imperial History', *Past & Present*, 164 (1999), pp. 198–243.

24 The flagship of the movement, the *Journal of World History*, was founded in 1990.

25 See William McNeill's pioneering study, *The Rise of the West: A History of the Human Community* (Chicago, 1963), and his re-evaluation, '*The Rise of the West* after Twenty-Five Years', *Journal of World History*, 1 (1990), pp. 1–22; idem, 'World History and the Rise and Fall of the West', *Journal of World History*, 9 (1998), pp. 215–36. Also Michael Geyer and Charles Bright, 'World History in a Global Age', *American Historical Review*, 100 (1995), pp. 1034–60. An accessible recent statement is Philip Pomper, Richard H. Elphick and Richard T. Vann (eds.), *World History* (London, 1998), though, perhaps surprisingly, it does not discuss globalization.

26 Mazlish and Buultjens, *Conceptualizing Global History*, is a valuable set of essays that deserves more advertisement than it has received. See also Bruce Mazlish, 'Comparing Global History to World History', *Journal of Interdisciplinary History*, 28 (1998), pp. 385–95. Note that this discussion is about the merits of world history and its variant, global history: it is *not* about the themes covered by the term globalization.

27 See, for example, Hopkins, 'Back to the Future', pp. 198–204, 240–3.

28 Especially of course by postmodernists who, interestingly enough, have so far made little imprint on the literature on globalization. One of the rare exceptions simply provides a restatement of ways in which the colonial era has been treated in the literature since the seventeenth century: Simon During, 'Postcolonialism and Globalization: A Dialectical Relation after All?', *Postcolonial Studies*, 1 (1998), pp. 31–47.

29 Ronnie D. Lipschutz, 'Reconstructing World Politics: The Emergence of Global Civil Society', *Millennium*, 21 (1992), pp. 389–400; Martin Shaw, 'Global Society and Global Responsibility: The Theoretical, Historical and Political Limits of International Society', ibid., pp. 50–82; Roland Robertson, *Globalization: Social Theory and Global Culture* (London, 1992).

30 Also referred to, marginally less felicitously, as 'McDonaldization'. See Robert J. Horton, *Globalization and the Nation State* (London, 1998), pp. 167–70.

31 This generalization refers to what might be called the mainstream literature flowing out of studies of international relations, international political economy and economic development. The fullest statement from a cultural perspective is Castells, *The Information Society*. Mike Davis, *Late Victorian Holocausts* (London, 2001) provides a wide-ranging study of famines.

32 I am grateful to my colleague, Dr Geoffrey Edwards, for discussing these issues with me and for commenting on an earlier draft of this chapter.

33 For example, Susan Strange, *The Retreat of the State: The Diffusion of Power in the World Economy* (Cambridge, 1996), pp. xii–xiii.

34 Answers to the question of how much globalization has taken place depend similarly on whether the term is defined broadly or narrowly.

35 See, for example, the definition adopted by Vivien A. Schmidt, which is strongly economic and entails the consequence that 'national autonomy' is undermined: 'Convergent Pressures, Divergent Responses: France, Great Britain and Germany between Globalization and Europeanization', in David A. Smith, Dorothy J. Salinger and Steven C. Topik (eds.), *States and Sovereignty in the Global Economy* (London, 1999), pp. 173–4.

36 W.K. Hancock, *Wealth of Colonies* (Cambridge, 1950), p. 1.

37 This is no exaggeration: see Andre Gunder Frank and Barry K. Gills, *The World System: Five Hundred Years or Five Thousand?* (London, 1993).

38 On the dangers of eliding globalization with other, established terms see Held *et al.*, *Global Transformations*, p. 28; also Geyer and Bright, 'World History in a Global Age'; Mazlish and Buultjens, *Conceptualizing Global History*; Mazlish, 'Comparing Global History to World History'.

39 I have adapted this summary from Held *et al.*, *Global Transformations*, p. 16. As Held puts it elsewhere: 'Globalization may be thought of initially as a widening, deepening and speeding up of world-wide interconnectedness in all aspects of contemporary social life, from the cultural to the criminal, the financial to the spiritual.' *Idem, Global Transformations*, p. 2.

40 This observation is unremarkable in itself, but it has had the effect of modifying established approaches to understanding the sources of foreign policy and the formation of international regimes by cutting across the 'great divide' between those who approach these issues from a cosmopolitan perspective and those who begin with domestic politics. The distinction is explored by Ian Clarke, *Globalization and International Relations Theory* (Oxford, 1999), ch. 1.

41 Linda Weiss, for example, has argued that, even today, most flows are international and 'cross-border'; only in the important but restricted case of finance can a strong case be made for a development that is both global and 'trans-border'. See 'Managed Openness: Beyond Neo-liberal Globalism', *New Left Review*, 238 (1999), pp. 126–40.

42 One of the most cited and most uncompromising statements is K. Ohmae, *The End of the Nation State* (New York, 1996). See also Strange, *The Retreat of the State*.

43 Robust statements from liberal and radical standpoints are Stephen D. Krasner, 'Globalization and Sovereignty', in David A. Smith, Dorothy J. Salinger and Steven C. Topik (eds.), *States and Sovereignty in the Global Economy* (London, 1999), pp. 34–52; Linda Weiss, *The Myth of the Powerless State: Governing the Economy in a Global Era* (Cambridge, 1998); M. Porter, *The Competitive Advantage of Nations* (London, 1990).

44 Kevin O'Rourke and Jeffrey G. Williamson, *Globalization and History: The Evolution of the Nineteenth-Century Atlantic World Economy* (Cambridge, Mass., 1999).

45 By exploring, for example, the rise of international non-governmental organizations (INGOs) and the developing international role of non-governmental organizations (NGOs) and non-state actors (NSAs). INGOs have been referred to, with some exaggeration, as 'the priests of the world polity'. See John Boli and George M. Thomas (eds.), *Constructing World Cultures: International Non-Governmental Organizations since 1875* (Stanford, 1999), p. 284.

46 Arjun Appadurai, *Modernity at Large: Cultural Dimensions of Globalization* (Minneapolis, 1996), combines both quantitative and qualitative dimensions in arguing that the key feature of globalization is the combination of mass migration and the mass media.

47 Ohmae, *End of the Nation State*; Strange, *Retreat of the State*. The best-known piece of triumphalism is Francis Fukuyama's *The End of History and the Last Man* (London, 1992).

48 Paul Hirst and Graham Thompson, *Globalization in Question* (Cambridge, 1996).

49 This being the majority position, citations are too numerous to mention here. However, representative examples include: J. Rosenau, *Turbulence in World Politics* (Brighton, 1990); J.G. Ruggie, *Winning the Peace: America and World Order in the*

New Era (New York, 1996); Suzanne Berger and Ronald Dore (eds.), *National Diversity and Global Capitalism* (London, 1996).

50 Fukuyama, *End of History*, is the most widely publicized presentation of this viewpoint.

51 Analysts in the United States have now produces a massive literature purporting to prove a universal principle, namely that democracy produces peace (and development for good measure). The initial point of reference was Michael Doyle's reflective essays: 'Kant, Liberal Legacies and Foreign Affairs', *Philosophy and Public Affairs*, 12 (1983), pp. 205–34 and pp. 323–52 , and 'Liberalism and World Politics', *American Political Science Review*, 80 (1986), pp. 1151–63, which gave new currency to Kant's previously obscure essay, *On Perpetual Peace* (on which see also note 17 above).

52 Both views are well represented in Smith, Solinger and Topik, *States and Sovereignty*; Boyer and Drache, *States Against Markets*; Mittelman, *Globalization*; Berger and Dore, *National Diversity and Global Capitalism*; Andrew Hurrell and Ngaire Woods (eds.), *Inequality, Globalization and World Politics* (Oxford, 1999).

53 The difference, roughly speaking, between the corporate capitalism found in Germany and France and the free-market version promoted in the United States and Britain. See Michel Albert, *Capitalism Against Capitalism* (London, 1993).

54 World Bank, *Accelerated Development in Sub-Saharan Africa: An Agenda for Action* (Washington, 1988), popularly known as the Berg Report. The original source of inspiration for the World Bank's change of mind was Peter B. Evans, Dietrich Rueschmeyer and Theda Skopol (eds.), *Bringing the State Back In* (Cambridge, 1985).

55 See the comments on the demonstrators in Prague in the *Independent*, 28 September 2000. Naomi Klein, *No Logo: Taking on the Brand Bullies* (London, 2000) shows what can be made of a one-sided argument.

56 Hurrell and Woods, *Inequality, Globalization, and World Politics* is a helpful introduction. David Miller's contribution, 'Justice and Inequality', pp. 187–210, provides a particularly lucid statement of what can and cannot be claimed under this heading. Practical action can be found in the new movement for 'fair trade'.

57 Buultjens, 'Global History and the Third World', pp. 71–91. Buultjens makes the additional point that gender history, too, is very Western in conception.

58 Holton, *Globalization and the Nation State*, pp. 12–14.

59 A proposal first put into circulation by *Le Monde* in 1974. Castells appears to have been unaware of this prior claim when he advanced the notion of a Fourth World 'made up of multiple black holes of social exclusion throughout the planet'. Castells, *The Information Age*, vol. III, p. 164.

60 I insert the qualification in deference to Daniel C. Bach, 'Les dynamiques paradoxicales de l'integration en Afrique subsaharienne: le mythe du hors-jeu', *Revue Française de Science Politique*, 45 (1995), pp. 1023–38, though it could be said that his interpretation is consistent with the majority view that, in important respects, sub-Saharan Africa has indeed become less closely integrated with the rest of the world than it was at the time of independence.

61 A representative example is P.W. Daniels and W.F. Lever (eds.), *The Global Economy in Transition* (London, 1996).

62 See for example James H. Mittelman (ed.), *Globalization: Critical Reflections* (London, 1996), chs. 6, 7, 8, and 9.

63 A similar criticism was made of William McNeill's *The Rise of the West: A History of the Human Community* (Chicago, 1964). An alternative approach was outlined by

Marshall G.S. Hodgson, *Rethinking World History: Essays on Europe, Islam and World History* (Cambridge, 1993). See also Geyer and Bright, 'World History in a Global Age'; and Peter N. Sterns, Michael Adas and Stuart B. Schwartz, *World Civilizations: The Global Experience* (New York, 1992). Immanuel Wallerstein, 'Eurocentrism and its Atavars: The Dilemmas of Social Science', *New Left Review*, 226 (1997), pp. 93–107, offers a restatement of the European perspective.

64 Edward Friedman, 'Reinterpreting the Asianization of the World and the Role of the State in the Rise of China', in Smith *et al.*, *States and Sovereignty*, pp. 246–63; *idem*, *The Politics of Democratization: Generalizing East Asian Experiences* (Boulder, Co., 1994). The role of Asia is also emphasized, though at a much more general level, by Giovanni Arrighi, 'Globalization, State Sovereignty, and the "Endless" Accumulation of Capital', in Smith *et al.*, *States and Sovereignty*, pp. 53–73.

65 Friedman, 'Reinterpreting the Asianization of the World', p. 249.

66 Starting points include: Philip D. Curtin, *Cross-Cultural Trade in World History* (Cambridge, 1984); Stephen Castles and Mark J. Miller, *The Age of Migration: International Population Movements in the Modern World* (London, 1993); Wang Gungwu, 'Migration and its Enemies', in Mazlish and Buultjens, *Conceptualizing Global History*, pp. 131–51; and the important set of essays in *idem* (ed.), *Global History and Migrations* (Boulder, Co., 1997).

67 John Torpey, *The Invention of the Passport* (Cambridge, 2000); D. Jacobson, *Rights Across Borders: Immigration and the Decline of Citizenship* (Baltimore, 1996); *idem*, 'Human Rights as Global Imperative', in Mazlish and Buultjens, *Conceptualising Global History*, pp. 173–204.

68 Frank and Gills, *The World System*, chs. 1, 3, 5.

69 Samir Amin, 'The Ancient World Systems Versus the Modern Capitalist World System', in Frank and Gills, *The World System*, p. 247; Immanuel Wallerstein 'World System Versus World Systems', ibid., pp. 292–6.

70 Eric Jones, *The European Miracle*, 2nd edn. (London, 1987).

71 J.M. Blaut, *The Colonizer's Model of the World* (New York, 1993); Kenneth Pomerantz, 'Two Worlds of Trade, Two Worlds of Empire: European State-Making and Industrialization in a Chinese Mirror', in Smith *et al.*, *States and Sovereignty*, pp. 74–98.

72 Among other criticisms of this kind made at the time, see A.G. Hopkins, 'Clioantics: A Horoscope for African Economic History', in Christopher Fyfe (ed.), *African Studies Since 1945* (London, 1976), pp. 31–48.

73 I agree here with Kevin O'Rourke and Jeffrey G. Williamson, 'When did Globalization Begin?', *National Bureau of Economic Research Working Paper*, 7632 (2000), pp. 1–2.

74 Amin, 'Ancient World Systems', p. 253. Amin is here also restating a Marxist position against Frank's radical but non-Marxist free-thinking.

75 Janet Abu-Lughod, 'Discontinuities and Persistence: One World System or a Succession of Systems?', in Frank and Gills, *World System*, p. 284. The full statement is in her book, *Before European Hegemony: The World System, 1250–1350* (Oxford, 1989).

76 Abu-Lughod, *Before European Hegemony*, p. 361.

77 Circuit 5 covers the Nile and the Red Sea but excludes west Africa.

78 Abu-Lughod concludes her study in the fourteenth century. However, none of the contributions to Frank and Gills, *World System*, makes any reference to the work of Lieberman and Reid cited here (notes 81–2 below). This is a serious empirical omission and also a telling indication of the persistence of an excessively Western

view of the world in the period after 1500. Andrew Gunder Frank, *Global Economy in the Asian Age* (London, 1998) advances the general proposition that Asia was the centre of the world economy before 1800 but couples this with the view that the rise of the West was a result of the fall of the rest – and of Asia in particular.

79 The high point of Ming sea-borne expansion occurred between 1405 and 1433, when Admiral Cheng Ho launched a series of explorations of westward 'rediscovery' that took his fleets to the east coast of Africa. Ships from Asia first reached east Africa around 200 BC. On this subject generally see G. Deng, *Chinese Maritime Activities and Socio-Economic Development, c. 2100–1990* (1997).

80 *Idem*, 'A Critical Survey of Recent Research in Chinese Economic History', *Economic History Review*, 53 (2000), pp. 5–6.

81 Anthony Reid, 'An "Age of Commerce" in Southeast Asian History', *Modern Asian Studies*, 24 (1990), pp. 1–30.

82 J.A. Goldstone, *Revolution and Rebellion in the Early Modern World* (Berkeley, 1991). The seminal works are by Victor B. Lieberman, *Burmese Administrative Cycles: Anarchy and Conquest, 1580–1760* (Princeton, 1984), and Anthony Reid, *Southeast Asia in the Age of Commerce, 1450–1680* (2 vols., New Haven, 1988, 1993).

83 Immanuel Wallerstein, *The Modern World System*, vol. II, *Mercantilism and the Consolidation of the European World Economy, 1600–1750* (New York, 1980), p. 258; see also pp. 2–9.

84 See also my Introduction and the essays by Bayly, Drayton and Ballantyne in this volume.

85 P.J. Cain and A.G. Hopkins, *British Imperialism, 1688–2000* (2nd edn., London, 2001); Linda Colley, *Britons: Forging the Nation, 1707–1837* (New Haven, 1992).

86 Colin Kidd, *British Identities Before Nationalism: Ethnicity and Nationhood in the Atlantic World, 1600–1800* (Cambridge, 1999), and his equally illuminating earlier work, *Subverting Scotland's Past: Scottish Whig Historians and the Creation of an Anglo-British Identity, 1689–1830* (Cambridge, 1993). A similar emphasis on the diversity of identities in the United Kingdom is apparent in Brendan Bradshaw and Peter Roberts (eds.), *British Consciousness and Identity: The Making of Britain, 1533–1707* (Cambridge, 1998).

87 David Hancock, *Citizens of the World* (London, 1995) deals with the Atlantic. The origins of this development have been authoritatively traced by Robert Brenner, *Merchants and Revolution: Commercial Change, Political Conflict and London's Overseas Traders, 1550–1653* (Princeton, 1993).

88 Tony Claydon and Ian McBride (eds.), *Protestantism and National Identity: Britain and Ireland, c. 1650–c. 1850* (Cambridge, 1998).

89 Some of the historiographical disjunctions arising from this fluidity are discussed by David Armitage, 'Greater Britain: A Useful Category of Historical Analysis?', *American Historical Review*, 104 (1999), pp. 427–45.

90 The key studies of this subject are Niels Steensgaard, *Carracks, Caravans and Companies: The Structural Crisis in the European–Asian Trade in the Early Seventeenth Century* (Copenhagen, 1973), and K.N. Chaudhuri, *The Trading World of Asia and the East India Company, 1660–1760* (Cambridge, 1978). There is only space here to note that Steensgaard has been criticized by Sanjay Subrahmanyam, *The Portuguese Empire in Asia, 1500–1700* (London, 1993); no one has yet attempted to refute Chaudhuri's complementary argument about the later period.

91 See here C.A. Bayly, 'The First Age of Global Imperialism, c. 1760–1830', *Journal of Imperial and Commonwealth History*, 26 (1998), pp. 29–47.

92 For example, Kathleen Wilson has shown how national liberty and the possession

of empire had become linked in the popular mind by the end of the eighteenth century: *The Sense of the People: Politics, Culture, and Imperialism in England, 1717–1785* (Cambridge, 1995).

93 H.V. Bowen, 'British Conceptions of Global Empire, 1756–83', *Journal of Imperial and Commonwealth History*, 26 (1988), pp. 5–7.

94 Especially, of course, after the loss of the American colonies. Anthony Pagden, *Lords of All the World* (London, 1995) provides a valuable point of entry into a vast and complex literature.

95 For a summary view and further references see Bayly, 'First Age of Global Imperialism'; Cain and Hopkins, *British Imperialism*, pp. 66–87; and, more briefly, Hopkins, 'Back to the Future', p. 207–9.

96 Cain and Hopkins, *British Imperialism*.

97 Ibid., chs. 1–2.

98 Ibid., pp. 64–5. Kant had already identified the National Debt as being the 'ingenious invention of a commercial people', but feared that the 'dangerous money power' standing behind it would encourage aggression by enabling wars to be fought more easily: *Perpetual Peace*, p. 88.

99 See my Introduction in this volume.

100 Anthony Reid, 'Historiographical Reflections on the Period 1750–1870 in Southeast Asia and Korea', *Itinerario*, 18 (1994), pp. 83–4, refers to 'a Chinese century' between 1740 and 1840. See also Deng, 'Recent Research', p. 4, and the additional citations given there.

101 Intra-Asian trade via Nagasaki remained significant after 1639; more important still, the period of closure was followed by far-reaching internal developments that made a vital contribution to Japan's economic 'miracle' after 1868. On these and allied themes see A.J.H. Latham and Heita Kawakatsu (eds.), *Japanese Industrialization and the Asian Economy* (London, 1994).

102 For reasons of space this remark is necessarily elliptical but refers to the blurring of the distinction between small trading polities and large agrarian states. The best introduction to these developments is C.A. Bayly, *Imperial Meridian: The British Empire and the World, 1780–1830* (London, 1989), chs. 1–2.

103 Ibid., ch. 2, and for their contribution to the 'world crisis' between 1780 and 1820, see ch. 6.

104 I am aware that there is an incongruity in referring to Islam as a non-state actor, but I do so here to establish the connection with the literature on globalization, which, broadly speaking, places religious and cultural themes in this category.

105 The first detailed account of the desert crossing was given by the celebrated Arab traveller, Ibn Battuta, in the 1350s.

106 Herman M. Schwartz, *States Versus Markets* (New York, 1994) and the symposium on globalization in the *Journal of Economic Perspectives*, 12 (1998) are helpful here.

107 Particular mention must be made of the work of Jeffrey Williamson and his associates cited in notes 109 and 112–14 below.

108 A valuable survey of these developments is Patrick O'Brien, 'Europe in the World Economy', in Hedley Bull and Adam Watson (eds.), *The Expansion of International Society* (Oxford, 1984), pp. 43–60. James Foreman-Peck (ed.), *Historical Foundations of Globalization* (London, 1998) presents a selection of primary and secondary materials on these themes.

109 On the 'amazing' decline in international transport costs see Philippe Aghion and Jeffrey G. Williamson, *Growth, Inequality and Globalization* (Cambridge, 1998), pp. 133–8.

110 China was the object of both diplomacy and force but was still not effectively integrated into the international system in the nineteenth century.

111 Measured, for purposes of comparison, as a percentage of GDP. See Paul Bairoch, 'Globalization Myths and Realities: One Century of External Trade and Foreign Investment', in Boyer and Drache, *States Against Markets*, pp. 173–92.

112 Jeffrey G. Williamson, 'Globalization, Convergence, and History', *Journal of Economic History*, 56 (1996), pp. 277–306; *idem*, 'The Evolution of Global Labour Markets since 1830: Background Evidence and Hypotheses', *Explorations in Economic History*, 32 (1995), pp. 141–96; *idem*, 'Globalization, Labor Markets and Policy Backlash in the Past', *Journal of Economic Perspectives*, 12 (1998), pp. 51–72.

113 Alan M. Taylor and Jeffrey G. Williamson, 'Convergence in the Age of Mass Migration', *European Review of Economic History*, 1 (1997), pp. 27–63; Kevin O'Rourke, 'The European Grain Invasion, 1870–1914', *Journal of Economic History*, 57 (1994), pp. 775–801. The Organization for Economic Co-operation and Development was founded in 1961 to represent 18 industrial countries in Europe, the United States and Canada. Today it covers nearly 30 countries, including Australia, New Zealand and Japan.

114 Kevin O'Rourke and Jeffrey G. Williamson, 'Late Nineteenth-Century Anglo-American Factor-Price Convergence', *Journal of Economic History*, 54 (1994), pp. 892–916; *idem*, *Globalization and History*; Jeffrey G. Williamson, 'Land, Labor and Globalization in the Pre-Industrial Third World', paper presented to the ESF Conference on Historical Market Integration, Venice, 1999. I am grateful to Professor Williamson for allowing me to see the text of his unpublished contribution.

115 *The Great Illusion* (London, 1910), pp. viii, ix.

116 Cain and Hopkins, *British Imperialism*, ch. 14.

117 Williamson, 'Globalization, Convergence and History'.

118 Cain and Hopkins, *British Imperialism*, pp. 472–3, 503, 508–11, 515–6, 520, 531, 553–4, 559, 609.

119 It need hardly be said that the economic theme has generated various sub-texts that cannot be considered here. One concerns the robustness of the statistical data and the value of GDP measurements; another concerns the extent to which free trade characterized the period 1850–1914. See, respectively, Aghion and Williamson, *Growth, Inequality and Globalization*, pp. 110–12, and Paul Bairoch, *Economics and World History* (London, 1993), chs. 2–3.

120 Stephen Krasner is among the most forceful exponents of this argument: 'Globalization and Sovereignty', in Smith, Solinger and Topik, *States and Sovereignty*, pp. 34–52.

121 For example, the development of Scottish identity *after* the Union with England in 1707: see Kidd, *Subverting Scotland's Past*; and John MacKenzie, 'On Scotland and the Empire', *International History Review*, 15 (1993), pp. 714–39.

122 Hopkins, 'Back to the Future' and the references given there. I would now add Janice E. Thomson's impressive study, which argues that national states cannot come into being until they have a monopoly of coercive power, and that this happened in the nineteenth century and not before: *Mercenaries, Pirates and Sovereigns: State-Building and Extra-Territorial Violence in Early Modern Europe* (Princeton, 1994).

123 Robert H. Jackson, *Quasi-States Sovereignty, International Relations and the Third World* (Cambridge, 1990).

124 See notes 112–15 above.

125 Rothschild, 'Globalization', p. 107.

126 This is an example of a neglected subject that needs to be opened up if the history of globalization is to be reconstructed. Some introductory information can be found in Craig C. Murphy, *International Organisation and Industrial Change: Global Governance since 1850* (Cambridge, 1994). Boli and Thomas, *Constructing World Cultures*, provide a set of detailed papers.

127 As it is termed today. See Lipschutz, 'Reconstructing World Politics'.

128 Britain had an ambiguous attitude towards the international organizations that her own activities had done so much to create, being suspicious of those she could not control and enthusiastic about those that were largely extensions of her own interests. See Murphy, *International Organisations*, pp. 78–9.

129 I cite these examples to offer suggestions for future research into topics that have been greatly understated in all standard histories of the period.

130 David Mikosz, 'Eurocentric Views of Universal Languages from 1605 to 1828', *Itinerario*, 22 (1998), pp. 103–15, shows how the attempt to create a universal language for describing the world as a whole ended in the extended use of English in the nineteenth century.

131 Here again is a topic that is at once obvious and yet neglected to an extraordinary degree, given the massive interest shown by postmodernists in the use of language. Yet, though the work of every major novelist has now been anatomized for signs of stereotyping and race prejudice, the development of the core language itself has escaped attention. A brief introduction is David Crystal, *English as a Global Language* (Cambridge, 1997).

132 *The Times*, 19 July 2000, p. 13. Duneton was intervening in the debate about whether French spelling should be simplified to make the language easier and therefore more popular, and thus be better equipped to fend off the invasion of English.

133 Kaoru Sugihara, 'Patterns of Asia's Integration in the World Economy, 1880–1913', in C. Knick Harley (ed.), *The Integration of the World Economy, 1850–1914*, vol. II (London, 1996), pp. 700–19.

134 See A.J.H. Latham, *The International Economy and the Underdeveloped World, 1865–1914* (London, 1978), pp. 76, 81, 85, 93–4, 144–7, and, for the importance of Burma in the story, pp. 151–2; A.J.H. Latham and Larry Neal, 'The International Market in Rice and Wheat, 1868–1914', *Economic History Review*, 36 (1983), pp. 260–80.

135 As explored by T.N. Harper in this volume.

136 This cautionary remark is prompted by the tendency in some of the contemporary literature not only to assume a state of Western dominance but to presume that the desirable goal of policy is to preserve the global capitalist world system. Elements of this thinking can be found, among other sources, in Jeffrey D. Sachs, 'Consolidating Capitalism', *Foreign Policy*, 98 (1995), pp. 50–64.

137 This is also my own view: see 'Back to the Future', pp. 238–43.

138 For example, Cox, 'A Perspective on Globalization'.

139 Further details are contained in Richard J. Barnet and John Cavanagh, 'A Globalizing Economy: Some Implications and Consequences'; Mazlish and Buultjens, *Conceptualizing Global History*, pp. 153–71; Bairoch, 'Globalization – Myths and Realities'; Mittelman, *Globalization;* Boyer and Drache, *States Against Markets*.

140 Mittelman, *Globalization*, p. 1, reports the striking estimate that in 1982 official remittances from expatriate Pakistanis (mostly in the Middle East) exceeded

Pakistan's total export earnings from other sources and amounted to over half the foreign exchange cost of the country's imports.

141 Imperial measures have given way to metric in the post-colonial era. The prime task of the Metre Convention is to secure agreement on uniform standards because 80 per cent of world trade in finished goods involves measurement. If this goal is to be achieved, the United States will have to adopt the metric system. See the *Financial Times*, 20 May 2000, p. 11.

142 Robert Brenner, 'Uneven Development and the Long Downturn: The Advanced Capitalist Economies from Boom to Stagnation, 1950–1998', *New Left Review*, 229 (1998), pp. 1–265.

143 Cox, 'Perspective on Globalization', pp. 21–2.

144 Immanuel Wallerstein, 'States? Sovereignty? The Dilemmas of Capitalism in an Age of Transition', in Smith *et al.*, *States and Sovereignty*, pp. 20–33; quotations on pp. 32 and 33.

145 Castells, *The Information Age*, vol. 3, pp. 164–5.

C.A. BAYLY

'Archaic' and 'Modern' Globalization in the Eurasian and African Arena, *c.* 1750–1850

In 1771 Captain James Cook crossed the Pacific on HMS *Endeavour* looking for specimens, taking sightings and observing peoples. He sailed to the coast of Java, already long controlled by the Dutch East India Company. He had taken with him his interpreter and intermediary from the Pacific island of Tahiti, a man called Tupia. Cook and Tupia landed at the East India Company's great emporium of Batavia, now Jakarta. Cook's journal reads:

> Of all the circumstances which engaged the attention of Tupia, nothing struck him so much as the variety of dresses worn by the inhabitants of Batavia; he enquired the reason of what appeared to be so extraordinary in his eyes, and being told that the people were of a variety of nations, and that all were dressed according to the mode of their own country, he requested permission to follow the fashion; this request being readily complied with, a person was despatched to the ship for some South Sea cloth, with which he soon clothed himself in the dress of Otaheite.[1]

This is a description of 'first contact' under the general rubric of globalization. The arena was an east Asian emporium which in most respects still functioned as any other of the great trading marts of the Mataram empire or, earlier, of the Hinduized state of Srivijaya which preceded it. Ethnic and cultural difference was marked through variety of dress, language and deportment. A newcomer from a completely alien cultural area was able immediately to understand the logic underlying this. By wearing his own dress and adapting his deportment to that of others in the city, Tupia was able to merge into his new environment. But there was no homogenization of styles, no aspiration to a common European or local ethnic norm. Tupia's sartorial cosmopolitanism was one among the processes which constituted what I shall call 'archaic globalization'. In another, more sombre, way Tupia became a symbol of the consequences of such global connections. Within the space of a few days he had died from a disease which was raging in the city, one among innumerable victims of the illnesses which had always spread over huge distances down the inter-regional trade routes.[2]

The encounter in Batavia was also symbolic of the confluence of older forms of globalization with proto-globalization: systems of trade and political organization which had been more recently generated at the heart of the developing capitalist world economy. Most of the capital accumulated in Batavia was of local origin, even when it was in the hands of the Dutch East India Company. But Amsterdam merchants and the London financiers, who already held a large stake in the Dutch capital markets, had made small but significant long-distance direct investments in regional trades. The Dutch East India Company had attempted to 'internalize protection costs' in the words of Niels Steensgaard[3] by producing a modern system of accounting which included military costs. Standing alongside Tupia and James Cook was one 'Mr Banks', a scientific observer whose project to categorize the whole of natural history and human society represented the beginnings of modern state-sponsored scientific and anthropological research in Britain.[4] A few months later Sir Joshua Reynolds drew a portrait of Tupia's countryman, Omai, who had survived the voyage.[5] Omai was shown in the flowing robes and turban of an eastern Raja, not the stiff, pounded bark product, 'south sea cloth'. The Tahitian was thus absorbed into the universal visual categories of the European Enlightenment. Finally, the voyage across the Pacific was more than a benign humanistic exploration. Cook's voyages, along with those of his French *alter ego*, Admiral Bougainville, marked the beginning of the export to the region of the vicious conflicts between European nation states which were to partition the world over the next 150 years.[6]

This essay seeks to isolate in time and discuss the logic of archaic forms of globalization and to show how they were subordinated by, but sometimes empowered, the modern forms of globalization which were emerging from the Atlantic world economy and the western European nation state at this time.[7] The broad scheme of the essay apparently bears some similarities to that employed two decades ago by Immanuel Wallerstein.[8] The difference is that I discuss a wider range of agents of what he called 'world empires' and 'the Atlantic world-economy' in action and inter-action over a particular period of time. In doing this, I seek to avoid the rigid teleology of his approach. I intend to show that the agents of archaic globalization could become active forces in the expansion of the Euro-American-dominated world economy and even survive and transcend it. Equally, I do not attempt to erase the competitive difference between Europe and other world civilizations in the early modern period, as André Gunder Frank so resolutely does in *ReOrientate*.[9]

Does the concept of globalization offer anything to historical debates which have long discussed the 'expansion of Europe', 'the Atlantic world economy' and 'Asia before Europe?'[10] The concept of globalization – a progressive increase in the scale of social processes from a local or regional to a world level – became fashionable because a variety of disciplines came to realize that the study of the village, province, nation state or regional bloc of human communities was inadequate to capture causation even within the 'fragment'. Economists concluded that international flows of capital were becoming so massive that no single government could control them. Anthropologists realized that even small and apparently isolated communities were now directly linked to each other and to the wider society through television, the mobile telephone, the internet and population movements. Sociologists recognized that diaspora and refugee communities were as worthy of study as the working classes of particular Western countries. Writers in the broad area of 'cultural studies' noticed that symbols of American consumer culture were now universal, but that baseball hat, trainers and Pokemon cards came to mean different things when transplanted to the Philippines or Inner Mongolia. In a memorable metaphor, Arjun Appadurai concluded that the global did not eliminate the local, but that the local and the global 'cannibalized' each other.[11]

In its most useful sense, 'globalization' is a heuristic device, not a description of linear social change. It draws attention to dynamics that transcend the old units of analysis in different academic fields and attempts to quantify or to model them. While at some periods globalization might appear to be a linear process, it was at best a very discontinuous one. Archaic globalization was itself a ruptured process, set back by the fall of ancient empires and the Mongol invasions. A new phase probably began in the thirteenth and fourteenth centuries, as Janet Abu Lughod has proposed.[12] This phase did not flow smoothly into proto-globalization and on into modern globalization. The shift between these forms was accompanied by disruptions in patterns of polities, cultures and economies. Periods when global interactions increased were followed by periods when these links were reduced or severed. Globalization had always stimulated countervailing trends to regionalism and localism.

Despite their apparent muteness in this debate,[13] some historians have long been studying varieties of globalization in practice. Imperial historians,[14] historians of international trade,[15] historical geographers of species diffusion[16] and historians of Islam[17] and Christianity[18] have all analysed globalization without benefit of modish jargon. The concept, however, holds out advantages for them since it points up a number of linkages between discrete disciplinary sub-fields and isolates a number of geographical and temporal convergences which need to be investigated more closely by historians. For instance, one feature of recent economic history and social anthropology, which could well be developed by world historians, is the relationship between new patterns of consumption and new patterns of production and trade. Jan de Vries[19] argues that 'industrious revolutions' in consumption values and the disposition of family labour were perhaps more fundamental even than 'industrial revolutions' in the creation of economic modernity. But his is a resolutely

Eurocentric view at present. Some historians and anthropologists have examined the cultural logic behind patterns of changing consumption outside Europe.[20] But we still have little idea of how culture, consumption and trade facilitated the expansion of Asian, African and, ultimately, European trade in the early modern period.

World economic and social history has been built around a centre–periphery polarity which was one of the problems with Wallerstein's approach. The concept of globalization helps us to remember that for centuries it was not clear what was the 'centre' and what the 'periphery'. Even after strong centralizing impetuses were generated by European capitalism in the early nineteenth century, forms of archaic globalization were still flowing strongly. In time, these could even generate their own centripetal forces. For instance, 'European expansion' before 1850 was accompanied by a Chinese diaspora and had been preceded by Arab and Gujarati Hindu diasporas. These networks of marriage, communication and credit have, in the twentieth and twenty-first centuries, served as agents of post-imperial globalization themselves.

This essay aims to illustrate some of these themes for the years 1750–1850 by deploying broad ideal types. This was a critical period because, even before the general diffusion of the electric telegraph, steamship or refrigerated transport between 1850 and 1880, the speed of the consignment and despatch of goods in international trade and government had apparently increased very substantially. The beginnings of the modern international system were driven, therefore, not so much by technological change, but by prior political and cultural change during what I have called 'the first age of global imperialism'.[21] The argument is that the period saw the subordination of older forms of globalization to new and yet inchoate ones emerging from Euro–American capitalism and the nation state. An essential feature of this proto-globalization was its continued utilization, or 'cannibalization' of forms of archaic globalization.

The Logics and Geography of 'Archaic Globalization'

The ideologies which were formative of modern globalization comprise at core nationalism, capitalism, democracy and consumerism. Before analysing the agents of the archaic globalization which linked much of Eurasia and northern Africa until the mid-nineteenth century, it would be useful to consider in abstract some of the ideologies and bodily practices which underpinned it. This will provide important indications of the nature of earlier global linkages and help to distinguish them from modern processes. Three linked ideologies appear to have inflected the activities of archaic consumers and producers from Europe and northern Africa to China and the Pacific, underpinning old globalization: the notion of cosmic kingship; universal religion and humoural understandings of the body and the land.

The idea of cosmic kingship stands in distinction to the more modern concept of the territorial nation state based on assumed ethnicity. It consequently set different cultural rules for consumption. The Chinese empire is the best-known example of the historic claim to universal rule or the Mandate of Heaven.[22] Recently, scholars have reminded us that the Qing also continued to see themselves as Manchu world conquerors, as great Khans whose rights and obligations extended to Tibet and central Asia as well as to the whole of Southeast Asia. The Ottoman, Safavid and Mughal emperors also blended together the concept of the Second Rome and succession to the Caliphate, both globalizing concepts.[23] Like the Qing, the Indian and central Asian Mughals also saw themselves as world conquerors endowed as a family with the light of God. Pre-modern European empires shared some aspects of this mentality, combining the duty of spreading Christ's dominion with the power of Rome, as Antony Pagden[24] showed for the Spanish and Portuguese empires.

Besides legitimating long-distance conquests, these claims encouraged pre-modern kings to 'cherish men from afar', to try to create inventories of universal knowledge and universal history and to consume tribute goods and choice products from beyond the boundaries of their immediate realms. The universal King was lord over the variety of God's creation: a myriad of holy sites, products, animals and men. His aim was to aggegate and order, not to assimilate this God-given variety into one.

This common ideology also inflected the logic behind royal consumption over much of Asia and beyond, bringing large quantities of graded goods and products into treasuries each tagged and docketed with the name of the ruler, chief and region from which it came and the auspiciousness of the day on which it was received.[25] But these patterns extended downwards through the courts of the nobles to the behaviour of the petty rulers and big men of the localities. It created a nexus of consumption, tribute-giving and gift exchange. Within it, the special qualities and savour of a great range of local producing units across the whole of Eurasia, stretching out into Africa and the Pacific, were preserved and cherished for their difference. In turn, this pattern underpinned the international trade of the great overland caravan traders and the sea-borne trading powers which will be discussed below.

Particular cultural and economic patterns created subtly different patterns of exotic consumption and deportment. The dress code and accoutrements of the Ming and Qing Chinese scholar gentry were generated out of a historicized notion of Confucian propriety which prized the discrimination of scholars as opposed to the vulgar acquisitions of the merely rich.[26] This evidently differed from the west Asian pattern of Islamic dress and consumption espoused by Safavid or Mughal rulers and passed on to their subjects.[27] But the implications for global trade, exchange and knowledge were equally profound. So, for instance, otter furs from what is now Bangladesh were traded as far as Beijing and northward between 1600 and 1800 because fine fur-trimming was a seemly form of dress depicted in Chinese painting of revered, earlier dynasties.[28] Rosewood Quran rests, prayer mats, precious books and scribes came into Mughal and post-Mughal India and Southeast Asia from the Middle East, bearing the charisma of the earliest realms of the Prophet's message. The movement of specialist and knowledgeable counsellors and administrative servants followed similar patterns, so that Persian families were found taking high office in Southeast Asia in the seventeenth and eighteenth centuries.[29] The Kashmir shawl, this region's finest product, became part of its tribute to Delhi. Mughal emperors passed shawls down to their subjects in rituals of royal incorporation. They became articles of prized consumption by aristocrats and even village leaders across Eurasia. Kashmiri scholars, administrators and intellectuals serving across the empire embodied these links.

These cultural integers of consumption therefore differed from modern capitalist consumption in that they emphasized the special products and qualities of distant realms. Whereas modern complexity demands the uniformity of Levis and trainers, the archaic simplicity of everyday life demanded that great men prized difference in goods, learned servants, women and animals and sought to capture their qualities. Modern 'positional' goods are self-referential to themselves and to the markets that create demand for them; the charismatic goods of archaic globalization were embedded in ideologies which transcended them. In one sense archaic lords and rural leaders were collectors, rather than consumers. What they did, however, was more than merely to collect because the people, objects, foods, garments and styles of deportment thus assembled changed the substance of the collector.

Secondly, archaic globalization was structured by the idea of cosmic religion. Great teachers had been given broad and concentric spiritual domains by God. This underlay a very different pattern from that of the national religious missions of the nineteenth century. All the major world 'religions' or, rather, cults, conceived of a world centred on places of special spiritual power, whether Jerusalem, Boddh Gaya or Mecca. All religions viewed prayer and sacrifice at these centres as specially efficacious thus supporting both traditions of lifelong eremetism and short-term pilgrimage. The world was, therefore, dotted with the traces of God and God-driven men. Wandering renouncers travelled huge distances bringing news from one place to another. Sufi orders, archaic globalizers *par excellence*, spread across Eurasia and Africa. Hindu renouncers visited shrines in central Hungary and Russia; Chinese Christians travelled to Jerusalem. By 1600, great periodic pilgrimages had brought into being a large infrastructure of transport, victualling and credit systems, making a large contribution to international trade. Hadhramauti Sayyids travelled to Southeast Asia and Javanese and Sumatran pilgrims returned to the Arabian peninsula in large numbers.[30] In a more sinister sense, the semi-observed Islamic command to take slaves from among non-believers pushed out Muslim armies and traders beyond the bounds of the *dār-al islām*, into sub-saharan Africa[31] and even as far as Ireland and Iceland, where the 'Barbary Pirates' raided as late as the seventeenth century.

Religious ideas penetrated to the level of bodily practice and modified consumption and trade. Clothing was influenced by religious norms. So too was food. In most Eurasian societies the 'royal table' of meat, game and wine products was set in contrast to the 'sacral table' of religiously sanctioned products. For instance, sugar played a part in Chinese ritual and this slowly domesticated it as a purely pleasurable consumable.[32] Japanese fish food bore the imprint of Shinto sacrifice, its cooks remaining priests of the kitchen. Ancient firms producing soy sauce bear witness to the economic importance of this pattern.[33] Brahminical food restrictions in India and old Southeast Asia powered the global spice trade.[34] The medieval western European fishing industry was supported by the needs of societies which could be legitimately abjured to switch from the royal to the sacral table once a week on Fridays in commemoration of Christ's Passion.

Thirdly, archaic biomedical and astrological systems designed to fortify the body and the land and to improve the individual's control over the future were predicated on notions of consonance between certain moral states and certain objects and natural products. Until late in the eighteenth century the central physiological and agricultural doctrines of Eurasia and Africa were humoural and had been generated from an ancient dialogue between China, the Islamic world and the inheritance of ancient Greece.[35] This put a premium on different types of medicinal plant, spice, precious metal or precious stone. The huge value commanded by these products was another stimulant to global trade and gift exchange, bringing disparate regions together with one another. The cultural logic underlying this notion of consonance between humours and substances[36] differed both from the fetishism of precious objects as signifiers of wealth and from the universalizing principles of modern medicine. The objects themselves were expected to transform the biomoral substance of the wearer. This idea still lies behind contemporary trade in rhinoceros horns, for instance. In this, its leading assumptions are in flat opposition to modern ecology which aims to protect, rather than strategically to consume diversity.

These cultural preferences for consumption were archaic, but not static. By the seventeenth century six newly desired products greatly modified the older types of consumption and acted as a breach through which the forces of European-led proto-globalization were ultimately to surge. Refined sugar, tobacco, tea, coffee and opium galvanized these earlier systems of consumption, trade and cultural exchange.[37] None was widely used throughout Eurasia before the fifteenth century. All five had become firmly entrenched in the world's major consuming centres before 1800. All five could be seen as 'addictive' commodities, in a chemical sense. But that is an inadequate explanation for their popularity. As sociologists from Werner Sombart[38] onward have pointed out, their consumption took place in certain cultural sites: in leisured courtly salons, in newly constituted units of household labour and in new forms of sociable public space. To Jan de Vries's idea of 'industrious revolutions' we could add 'revolutions of sociability', which brought into being simultaneously London coffee houses and Chinese opium parlours.[39] These commodities, though the harbingers of modern capitalism and colonialism in Eurasia and Africa, also fitted into the biomoral logic previously discussed. They were expected to enhance taste, health, mental acuteness and sexual pleasure and to improve the quality of archaic lordship.

Finally, silver and gold, key catalysts to the velocity of global trade had something of this two-sided aspect: they responded to the values of archaic consumption but also pressaged proto-globalization and market-driven exchange. The building-up of hoards in royal and family possession was an aspect of archaic consumption.[40] At the same time, the widening use of money in the early modern period across the world was a marker of the growth of the state. The currencies of all the Eurasian empires were dependent on imports from Mexico and Peru before 1700. But later, this archaic fiscal globalization was severely ruptured by consequences for the new world of the Napoleonic Wars. The collapse of the *ancien régime* in Europe was distantly linked to contemporary Asian convulsions. The end of the Spanish empire, for instance, helped to deepen the crisis which began with the White Lotus Rebellion in China.[41] It exacerbated the problem of silver supply, already diminished by the outflow to cover imports of opium.

Some scholars have argued in regard to post-colonial globalization that it should really be seen as a process of regionalization. It is marked by the emergence of the European Union, the American free-trade area and other regional economic entities, rather than by a truly world flow of capital and trade. This idea has some resonance for archaic globalization which tended to link complementary zones together into regions. Social processes in central Asia had long spilled over periodically into India and China; Chinese taste, trade and forms of state-building pushed trade into the Nanyang, Southeast Asia. The sea slugs and birds' nests which drove entrepreneurs to the shores of Australia played very specific roles in Chinese scholar–gentry cuisine. But some relatively new inter-regional links, as far as large-scale trade and cultural exchange were concerned, seem to have developed in the period between 1500 and 1800. Indian influence and desire for household slaves and exotic trade goods integrated Southeast Asia and the 'Swahili coast' of Africa into the broader Indian Ocean with the growth after 1300 of large emporia such as Malindi in east Africa. Similarly, southern European commercial and political influences in the Mediterranean Sea and its southern hinterland increased markedly in the eighteenth century.

Some truly global linkages however, were established. As we know, silver exports across the Atlantic and Pacific Oceans were the most striking case. The Portuguese overseas empire which displayed some features of an archaic thalassocracy writ large and some features of proto-capitalism was another case in point. By the eighteenth century, Indian blue cloth had become a mark of honorific status in west Africa. Maori whalers had been settled in southern Africa. Cultural forms seem to have begun to transcend regions and become global, too. The Iberian notion of caste, *casta*, represented an old Mediterranean juridical status category melded with an Atlantic slave terminology which placed African slave blood in antithesis to Christian European purity[42] In the East, these concepts merged in turn with an Indian notion of of purity and pollution which had already been filtered through the judicial categories of Muslim law. If the Indian 'caste system' was, indeed, an invented category, its invention was already well under way in the globalizing pre-modern society· and did not await the coming of British imperialism to India.

'Economy' and 'Culture'

Here we should pause and ask what relations between the two abstractions 'culture' and 'economy' have been proposed thus far. This essay seeks to avoid simplistic cultural reductionism as well as simplistic economic reductionism by re-integrating value-driven and profit-driven approaches to archaic societies.[43] In a sense, all economic activity was and is 'cultural'. But that does not get us very far because with equal plausibility we might assert that all cultural activity is economic, as rigorous Marxists used to do. Instead, the chart overleaf attempts to chart what is implied by this essay. Certain products, such as basic grains and basic cloth were more or less universally required and universally produced in all pre-modern agrarian economies. Economic activities based on production and consumption at this level were predictable and differed little from one civilization to another. They were determined by the harvest, distance to markets, the relationship of supply and demand. Their exchange summoned up all the common attributes of economic man. By contrast, there were other products and patterns of consumption which were both geographically specific and heavily determined by cultural preference: Arab horses, otter skins, certain types of medicinal spices and diamonds, for instance.[44] There were also products which carried a heavy freight of cultural value and reputation, but which were produced fairly evenly across regions: flowers and fruit, for instance.

Intermediate and long-distance trade in early modern Eurasia was not simply a matter of preciosities, as used to be said, though transport costs were critical. However, trades and complementary patterns of consumption with both a high geographical and high cultural specificity were disproportionately important in regional economies and in emerging patterns of global connection for a number of reasons. First, they attracted silver and gold as media of exchange: one preciosity attracts another. This focused the attention of states and their agents on exploiting and protecting such products. Secondly, their production involved the use of rare embodied labour skills, knowledge and reputation, which could not easily be reproduced. The opportunity cost of

A. 'Old' global society, *c*.1650 ('archaic globalization')

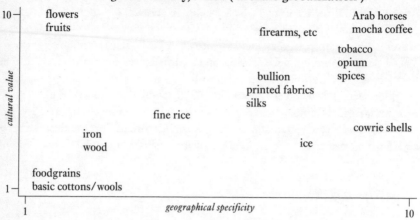

B. 'Early modern' global society, *c*.1750 ('proto-globalization')

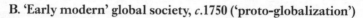
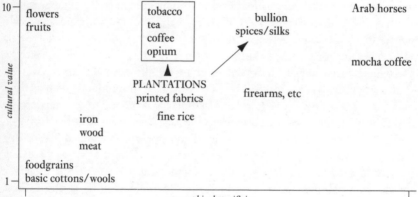

C. Modern global society, *c*.1880

training a silk-weaver in a poor economy was very great. Eurasian rulers, therefore seized and 'repatriated' specialist weaving and artisan communities. There was little notion of the transfer of skills to their own populations through education or economic development: these are modern ideas. Labour was captured not trained. Conversely, rulers went to great lengths to protect the trade secrets of production and merchant intermediaries to promote the reputation of their products. The Republic of Venice, for instance, forbade the dissemination of the secrets of Murano glass factories on pain of death. Apocryphally, the factors of the East India Company cut off the thumbs of specialist Bengali weavers. Reputation and rarity ensured the development and continuation of global patterns of land and sea-borne trade in these commodities.

The first wedge of what the Introduction has termed proto-globalization was represented by the plantation and American slave system. This was designed to re-distribute what had been geographically specific commodity production and labour while maintaining reputation and the cultural specificity of consumption. Dutch and later English plantation-produced coffee, for instance, was soon cultivated in areas far distant from the old production areas of southern Arabia. But by controlling supply and maintaining the link between its consumption and elite sociability and medicinal reputation, the companies were able to ensure that coffee remained an expensive rarity which families locked away in hardwood boxes. Labour was coerced and new modes of production diffused at a global level, but the agents of early capitalism were happy to maintain archaic ideologies of consumption because this helped to increase profits, at least in the medium term.

Agents of old globalization and their modern fate

(1) TRIBAL DYNASTIC MIGRATIONS AND PIONEER HORSEMEN

This essay now moves on to examine some of the agents of archaic globalization in greater detail. It considers the form of their decline in the period of proto-globalization, but also shows how some of these agents persisted into the nineteenth century and beyond because they could play a functional role in the new world division of labour and knowledge.

First, the periodic irruption of nomadic soldiers, founding new dynasties, disrupting patterns of trade but eventually creating new polities and new commercial links, was an ancient feature of Eurasian and African society. Invasive warrior dynasts from Alexander and Attila through Genghis Khan and Tamberlaine to Nadir Shah[45] in the eighteenth century, were genuine agents of global change. They traversed huge tracts of land, bringing local, often tribal and shamanistic, practices to new regions. Their destruction or revamping of political systems brought into being new patterns of government.

This form of warrior globalization declined in importance between 1750 and 1850. By the end of the nineteenth century, it was reduced to a small-scale local phenomenon.

The eighteenth century in Asia still saw several important movements of this sort. The Persian King Nadir Shah attacked the Ottomans and struck deeply into India in 1739. He pulled together an alliance of free cavalry soldiers (*kazak*s) from the tribal groups of the Iranian and central Asian peripheries. In the 1750s and again in the 1790s, Durrani tribesmen from Afghanistan invaded and destabilized India, continuing an old pattern in which Pathan soldiers descended on the subcontinent and often settled there.[46] In the second half of the eighteenth century the Wahhabi tribal and religious movement of the Najd in the Arabian peninsula broke out into the satrapies of the Ottoman Empire. The holy places of Mecca, Medina and Karbala were sacked and the trade of Egypt threatened. Throughout, the expansion of the Tsarist empire was preceded by a form of tribal predatory settlement pioneered by the Cossacks. In Africa the *jihad* of Dan Fodio across west Africa in the 1820s displayed some of these features.[47]

Historically, these movements had a number of features in common. Firstly, they were successful because they deployed a novel combination of men and weaponry. The horse-archer of the Mongols; the combination of heavy cavalry and artillery of the Manchus and Mughals; the Russian-style combination of fast cavalry and artillery of Nadir Shah – all these were innovations in their time. Secondly, these tribal globalizers combined military with economic power. By threatening trade routes valuable to urban centres of power in the settled territories, they could either starve or force their rulers to terms. Caches of captured silver allowed them to employ specialist soldiers, artisans and, later, administrators to police newly created realms. Thirdly, young men followed these dynastic invaders because the high valleys, the steppe and the desert fringes were too poor to support an expanding population. In time, as conquering elites in rich agricultural lands the new dynasts encouraged further outflows of young men from the marginal tracts which had once been their homes. Finally, in the Islamic context, the leaders of these great movements summoned up memories of the Prophet's progress to Medina, though Alexander, 'Iskander', was the most common exemplar.

In the eighteenth century these movements did not create new cosmic empires, as they had done earlier. They did, however, weaken the remaining old empires and they drove capital to the enclaves of the new Euro-American proto-global economy. Contemporaries noted that Bengal, for instance, was largely immune to the effects of Nadir's invasion,[48] but many Indian capitalists moved from Delhi, Agra and Lahore into the coastal territories where the English East India Company was increasingly powerful. An off-hand comment by Warren Hastings of 1786 suggests that the looting of north India's bullion had allowed Iran and Iraq to continue to purchase Indian goods in the latter part of the eighteenth century, so helping to maintain the Company's financial health in western India.[49] The last spasms of this form of archaic globalization, therefore, seem to have aided the financial empowerment of the new quasi-capitalist European one.

Zaman Shah Durrani's invasion of India in 1798 was perhaps the last flicker of these old pan-Eurasian bush fires. Why then did this pattern of global change decline in the nineteenth century? The reason was partly a military one. The new European-style armies, including the troops of Muhammad Ali in Egypt and the rulers of early Qajar Iran could stop tribal cavalry charges dead and outgun tribal artillery. The British in India and the French in north Africa created stud farms to breed big Arab horses which outclassed the wiry nomadic horses of central Asia or the Sahara. Again, the extractive nature of the new colonial and para-colonial regimes gave them resources and a degree of credit much greater than those of the older polities; hence they were less vulnerable to predatory attack. But, thirdly, the political and military policies of the colonial and para-colonial powers allowed them to avoid the 'locust-like' massing of small tribal warbands into larger coalitions. Political officers and military governors kept the tribesmen divided and ruled. Recruiting officers coralled the younger sons into tribal regiments of the colonial governments. In the early stages of European colonial empires, these cavalry bands were still employed to extract political tribute for the European rulers. But the context in which they operated had changed out of recognition.

(2) · MERCHANT DIASPORAS AND SEA-BORNE TRADING POWERS

In the case of the tribal raiding movements, the individual free cavalryman was the basic unit. Cavalrymen massed together on lines of kinship and patronage under the aegis of a great war leader. Another distinct type of archaic globalization consisted in the linked long-distant networks of sea-borne merchant communities. Here the basic unit was the shipowning captain, or partnership of merchant and shipowner. But these units bonded together in 'shoals' (the equivalent of the land-based 'locust' phenomenon) under the aegis of port kings or corporations who offered them protection and well-fortified central places within which to trade. These long-distant trading communities were communities of mercantile trust, sometimes underpinned by long-range marriage connections and often by common religious confession. Much has been written to show how Islam acted as a bonding agent across the whole area from the ports of the eastern Mediterranean to the Indonesian archipelago.[50] But beneath this broad umbrella of similarity in religious practice, there existed many smaller communities defined by a loose allegiance to a common headman, prince or sultan who embodied a degree of religious authority. Networks of mosques and the tombs or hospices of Sufi teachers acted as the central places where these communities overlapped with each other. As with the great tribal leaders of the nomadic-warrior caravans or armed bands, big commercial men were able to fund and support shipowners and smaller merchants, so concentrating power and authority and giving these diasporic communities a degree of internal political coherence.

In the seventeenth century and early eighteenth century, these linked communities formed a commercial ecumene from the north-west African coast to the northern tip of Australia and Mozambique. The most important sea-borne trading powers or thalassocracies which dominated the trading life of the seventeenth century were the Beys of Algiers (the 'Barbary Pirates'), the Knights of St John of Malta, the Republic of Venice, the Greek merchants of the Dodecanese, the Arabs of Muskat and Oman, the Bohras of the western Indian coast and the Bugis of the Malay world.[51] All of these corporations or sea-borne monarchies were formerly subject to great external emperors or kings, but they all retained considerable local political power and the power to arbitrate commercial disputes.

This form of sea-borne commercial culture survived into the nineteenth century. As Rajat Ray [52] has shown, the maritime bazaar economy formed an essential underpinning of the expansion of capitalist finance and production across the Eurasian and north African world throughout the colonial period. In many respects it was more resilient than the larger and newer capitalist enterprises that overlay it and weathered the slumps in the north Atlantic economy better. Still, the dominant trend was for the subordination of the old-style merchant diasporas and thalassocracies to larger forms of state and commerce. This was in part the result of a a long-term change in economic management. Niels Steensgaard argued that the Portuguese 'sea-borne empire' was in effect a version of pre-modern thalassocracy writ large. He went on to suggest that by 'internalising protection costs' the Dutch effectively replaced this type of international peddling trade with something more like capitalist production.[53] Here production is adjusted to raise final prices to the consumer at an international level and to suppress local production costs. K.N. Chaudhuri followed this by showing that the English East India Company was able to exert a surprising degree of control over purchase of its cotton goods in India and sale in Europe. It was in fact, capable of the fine price control which characterize modern corporations.[54]

The deployment of new forms of political authority and military power was equally important in the decline of the thalassocracies. Studies of the Mediterranean have shown that the great powers were already beginning to exercise a form of proto-nationalist hegemony in the early eighteenth century.[55] French control over trade was diminishing the room for manoeuvre of the Knights of Malta and the Venetians. Meanwhile, the Ottoman government was extending its control over the eastern Mediterranean. Further east, the British in Bombay were flexing their muscles against the mercantile kingdoms in an attempt to force down the prices of Mocha coffee.[56]

By 1830, despite a temporary revival of Muscat and the Bugis during the Napoleonic Wars, indigenous shipping and the old indigenous merchants of the coast and the port kings were all in full decline again.[57] The dominance of the Royal Navy (and to a much lesser extent of the French and Ottoman navies) had been confirmed. Punitive action by the British against the Muskat Arabs and Bugis, by the Americans against the Barbary pirates, along with the ending of the rule of the Knights of Malta, had circumscribed the political power of the older forms of mercantile community. Indigenous shipping found increasing difficulty in finding insurers and meeting the legal requirements imposed by European mercantile law. Many of these changes were in place before the major technical changes which accompanied the steamship and the electric telegraph in the 1840s. By 1860 the bulk of world shipping was controlled by the merchant fleets of the great European powers and the United States with the result that the older sea-borne trading powers were reduced to the status of local adjuncts to a system of maritime finance and control which was based on London, Amsterdam, New York and Marseilles.

(3)   THE LAND CARAVAN TRADE

Similar in structure to the thalassocracies were the extensive networks of the great land-based merchants operating across Eurasia since the time of the silk-route. At the height of the Islamic and early Tsarist empires, these may well have accounted for a considerable element of global trade. Items of exceptionally high value, such as Arab horses, medicines and silks, passed along these routes. Their importance was enhanced by the important role they played in distributing new-world silver from western and central Europe through the Middle East to India and China. Silver and gold were attracted in large quantities to India where it became stores of value in the form of family jewellery.

The merchants operating on these routes were varied and trade was by no means entirely circumscribed by ethnic–legal categories. Still, among the most important traders were the Armenians who fanned out from the Iranian city of Julfa, westward into the Ottoman Empire and Russia and eastward through India as far as Burma and Thailand.[58] Armenian families were prominent in eighteenth-century Burma, for instance, where they played a major part in the trade in raw cotton, birds' nests and sea-slugs into western China. Muslim Kashmiri traders plied routes from eastern India through Tibet into central Asia. Indian Khattri and Sindhi merchants traded down into south India and up into Russian central Asia where thay had a large colony in Astrakhan on the Caspian sea.[59] These traders are best described as medium-term diasporic communities. Family members went off to run branch agencies in distant cities for five years or more, sometimes marrying local women, but eventually returning to their home cities. Inter-regional movements of this sort generalized sophisticated double-entry bookkeeping methods along with disciplines of accountancy and categorization. In some cases, they diffused new forms of religious observance.

As with the thalassocracies, these agents of archaic globalization suffered both a cyclical and a structural decline in the period from 1750 to 1850. They had flourished with the rise of the Islamic world empires and had contributed to their growth. The fragmentation of these polities raised protection costs against them. While every individual regional or local ruler may have had an interest in keeping trade flowing, no one had the authority to enforce their protection as a common good. Exactions severely damaged these trades and the patterns of cultural exchange which accompanied them. The general crisis of the towns of Iran, central Asia and north India affected them,[60] as did the decline of old consuming elites in other parts of Asia with the onset of colonialism. It seems possible, too, that the severe specie crisis caused first by the East India Company's halt to bullion imports into India after 1757 and later by the collapse of production in Mexican and Peruvian mines after 1805 acted to choke off commerce. At the same time, the economies of scale and protection costs offered by the British domination of sea-trade after 1805 meant that sea-trade increasingly outstripped land-trade, fortified as it was with better systems of insurance and quality control.

Similar merchant communities did, of course, continue to trade in the nineteenth and twentieth centuries. Claude Markovits has recently shown how Sindhi traders linked the manufacture of Japanese exotica with clients in Egypt and even as far afield as central America in the late nineteenth century. At the same time they penetrated deeply into Russia, raising administrative difficulties for the British and Russian empires.[61] But such communities were definitely subordinate to the wider structure of the European capital markets, manufacturing system and national and imperial states. It is perhaps true that the modern descendants of some of the most archaic diasporas have rediscovered their independence in the era of post-colonial globalization. Yet the international division of labour and global information order in which they operate is now so radically different that continuities remain only at the level of language, legend and worship.

Responses to Archaic Globalization

The various globalizing agents discused here have long been considered by specialist historians. What 'globalization' as a heuristic device may be able to do is to cause them to be viewed in a different light. Rather than being 'noises off' in the history of the expansion of Europe or fodder for study in the more pettifogging of departments of Oriental Studies, they can be better seen as integral dimensions of archaic globalization, that is of a pattern of commerce and culture with a degree of functional coherence.

The same may be true of the relationship between old globalization and the local. An essential part of the model of modern globalization is the assumption that the global and the local are in constant dialogue and conflict. One informs the other; neither is prior to the other. Thus José Bove the French environmental activist or 'Gandhi des Brebis', is a 'construction' of 'McDonald-ization', rather than being an organic representative of 'la France profonde' perduring through history. This is of relevance to historians of the seventeenth and eighteenth centuries who may need to reassign the weight given to external, globalizing phenomena in their understanding of the development of the early modern state or the regional identities which preceded the nineteenth century.

It is true that some historians have always assigned great weight to such forces in their accounts of the development of particular culture areas or proto-nations. Most historians of Southeast Asia, but notably Anthony Reid, [62] have persistently argued that diaspora and international trade have been critical factors in the creation of 'Indonesian' states and identities. Again, some historians of the Islamic world such as Marshall Hodgson and Andre Wink[63] have gone very far in tying all developments in Islamic Eurasia and Africa to the international spread of trade, Islam and gunpowder. On the other hand, most histories are still predicated on the assumption that it was essentially internal developments, such as the growth of agricultural production, internal class formation and the movement from lineage to state, which determined the emergence of proto-nations, be they England or Syria. External factors have generally been seen as contingent.

Though we cannot develop the point very far here, the concept of archaic globalization may give a different picture of the emergence of the early modern state and early modern patriotic identities. In a negative sense, for instance, the periodic irruptions of 'the Turk' from the outside world into India, Iran, China and the Arab lands seem to have been an important force in the creation of the fluid senses of regional identity and patriotism which were apparent even before the eighteenth century in these societies. [64] By the eighteenth century the Indian Marathas, laying claim to the mantle of the Mughals, asserted that 'no king of Iran or Turan has ever held dominion in Hindustan'[65] in response to Nadir Shah's incursion. Again, Sri Lankan historians have shown how far a Sri Lankan patriotism had come into being before 1750, defined in part by the perceived twin threat from Tamil south India and the Portuguese.[66]

On the positive side, the speed of state-building in India, China and Southeast Asia between 1500 and 1800 was greatly increased by the influx of precious metals along a myriad of trade routes, including the overland caravan and sea-borne links. Military technology which spread faster even than bullion also helped Asian and African state-builders. Often it was disseminated from Chinese or Ottoman, rather than from European sources. Here knowledge from the wider world was turned inward to build stronger regional powers.[67] Historical data reinterpreted in this light might help to put African and Asian state-building into the same broad context as Europe's where recent work has emphasized again the importance of inter-state relations and global conflict in the formation of 'enlightened despotisms'.

Proto-globalization: The Origins of Modern Globalization

When Tupia the Tahitian came to Batavia he fitted into a dimension of this archaic pattern of globalization, becoming representative of another 'nation' of long-distance merchant communities in a multi-ethnic emporium. But, by the eighteenth century, there were distinctly new forces creating parallel and encompassing patterns of globalization. These were in some respects new in scale, in some respects new in quality. Tupia was carried into the Dutch East Indies on Cook's *Endeavour* which repesented these forces.

There had long been merchant capitalism across the breadth of Eurasia. Indian, Chinese and Arab merchant communities had developed complex systems of credit and double-entry bookkeeping which paralleled those of Europe. Governments struggled to control the unintended moral consequences of the expansion of commerce which larger states and the spread of archaic consumption entailed.[68] What distinguished eighteenth-century Europe, the Caribbean and the east coast of north America in the era of proto-globalization, however, was the way in which capitalist relations of production had expanded in scale. By the eighteenth century large sections of whole societies were fully geared to the reproduction of capital. The disposition of land, labour and status operated increasingly through the market. The cultural logics of consumption were driven by the need to display wealth as an external indication of a homogenized social power. It ceased to be a mark of actual bodily practice.[69] Taste was driven by the teaching of the market by advertising, rather than by the search for affinities and the matching of products to persons.

In this period, the global reach of the European companies and financiers also greatly increased. Direct foreign investment was beginning to overtake the earlier form of local partnership or *commenda*, which had served European adventurers abroad. The most globalized dimension of this proto-capitalist economy was the Atlantic plantation system, especially as it became predominantly a slave-labour system after the mid seventeenth century. While brutal forms of primitive accumulation and the looting of labour underpinned it, the plantations saw new flexible patterns of management, labour control over time, and middle-level technologies. They were vast estates run for profit, central to Britain's creditworthiness.[70] Management was often divorced from ownership and finance, which was a typically 'modern' pattern of business. Protection was guaranteed by the British, French and Dutch states. The distribution of the produce of the plantations was regularized through large-scale marketing, and increasingly in the eighteenth century novel systems for raising finance, insurance and advertising sales came into vogue. Large economies of scale in shipping and transport were possible on the Atlantic routes and these advantages were deployed at a global level. Cook's junior officer, William Bligh, soon visited Tupia's relatives in search of calorific economies of scale in slave food.

Most important, perhaps, to new globalization was the re-orientation of consumption captured well in de Vries's theory of 'industrious revolutions'. The plantation system flattened out the picture of geographical specificity portrayed in the chart by generalizing the production of commodities, such as sugar, tobacco and tea, over a much wider geographical area. With the later development of beet sugar, production became universal. Even fine-cloth production was, in a sense, generalized now that Paisley and other manufactures could produce simulacra of Chinese and Indian textiles. At the same time consumption patterns had been flattened and regularized by two factors. Firstly, class formation at a world level had created classes of consumers who had a common interest in acquiring positional goods that homogenized their status, first in Europe[71] and later outside.[72] Secondly, the international confluence of 'industrious revolutions' created a massive growth in retailing in which shopkeepers through the local print media actively helped to advertise and promote goods as such markers of status. Collectors of prized, exotic and charmed goods slowly became consumers living virtually identical life-styles.

International trading bodies which originated in the age of old globalization transformed themselves. K.N. Chaudhuri and Om Prakash[73] have shown that the European East India Companies also achieved a high degree of stock control, creating a transparent market and using skills of advertisement. The form of a public company issuing its own bonds and stock formed an excellent machinery for raising capital quickly. Political and legal safeguards protected this property[74] to an extent unknown in Asian or north African financial sectors which were always at risk from the forced loan or amercement. All this, if nothing else, refutes André Gunder Frank's polemical attack on the notion that there was anything intrinsically more socially competitive about Europe during its rise to brief world domination.

On the other hand Gunder Frank is surely right to insist that non–European societies were active as well as passive agents in this new capitalist globalization. Arjun Appadurai remarked that in the modern age globalization 'cannibalizes' localism, and vice versa. For the period 1780–1830, it is perhaps more persuasive to argue that new globalization created a hierarchy in which the fractured patterns of archaic globalization were subsumed and put to use as the link between the global and the local. We have already suggested that the old pattern of periodic invasion by world-conquering dynasts drove capital and expertise to the European enclaves in eighteenth-century Asia. In addition, by inheriting and making use of the old predatory Cossack-style raider, the European powers sucked money into their revenue systems and protected expanding agrarian settlements. Until the 1830s in central and south India, British-sponsored regimes continued to employ cavalry corps often made up of Afghan mercenaries to collect the land revenue.[75] Genghis Khan and Nadir Shah would have felt immediate affinity with these 'rascally *banditti*' who were nevertheless front-line agents of the gentlemanly capitalists of Leadenhall Street.

More generally, tribute in silver derived from a land-revenue system which reflected patterns of archaic globalization underpinned the supposedly capitalist power of the European companies. Primitive accumulation underlay capitalist cunning. Since 1764, the Indian land revenues had been used to bail out the finances of the East India Company's trade account. But as B.R. Tomlinson, has recently reiterated,[76] East India Company trade in the early nineteenth century was a mechanism by which political profit could be repatriated to Britain through 'false' commerce in Indian piece goods and commodities, such as indigo, which could not be sold at a real profit. The East India Company indirectly helped spread Western-style capitalism and, later, industrial products around the world. But embedded in its core was a tribute-taking merchanism which was the residue of older forms of global military fiscalism.

By the same token, the expansion of industrial production and capitalist relations in Eurasia took place on the back of older global networks of trade. Trade diasporas and thalassocracies, such as the Maltese or the Muskat Arabs, distributed European goods and bulked up local primary produce for transport to European enclaves until well into the nineteenth century. The old south and west Asian system of merchant credit-notes along with the Hakka Chinese equivalent in east and Southeast Asia, continued to move the capital of European traders and governments until the mid century. At a global level, European capitalism was not marked by an inevitable and rapid transition to modern markets and systems of production. Instead, it was modern global capitalism's power to subsume and manipulate earlier social connections and commercial mechanisms which was so striking. The monopoly of power which colonial states tried to secure in Asia and Africa greatly reduced the protection costs incurred by the more archaic networks, so preserving but subordinating them.

Consideration of the state reminds us that the early nineteenth century also saw profound new cultural changes in the global expansion of the European-style nation state and, ultimately, the globalization of nationalism itself. Paradoxically, a state form which was more homogenized than ever before tended to divide regions one from another in a way that the old universal empires never did. Global connections increasingly became international connections in the precise sense that they were structured through the external dialogues of nation states. Old universal empire-building was based on the idea of service to lords in multi-ethnic aristocracies. New empire-building was based on the notion of allegiance to a nation state, often defined around an exclusive idea of racial identity. National governing bureaucracies replaced the old migrations of German administrative families to Russia, or Persians to Burma. Even the overseas expansion of religion was closely annexed to nationalism. The universal search of men of many nations for traces of God on earth was transformed into the idea of the national mission to civilize the pagan. Missionary societies mimicked the forms of the official report, counting 'souls' in much the same way as their administrative peers counted 'subjects' and enumerated revenue-holdings. The great Sufi orders, bearers of a global message of culture and humanity, were penned in to national boundaries both by government officials and by the agency of normalizing religious 'reformers'.[77]

In time as Arjun Appadurai, Partha Chatterjee[78] and Prasenjit Duara[79] have pointed out, Asian and African people began to take up and adapt a concept of 'religion' and 'nation' which was in some essential sense 'derivative' of Western discourses. In this sense, the nation state and doctrinally differenti-ated religions were globalized even though their tendency was to fragment and enhance difference between societies.

Yet, at the same time, the same point can be made about nation states and modern religions that we have made about the world capitalist economy. They expanded by subsuming earlier globalizing traditions, sentiments and practi-ces. In the early modern period norms of good conduct and good rulership, derived from west Asian ethical traditions (akhlaq) and norms of Confucian government, had spread internationally. Rooted to the memories, histories, languages and territories of particular regions, these became local patriotic and religious traditions.[80] In the same way the universal message of the great religious teachers was embedded in different regional forms of Islam, Buddhism and Christianity.[81] Modern nationalism and modern religious belief did not erase these earlier formations. Instead ancient religion and old patriotisms were subsumed into the new forms of nationalist and religious ideology. In turn they helped root them in particular terrains. During the Indian Rebellion of 1857, Indian insurgents accused the British of violating principles of good government which were derived more from Aristotle than from the ancient Sanskrit texts.

The Tahitian Tupia insisted on wearing his Tahitian dress even in the old global city of Batavia; within a hundred years the protection of indigenous forms of dress and deportment and indigenous forms of weaving had become important for the first generation of nationalists all over the world. Gandhi's swadeshi movement, which urged Indians to turn back to consuming the produce of their own weavers and artisans, has been seen as a movement back to the villages. But what Gandhi was distantly invoking was an archaic world in which chains of local producers and consumers stretched across a whole globe as yet undivided by intrusive nation states.

Conclusion

The concept of archaic globalization outlined in this essay is an ideal type or heuristic device. It can help us to investigate discontinuous and ruptured processes which brought large areas of the world into contact with each other before the age of the nation state and the international industrial economy. Though its origins stretched back over many millennia, the pattern of archaic globalization ran particularly strongly from the thirteenth to the eighteenth centuries when great land-based, loosely textured empires stretched across Eurasia and Africa, providing a benign context for the movement of traders, mystics, learned administrators and soldiers of fortune on horseback. Many historians, notably Janet Abu-Lughod and K.N. Chaudhuri have analysed this world in terms of trade contacts and state forms. This essay has argued that the particular features of archaic globalization represent a realization in society of a set of ideologies and bodily practices which were mediated through forms of consumption. Economic life was not innocent of the notion of profit. There existed well-developed markets. Economic man had already evolved. Yet social and economic links beyond the locality were heavily inflected by ideologies of power, sanctity and humoural balance. Already, in the period 1750–1850, features of proto-globalization based on the supremacy of market-driven, profit-maximizing forces emanating from Euro-American capitalism and the nation state were apparent. They emerged in symbiosis, and later conflict with trends towards commercialization and 'industrious revolutions' in other societies, where archaic consumption had stimulated status emulation among middle-ranking people. The rise of long-distance joint-stock trading companies and the slave-plantation system were economic changes of a different order. However, agents of archaic globalization were slowly subordinated to these forces rather than being wiped out by them. Modern and post-colonial globalization built on and was in turn modified by these earlier social formations, contributing to the persistence of long continuities of form even under modern capitalism.

Notes and References

1 *Captain Cook's Voyages of Discovery*, Everyman edn. (London, 1906), p. 97.
2 Ibid., p. 102.
3 N. Steensgaard, *Carracks, Caravans and Companies: The Structural Crisis in the European-Asian Trade in the Early Seventeenth Century* (Copenhagen, 1972), but see L. Blussé, *Strange Company: Chinese Settlers, Mestizo Women and the Dutch in VOC Batavia* (Dordrecht, 1986).
4 J. Gascoigne, *Science in the Service of Empire: Joseph Banks, the British State and the Uses of Science in the Age of Revolution* (Cambridge, 1998), Richard Drayton, *Nature's Government: Science, Imperial Britain and the 'Improvement' of the World* (London, 2000).

5 Sir Joshua Reynolds, 'Omai' pen and ink sketch, National Portrait Gallery, London.

6 For the beginnings of the globalized national gaze, see K. Wilson, *The Sense of the People: Politics, Culture and Imperialism in England, 1715–1785* (Cambridge, 1995).

7 See the discussion by A.G. Hopkins in the Introduction to this volume and his own essay, 'The History of Globalization – and the Globalization of History?', which develops these points into the modern era.

8 Immanuel Wallerstein, *The Modern World System*, vol. II, *Mercantilism and the Consolidation of the European World Economy, 1600–1750* (New York, 1980).

9 A.G. Frank, *ReOrientate: Global Economy in the Asian Age* (Berkeley, 1998). But see the sophisticated approaches to this theme of R. Bin Wong, *China Transformed: Historical Change and the Limits of European Experience* (Cornell, 1997); K. Pomeranz, *The Great Divergence: China, Europe and the Making of the Modern World Economy* (Berkeley, 1999).

10 K.N. Chaudhuri, *Asia Before Europe: Economy and Civilization of the Indian Ocean from the Rise of Islam to circa 1750* (Cambridge, 1990).

11 Arjun Appadurai, *Modernity at Large: Cultural Dimensions of Globalization* (Minneapolis, 1996).

12 J. Abu Lughod, *Before European Hegemony: The World System, 1250–1350* (Oxford, 1989).

13 *Public Culture*, the major journal on the globalization of culture, though edited by a historian–anthropologist, has never published an article on the history of globalization in its decade of life; but see F.J. Lechner and J. Boli, *The Globalization Reader* (London, 2000).

14 A.G. Hopkins, 'Back to the future: From National History to Imperial History', *Past and Present*, 164 (1999), pp. 198–243.

15 K.N. Chaudhuri, *Trade and Civilization in the Indian Ocean: An Economic History from the Rise of Islam to 1750* (Cambridge, 1985); A. Das Gupta, *Indian Merchants and the Decline of Surat* (Wiesbaden, 1979); *idem, Malabar in Asian Trade, 1740–1800* (Cambridge, 1967); Om Prakash, *European Commercial Enterprise in Pre-Colonial India: New Cambridge History of India*, vol. II, 5 (Cambridge, 1999); P. Chaunu, *L'Expansion Européenne du XIII au XV Siècle* (Paris, 1976); J. Abu Lughod, *Before European Hegemony*.

16 W.A. Crosby, *Ecological Imperialism: The Biological Expansion of Europe* (Cambridge, 1994).

17 Marshall G.S. Hodgson, *Rethinking World History: Essays on Europe, Islam and World History* (Cambridge, 1993).

18 K.S. Latourette, *A History of the Expansion of Christianity*, 5 vols. (New York, 1937–45); for a typical recent revision, see R. Gray, *Black Christians and White Missionaries* (London, 1990).

19 J. de Vries, *The First Modern Economy: Success, Failure and Perseverence of the Dutch Economy, 1500–1815* (Cambridge, 1997). I am also beholden to Professor de Vries's Ellen MacArthur Lecture series at the University of Cambridge, 2000; see the attempt to generalize this concept in K. Pomeranz, *The Great Divergence*.

20 See A. Appadurai (ed.), *The Social Life of Things: Commodities in Cultural Perspective* (Cambridge, 1986); F. Bray, *Technology and Gender: Fabrics of Power in late Imperial China* (Berkeley, 1997); anthropologists have explored these issues much more fully, see D. Miller, 'Consumption and Commodities', *Annual Review of Anthropology*, 24 (1995), pp. 140–61.

21 C.A. Bayly, 'The First Age of Global Imperialism, *c.*1760–1830', *Journal of Imperial and Commonwealth History*, 26 (1998), pp. 5–10.

22 J. Hevia, *Cherishing Men from Afar: Qing Guest Ritual and the Macartney Embassy of 1793* (London, 1995); E.Rawski, *The Last Emperors: A Social History of Qing Imperial Institutions* (Berkeley, 1998).

23 See Amira K. Bennison's essay in this volume.

24 A. Pagden, *Lords of all the World: Ideologies of Empire in Spain, Britain and France, c. 1500–1800* (New York, 1995).

25 The best example is the Mughal court, see Abul Fazl, trans. H. Blochmann, *Ain-i-Akbari*, vol. I (Calcutta, 1993), pp. 91–3; see also C.A. Bayly, 'The origins of *swadeshi* (home industry): Cloth and Indian Society 1700–1930', in A. Appadurai (ed.), *Social Life of Things*. But Ottomans, Safavids and Southeast Asian rulers had similar procedures for royal accumulation. They bear some resemblance to old court rituals in Europe, the Pacific and sub-Saharan Africa.

26 These issues are broached in Timothy Brook, *The Confusions of Pleasure: Commerce and Culture in Ming China* (Berkeley, 1998), pp. 75–7 *passim*; see Rawski, *Last Emperors, pp.* 46–7 for Qing 'patriotic' consumption of Manchurian food and products.

27 Little apparently has been written on the culture of west-Asian consumption, but much can be gleaned from works on the arts, e.g., A.V. Pope and P. Ackerman, *A Survey of Persian Art: From Prehistoric Times to the Present*, vol. V (New York, 1964); vol. VI (New York, 1967), *passim*. Persian carpets were used as a kind of heraldic banner and hung out on the balcony of houses; this usage passed through Venice to northern Europe. The global trade in oriental carpets originated, therefore, in competitive displays of genealogical 'fineness'.

28 William Moorcroft's memorandum to John Adam on trade in central Asia, 15 September 1814, Home Miscellaneous Series, vol. 645, Oriental and India Office Collections, British Library, London.

29 S. Subrahmanyan (ed.), *Merchant Networks in the Early Modern World* (Aldershot, 1996).

30 For the classic study of pilgrimage see A. Pesce (ed.), *Makkah a Hundred Years Ago. C. Snouck Hurgronje's Remarkable Albums* (London, 1986).

31 E.N. Saad, *Social History of Timbuktu: The Role of Muslim Scholars and Notables, 1400–1900* (Cambridge, 1983), p. 139; A.G.B and H.J. Fisher, *Slavery and Muslim Society in Africa: The Institution in Saharan and Sudanic Africa and the Trans-Saharan Trade* (London, 1970).

32 Pomeranz, *Great Divergence*, pp. 119–20.

33 Kikkoman Soy sauce, for instance, has been produced continuously since 1630 (see the Company's beer-mat). It has now become an important branded ingredient for the new global taste for Japanese *sushi* and *sashimi*.

34 South-Indian quality food was patterned on the *prasada*, or offerings of rice and vegetables made at temples. From the sixteenth century it was spiced up with the chili plants which spread east alongside silver bullion from the Spanish New World.

35 E.g., Allan Chapman, 'Astrological Medicine' and Charles Webster, 'Alchemical and Parcelsian Medicine' in Charles Webster (ed.), *Health Medicines and Mortality in the Sixteenth Century* (Cambridge, 1979), pp. 275–300, 301–34. The predispositions of Chinese external trade before the opium revolution bear on all the preceeding points. Admiral Cheng-ho's voyages were designed in part to secure medicinal plants and exotic animals for the imperial menagerie; later trade through Macao centred on spices, medicinal oils, frankincense and luxury woods,

commodities directed to 'medicinal', ritual and luxury consumption respectively, see K.C. Foc, 'The Ming Debate on How to Accommodate the Portuguese and the Emergence of the Macao Formula', *Revista Cultura* (Lisbon), 13, 14 (1991), p. 336.

36 A similar point was made by M. Foucault, *Words and Things* (London, 1989).

37 The best short account of the new commodities remains G.B. Mansfield, 'Crops and Livestock', in E.E. Rich and C. Wilson (eds.), *Cambridge Economic History*, vol. IV, (Cambridge, 1968), pp. 276–99; see also the classic study by Sidney Mintz, *Sweetness and Power: The Place of Sugar in Modern History* (New York, 1985).

38 W. Sombart, *A History of the Economic Institutions of Modern Europe* (New York, 1933).

39 The use these commodities and of tobacco in both Europe and Asia was closely connected to the emergence of new patterns of leisure, see E. Rawski, D. Johnson and A. Nathan, *Popular Culture in Late Imperial China* (Berkeley, 1985); J. Ovington, *An Essay upon the Nature and Qualities of Tea* (London, 1689); Anon., *The Natural History of Coffee, Chocolate, The, Tobacco* (London, 1682).

40 Such consumption patterns, differing from modern-market sensitive consumption still prevail in the case of Indian gold and jewellery, see Helen Ward, 'Worth its Weight: Gold, Women and Value in North West India', Ph.D. dissertation, University of Cambridge, 1999.

41 The economic fragility of Qian Long's China is best depicted in P. Kuhn, *Soulstealers: The Chinese Sorcery Scare of 1768* (Cambridge, Mass. 1996), esp. ch. 1.; see also J.K. Fairbank and D. Twitchett (eds.), *The Cambridge History of China*, vol. 10.1, *The Late Ch'ing* (Cambridge, 1978), pp. 163–208.

42 M.C.G. Saiz, *Las Castas Mexicanas. Un Genero Pictorico Americano* (Mexico City, 1989); S.B. Bayly, *Caste, Society and Politics in India from the Eighteenth Century to the Modern Age* (Cambridge, 1999), pp. 97–102.

43 For an example of cultural reductionism in the tradition of Karl Polanyi see S. Sen, *Empire of Free-Trade: The East India Company and the Making of the Colonial Marketplace* (Philadelphia, 1998). By contrast see Frank, *ReOrientate*, which reduces capitalism to exchange.

44 The distinction I am making here relates to the anthropologists' distinction between ordinal and cardinal systems of ranking in spheres of exchange. There was a global sphere of quality (ordinally denominated) exchange, before quantity (cardinally denominated) exchange developed, see J.M. Keynes 'Ancient Currencies' in D. Moggridge (ed.), *Collected Works* (New York, 1982); P. Bohannan, 'The Impact of Money on an African Subsistence Economy', *Journal of Economic History*, 19 (1959), pp. 491–503; S. Campbell, 'Attaining Rank: A Classification of Shell Valuables', in E.J. and J. Leach (eds.), *The Kula: New Perspectives on Massim Exchange* (Cambridge, 1983); C. Gregory, 'Exchange and Reciprocity', in T. Ingold (ed.), *Companion Encyclopaedia of Anthropology* (London, 1994), pp. 911–40. I am grateful to Dr. S. Bayly for these references.

45 L. Lockhart, *Nadir Shah: A Critical Study Based Mainly on Contemporary Sources* (London, 1938).

46 J. Gommans, *The Rise of the Indo–Afghan Empire, c. 1710–1780* (Leiden, 1995).

47 M. Hiskett, 'The Nineteenth-Century *jihads* in West Africa', in J.D. Fage and Roland Oliver (eds.), *Cambridge History of Africa*, vol. IV (Cambridge, 1976), pp. 125–69.

48 'Abstract of Letters received from the Coast and Bay, 1739' by Court of Directors, cited in K.N. Chaudhuri, *The Trading World of Asia and the English East India Company* (Cambridge, 1978), p. 576, n. 44.

49 Warren Hastings, 'Persia', in *The Present State of the East Indies* (London, 1786), p. 114 ff.

50 D. Richards (ed.), *Islam and the Trade of Asia* (Oxford, 1970).

51 A. Plaisse, *Le Rouge de Malte* (Renne, 1991); J.B. Wolf, *The Barbary Coast: Algiers under the Turks 1500–1830* (New York, 1979); P. Risso, *Oman and Muscat: An Early Modern History* (London, 1986); C. Pelras, *The Bugis* (Oxford, 1996).

52 R.K. Ray, 'Asian Capital in the Age of European Dominion: The Rise of the Bazaar, 1800–1914', *Modern Asian Studies*, 29, 3 (1995), 469–554.

53 Steensgaard, *Carracks*. The various criticisms of Steensgaard by S. Subrahmanyam and others have revealed a large Portuguese 'private trade' and a shift towards a more modern form of commerce under the Habsburgs. I do not believe that his basic characterisation of the early Estado da India has been undermined.

54 Chaudhuri, *Trade of Asia*.

55 On the French and the Mediterranean, see F-X. Emmanuelli, *La Crise Marseillaise de 1774 et La Chute des Courtiers* (Paris, 1979).

56 Chaudhuri, *Trade of Asia*, pp. 372–3.

57 Of course, as T.N. Harper shows in his essay in this volume, this did not deprive the merchant diasporas of their commercial importance, particularly in an area such as Southeast Asia.

58 E. Herzig, 'The Armenian Merchants of New Julfa (Isfahan), 1600–1750', D.Phil. dissertation, Oxford, 1991; M.J. Seth, *The Armenians in India from the Earliest Times to the Present Day* (Calcutta, 1937); for Armenians in Burma in the late eighteenth century, see Sarkies Manook to Commissioners, Yandaboo, 25 February 1826, Home Miscellaneous, vol. 668, Oriental and India Office Collections, British Library, London; Ina Baghdiantz McCabe, *The Shah's Silk for Europe's Silver: The Eurasian Silk Trade of the Julfan Armenians in Safavid Iran and India (1590–1750)*, (Philadelphia, 1999).

59 S. Dale, *Indian Merchants and Eurasian Trade, 1600–1750* (Cambridge, 1994); C.A. Bayly, *Rulers, Townsmen and Bazaars: North Indian Society in the Age of British Expansion, 1780–1870* (Indian edn., Delhi, 1992), pp. 140–1, *passim*; C. Markovits, *The Global World of Indian Merchants, 1750–1942* (Cambridge, 2000).

60 M. Alam, *The Crisis of Empire in Mughal North India* (Delhi, 1986), pp. 134–55.

61 Markovits, *Global World*.

62 A. Reid, *Southeast Asia in the Age of Commerce*, 2 vols. (London, 1988–93).

63 A. Wink, *Al-Hind: The Making of the Indo-Islamic World*, 2 vols. (Leiden, 1990–7).

64 V.N. Rao, S. Subrahmanyam and D. Shulman, *Symbols of Substance: Court and State in Nayaka Period Tamilnadu* (Delhi, 1992), p. 6; C.A. Bayly, *Origins of Nationality in South Asia*; S. Pollock, 'Ramayana and Political Imagination in India' Journal of Asian Studies, 52, 2 (1993), pp. 261–97; J. Whaley-Cohen, 'Commemorating War in Eighteenth-Century China', *Modern Asian Studies*, 30, 4 (1996), pp. 869–99.

65 Raghoba's letter from Lahore, in T.S. Shejwalkar, *Panipat 1761* (Pune, 1946), p. 124.

66 M. Roberts (ed.), *Sri Lanka: Collective Identities Revisited* (Colombo, 1997).

67 G. Parker, *The Military Revolution: Military Innovation and the Rise of the West, 1500–1800* (Cambridge, 1988); D. Ralston, *Importing the European Army: The Introduction of European Military Techniques and Institutions into the Extra-European World* (London, 1990).

68 Brook, *Confusions of Pleasure*.

69 See the many works listed in, e.g. G. Snookes (ed.), *Was the Industrial Revolution*

Necessary? (London, 1994); Pomeranz, *Great Divergence*; Bin Wong, *China Transformed*; P. O'Brien, 'European Industrialisation from the Voyages of Discovery to the Industrial Revolution', in H. Pohl (ed.), *The European Discovery of the World and its Economic Effects on Pre-Industrial Society, 1500–1800* (Stuttgart, 1990).

70 See Drayton, *Nature's Government.*

71 N. McKendrick, J. Plumb and J. Brewer, *The Birth of a Consumer Society: The Commercialisation of Eighteenth-Century England* (London, 1982).

72 See, e.g., C. Bayly, 'The Origins of *swadeshi* (Home industry)', in A. Appadurai (ed.), *The Social Life of Things*; E. Tarlo, *Clothing Matters: Dress and Identity in India* (London, 1996); N. Thomas, *Colonialism's Culture: Anthropology, Travel and Government* (London, 1994).

73 Chaudhuri, *Trade of Asia*; Om Prakash, *European Commercial Entrerprise.*

74 A.G. Hopkins and P.J. Cain, *British Imperialism, 1688–2000* (London, 2001), chs. 1–15.

75 S. Alavi, *The Sepoys and the Company* (Delhi, 1994).

76 B.R. Tomlinson, 'The East India Company and the Weavers of Bengal', *Kansai: The Bulletin of the Osaka University of Foreign Studies*, March 2000.

77 See, e.g., B.D. Metcalf, *Islamic Revival in British India* (Princeton, 1969).

78 P. Chatterjee, *Nationalist Thought and the Colonial World: A Derivative Discourse?* (London, 1996).

79 P. Duara, *Rescuing History from the Nation: Questioning Narratives of Modern China* (London, 1993).

80 C.A. Bayly, *Origins of Nationality in South Asia: Patriotism and Ethical Government in the Making of Modern India* (Delhi, 1997).

81 See Amira K. Bennison's essay in this volume; J. Whaley Cohen, 'Commemorating War in Eighteenth-Century China', *Modern Asian Studies*, 30, 4 (1996), pp. 869–99.

AMIRA K. BENNISON

Muslim Universalism and Western Globalization

In any historical investigation of globalization and its evolution world systems other than those generated by the West should loom large as precursors and contributors. This essay addresses both these dimensions by looking at the Islamic world as a particularly successful example of archaic globalization, a participant in proto-globalization, and an area challenged by and challenging modern and post-colonial globalization. In some respects, contemporary globalization is certainly new, in particular in the speed of communications enabled by innovative information technologies, and mass individual participation in trans-national communications and economic exchanges. At the same time it has significant antecedents in the past, both the recent imperial past and the sweep of non-European history over a much longer timespan, which Braudel calls the *longue durée*. International economic exchanges, migrations and global ideologies within and without state structures are not the sole preserve of late twentieth or early twenty-first-century Western societies but have been developed, promoted and upheld by many world systems which, although not necessarily global in reach, certainly maintained universal, and thus global, aspirations.

One of the most striking examples of an earlier world system with impressive reach is the Islamic œcumene which, like the global society emerging today, exhibited the subsistence, interaction and engagement of the local and universal in the economic, political and cultural spheres. The geo-political configuration of the Islamic world altered tremendously over time but between the late seventh century AD and its sub-division into nation states by European imperial powers, it was a vast domain across which capital, commodities, ideas and people moved continuously. The establishment of the Islamic world system began with the newly Islamized Arabs, but quickly incorporated the peoples of the Near-Eastern Byzantine and Sasanian empires. Further expansion brought Berber north Africa, the Iberian peninsula, Turkic central Asia and northern India into the Muslim sphere. Trade consolidated

Muslim politico-military achievements and pushed the Islamic frontier south into sub-Saharan Africa and Indonesia and east along the silk route through central Asia to China. Despite the temporary setback of the Crusades in the twelfth and thirteenth centuries, and the loss of Iberia to Christian Spain in the fifteenth century, Muslim powers such as the Ottomans and Mughals brought new areas into the Islamic world system during the era of proto-globalization, as did Hadhrami Yemeni traders in the Indian Ocean.

This essay seeks to elucidate the universalizing elements which arose out of the Muslim conquests and flourished alongside the subsequent spread of Muslim commercial networks. It will begin with a series of general comments about the formative eighth to twelfth centuries, during which the foundations of a universal Muslim culture and civilization were laid, and their maintenance prior to the emergence of Europe as a global player in the fifteenth and sixteenth centuries. It will then analyse the interaction between the Islamic world and Europe in the periods of proto-globalization and modern globalization in closer detail, using the Mediterranean and African Islamic regions as case studies for phenomena which also occurred in the Asian parts of the Islamic world considered in C.A. Bayly and T.N. Harper's chapters in this volume. Broadly speaking, this entails a consideration of the Ottoman empire, the largest Islamic state of the period between 1600 and 1922, the Ottoman provinces of north Africa and the 'Alawi sultanate of Morocco.

Archaic Globalization: The Muslim Example

Muslim political and commercial successes went in tandem with the dissemination of a universalist ideology which shaped political systems, cultural attitudes and modes of exchange, and a lingua franca: Arabic, Islam's sacred language. Although many Muslims did not speak Arabic, its vocabulary and script had a profound influence across the Islamic lands and acted as a vehicle for archaic Muslim globalization. The original Muslim universalizing impulse rested on the idea, shared with Christianity, that the faith would ideally become the sole religion of mankind. It differed in that it was initially promoted by an expanding empire with the ability to structure local political, economic and cultural life using a series of shared religious categories.

The first of these normative categories was the universal Muslim community, the *umma*; the second the binary division of the globe into the dominant *dār al-islām* (land of Islam) and the peripheral *dār al-harb* (land of war); the third the caliphate (*khilāfa*), the political concomitant of the *dār al-islām*, which engendered shared Islamic visions of politics and statehood. Myriad networks transmitted and reiterated this tripartite conceptual framework throughout the Islamic lands, where it provided the means for Muslims to envisage their place in the world and their centrality to it. It also enabled them to imagine and experience the local as part of a larger Islamic universal whole, a process facilitated by the assumption that local practices not specifically prohibited by Islam were Islamic.

The *umma* had no territorial or political bounds but included every Muslim wherever he or she may be, a concept readily adapted to trans-state migrations. The term *umma* came from the pre-Islamic Arabic, where it meant a tribe or people, and was adopted by the early Muslims to denote the new, radically different, non-tribal or supra-tribal community engendered by Muhammad's message. The *umma* writ large was neither ethnic nor political. Instead, it gained tangible form in the juridical sphere: to be a Muslim meant adherence to Islamic law, the Shari'a, and membership of one of the schools of law (*madhāhib*). Five such schools, based on the legal rulings, opinions and methodologies of key early Muslim scholars, coalesced between the ninth and twelfth centuries.[1]

The Shari'a defined broad parameters by means of the religio-legal bounds (*hudūd*) of human behaviour specified in the Qur'ān which did not homogenize Islamic societies but fostered a recognizable religio-cultural framework for social and commercial interactions between members of the *umma*. The contextualized opinions of the jurists of each law school constantly elaborated these parameters, enabling subtle interactions between the local and the universal. Jurists and judges emphasized the standardization of processes rather than outcomes and produced divergent opinions and rulings in response to local exigencies.[2] However, the dominance of four Sunni schools of law and one Shi'i school gave each an extensive geographic reach, enabling jurists of the individual schools to seek and apply the rulings of one locale in distant territories. Secondly, although political authorities controlled criminal proceedings, the codification of the Shari'a by scholars, not states, meant that the schools of law transcended political boundaries and functioned in tandem as an internationally recognized legal system.

The socio-cultural framework fostered by the Shari'a was constantly reiterated and renegotiated by the religious scholars ('*ulama*'), mystics, merchants and pilgrims, who traversed the Islamic lands carrying normative values, knowledge and skills with them. Scholars, who were frequently also traders, played a vital role in this process by travelling widely in pursuit of religious knowledge and patronage. From earliest Islamic times, when devout Muslims travelled to the farthest reaches of the *dār al-islām* to gather the sayings (*hadīth*) of the Prophet from his companions and their associates, mobility was a common part of a scholar's lifestyle.

Whilst travel was neither easy nor always safe, scholarship gave its holder a *de facto* passport to traverse political boundaries within the *dār al-islām*, relative immunity from the depredations of rulers and highly transferable skills, including a knowledge of Arabic. Although the search for knowledge (*talab al-'ilm*) was a prominent justification for travel, scholars also transmitted knowledge by teaching in the mosques, *madrasas* and Sufi lodges which came to form the religious networks of the Islamic lands by the twelfth century.

They could also replenish their funds by serving in local judiciaries or bureaucracies, although the most morally scrupulous avoided such employment as being corrupting. Travel could generate perceptions of difference but such feelings were tempered by an over-arching sense of cultural and religious community.[3] Indeed, comment on differences between Muslim societies and laments about disunity assumed a shared Islamic framework which served as a benchmark for comparison and criticism, a measure for deviation and conformity.[4]

Whilst the *umma* was and is the international community of believers, the *dār al-islām* was the geographic area in which rulers recognized God's ultimate sovereignty and implemented His law, the Sharī'a.[5] The inhabitants of this area submitted to God's ordained religio-political order either as Muslims, literally 'those who have submitted [to God]', or as *dhimmis*, non-Muslims who exchanged political submission for religious freedom and protection, a system instituted during the seventh to eighth-century conquest era and maintained henceforth. Over time, the geo-political balance within the *dār al-islām* swung from the eastern Mediterranean to Iraq, Iran and other areas, but its conceptual and religious heart remained in the pivotal holy cities – Mecca and secondarily Jerusalem – the points of perfect communion between God and man, represented by the meteorites housed in the Ka'ba and the Dome of the Rock.

The early development of the annual *hajj* and *'umra* rituals of pilgrimage, modelled on the Prophet's own actions and instructions, consolidated the symbolic centrality of Mecca, the navel of the earth, and ensured that the 'gateway' cities on the pilgrimage routes, Cairo, Damascus and Baghdad, retained metropolitan cultural, if not political, status. Scholarly itineraries usually included performance of the *hajj* and thus sojourns in the 'gateway' cities, making them pivotal nodes in networks from all parts of the *dār al-islām*, and the *loci* for exchanges of culture, commodities and information. The symbolic centering of the *dār al-islām* on Mecca and the Near East for all Muslims, whatever their sectarian and political affiliations, enabled it to weather numerous religio-political upheavals which might otherwise have permanently ruptured its tenuous conceptual unity.

The *dār al-islām* was also a series of connected economic units within which luxury commodities, bulk goods and labour circulated according to archaic patterns. Muslim and Jewish merchants constructed elaborate networks spanning borders both within the *dār al-islām* and into neighbouring parts of the *dār al-harb*: Mediterranean Europe, sub-Saharan Africa, southern India and China.[6] The extensive mercantile networks of the *dār al-islām* have been studied elsewhere but it is worth emphasizing some of their global aspects. Firstly, mercantile networks transcended religious and political boundaries. Secondly, they relied heavily on common accounting techniques which drew on the sophisticated Indo-Arabic mathematical tradition and on Sharī'a codes of good market practice and public morality (*hisba*), which provided a shared ethical framework for industry and commerce.[7]

The area of the globe outside the Muslim political and cultural sphere was the *dār al-harb*, the lands of war. This was the geographic area governed by non-Muslims who had not submitted to God, did not recognize His sovereignty, and did not implement His order on Earth. This placed them in a state of opposition not necessarily to Muslims but to God. The concept that non-Muslim rulers and their subjects existed outside the Muslim nexus meant that the most important boundary for many Muslims was the frontier between the *dār al-islām* and the *dār al-harb*, rather than boundaries within the *dār al-islām*. To facilitate commercial and diplomatic relations across this frontier, jurists defined a third zone, the *dār al-sulh* (land of truce), a theoretically temporary space created by treaties and truces of specified duration between Muslim and non-Muslim powers.

The unity of the *dār al-islām* found political and symbolic expression in the caliphate (*khilāfa*), universal Muslim rule by a deputy or caliph (*khalīfa*). The title *khalīfa* was originally applied to those who succeeded the Prophet as heads of the *umma* and deputized for him. As the empire expanded and Islamic religio-political discourse absorbed Byzantine and Iranian ideas of sacred monarchy, it gained the connotation of God's deputy on Earth. The caliph became God's anointed religious, political and military head of the community. The totality of his power and authority were reflected in his titles: *imām*, denoting religious leadership; *amīr al-mu'minīn*, denoting military leadership; and *zill allah fi'l-ard* (the shadow of God on Earth), denoting his unique position as God's representative.[8]

Despite such theocratic constructs, the 'Abbasid caliphs had become religious figureheads by the tenth century. On the one hand, the emergent scholarly establishment succeeded in wresting from the caliph's grasp the definition of doctrine and maintenance of Islamic normative values, a fact which forestalled the religious fragmentation of the *dār al-islām* by preserving a consensual and diffuse, rather than authoritarian, model of religious leadership. On the other hand, real political power passed to caliphal rivals, provincial governors and temporal rulers, termed sultan, a word meaning both temporal power and its holder.

The unitary caliphal model nonetheless remained crucially important. The first sultans, the eleventh-century Turkic Seljuqs, could construct legitimacy only by presenting themselves as protectors of the enfeebled 'Abbasid caliphs and Islam. After the destruction of the caliphal line by the Mongols in 1258, this idea of temporal rulers as defenders of the faith legitimized the shift from the caliphal model to Muslim political multiplicity: sultans ceased to be the protectors of the caliphs but became mutually independent protectors of the Sharī'a. Despite such fragmentation, sultans inherited the caliphal responsibility to defend the *dār al-islām* in its entirety, obliging them to maintain at least a notional sense that a Muslim 'commonwealth' or 'league' of states existed.

Moreover, unity under a caliph remained a latent ideal, a seductive ambition for rulers and a utopian vision for their subjects.

The basic premise underlying both the caliphal and subsequent common-wealth paradigms of Muslim politics and the division between 'Islam' and 'war' was that ultimate sovereignty lay with God. From the Muslim perspective, rulers were thus servants of God rather than independent actors, and politics, domestic and international, were a series of negotiated relation-ships: the relationship between a ruler and God, the relationship between a ruler and his subjects and the relationship between the lands of Islam and the lands of war. This emphasis on the relational meant that the political boundaries which emerged within the *dār al-islām* after the fall of the caliphate were not primarily territorial or national but contractual. Although rulers made territorial claims, they were rarely physically represented upon the ground, and political space was structured by constantly renegotiated covenants between rulers and local communities.

The first of these covenants was the implicit contract between God and rulers which gave the latter the right to command obedience and levy taxes in return for fulfilling their responsibilities to defend the faith. Defence of the faith included preservation of security on pilgrimage routes, provision of water, shelter, and religious space for Muslims to fulfil their religious obligations, and military protection of the Muslim frontier. Since rulers were perceived as divinely appointed trustees, their relations with their subjects were also contractual. This gave the ruled communal rights of negotiation and dissent, expressed in the oath of allegiance (*bay'a*) extended to a ruler on his accession to power.

Although often a technicality, the *bay'a* was not an unconditional oath but a contract offering obedience in return for security and justice. When a ruler appeared not to be upholding his part of the *bay'a*, religious admonition (*nasīha*), and revolt were mechanisms by which the ruled could remind rulers of their political duties. Their desire and ability to do so varied widely in time and space. In general unarmed sedentary communities had less of a voice than urban elites, represented by scholars ('*ulama*') and descendants of the Prophet (*ashrāf*), who could wield economic and religious sanctions; and tribesmen in possession of arms. The pact (*dhimma*) between Muslim authorities and non-Muslim communities exhibited similar characteristics, but the latter had less ability than their Muslim fellows to press for its fulfilment.

As in the juridical sphere, similarities of process and perception linked diverse Muslim state structures into a recognizable whole, comparable to modern state systems theoretically founded on shared values. Of course, the ideologies of ruling and religious elites were not upheld uniformly throughout the *dār al-islām*. The city (*madīna*), a word meaning the locus of religion, law and exchange, was the crucial node in networks of scholarship, pilgrimage and trade, and in general the base of political power. Conversely, rural and tribal areas remained less easy to reach. However, as C.A. Bayly has observed,[9] one of the motors of archaic globalization were groups of tribal warriors coming from the periphery to replace their decadent and weary urban-based predecessors in movements described by the fourteenth-century north African scholar, Ibn Khaldun.[10] By their actions, these warrior groups strengthened links between the Islamic heartlands and the periphery, and in fact expanded the reach of the Muslim world order, despite periodically destabilizing its centre.

In addition, the desire of new rulers from the tribal periphery to model their courts according to metropolitan Muslim patterns drew intrepid scholars out to frontier regions to consolidate the Islamic infrastructure. Such migrations replicated political systems across the *dār al-islām*.[11] For instance, Ibn Battuta, a native of Tanger in Morocco, was able to find employment with rulers in Delhi, the Maldives and west Africa among other places.[12] Similarly, rulers often forcibly moved cohorts of artisans, craftsmen and soldiers, whose skills were thereby transferred to new locales. For instance, in 1402 Timur moved large numbers of Damascene craftsmen to Samarkand to embellish his capital. A century later the Ottomans forced Cairene artisans to migrate to Istanbul for a similar purpose.

Muslim Universalism and Proto-Globalization: A Partnership of Equals?

The classical *dār al-islām* was, to use Ross Dunn's phrase, 'a trans-hemispheric civilisation' and probably the most successful, long-lasting and far-reaching example of archaic globalization.[13] Envisaged by an expanding empire, it actually became a cultural and economic reality after that empire had fragmented into smaller political units, which nonetheless maintained the ideal of unity. However, Muslim regimes never managed to conquer or convert and acculturate either the north-western portion of the *dār al-harb*, Europe, or the eastern portion centred on China, despite trade links with both. This meant that the Muslim commonwealth, which reached maturity after the rise of military absolutist gunpowder empires in the sixteenth century, came face to face with the proto-globalizing impulses coming out of Europe between 1648 and 1850. This period was characterized by the perpetuation of archaic globalization and the parasitic appropriation of many of its modes by proto-global systems such as the Portuguese and Dutch overseas trading empires. It witnessed European penetration into the *dār al-islām*, the attachment of new parts of the globe – the Americas, southern Africa and later Australasia – and the development of a European vision of global centrality.

The *dār al-islām* was not static during this time, and from the perspective of the Islamic Old World, the shift of centrality to Europe was neither self-evident nor inevitable. During the seventeenth and eighteenth centuries Muslim expansion occurred along the southern frontier of the *dār al-islām* in

Africa, the Indian Ocean and Indonesia, and Muslim powers, such as the Ottomans, the Moroccans and the Safavids, developed a Muslim 'proto-global' monarchical state system which shared features with the European state system defined by the Treaty of Westphalia. This process again suggests similarities which historical outcomes obscure. The imperial impulses to plunder, colonize and civilize identified by Richard Drayton[14] can be identified in Muslim lands as in Europe, and eighteenth-century European cosmopolitanism, with its presentiments of late twentieth-century globalism, was a phase which crossed Christian–Muslim confessional lines to a degree which seemed inconceivable in the subsequent chauvinistic, modern globalizing phase.

Like other forms of globalization, Muslim proto-globalization sometimes relied on and sometimes transcended state structures. At the state level, the attempt of the Sa'di sultan of Morocco, Ahmad al-Mansur (1578–1603) to establish a sugar industry at Shishawa near Marrakesh and colonize the western Sudan to plunder its gold and perfect its practice of Islam was conceptually similar to, although smaller scale than, Spanish and British initiatives in the New World. At the other end of the *dār al-islām*, Ottoman activities in east Africa, Arabia and India suggest that they were as interested in tapping the wealth of the Indies as European empires of the time.[15] They pursued their ends by offering gunpowder technology and Islamic solidarity to secure alliances across the Indian Ocean.[16]

In the Mediterranean, Muslim and Christian states participated in a web of alliances in which traditional religious prejudices were maintained in theory but subsumed in practice. By the seventeenth century several different types of government existed within the western Muslim sphere. Theoretically, the two main powers were the Ottoman and Moroccan 'Alawi sultanates, and the main political boundary lay between their domains. However, the Ottoman provinces of north Africa had gained considerable autonomy under different regimes: a military oligarchy under a non-dynastic *dey* in Algiers; and governorial dynasties in Tripoli and Tunis. They enjoyed the sovereign freedom to negotiate treaties independently, but remained bound to the Ottoman system. Their right to rule lay in their confirmation by the Ottoman sultan, and his ultimate sovereignty was recognized by his acknowledgement in the Friday prayer in Algiers, Tunis and Tripoli. Despite this, the Ottoman and Moroccan parts of the Maghrib were considered to be a single unit from the perspective of political economy. All *maghāriba* (Westerners) paid duties on merchandise when they entered and exited Egypt, whether they came from the Ottoman provinces or the 'Alawi sultanate.

Muslim rulers assumed that European monarchies and peoples (*jins*, *ajnās*) interacted in a similar variety of ways within a comparable Christian state system. They considered bi-lateral alliances across the Muslim–Christian divide acceptable as long as the welfare of the *dār al-islām* was not jeopardized. Many of the treaties they made had a distinctly 'modern' flavour. They were characterized by reciprocity, use of signatures, and circulation among

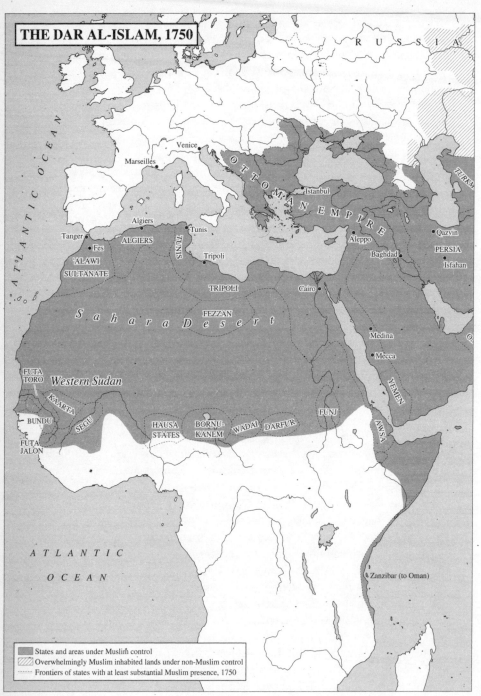

THE DAR AL-ISLAM, 1750

RUSSIA

ATLANTIC OCEAN

Venice

Marseilles

OTTOMAN EMPIRE

Istanbul

TURKM

Algiers

Tunis

Aleppo

Qazvin

Tanger

Fes

ALGIERS

TUNIS

Tripoli

Baghdad

PERSIA

Isfahan

'ALAWI
SULTANATE

TRIPOLI

Cairo

Sahara Desert

FEZZAN

Medina

Mecca

FUTA
TORO

Western Sudan

YEMEN

KAARTA

BUNDU

SEGU

HAUSA
STATES

BORNU-
KANEM

WADAI

DARFUR

FUNJ

AWSA

FUTA
JALON

ATLANTIC

OCEAN

Zanzibar (to Oman)

	States and areas under Muslim control
	Overwhelmingly Muslim inhabited lands under non-Muslim control
	Frontiers of states with at least substantial Muslim presence, 1750

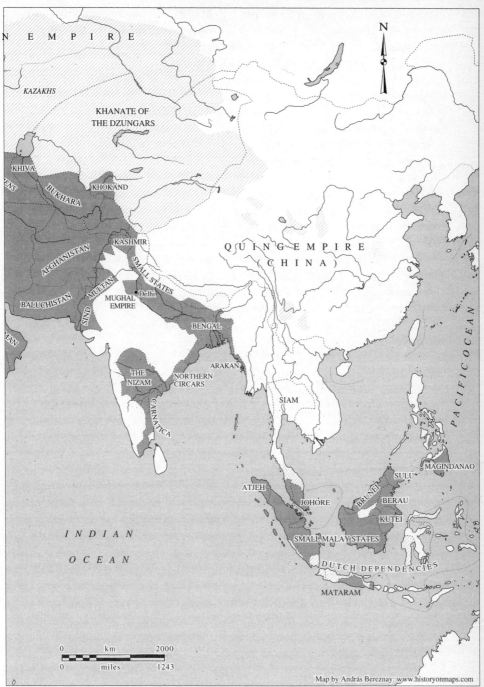

neighbouring states who then demanded similar conditions from European powers. For instance, Dutch treaties with Algiers were used as models by the Husaynids of Tunis,[17] and Venice made a treaty with Morocco on the same terms as a previous Venetian treaty with Algiers.[18]

On the theoretical side, traditional ideas of Muslim solidarity and superiority were maintained in a variety of ways. Relations between Muslim states were not necessarily harmonious, but when European powers became involved a Muslim community of interest could exist. In 1770–1 the 'Alawi sultan, Sidi Muhammad, objected to a French attack on Tunis because, 'tout le monde savait que les Maures ayant une seule religion, ils étaient tenus de s'assister les uns les autres' ('everyone knows that the Moors, being of one religion, are obliged to assist each other'). The somewhat startled French consul replied that France had not expected to offend the 'Alawi sultan since, 'les princes d'Europe considéraient la Tunisie comme un pays distinct du Maroc' ('the princes of Europe consider Tunisia a country separate from Morocco').[19] The sultan demonstrated a similar perspective when he asserted that there was no Christian norm to justify his attacks against the Spanish enclaves of Ceuta and Melilla in 1774 because they were inspired, 'seulement pour défendre notre religion' ('solely in order to defend our religion'). They did not imply war with Spain but an effort to regain land which belonged to the *dār al-islām*:

> En ce qui concerne les forteresses qui se trouvent sur nos côtes et que le roi d'Espagne déclare lui appartenir, elles ne sont ni à nous, ni à lui, elles appartiennent à Dieu le Suprême et a celui à qui Il les donne ou qui peut les prendre.[20]
>
> (With respect to the fortresses which are situated on our coasts and which the king of Spain claims belong to him, they belong neither to us nor to him but to God Most High and to whomever He gives them or who can capture them.)

Relations between Istanbul and the 'Alawi sultanate demonstrated a similar trans-national sense of political community. Although both dynasties used caliphal titulature to suggest their primacy within the *dār al-islām*, thereby implying a denial of the other's legitimacy, three 'Alawi embassies went to Istanbul during the reign of Sidi Muhammad (1757–1790) and agreed pacts of mutual help against the 'infidels'.[21]

At home, Muslim states took precautions to present encounters with Europeans in ways that suggested Muslim superiority and centrality to their subjects. Firstly, all the north African states maintained or patronized corsairing crews whose publicized purpose was to wage 'maritime *jihād*' (*al-jihād fi'l-bahr*). They also described associated practices, such as the redemption of captives and the disposal of booty, as *jihād*.[22] Secondly, where treaties with European states existed, Muslim rulers insisted on lavish gifts and annual tribute as symbols of infidel submission. The Moroccan sultans also signalled their superiority by limiting access to their presence. They rarely granted European merchants and envoys court audiences; when they did, they treated them in ways designed to force them into symbolic and real modes of submission. Sidi Muhammad, a ruler keen to promote foreign trade and contact with European countries, nonetheless physically maltreated European nationals, forced them to transfer their place of residence and even to construct houses at his pleasure.[23] Such strictures placed Europeans in a symbolic *dhimma* relationship with the sultan, analogous to that of the indigenous Jews. Christian powers maintained their own fictions of superiority.[24]

State ideological constructs, Muslim and Christian, masked a growing cultural convergence, symbolized by the spread of coffee drinking in the seventeenth century. Gift exchange ensured that the circulation of luxury commodities and elite culture proceeded in all directions. European envoys presented Muslim monarchs with silver and gold-plated coffee and later tea services, bejewelled watches and military hardware from the seventeenth century onwards, thereby stimulating elite desire for European commodities, while European elites eagerly received exotic products, silk ribbons and brocades. In addition, the cultural norms of contemporary Europe began to impinge on the ordering of Muslim ceremonies. In eighteenth-century Morocco, Sidi Muhammad screened himself from European view in a European carriage and on other occasions presented his wives to European consuls to demonstrate their education.[25] Elsewhere, European artistic forms meshed with local Islamic artistic vocabularies to become elite markers of distinction: the Qajars and Mughals incorporated Italianate floral motifs, while the Ottoman Baroque flourished in Istanbul.

Outside the confines of the state, Muslim networks adapted to changing economic realities and developed new connections to European networks that created a shared proto-global system. Two examples are Mediterranean trading networks operated by interstitial communities, which mediated economic and cultural exchange across the Christian–Muslim divide, and religious brotherhoods such as the Nasiriyya and Qadiriyya, which connected the trans-Saharan trade to Atlantic outlets. In the Mediterranean, British, French, Dutch and Spanish carriers predominated, but European merchants were restricted in their movements on land, where the development of their trade was almost exclusively in the hands of local intermediaries, who were therefore the beneficiaries of, and the agency for, commercial expansion. The detailed and insightful commentary of the eighteenth-century traveller, Venture de Paradis, on the government and industry of Tunis and Algiers suggests that these links created a cosmopolitan Mediterranean sensibility which crossed the religious divide.[26]

In the Balkans, Istanbul, the Levant and Egypt, Greeks played the main role in developing commercial contacts with Europe.[27] In north Africa, Sephardic Jews played a comparable role through their networks connecting Tanger, Algiers and Tunis to Gibraltar, Marseille, Livorno and the Levant. Another group were the Levantine dragomen, translators for European consuls and commercial agents, recruited among Levantine Christians and Italians who had resided in the Ottoman empire so long that Europeans no longer considered them 'Western'. European consuls themselves supplemented their meagre salaries by participating in complex banking and loan arrangements with Muslim merchants to redeem captives.[28] A final group were the renegades, Mediterranean Christian converts to Islam, who served in Morocco, Algiers and Istanbul and acted as transmitters of European science and technology.

The trans-Saharan trade networks organized by religious brotherhoods did not have the cosmopolitan character of Mediterranean networks, but they also linked European and Muslim trading zones in new ways in the seventeenth century and played a dynamic 'universalizing' role on the southern Islamic frontier in the eighteenth century. Muhammad b. Nasir founded one such brotherhood, the Nasiriyya, in the mid seventeenth century at Tamgrut, a small oasis settlement below the High Atlas on the western-most trans-Saharan route. The Nasiriyya quickly developed an extensive network of religious lodges (*zawāyā*) which offered financial, social and religious services to local communities and Muslim merchants trading between Timbuktu, the Moroccan sultanate and Europe via Moroccan Atlantic ports.[29]

The Nasiriyya offered credit arrangements, warehousing and access to information to their affiliates. They were able to do this as a result of their religious prestige and their embeddedness in local, regional and international networks based on the circulation of financial, social and symbolic capital. They stored grain and then fed hungry tribesmen during times of famine, thereby securing their forbearance from attacking Nasiri-sponsored and protected caravans; they built up capital using gifts from grateful merchants whose caravans arrived safely at their destination as a result of Nasiri protection; and they offered loans repaid in excess by clients keen to secure the saint's blessing (*baraka*) for future undertakings. The Qadiriyya offered similar services on the southern edge of the Sahara.

The cultural and political impact of the brotherhoods was quite different from that of the metropolitan Mediterranean networks. Whilst Mediterranean connections fostered a cosmopolitan attitude which blurred the line between non-Muslim and Muslim, the brotherhoods embarked on Muslim globalizing projects which sharpened the distinction. This reflected the fact that the brotherhoods operated on frontiers, the internal frontier between the desert and the sown, and the southern African frontier between the *dār al-islām* and the *dār al-harb*, where both Christian and Muslim powers felt free to plunder, exploit and enslave. However, while European slave-traders made no distinction between Muslim and non-Muslim Africans, this distinction was crucial from the perspective of local Muslim religious leaders who saw the economic, social and political viability of regional Islam being undermined by slave raiding and trading.[30]

In response, several religious brotherhoods, beginning with the west-African Qadiriyya, launched initiatives to 'civilize' local Muslim communities by insisting on their full Islamization and political separation from local non-Muslims.[31] The resulting *jihād* movements were part of a wider phase of Islamic renewal (*tajdīd*) which criticized existing religious and political practices and called for their reform by means of renewed creative engagement (*ijtihād*) with the fundamental texts of the faith and active struggle (*jihād*) to implement the norms encapsulated within them. Renewal entailed, in essence, projects to (re)establish the normative religious (basic knowledge of Muslim rites), social (welfare, education, security) and economic (payment of alms) conditions for the full integration of 'marginal' communities into the *umma* and the *dār al-islām*.

Whilst religious renewal was a periodic phenomenon in Islamic history, in the eighteenth century it was characterized by synchronic movements across the *dār al-islām* in Africa, Arabia and Asia, which exhibited a strong urge to homogenize religious practice and consolidate Islamic political structures. In general reformers possessed a strongly integrative Muslim vision, expressed in their production of orthodox textual versions of Islam, to counteract local practices now seen as deviant and their desire to debate their views in the international Muslim arena.

Religious reformism owed its international profile in part to modern forms of communication which invigorated Muslim intellectual networks. Between 1750 and 1850, a growing number of north-west African pilgrims took European ships from Maghribi ports to Alexandria *en route* to Mecca, thereby considerably reducing the pilgrimage's duration.[32] This meant that information about reformist movements quickly circulated and could be discussed by scholars in numerous places. Secondly, exposure to wider Muslim intellectual currents through travel was a catalyst to reformism in itself: the majority of reformers had performed the *hajj*, and the difference between their ideals and reality in multiple Islamic centres spurred them to action.[33]

The debates aroused by the Wahhabi movement demonstrate the point. The central Arabian Wahhabis gained widespread notoriety after they captured Mecca but their attempt to reconstitute the early Islamic state by force was not as influential as the extensive discussion of Muhammad b. 'Abd al-Wahhab's reformist doctrines in the Azhar mosque in Cairo, the Zaytuna mosque in Tunis, and the Qarawiyyin mosque in Fes between 1818 and 1820.[34] Simultaneously, north African mystics and scholars promoted their own vision of regeneration in Cairo and the Hijaz where they interacted with local '*ulama*' and reformist scholars from the Indo-Persian half of the *dār al-islām*.[35]

The pro-active attitudes of these scholars and their homogenizing vision of Muslim universalism suggest a new phase in Muslim globalization which coincided with the transition from proto- to modern globalization. Scholarly debates in the early nineteenth century certainly set the tone for the pan-

Islamist philosophies of the ensuing era. However, the exact relationship between Islamic renewal, proto-globalization and early modern globalization is difficult to gauge and has scarcely been researched at present. Muslim territorial losses in central Europe, the Caucasus and Crimea, central Asia, India, and Africa generated a sense of impending crisis which Muslims tended to identify as divine punishment for their religious laxity. However, in the Arabo-Islamic world we have few explicit links between the two phenomena before the 1830s, when north Africans interpreted the French conquest of Algiers as God's retribution and insisted that unless local Muslims established a just Islamic socio-political order they would not be able to expel the French.[36]

Muslim Unity and Division in the Age of Modern Globalization

Between 1648 and 1850, intermediaries and ritual maintenance of traditional relations facilitated European–Muslim contact and created, in the Mediterranean at least, a system characterized by shared cultural and commercial practices rather than by religious conflict. From the late eighteenth century, exchanges between the Islamic world and Europe intensified and this fragile equilibrium faltered. During the nineteenth century the often violent construction of European empires destroyed the cosmopolitanism of the eighteenth century and remade the binary division between the *dār al-islām* and the *dār al-harb*.

Some Muslim powers attempted to adopt and Islamize the political paradigms offered by modern globalization in order to compete and participate in the emerging world order, but Muslim societies fell back on older concepts of social and political unity revived by the Islamic renewal movements which continued to push for universal religious conformity. Although 'fundamentalist' in character, they were considered politically innovative and subversive by contemporary Muslim regimes because they were not constrained by the political boundaries which they, and European imperial powers, wished to consolidate. At the level of both state and society, however, European concepts of nation, nation state and nationalism permeated the *dār al-islām* only to be re-imagined with reference to the world order of which Muslims were, and continue to be, part.

Although 1850 is a convenient date for the start of modern globalization, Napoleon's expedition to Egypt (1798–1801) initiated the change in Christian–Muslim relations in the Mediterranean.[37] From 1798 Muslim states found it increasingly difficult to persuade their subjects that they had European powers at their beck and call. They faced European-imposed constraints on corsairing, protectionism in European markets, and the threat of bombardment if they failed to accept new 'international' concepts of sovereignty and territoriality. They responded by trying to compete with their European counterparts by adopting their military technology and tactics, rationalizing government and reluctantly accepting territorial definitions of statehood.

Muslim regimes called the military restructuring which they undertook the *nizām-i cedīd*, the New Order, and it was just that. It replaced traditional socio-political categories with conscription, new types of taxation and legal status, and promoted new ideas of territorial statehood by placing the population of defined regions under more efficient central administrations.[38] European states welcomed the *nizām-i cedīd*, sold Muslim regimes artillery and sent them military instructors. They did this because they consciously recognized the *nizām-i cedīd* as an agent of imperial globalization which would assist their mission to order and 'civilize' potential colonial spaces. In the 1840s both the French and British commented that Moroccan military modernization should be promoted to enable the sultan to control his subjects and uphold Morocco's new border with French Algeria.[39]

In order to counter domestic criticism that the *nizām-i cedīd* was an infidel importation, many regimes described their new armies as instruments for the *jihād* to defend the *dār al-islām* from Europe's new crusade. The Ottoman sultan Mahmud II (1808–1839) called his new army the *asākir-i muhammadiye mansūriye* (the victorious Muhammadan troops) while *nizām-i cedīd* textbooks from Egypt and Moroccan apologetics for it both contained extensive jihadist vocabulary.[40] State utilization of jihadist justifications for the *nizām-i cedīd* demonstrated the ambiguity with which Muslim states viewed the rise of the West. On the one hand, they tacitly acknowledged and promoted the new world order by acquiring its technologies, using non-Muslim European instructors, and sending educational missions to Europe. On the other hand, they envisaged the *nizām-i cedīd* as the means to combat Eurocentric globalization, consolidate the states of the *dār al-islām*, and fortify the border with the *dār al-harb*. As the chief minister of the Moroccan sultan enthusiastically stated in 1845, when describing the *nizām-i cedīd* army: 'My brother, if you had only seen its resolve and courage, you would realise that it is the very thing to tear down the defences of the infidel.'[41]

To this end Muslim regimes offered each other moral and material support against European powers, circulated *nizām-i cedīd* textbooks and exchanged Muslim military instructors. In the 1840s the sultan of Morocco received Ottoman offers of artillery and instructors to stiffen local resistance to French expansion in Algeria. He also received envoys from Husaynid Tunis, military instructors from Algeria, and *nizām-i cedīd* textbooks from Egypt. Meanwhile, jihadist regimes in conflict with the French in Senegal looked to the Moroccan and Ottoman sultans as symbols of Muslim solidarity and possible sources of material assistance, as did Muslims in India.[42]

Attempts to promote greater inter-state solidarity were part of a communal re-imagining of the division between the *dār al-islām* and *dār al-harb* and renewed nostalgia for the religio-political unity symbolized by the caliphate. This shift in popular attitudes, galvanized by Islamic renewal, expressed the disquiet generated by the apparent marginalization and subjugation of the *dār al-islām* within a non-Muslim global order. Many Muslims did not consider the *nizām-i cedīd* a new order but the overturning (*inqilāb*) of the established Islamic order. They opposed it because it ruptured the contract between sultan and subject institutionalized in the *bay'a* and *dhimma*, and enshrined non-divine principles of order dependent on the mechanization and subjection of the individual to rational military and governmental structures, and the substitution of bounded territorial sovereignty for divine sovereignty.

Nevertheless modern European political concepts of the nation, the national homeland and the nation state, penetrated the Middle East steadily during the nineteenth century. They were first adopted by Christian intellectuals who had to circumvent old elites and persuade their peasant fellows that they belonged to nations rather than to the orthodox Christian commonwealth.[43] But it was not just new Christian elites who aspired to transplant the nation state. The Ottoman state itself embarked upon a project of political modernization, the Tanzimat, which triggered the development of Ottomanism, an innovative ideology which transposed the idea of the national homeland to the Ottoman context.[44] The proponents of Ottomanism, a secularized elite group known as the Young Ottomans, equated the *patrie* with the *vatan* (*ar.watan*), the natal locality. They hoped that the *vatan* would act as a focus for the political loyalty of all Ottoman subjects, whatever their ethnicity, religion or language.[45] Internationally, they expected that this would enable the Ottoman empire to take its place in the modern global order as a partner of the European imperial powers.

They faced problems on all fronts. Loyalty to the Ottoman empire was not territorial but inter-personal; it lay in the religiously defined contract between sultan and subject ruptured by the *nizām-i cedīd* and Tanzimat. Secondly, Ottomanism could not define 'Ottoman' in ethnic terms because the ruling elite was recruited from all over the empire: 'Turk' was a socio-linguistic not ethnic distinction which included members from the Balkans, Anatolia, the Arab lands and renegades from European societies. Nor could the Young Ottomans delineate a metropolitan space since the heartland of the empire, Rumelia, had already been partitioned by the secession of Greece. The Ottoman *vatan* was therefore a vague domain rather than a defined territory, and lacked a nation at its centre.

On the international front, the European powers admitted the Ottoman empire to the Concert of Europe in 1856 but did not view it as a true partner in the imperial world order. From the European perspective, the Christian 'nations' of the Balkans and proto-national units such as Egypt were the carriers of modern globalization, not the Ottoman empire, the 'sick man of Europe'. Imperial hierarchies of power assumed that metropolitan space was European (and Christian), and that non-European space entered the system as a colony or a client, not as a metropolitan equal. The Ottoman empire could only be an object not a determinant in the modern global order and its emulation of European empires excluded rather than integrated it.

As in other eras, however, modern globalization also operated beyond the confines of the state using the links between the *dār al-islām* and Europe multiplied by imperial communications. The most influential beneficiaries of these connections were Muslim scholars, the traditional guardians of Islamic values, some of whose peregrinations now included sojourns in European metropoles and who used the nascent Middle Eastern press to promote their ideas.[46] These Islamic modernists affirmed the validity of Muslim universalism and its compatibility with modernity. They insisted that the *umma* had to engage with European science, politics and culture, and select what was appropriate for Muslim benefit. To legitimize this process they used the methods of Islamic renewal – creative interpretation of the Islamic sources (*ijtihād*) – to equate European and Islamic institutions. One such equation was the comparison of parliamentary democracy to *shūrā*, the practice of consultation.[47]

The extensive debate as to whether such associations were valid is not relevant here. Islamic modernism was important because it defined the parameters of a new Muslim global discourse in a dialectic rather than a purely emulative relationship with ideas emanating from Europe, a situation perpetuated into post-colonial globalization. The Islamic modernists also challenged Muslim regimes for failing to fulfil either old or new political obligations and provided a framework for the synthesis of those obligations in the form of Pan-Islamism, a doctrine of international mass Muslim solidarity against European imperialism and decadent domestic regimes.[48]

In response to European imperialism, Islamic modernism and Pan-Islamism, the Ottoman sultan, Abdülhamid II (1878–1909), reactivated the caliphate. His decision was influenced by the disruptive and divisive dimensions of modern globalization. First, the Ottoman demographic balance between Christians and Muslims had shifted decisively in favour of Muslims owing to the secession of Christian areas and the migration of five to seven million Muslim Turks, Kurds and Circassians from the Balkans and the Russian empire (1850–1914).[49] This movement transformed a multi-confessional empire into a more monolithic Muslim block. Second, immigrant experiences of Pan-Slavism encouraged them to counteract 'Christian' European imperialism with alternative Turkic and Muslim paradigms which radicalized Ottoman politics. The ideologies which emerged were Turkism, Pan-Turanism and Ottoman caliphal ideology, which sought to connect Muslims across the *dār al-islām*, inside and outside imperial systems, into a symbolic unit analogous to the Christian Orthodox community under the Russian Tsar.[50] Although designed in part to disquiet the British and French imperial administrations, the Ottoman caliphate also sought to give the *umma* a new focus in a world characterized by extensive economic networks but also by division between European metropolitan and non-European colonial spaces, and the destruction of the free movement previously enjoyed by Muslims within the *dār al-islām*.

European powers viewed Pan-Islamism and the Ottoman caliphate as reactionary phenomena indicative of Muslim 'fanaticism'. In reality, they were modern responses in an Islamic idiom to the exclusivity of the imperial age and its hierarchies of power which deprived the states of the *dār al-islām* of the partnership implied by proto-globalization and constrained the movements of Muslims. Many Muslims also rejected the Ottoman caliphate but for different reasons. Arab and Turkish intellectuals inspired by political secularism rejected the religious dimension, while devout Muslim Arab scholars influenced by new ideas of nationality rejected the 'Turkish' appropriation of an 'Arab' prerogative, a position expressed most strongly by al-Kawakibi, an Aleppan scholar.[51] Therefore, ironically, the efforts of the Ottomans to become a partner of the European imperial powers did not secure them European recognition but the recognition of their subject peoples, who then rejected imperialism in both Ottoman and European guises.

Local Muslim opposition to imperialism took the form of a new and sometimes contradictory synthesis between secular nationalism and Muslim universalism. Nationalists in the Arab lands posited the idea that the peoples (*ajnās*) of the *dār al-islām* were actually discrete (national) communities (*umam*) within the larger universal (religious) community (*umma*). These nations were connected by the linguistic and cultural heritage of the *dār al-islām* shared by Muslims and non-Muslims alike.[52] The contradiction in making the *umma* both national and universal, secular and religious, was alleviated, but not resolved, by the fact that the *umma* had been politically fragmented for centuries. The nation state came to subsist, sometimes uncomfortably, with alternative ideologies such as Pan-Arabism which yearned for greater integration. As a result many saw it as a transitional phase in the political reunification of the *dār al-islām*.

Muslim Universalism in the Post-Colonial World

Using a universalizing religious ideology, Muslims produced a dynamic form of archaic globalization which incorporated large parts of the globe into a system of shared values, cultural practices and commerce. Interaction between this Islamic sphere and competing global systems emerging from Europe from the sixteenth century onwards took several forms which altered radically over time. During the phase which this volume defines as proto-globalization, strong parallels existed between processes in the western *dār al-islām* and Europe. The development of systems of expanding states, Muslim and Christian, was in many ways a mutually reinforcing process. Although parasitic on occasion, European exploitation of non-European trade networks contributed to the consolidation of Muslim state structures on the African frontier, while both European and Muslim states utilized middlemen in the Mediterranean to their own commercial benefit. Proto-globalization was, in effect, a multi-centred phenomenon, strengthened by the active participation of Muslim elements.

As the transition from proto-globalization to modern globalization occurred, what had appeared potentially to be a partnership of equals evolved into the subjugation of the states and peoples of the *dār al-islām* within European-dominated imperial systems. Even at this juncture, however, the Islamic world was not a passive recipient, as the attempt of the Ottomans to restructure and re-imagine their empire according to new European imperial norms indicates. The creative adaptation of the idea of the nation by Arab intellectuals demonstrated similar engagement with, and reformulation of, the European concepts being exported around the globe.

Relations between the *dār al-islām* and the modern European global order reached their nadir during the inter-war period. Until World War I, many Muslim intellectuals believed that their embrace of the principles of the modern European order – nationalism, secularism and democracy – entitled them to independence. Certainly, Middle Eastern nationalists hoped that the European powers would support their aspirations for independence as they had supported Christian separatism during the nineteenth century. The demise of the Ottoman empire after the war and its division into British and French mandates demonstrated their naivety. Mature modern globalization meant the fragmentation of the *dār al-islām*, the isolation of its constituent parts within closed colonial borders, and prohibitions on Muslim movements, including pilgrimage to Mecca. Global economic integration meant the exploitation of the *dār al-islām*'s resources for the benefit of foreign companies and colonists and frequently the impoverishment of indigenous peoples. Travel and migration were redirected towards European metropoles, where Muslims served as cheap labour and cannon fodder.

For many Muslims, the first half of the twentieth century was a period of humiliation which could only be ended by independence. Modern imperial globalization seemed an anomalous phase in comparison to archaic and proto-globalization during which the *dār al-islām* maintained its own sense of centrality and importance and contributed in manifold ways to the circulation of knowledge, commodities and people. The stress on secular national categories of identity by the governments of most post-colonial states masked the religious dimension of politics in the *dār al-islām* for many decades. However, restoration of Muslim self-confidence in the post-colonial world required the reconstitution of the *dār al-islām* in a new form which would enable Muslim nations to take their place as equals in a truly global order.

The formation of the League of Arab States in 1945, the popularity of the pan-Arab rhetoric of Gamal 'Abd al-Nasir in the 1950s and 1960s, and latterly the formation of the Islamic Conference were all steps in this direction, but it has yet to be seen whether the *dār al-islām* can be integrated into the modern global order in a coherent way. Most global systems, archaic and modern, have required the existence of agents and recipients, thus implying that global systems are inherently bipolar. The most trenchant criticism of contemporary globalization is that it is simply an alternative name for Western and particularly American political, cultural and economic dominance, a view held not only by Muslims but also by Australians and others whose economies are tied to the US dollar. Conversely, when Muslims adopt and exploit new global media, many commentators in the West chose to see their activities as part of a subversive global Islamic fundamentalist movement which threatens democratic 'civilization'.[53]

Another problem is grass-roots Muslim ambivalence towards the nation state, which remains the dominant political form within the current global system, whatever its future may be. The formation of Muslim states using the idiom of nationhood was a means to escape the colonial bind, but such states lacked authenticity and historical validity. Such ideological problems could have been overcome by real achievements in the social, political and economic spheres, but these have not been forthcoming. Moreover, many Muslim migrants to the nation states of the West have been unable to find a meaningful place in their host societies. In such a climate, Muslims have naturally turned to Islamic solutions. These provide ideals of integrity and integration which contemporary globalization offers but has not produced for most Muslims. The challenge of the present is to rethink globalization, to move away from inherited notions of bipolarity and assumptions about the inherent superiority of the nation state, and recognize a multiplicity of global visions and the distinct world civilizations which have generated them.

Notes and References

1 Although texts generally talk about four schools of law, the Maliki, Hanafi, Shafi'i and Hanbali schools, it is appropriate to include the Shi'i school of law based on the work of the sixth Shi'i imam, Ja'far al-Sadiq, in this context.

2 A stimulating discussion of the importance of the procedural and relational in Islamic law is Lawrence Rosen's *The Justice of Islam* (Oxford, 2000).

3 Ian Richard Netton (ed.), *Golden Roads: Migration, Pilgrimage and Travel in Modern and Medieval Islam* (London, 1993) and Dale Eickelman and James Piscatori (eds.), *Muslim Travellers: Pilgrimage, Migration and Religious Imagination*, (London, 1990) contain several articles exploring the ambiguities of travel within the *dār al-islām*.

4 William Wright (ed.), *Riḥlat Ibn Jubayr*, revised by M.J. de Goeje (Leiden, 1907). Throughout this account of his pilgrimage, the eleventh-century Granadan traveller, Ibn Jubayr, assumes that there are Islamic norms which are as relevent to Egypt, Syria and the Hijaz as to Granada.

5 I use the past tense because the *dār al-islām* no longer exists in the form I describe due to political secularization and the introduction of the equality of all citizens regardless of their religion.

6 Kirti Chaudhuri, *Trade and Civilisation in the Indian Ocean: An Economic History*

from the Rise of Islam to 1750 (Cambridge, 1985); Olivia R. Constable, *Trade and Traders in Muslim Spain* (Cambridge, 1994).

7 See 'Hisba' in the *Encyclopedia of Islam*, vol. 2, (Leiden).
8 For a discussion of the evolution of caliphal ideology, see Patricia Crone and Martin Hinds, *God's Caliph: Religious Authority in the First Centuries of Islam* (Cambridge, 1986).
9 See C.A. Bayly's essay in this volume.
10 N. Dawud (ed.), *Ibn Khaldun: The Muqaddimah*, trans. Franz Rosenthal (Princeton, 1969).
11 Ross Dunn, 'International Migrations of Literate Muslims in the later Middle Period: The Case of Ibn Battuta', in Netton, *Golden Roads*, pp. 77–80.
12 H.A.R. Gibb, *The Travels of Ibn Battuta*, vol 3, (Delhi, 1993); Ross Dunn, *The Adventures of Ibn Battuta: A Muslim Traveller of the Fourteeth Century* (1986); Said Hamdoun and Noel King, *Ibn Battuta in Black Africa* (Princeton, 1994).
13 Dunn, 'International migrations', p. 76.
14 See Richard Drayton's essay in this volume.
15 Salih Ozbaran, *The Ottoman Response to European Expansion: Studies on Ottoman–Portuguese Relations in the Indian Ocean and Ottoman Administration in the Arab Lands during the Sixteenth Century* (Istanbul, 1994).
16 Salih Ozbaran, *Ottoman Response*, pp. 61–6.
17 Alexander de Groot, 'Barbary Legend Revisited: Ottoman Peace Treaties from Algiers (17th–18th centuries)', unpublished paper presented at the Skilliter Centre Conference: Piracy in the Ottoman Empire, Cambridge, 2000.
18 Georg Høst, *Histoire de l'Empereur du Maroc Mohamed Ben Abdallah* (Copenhagen, 1791), Trans. by F. Damgaard and P. Gailhanou (Rabat, 1998), p. 33.
19 Høst, *Histoire*, p. 62.
20 Høst, *Histoire*, p. 80.
21 Sidi Muhammad's chief minister, al-Zayyani, recounts his mission to Istanbul in his, *al-Turjumāna al-Kubrā fī akhbār al-Ma'mur Barran wa Bahran*, ed. 'Abd al-Karim al-Filali, (Casablanca, 1967); M'Hammad Benaboud discusses two embassies in his article, 'Authority and Power in the Ottoman State in the Eighteenth Century', in Caesar Farah (ed.), *Decision-Making and Change in the Ottoman Empire* (Missouri, 1993), pp. 67–79.
22 Ahmad al-Ghazzal, 'Natījat al-Ijtihād fi'l-Uhadāna wa'l-Jihād', Manuscript D107, Bibliotheque Generale, Rabat.
23 Høst, *Histoire*, pp. 33–6, 58, 74–5; al-Du'ayyif al-Ribati, *Tārīkh al-Dawla al-'Alawiyya al-Sa'īda* (Casablanca, 1988), p. 324.
24 For examples of French attitudes, see Younès Nékrouf, *Une amitié orageuse: Moulay Ismaïl et Louis XIV* (Paris, 1987).
25 Høst, *Histoire*, pp. 70, 97–8.
26 Jean-Michel Venture de Paradis, *Tunis et Alger au XVIII siècle*, ed. J. Cuoq (Paris, n.d.).
27 Charles Issawi, *Cross-Cultural Encounters and Conflicts* (Oxford, 1999), pp. 101–17.
28 Pal Fodor, 'Piracy, Ransom, Slavery and Trade: French Participation in the Liberation of Ottoman Slaves from Malta', unpublished paper presented at the Skilliter Centre Conference: Piracy in the Ottoman Empire, Cambridge, 2000.
29 I have taken much of the detail in this paragraph and the next from David Gutelius's unpublished paper, 'The Nasiriyya *tarīqa* and economic change in the early modern world', presented at the American Institute for Maghrib Studies Conference: The Maghrib in World History, Tunis, 1997.

30 Many rural west-African Muslim communities were involved in other forms of trade with European powers, the grain trade in particular, and sought cohesion and protection against semi-pagan domestic regimes. Nehemia Levtzion, 'The Eighteenth-Century Background to the Islamic Revolutions in West Africa', in Nehemia Levtzion and John Voll (eds.), *Eighteenth-Century Renewal and Reform in Islam* (Syracuse, 1987), pp. 21–38.

31 The most famous of these movements was the mid-eighteenth century *jihad* of the Qadiri shaykh, Usuman dan Fodio, which led to the establishment of the Sokoto caliphate: see Louis Brenner, 'Muslim Thought in 18th-Century West Africa: The Case of Shaykh Uthman b. Fudi', in Levtzion and Voll, *Reform in Islam*, pp. 39–68

32 Høst, *Histoire de l'Empereur*, p. 50; Venture de Paradis, *Tunis*, p. 134; H. Norris, *The Pilgrimage of Ahmad, Son of the Little Bird of Paradise* (Warminster, 1977).

33 John Voll, 'Linking Groups in the Networks of Eighteenth-Century Revivalist Scholars: The Mizjaji Family in the Yemen', in Levtzion and Voll, *Reform in Islam*, pp. 69–92.

34 Mohamed El Mansour, 'Al-haraka al-wahhābiyya wa'l-radd fa'l al-maghribi fi bidāyat al-qarn al-tāsi' 'ashar.', in *al-Islāh wa'l-Mujtama' al-Maghribi* (Rabat, 1986), pp. 175–89.

35 Several of these Maghribi scholars and Sufis have been the subject of monographs, see: R.S. O'Fahey, *Enigmatic Saint: Ahmad Ibn Idris and the Idrisi Tradition* (London, 1990) and Knut Vikør, *Sufi and Scholar on the Desert Edge: Muhammad b.''Ali al-Sanusi and his Brotherhood* (London, 1995).

36 Norris, *Pilgrimage of Ahmad*, pp. 83–93; Muhammad b. 'Abd al-Qadir, *Tuhfat al-Zā'ir fi Tārīkh al-Jazā'ir wa'l-Amīr 'Abd al-Qādir* (Beirut, 1964) pp. 157–8.

37 See: 'Abd al-Rahman al-Jabarti, *Ajā'ib al-Athār fi'l-Tarājim wa'l-Akhbār*, vol. 3, (Beirut, n.d.); Mohamed El Mansour, 'Le commerce maritime du Maroc pendant le régne de Moulay Slimane (1792–1822)', *Maghreb Review*, 12 (1987), pp. 90–3.

38 For an introduction to military and governmental modernization in the Muslim Mediterranean, see Carl L. Brown, *The Tunisia of Ahmad Bey* (Princeton, 1974); R. Davison, *Essays in Ottoman and Turkish History 1774–1923: The Impact of the West* (London, 1990); Carter Findley, *Bureaucratic Reform in the Ottoman Empire: The Sublime Porte 1789–1922* (Princeton, 1980); W. Polk and R. Chambers, *The Beginnings of Modernization in the Middle East* (Chicago, 1968); Afaf Sayyid-Marsot, *Egypt in the Reign of Muhammad Ali* (Cambridge, 1983); Stanford J. Shaw, *Between Old and New: The Ottoman Empire under Selim III* (Cambridge, MA, 1971).

39 FO99/26: Hay to Aberdeen, 13.5.1845 and 26.6.1845, Public Record Office, London.

40 Muhammad al-Khuja, 'Risāla fī Tanzīm al-Jaysh', Manuscript K2733, Bibliotheque Generale, Rabat; Ahmad al-Kardudi, 'Kashf al-Ghumma bi-Bayān inna Harb al-Nizām Haqq 'ala al-Umma', Manuscript D1281, Bibliotheque Generale, Rabat.

41 Muhammad b. Idris to Bu Silham, 21 Rajab 1261. al-Tartib al-'Amm, Correspondance Generale, Direction des Archives Royales, Rabat.

42 West-African Muslim leaders viewed both the Moroccan and Ottoman sultans as possessing the 'caliphal' right to 'unite the whole community'; the Ottoman sultan because he controlled vast territories and the Moroccan sultan because he was a descendant of the Prophet and therefore religiously sanctioned. See A. Zebadia, 'The Career and Correspondence of Ahmad al-Bakkay', unpublished Ph.D. thesis, University of London, 1974, p. 181.

43 See Dimitris Livanios, 'Conquering the Souls: Nationalism and Greek Guerrilla

Warfare in Ottoman Macedonia, 1904–1908', *Byzantine and Modern Greek Studies*, 23 (1999), pp. 195–221.

44 R. Davison, *Reform in the Ottoman Empire, 1856–1876* (Princeton, 1963); Kemal Karpat, 'The Transformation of the Ottoman State 1789–1908', *IJMES*, 3 (1972), pp. 234–44.

45 The classic work on the Young Ottomans is still Serif Mardin's *The Genesis of Young Ottoman Thought* (Princeton, 1962).

46 The Cairene press, established by Christians from Lebanon and Syria, was particularly active in publishing the works of secular and religious intellectuals such as Muhammad 'Abduh, see Albert Hourani, *Arabic Thought in the Liberal Age, 1798–1939* (Cambridge, 1983), pp. 132–3.

47 See Khayr al-Din, *The Surest Path*, trans. by C. L. Brown (Cambridge, MA, 1967); Malcolm Kerr, *Islamic Reform: The Political and Legal Theories of Muhammad Abduh and Rashid Rida* (Berkeley, 1966).

48 The most renowned exponent of Pan-Islamism was Jamal al-Din al-Afghani, an Iranian Shi'i scholar who passed himself of as an Afghan Sunni and travelled extensively in India, Iran the Ottoman empire and Europe trying to find rulers who would co-operate in defending the *dār al-islām* against European imperialism. His resulting disillusionment with Muslim ruling elites led him to identify Islamic modernist scholars as a new generation of community leaders with a responsibility to educate and direct the Muslim masses in the modern world. See Nikki Keddie, *An Islamic Response to Imperialism: Political and Religious Writings of Jamal al-Din al-Afghani* (Berkeley, 1983).

49 Kemal Karpat, 'The *hijra* from Russia and the Balkans', in Eickelman and Piscatori, *Muslim Travellers*, pp. 131–52.

50 See Selim Deringil, *The Well-Protected Domains: Ideology and the Legitimation of Power in the Ottoman Empire, 1876–1909* (London, 1998).

51 'Abbas Mahmud al-'Aqqad, *'Abd al-Rahman al-Kawakibi* (Cairo, 1959), pp. 64–74.

52 Many early Arab nationalists were Christians who realized the importance of bridging the Muslim–Christian confessional gap but also genuinely recognized that the history of the Arabs was also largely the history of Islam. Their solution was to consider Islamic civilization a shared Christian and Muslim Arab heritage and to present secular nationalism as the modern equivalent of Islam. This is particularly evident in the writings of Michel Aflaq who founded the Ba'th party in the 1920s.

53 Martin Kramer, *Arab Awakening and Islamic Revival* (London, 1996), pp. 265–78.

RICHARD DRAYTON

The Collaboration of Labour: Slaves, Empires, and Globalizations in the Atlantic World, *c.* 1600–1850

How we delineate 'globalization' depends on the interpretive use we plan for the category. For journalists and political scientists it is a name for a contemporary order of things.[1] For historians it may merely be a new flag to fly over the old question of the origins of the modern world. Even among them there will be serious disagreements about modernity and the world they seek to explain and, in consequence, about process and periodization. The division of 'globalization' into 'archaic' or 'modern' or 'proto' phases, as a generation ago with 'modernization' and 'industrialization', may generate more questions than answers.

This essay, in part, complements others in this collection, adding to it the Atlantic world in the early modern period. It questions, like them, the teleological construction of the 'global', common to so many contemporary accounts, and argues for the non-cumulative and plural character of world history. No cultural, political, technological or economic regime has ever integrated more than part of the planet, and later systems failed to subsume the worlds created by earlier ones. What distinguishes this essay from its companions, however, is its focus on human labour. It proposes the organization and co-ordination of work in different parts of the planet as the key to 'globalizations' and, if we choose, to 'globalization' understood in its Whiggish singularity. We would do well to heed Adam Smith's advice, rarely understood by most who invoke Smith, that 'It was not by gold or by silver, but by labour, that all the wealth of the world was originally purchased'.[2] While Smith's transcendant theme was the division of labour, we may instead choose to elucidate its collaboration.

This essay explores how an alliance of New World plantation slavery and semi-free Old World labour between 1500 and 1900 generated global circuits of bullion, sugar, cotton, wheat, beef and debt, and cycles of colonial expansion and European settlement on every continent. At its centre is the story of the sugar plantations of Brazil and the Caribbean and their economic, political and cultural impact on the international system.[3] It is a parable of the periphery acting as centre, and of a past still present with us in the wealth and squalor of our contemporary globalizations.[4] It is probable that the world might have been integrated had there been no sugar; what is certain, however, is that Africans, as labour, capital and currency, shaped the terms of integration over four hundred years.

Resituating the 'Sugar Plantation Complex'

All human history is the story of the elaboration of increasingly complex systems of work and play. By 'work' I mean that collective activity through which nature is turned into the path of human history, and by 'play', the capacity for imaginative manipulation, through which the world and the self are experienced and transformed. Any social arrangement may easily be unlocked by the questions: how is work organized, who orders whom, and how are the good things work yields distributed? And in 'play' lie the keys to the vanity of proconsuls and economists, our hunger for music and our curiosity for the causes of things.

Work begins in the attempt by communities to recruit from nature what they need to survive. What changes, however, is how humans understand 'necessity' and 'survival', and with it the modes of work, the social organization, modes of knowledge, sensibility, and identity, which order a particular relationship to nature. For the play instinct is quick to expand the boundaries of necessity, to seek that excess which is luxury, and to project, onto external things, images of the deepest and most irresistible human urges and passions. This is the process at the heart of the evolution of ideas of value, which finds one expression in the elaboration of moral codes, the registers of sensibility and obligation against which the individual finds his or her agency meaningful, and another in the displacement onto gold and cowries, tobacco, silver or paper of the right to command goods, services, loyalty. What we might call 'globalizations' are moments in this evolution: particular contexts in which labour, under various forms of compulsion, is allied across an expanse of the planet towards meeting what one party understands to be its needs, and may ultimately perhaps persuade others to desire. This co-ordination of labour is mediated by new kinds of kinship bonds, fears of violence and scarcity, hopes of protection or plenty, ideas of debt, and changing tastes for foods, ornaments, and intoxicants.

There is perhaps no better example of this process than the system of events which flowed out of the human palate's bias for sweetness. The taste for the sweet is hard-wired into the brain as a means of guiding the species towards fruits and vegetables. The intense sweetness of a giant New Guinea grass thus led to its cultivation in India, then Egypt and the Arab Mediterranean, where sucrose, with great difficulty, was extracted from it.[5] Its crystals, products of alchemical expertise, bewitched all who came in contact with them, a pound of sugar going for more than its weight in precious metals in late medieval Europe. Christendom's crusaders learned in Crete, Cyprus and Sicily how it was made: the heavy labour of growing, cutting, hauling, chopping, grinding, and the arts of boiling and curing. Local people were coerced into sugar production, and small amounts were made at mills which would otherwise have ground cereals. But where flight of indigenes, or their deaths, intervened, sugar was valuable enough to justify the purchase of slaves. Captives from eastern Europe and the British isles, and ultimately from the Maghreb and West Africa, once cane was planted in Portugal's Atlantic islands, were imported to cut and mill cane.[6] In Madeira and São Tomé, investments in labour and machines were so substantial that sugar could not be profitably produced on a small scale. A pattern of linked environmental, social, and economic change thus emerged which would later be imprinted on the islands of the Caribbean: the clearing of large tracts of land on these islands, and with it deforestation and desertification, the coercion and destruction of local populations, the importation of slaves, the whole initiative based on substantial capital and credit flows justified by an economy streamlined to export one valuable product.[7]

It has now, indeed, become conventional to talk of a 'sugar plantation complex', migrating ultimately to sixteenth-century Brazil, and then to Barbados, diffused to the rest of the Caribbean and ultimately the wider world.[8] The efficiency of this model has recently come under attack: did this 'institution' spring fully formed like Athena from Zeus in the thirteenth century, and how much in this 'complex' are the peculiar stories of seventeenth-century Barbados and eighteenth-century Jamaica being imposed on, and made normative for, an intricate chain of events and interactions?[9] J.C. Miller urges an approach more sensitive to context and process, and more careful about the particularity of the phenomena which the model attempts to aggregate. This essay is, in part, a response to this challenge, but it is also moved by another concern: to what extent is the prevailing description of an exotic conjuncture of sugar and slaves not complicit with an approach to world history which, paradoxically, balkanizes that history into regional ghettos? Might we not, following Eric Williams and Sidney Mintz, place the sugar plantation complex into our narratives of temperate as well as tropical history? Sugar, in several theatres of human experience, was ultimately a reason for putting the world to work.

The Modernity of the Sugar Plantation

Sugar production superficially resembles wine-making: canes, like grapes, must be planted, harvested, and pressed before they rot. In tenth-century Cyprus and eleventh-century Sicily, the canefield was often the successor to the vineyard. But wine and sugar are wholly different in the raw material to final product ratio, and once production was perfected in the regime of the fifteenth- and sixteenth-century Atlantic colonies, sugar involved heavy machinery, and a chain of processes, which required an entirely different scale of production. The production of sugar came to resemble that of metals: an ore, which needed cultivating, had to be mined and transported to a centre where it was smelted into a form valuable enough to be worth transporting to centres where it would be refined into a final product.

The sugar mill – *engenho* (Portuguese), *ingenio* (Spanish, the word finding itself, untranslated, in the subtitle of Ligon's 1657 *History of Barbados*), literally 'the engine' – was the centre of an agricultural regime which, in its mature form, held several hundred acres and many scores of slaves under its discipline. It was a machine for colonization, in the classic Roman sense: it consumed the indigenous, sucking into its furnaces as much timber as could easily be brought to it, and implanted the foreign in the local environment. Oviedo in the *Historia General y Natural de las Indias* described the massive investment required to make sugar in the Caribbean: as much as fifteen-thousand ducats in order to pay for the building of the mill, its boiling-house, the houses where the sugar is cured, the hundred and twenty negroes needed to keep the machines moving, thousands of head of cattle, and stores of timber and food.[10] Hispaniola's sugar production thus depended on inflows of capital and debt – Oviedo noted, in particular, the investments in *ingenios* of the Welsers and the Genoese. All the subsequent re-enactments of the 'sugar revolution', from seventeenth-century Barbados to eighteenth-century Saint Domingue and nineteenth-century Cuba, would depend on similar capital infusions. But it also required the intervention of the state; it was, in F. Ortiz's phrase, 'una espécie de capitalismo privilegiado'. Decrees of Charles V in 1518, 1519, 1529 and 1538 encouraged sugar production through facilitating public grants of land to *ingenios*, removing taxes on imported inputs, encouraging the migration of skilled craftsmen from the Canaries, and, most strikingly, protecting slaves and machinery from their owners' creditors in the event of insolvency.[11] In the decree of Charles V of 1538, the Crown's protection was extended at the same time to mills smelting metals and manufacturing sugar, with their slaves, instruments, and machinery, 'that they might not cease to prosper for the common good of these kingdoms and of the Indies'.[12] Repayment was to be made in the product of the mills, and indeed over several centuries, the perpetually indebted and failing New World planters, buying overpriced imports from Europe, more than repaid their debts in the form of sugar, molasses and rum, and in the downstream supply-and-demand flows based on these commodities.[13]

We need to recover a clear sense of the modernity of the mature sugar plantation, because Liberals and Marxists alike are prone to treat slave

production under state protection as a medieval relic.[14] This is a misunderstanding: the sugar plantations of Barbados, and later Jamaica and St
Domingue, were in fact at the cutting edge of capitalist civilization, whether
we look at the size of the labour force attached to single enterprises, its task
specialization, its subordination to a time discipline, its alienation from its
tools, its wholly expatriate character, the capital and machine-intensive nature
of sugar production, its extensive economies of scale, and its dependence on
long-distance trade for inputs and for exporting its product. African slavery
involved the ultimate commodification of labour and it was, moreover, a
modern rational, legal condition: it exemplified the apotheosis of both the law
of property and the right of government to decide the identity and conditions
of all who lived under it.

Yet the complexity of the 'modern' needs also to be emphasized, for the
New World, with its coerced labour, is commonly and incorrectly juxtaposed
to an Old World in which labour was mainly disciplined by money.[15] Even in
Amsterdam or London many unfree labour regimes were spliced to the
monetized economy: apprentices in guilds; warriors pressed under naval and
military discipline; women, children and dependants, within the family;
tenants, sharecroppers, indentured servants, on nearby farms. The plantation
slavery of Ligon's Barbados, indeed, may be said to represent an assimilation
of an Iberian institution, embodied in the Spanish loan word 'negro', to
English agrarian practices of purchasing labour services, via contracts of
indenture.[16] In the early stages of all the plantation colonies, moreover, the
binding of local labour, in particular the kidnapping and barter for
Amerindians, was initially more common than the very expensive business of
purchasing African slaves.[17] The 'sugar revolution' in Brazil, and later
Barbados and Jamaica, was initially financed by capital organized within the
New World, in the form of labour, dyewoods and other timber, and bullion
extracted from the region. Most crucially the growth of cities like Amsterdam
or London, or Bristol, Nantes, and Bordeaux, was directly connected to that of
peripheries of unfree labour. New World slaves were not the only tortured
collaborators of urban Europe. As Ferdinand Braudel reminded us, simultane-
ous with the rise of the trading cities of western Europe and the slave
plantations of the Atlantic came the 'second serfdom': east of a line which
stretched from Hamburg to Venice, peasants who were already emancipated
when Columbus reached Guanahani, found themselves re-subordinated, over
the course of the sixteenth century, to a fierce discipline which ensured that
wheat flowed to Danzig, Riga, Stettin and Wismar, and the luxuries of
Hamburg, Amsterdam and Paris, including the products of the East and West
Indies, flowed to their masters.[18] Two spheres of apparently 'pre-capitalist'
social relations thus arose in connection with the rise of the market economies
of western Europe: Polish serfs worked seven days a week, and slaves in
Martinique and Jamaica six, in order that Swedes and Prussians might drink
sugared coffee in Chinese porcelain, and gentlemen in Hamburg, Bordeaux

and London might add credits to their ledgers. It is a pity that Europe's historians tend, like their ancestors, to create separate accounts of profit and loss for each node of global economic systems.

Slaves and the City

We might describe the slave and serf peripheries of early modern capitalism as examples of the displaced despotism of the market. James Scott has described how planned cities like Washington and Brazilia are always flanked by chaotic suburbs and slums which make possible the ordered regime at the centre.[19] Had he extended his gaze to the rational and civilized Western centres of the world economy, where labour, weights and measures, security of person and social welfare are regulated, he would have found them always surrounded by overseas zones of plunder, coerced labour and limited rights. For trading cities like Amsterdam and London, often fair and pleasant places for those who lived near them, prospered on the right to exchange commodities which were very rarely the product of their vendors' efforts, on work disciplined by direct and indirect violence in other regions, and on currencies and terms of trade structured to the benefit of the central market.

Yet we must keep to a distance the assumption, central to Immanuel Wallerstein and indeed Braudel, that what really mattered for the process was the emergence of the city.[20] The metropolis should not be conceived as the first cause of the modern. Consumption, the focus of many useful recent attempts to understand early modern Europe, was often driven by new supply.[21] This is visible, for example, in the evolution of the price of sugar in the sixteenth century: as Bartholomé de Las Casas noted in the *Historia de Las Indias*, an arroba of sugar, worth one ducat when only Valencia and the Canaries fed Spain's consumers, was worth twice this by the middle of the century, when Hispaniola and Puerto Rico were also 'under cane'. The eighteenth-century English consumer, the hero of C. Shammas and J. Brewer, was similarly responding to the influx of tropical foods and drugs. We need to recover a sense of the co-evolution of the centres and peripheries in response to supply and demand at many centres. The point is not that the development of Europe was made possible by expropriating wealth from the rest of the world. It is rather that what we now call Europe, Africa, the Americas and Asia were constructed together in the midst of a relationship, at once economic and cultural, military and political, which tended and still tends to allocate to the West a disproportionate share of the power to command and consume resources. The semi-voluntary 'industrious revolutions' at the centre depended on coerced latifundial labour at frontiers, and the consequences of both continue. Kenneth Pomerancz's *The Great Divergence* makes precisely this argument: that it was access to the resources (and labour power) of the

Atlantic which gave Europe real advantages over China in terms of long-term growth.[22]

The significance of Eric Williams's *Capitalism and Slavery* (1944) has often been misconstrued by those who assumed that his argument concerned the impact of the direct profits of slaving on Britain's economy and society.[23] This approach may be compared to an attempt to understand the signficance of the opium trade for Britain, India and China by merely examining the accounts of the merchants involved. Summing the profits yielded by the exchange of Jamaican and Rhode Island rum or East Indian and Lancashire cottons or Birmingham guns on the Guinea coast for labour power is a similarly incomplete way to explore the meaning of slaving. In both these cases, we ignore the immediate stimulus to some (and paralysis to other) economic activity which such trades provide, and neglect completely long-term social and economic effects. Such calculations are founded on the error of taking exchange value to be a fair guide of use value, and indeed of taking money, the most mercurial and mythical of 'real' measurable things, as a means of judging the meaning of an exchange between two economic systems. Williams, as J.E. Inikori has argued, saw the real significance of the slave trade and plantation slavery not in profits or capital generated, but in the dynamism it gave to world trade between the fifteenth and the nineteenth centuries, and the new structures of capital, labour, production and services it mobilized.[24]

By 1690, Dalby Thomas could write that 'sugar has contributed more to England's pleasure, glory, and grandeur than any other commodity we deal in or produce, wool not excepted'.[25] Davenant, a few years later, estimated that the plantation trade accounted for £720,000 of England's £2 million external commerce, and much of his estimate for European trade amounted to re-exports.[26] Around slaving and the plantation trade emerged ship-building, insurance (the original business of the gentlemen of Lloyd's coffee house), banking (the basis of the Barclay family's enterprise), and a great deal of textile and metal manufacture. What the building of ships for the transport of slaves did for Liverpool, Eric Williams noted, the manufacture of cotton goods to clothe slaves did for Manchester: 'The first stimulus to the growth of Cottonopolis came from the African and West Indian markets.'[27] The aggregate trade figures conceal the importance of these peripheries in the statistic that Europe in the mid eighteenth century provided 47 per cent of imports and 62 per cent of exports: the Atlantic represented Britain's fastest growing markets.[28] The literally captive markets of the New World kept British wool workers employed in an era in which competition drove their products from Europe.[29] In 1772, 72 per cent of Yorkshire woollens and 90 per cent of broadcloth, and about 40 per cent of all English copper and brass was going abroad chiefly to Africa and the New World.[30] Estimates of the changes in British pig-iron output and export relative to raw material supply similarly argue the importance of export into the Atlantic trade system.[31] Atlantic trade, dominated by sugar and slaves, was the most dynamic sphere of Britain's eighteenth-century economy.[32] It was vital to the growth of London and Bristol, Glasgow and Liverpool, to cotton and iron working, shipping, insurance, banking, and to the three million new urban jobs created between 1700 and 1801 which were the reality behind Smith's vision of 'division of labour'. From the end of the seventeenth century until the 1820s, sugar was consistently the most valuable British import until it was replaced by another slave-grown commodity: cotton.[33] The slave plantations were also an important debt frontier: the perpetually insolvent plantations, and their commodities, were important objects of financial speculation, and a source of direct and indirect revenue streams.

The Old World was tugged into the modern by the New. The first British working class had been made on the sugar plantations of the New World in the 1660s, 1670s, and 1680s.[34] Plantation sugar production, as we noted earlier, was large scale, capital intensive, and machine dependent like no other industry in Britain before the mid eighteenth century. Structured gangs were composed of free and semi-free whites, and black slaves worked in units of over a hundred, divided into a variety of different tasks, operating in harmony with the *ingenio* under the strict time discipline of its bell. Slave populations, like the factory workers of nineteenth-century Clydeside or the Ruhr, lived several hundred to the square mile, and depended completely on long-distance trade for food and other supplies and for the sale of their produce. Across the water in Europe, in suceeding decades, men and women, in response to this tropical industrial revolution, were pulled into new kinds of work as dockers, woollen and cotton cloth-makers, shipbuilders, sugar refiners, gunsmiths, and iron mongers, on the one hand, and bankers, *armateurs*, insurers, on the other. A hundred and fifty years later, the Mississippi-born African at the cotton gin, and the operatives in Lancashire's *ingenios*, were similarly collaborating in creating another new economy. In the 1840s, moreover, over two million sterling of abolitionist Manchester's textiles were destined for the backs of the slaves who toiled on the cane fields of north-eastern Brazil. Wages earned in England spinning slave-grown cotton for slave consumers went to purchase bread and woollen cloth imported from the temperate Americas and the Antipodes: helping thus to finance new new frontiers of white 'free-labour' settlement. Recognizing this, we can better understand the non-environmental facts which made possible what Alfred Crosby and Tom Tomlinson have teleologically styled the 'neo-Europes'.[35] One globalization, sugar-centred, underlay other, later moments in the global mobilization of land and labour.

Slaves and Three Kinds of Imperialism

It is to this theme, the wider significance of slavery for the cycles of European expansion, that we now turn.

Plunder or asset-stripping is the most common original motive for

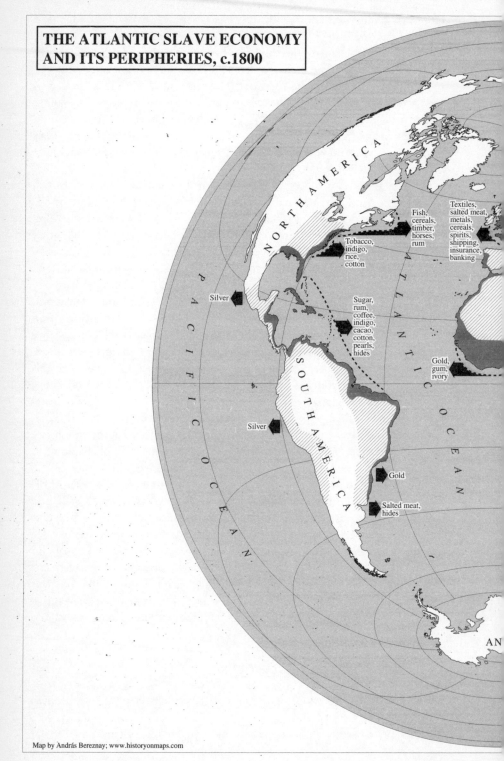

THE ATLANTIC SLAVE ECONOMY
AND ITS PERIPHERIES, c.1800

NORTH AMERICA

Fish, cereals, timber, horses, rum

Textiles, salted meat, metals, cereals, spirits, shipping, insurance, banking

Tobacco, indigo, rice, cotton

Silver

Sugar, rum, coffee, indigo, cacao, cotton, pearls, hides

PACIFIC OCEAN

ATLANTIC OCEAN

Gold, gum, ivory

SOUTH AMERICA

Silver

Gold

Salted meat, hides

AN

Map by András Bereznay; www.historyonmaps.com

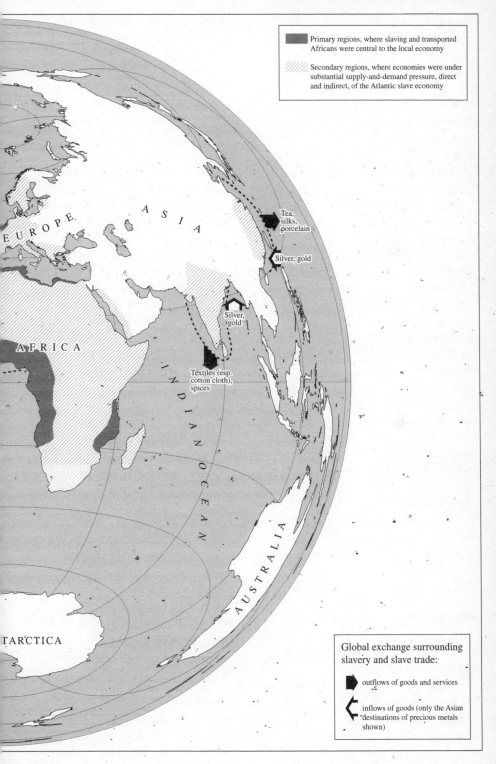

Primary regions, where slaving and transported Africans were central to the local economy

Secondary regions, where economies were under substantial supply-and-demand pressure, direct and indirect, of the Atlantic slave economy

Tea, silks, porcelain

Silver, gold

Silver, gold

Textiles (esp. cotton cloth), spices

EUROPE

ASIA

AFRICA

INDIAN OCEAN

AUSTRALIA

ANTARCTICA

Global exchange surrounding slavery and slave trade:

outflows of goods and services

inflows of goods (only the Asian destinations of precious metals shown) expansion, and until the seventeenth century it was the dominant one. Europeans went abroad principally in the hope of seizing exotic resources which would quickly make them rich at home. Sometimes this meant simple plunder; elsewhere it involved trade with parties from whom information about the real value of commodities was withheld. The New World, Africa, and Asia, were short-term means to Old World ends. The settlement of Spanish America flourished only where commodities might be easily extracted, and retreated, as in Hispaniola and Cuba, where these resources dwindled. Sugar production was introduced to the Spanish Caribbean principally as a means of rapidly extracting wealth; when other more direct forms of plunder appeared in Mexico and Peru, it quickly declined.

Slaves, in this first context, were more a currency, a kind of portable wealth, which might be extracted from a territory and sold where it was valuable. Columbus, for example, recommended to Ferdinand and Isabella that his domains might enrich the Crown, and help pay for the liberation of Jerusalem, by providing cargoes of Amerindian slaves for sale in the Mediterranean.[36] Hawkins and Drake, and three centuries of later English, Dutch and French slave traders, sought similarly to acquire bullion through the legal and illegal sale of Africans in Spanish America and Brazil. Slaving was central to the bullion flow which powered the massive expansion of the money supply in early modern Europe. The cod-hunters of St Malo and La Rochelle, and the herringmen of Bristol, converted themselves into fishers of men, and returned home with Guinea and Brazilian gold, and silver Spanish dollars. The luxuries of Calcutta and Canton – silks, calico, spices and tea – depended, in significant part, on bullion earned in selling Africans in the Americas. The recouping as specie of the profits of the East India companies, remitted in the form of cotton cloth to Europe, also depended significantly on export markets in Africa.[37] African slaves were thus a currency which, even at the dawn of the nineteenth century, were ultimately enabling the growth of European commerce and empire in Asia.[38]

Colonization, in the classic Roman sense of the imposition of a settlement on a new landscape, is the second idiom of imperialism. It was for internal European strategic reasons that it became a priority at the end of the sixteenth century: the union of the Spanish and Portuguese Crowns, in the context of Philip II's aggressive confessional politics, stimulated English, Dutch and French commercial and colonial effort after 1580. In the Treaty of London (1604) and the Treaty of Antwerp (1609), Spain was forced to retreat from the presumptions of the Treaty of Tordesillas, and to concede that effective occupation of empty territory granted sovereign right. It was essentially for political, and not economic reasons, that plantation colonies were formed in the West Indies, and settlements in North America, in the first decades of the seventeenth century: agriculture was viewed essentially as an instrument of policy. Europeans were forced to inhabit Amerindian lifeways to survive: sleeping in hammocks and eating manioc, their poor and tiny settlements clustered near sources of fresh water. Bayly's European abroad of the 1770s, imposing his style on the periphery, is an artifact of an era in which colonial 'bridgeheads' had prospered.[39] Sugar cultivation was, initially, too difficult, and African slaves too expensive, to allow the implantation of the São Tomé regime.

Plunder, in different centuries for the Americas and Africa, subsidized colonization. The extraction of Amerindian labour, brazil wood and other dyestuffs, timber, furs and meat, quite apart from precious metals, made settlement possible. When Adam Smith argued that development and prosperity of the sugar islands were 'owing to the great riches of England of which a part had overflowed', he did not know that Dutch wealth, made in the Americas, financed the 'sugar revolution' in Brazil, Barbados and St Christopher, while plundered Spanish bullion paid for the development of Jamaica.[40] The sugar plantation was itself, for reasons discussed above, an extractive industry, but the plantation economies of the British and French West Indies prospered in a political context in which settlement had become a priority in its own right.

Slaves made sugar and tobacco settlement possible, and plantations were the cause of a massive wave of migration: perhaps as many as three out of every five people who crossed the Atlantic before 1800 were African.[41] How many million Africans crossed the Atlantic will never be known with certainty but, given that many entered as unregistered contraband, we may guess that Curtin's famous estimate of less than ten million was far too low.[42] Much of this life was wasted: in a context where a slave could be purchased for two-thirds of a ton of sugar, it was profitable to work him or her to death in three or six years, and life expectancy in the heyday of the sugar islands fell to as low as seven to nine years for new African arrivals.

The 'free-labour' farms of British North America depended on the consumption of the slave plantations of the West Indies.[43] It is worth noting, in passing, Pitman and Williams's surprising statistics on the relative importance to Britain of the West Indies and North America: in 1697 British imports from Barbados were five times in value those from the 'bread colonies', while imports from Jamaica in 1773 were similarly five times those from all the mainland settlements. Between 1714 and 1773, Montserrat (24 square miles) produced three times the value of British imports from Pennsylvania, Nevis (around 60 square miles) three times as much as New York, and Antigua (about 100 square miles) three times those of New England put together. The timber, wheat, fish, shingles, horses and cattle imported by the plantations thus made possible the growth of white settlement in the north, much as slave labour made possible the tobacco, indigo and rice colonies to the south. The merchants of Boston, and in particular Newport, came themselves to specialize in their own triangular trade, purchasing slaves in Africa with their famous 'double distilled' rum, which they sold in the West Indies, returning with molasses with which to make more rum. The cities of 'white' North America thus grew, like its farms, in response to distant tropical plantations. In time, the Yankees' wish to purchase molasses from the French West Indies would be an important fact in their revolutionary politics.

Settlement colonization came to depend on the idea of 'improvement': the proposition that nature might be made more fruitful through its appropriation by Locke's 'industrious and rational' men. The idea of 'improving' land led easily to the idea of 'improving' people. A third kind of imperialism was driven by those who understood themselves as cosmopolitans, and as the diffusers of universal progress. Raffles, in his memoir on British Commercial Policy in the East Indies of 1819, provided the most eloquent expression of this utopian self-delusion so central to the liberal despotisms of the nineteenth and twentieth centuries: 'Our interests are so manifestly connected with the advancement and improvement of the native states, that it is obvious we can have no views which are not equally to their advantage.'[44] We may call it the imperialism of the division of labour, to give credit to the proposition which best expressed its genius. By the late twentieth century, the logic of cosmopolitan expansion was carried to its ultimate anti-colonial conclusion, and a bouquet of new flags adorned the powerless General Assembly of the United Nations.

The place of slaves in this third idiom of imperialism was complex and contradictory. On the one hand, division-of-labour imperialism presumed a world of free labour, of contracts freely entered into, and indeed its allies supported the anti-slavery movement. Yet the slaves of Brazil and Cuba, and the semi-slaves of the Dutch and British East Indies, were, as we have noted, important producers and consumers well into the nineteenth century, as important for the factories of Lancashire as they were for the progress of 'free-labour' settlement in Argentina and Uruguay. In our own age, one of the peculiar characteristics of the division of labour remains the dependence of the centres of global consumption on frontiers of coerced and sweated labour. Wage slavery, in Guatemala, the Philippines or China, is not always simply a metaphor. Somehow, classical political economy's dream of universal peace and abundance seems always to be deferred for those who live at lower latitudes, and increasingly too, as chronic malnutrition and diseases like tuberculosis extend their empires in the former Eastern bloc, for significant parts of the northern hemisphere. This is the space inhabited by what we today call 'globalization'. How far it stands from the old imperialisms remains to be demonstrated. There is no evidence that we have entered, definitively, an age in which the sovereignty and rights of peripheral peoples will be respected.[45]

The Ghost of Globalization Past

Slave-powered globalization reached its climax in the early decades of the nineteenth century, when it was the partner of industrialization and urbanization within Europe, and a principal direct and indirect cause of the settlement of European populations on new continents. It shared a world with newer regimes of taste and technology, religious and economic ambition, which it had helped to bring into being, and which in time would destroy it. In a few generations, emancipations would remove the whip and chain from the plantations, and crystals and syrups extracted from beet and maize would drive down the price of sugar. But the plantations remained, and spread their discipline into Africa, south Asia and the Pacific. Their legacies continue in the destructive ways we price labour and human life and share the resources of the planet, all the world of darkness which surrounded our self-congratulatory millennium fireworks.

Notes and References

1 D. Held, A. McGrew, D. Goldblatt and J. Perraton, *Global Transformations* (Oxford, 1999).

2 Adam Smith, *The Wealth of Nations*, I: ch. 5, para. 2/42.

3 Even the most skeletal outline of the historiography on the slave-sugar complex and its role in the development of the West would require a substantial essay; important recent interventions include R. Blackburn, *The Making of New World Slavery: From the Baroque to the Modern, 1492–1800* (London, 1997); D. Eltis, *The Rise of African Slavery in the Americas* (Cambridge, 2000); B. Higman, 'The Sugar Revolution', *Economic History Review*, 53 (2000), pp. 213–36.

4 What needs to be emphasized is the role of slavery and the Atlantic frontier in quickening new kinds of international exchange and the development of 'leading edge' sectors of commerce, finance and industry within Europe. For it is common, distracted by aggregate figures for the 'home' economy, for historians to lose sight of the central contribution of long-distance trade, for which slaves were central, to dragging 'the West' into the modern world. D. Eltis and S. Engerman in 'The Importance of Slavery and the Slave Trade to Industrializing Britain', *Journal of Economic History*, 60 (2000), pp. 124–44, for example, casually note that Barbados's product in 1700 was only the value of Rutland's (p.128), forgetting that the island was however a magnet for London's sail and the reason for a dozen new industries.

5 S. Mintz, *Sweetness and Power* (Baltimore, 1985) and J. Galloway, *The Sugar Cane Industry: An Historical Geography from its Origins to 1914* (Cambridge, 1989). See also N. Deerr's classic *History of Sugar*, 2 vols. (London, 1949).

6 C. Verlinden, *Esclavage dans l'Europe medievale*, 2 vols. (Bruges, 1955); O. Patterson, *Slavery and Social Death* (Cambridge, Mass., 1986).

7 The sugar plantation complex is most elegantly described by Braudel in his chapter on islands, although few later discoverers seem to remember his passage: F. Braudel, *La Méditerranée et le monde méditerranéen à l'epoque de Philippe II* (Paris, 1966 [1949]), pp. 139–40. Among contemporary authorities, see S. Greenfield, 'Madeira and the Beginning of New World Sugar Cane Cultivation and Plantation Slavery', in V. Rubin and A. Tuden (eds.), *Comparative Perspectives on Slavery in New World Plantation Societies* (New York, 1977), and W.D. Phillips,

'The Old World Background of Slavery in the Americas', in B. Solow (ed.), *Slavery and the Rise of the Atlantic System* (Cambridge, 1991).

8 S.B. Schwartz, *Sugar Plantations in the Formation of Brazilian Society: Bahia, 1550–1835* (Cambridge, 1986); D. Watts, *The West Indies* (Cambridge, 1988); P.D. Curtin, *The Rise and Fall of the Plantation Complex* (Cambridge, 1990).

9 J.C. Miller, 'The Southern Atlantic in Global Perspective', unpublished essay, 1999. I am grateful to Professor Miller for the opportunity to read a draft of this essay. Miller, without knowing it, echoes exactly the concern of Jean Meyer that 'La réalité pré-brésilienne reste cependant bien modeste', in Meyer, *Histoire du sucre* (Paris, 1989), p. 77.

10 G.F. de Oviedo y Valdes, *Historia General y Natural de las Indias* (1535–57), vol. I, pp. 224–6.

11 F. Ortiz, *Contrapunteo Cubano de Tabaco y el Azúcar* (Havana, 1940), pp. 276–9.

12 E. Williams (ed.), *Documents of West Indian History* (Port of Spain, 1963), p. 29.

13 Richard Pares, *Merchants and Planters* (Cambridge, 1960), still provides the best portrait of this system of trade and debt.

14 Even Robin Blackburn, surprisingly, seems to share in this misunderstanding when he writes that '[John] Locke's apparent endorsement of the development of the slave plantations does seem to argue the presence of what is, strictly speaking, a non-capitalist strand in his thinking', in Blackburn, *The Making of New World Slavery*, p. 275, n. 90.

15 I merely add here to that exploration of the spectrum of 'free' and 'slave' labour visible, *inter alia*, in S. Engerman (ed.), *Terms of Labour: Slavery, Serfdom and Free Labour* (Stanford, 1999) and S. Amin and M. van der Lingen (eds.), *'Peripheral' Labour? Studies in the History of Partial Proletarianization* (Cambridge, 1997).

16 H. McD Beckles, '"Black Men in White Skins": The Formation of a White Proletariat in West Indian Slave Society', *Journal of Imperial and Commonwealth History*, XV (1986), pp. 5–21; *idem, White Slavery and Black Servitude in Barbados, 1627–1715* (Knoxville, 1989).

17 As was written of sixteenth-century Brazil: 'escrividão negra e indígena coexisteram desde o início da colonizacão', M. Correia de Andrade, *A Terra e o Homem No Nordeste* (São Paulo, 1986), p. 60.

18 F. Braudel, *Civilisation matérielle, economie et capitalisme, II (Les jeux de l'échange)* (Paris, 1979), pp. 310–17.

19 J. Scott, *Seeing Like a State* (New York, 1998).

20 I. Wallerstein, *The Modern World System*, vol. I (New York, 1974) and vol. II (New York, 1974); Braudel, *Civilisation matérielle, passim*.

21 N. McKendrick, J. Brewer, J. Plumb, *The Birth of a Consumer Society: The Commercialization of Eighteenth-Century England* (Bloomington, 1982), and C. Shammas, *The Pre-Industrial Consumer in England and America* (Oxford 1990).

22 K. Pomerancz, *The Great Divergence: Europe, China, and the Making of the Modern World Economy* (Princeton, 2000).

23 See, for example, Roger Anstey, *The Atlantic Slave Trade*, p. 47–59, and S. Engerman, 'The Slave Trade and British Capital Formation in the Eighteenth Century: A Comment on the Williams Thesis', *Business History Review*, 46 (1972). The best general critique of Williams's critics is Cedric Robinson, 'Capitalism, Slavery, and Bourgeois Historiography', *History Workshop Journal*, 23 (1987), pp. 122–40.

24 J.E. Inikori, 'Market Structure and the Profits of the British African Trade in the Late Eighteenth Century', *Journal of Economic History*, 61 (1981), p. 746.

25 Dalby Thomas, *An Historical Account of the Rise and Growth of Our West-India Colonies, And of the Great Advantages they are to England, in respect of Trade* (London, 1690), p. 14.

26 See C. Whitworth, *The Political and Commercial Works of Charles Davenant* (London, 1781), vol. II, p. 18.

27 Eric Williams, *Capitalism and Slavery* (London, 1964 [1944]), p. 68.

28 J. Brewer, *The Sinews of Power*, p. 185; P.J. Cain and A.G. Hopkins, 'The Political Economy of British Expansion Overseas, 1750–1914', *Economic History Review*, 33 (1980), pp. 469–70. As David Richardson notes in 'The Slave Trade, Sugar, and British Economic Growth, 1748–1776', *Journal of Interdisciplinary History*, 17 (1987), pp. 757–63, 'an analysis of export demand which is based primarily on aggregate trade and output figures and neglects to examine the changing composition of British exports after 1748 . . . is misleading about the contribution of exports to Britain's industrial performance between 1750 and 1780'.

29 See P. Cain and A. Hopkins, 'Gentlemanly Capitalism and British Overseas Expansion. I. The Old Colonial System, 1680–1850', *Economic History Review*, 39 (1986), pp. 501–25, see p. 520; R. Davis, 'English Foreign Trade, 1700–1774', in W. E. Mitchinson (ed.), *The Growth of English Overseas Trade in the Seventeenth and Eighteenth Centuries* (London, 1969), pp. 105–6.

30 See Richardson, 'The Slave Trade, Sugar, and British Economic Growth', and Richard G. Wilson, *Gentleman Merchants* (Manchester, 1971), pp. 41–2.

31 Richardson, 'The Slave Trade, Sugar, and British Economic Growth'; Philip Riden, 'The Output of the British Iron Industry before 1870', *Economic History Review*, 30 (1977), pp. 442–59.

32 See P.K. O'Brien and S.L. Engerman, 'Exports and the Growth of the British Economy from the Glorious Revolution to the Peace of Amiens', in Barbara L. Solow (ed.), *Slavery and the Rise of the Atlantic System* (Cambridge, 1991), pp. 177–209.

33 Ralph Davis, *The Industrial Revolution and British Overseas Trade* (Leicester, 1979), p. 43.

34 Mintz notes, 'The plantation as a synthesis of factory and field . . . was really quite unlike anything known in mainland Europe at the time . . . [it was] probably the closest thing to industry that was typical of the seventeenth century', *Sweetness and Power*, pp. 47–8.

35 The rise of Alfred Crosby's 'neo-Europes' was driven more by the economic consequences of slave-sugar globalization than by ecological necessity; for the opposing argument see A. Crosby, *Ecological Imperialism: The Biological Expansion of Europe, 900–1900* (Cambridge, 1986), and B.R. Tomlinson, 'Economics and Empire: The Periphery and the Imperial Economy', in A. Porter (ed.), *The Oxford History of the British Empire: The Nineteenth Century* (Oxford, 1999), pp. 53–74.

36 Las Casas, *Historia de las Indias*, vol. II, chapter xc.

37 East India textiles made up some 25 per cent of Britain's exports to Africa; see Richardson, 'Slaves, Sugar, and Growth', p. 763.

38 See J.C. Miller's magisterial *The Way of Death: Merchant Capitalism and the Angolan Slave Trade, 1730–1830* (Madison, 1988), especially chs. 2 and 3; and J. Thornton, *Africa and the Africans in the Making of the Atlantic World, 1400–1680* (Cambridge, 1992).

39 For the useful category of the 'bridgehead', that is the exotic enclaves from which future waves of immigrants might impose themselves on a new environment, see P.J. Marhall, *Bengal: The British Bridgehead: Eastern India, 1740–1828* (Cambridge,

1987), and J. Darwin, 'Imperialism and the Victorians: The Dynamics of Territorial Expansion', *EHR*, 112 (1997), p. 641.

40 Nuala Zahediah, 'Trade, Plunder, and Economic Development in Early English Jamaica, 1655–89', *Economic History Review*, 2nd series, 39 (1986), pp. 205–22. For the debate on West Indian profitability see R. Sheridan, 'The Wealth of Jamaica in the Eighteenth Century', *Economic History Review*, 2nd series, 18 (1965), pp. 293–311; R.P. Thomas, 'The Sugar Colonies of the Old Empire: Profit or Loss for Great Britain', *Economic History Review*, 2nd series, 21 (1968), pp. 30–45; P.R.P. Coelho, 'The Profitability of Imperialism: The British Experience in the West Indies, 1768–1772', *Explorations in Economic History*, 10 (1973), pp. 253–80; J.R. Ward, 'The Profitability of Sugar Planting in the British West Indies, 1650–1834', *Economic History Review*, 2nd series, 41 (1978), pp. 197–213; Seymour Drescher, *Econocide: British Slavery in the Era of Abolition* (Pittsburgh, 1977).

41 D. Eltis, S.D. Behrendt, D. Richardson, and H.S. Klein, *The Trans-Atlantic Slave Trade: A Database on CD-ROM* (Cambridge, 1999); Eltis, *The Rise of African Slavery in the Americas*, p. 11.

42 J.E. Inikori, 'Measuring the Atlantic Slave Trade: An Assessment of Curtin and Anstey', *Journal of African History*, 17 (1986), pp. 197–233, P. Lovejoy, 'The Volume of the Atlantic Slave Trade: A Synthesis', *Journal of African History*, 23 (1982), pp. 473–501.

43 R. Pares, *Yankees and Creoles: The Trade Between North America and the West Indies Before the American Revolution* (London, 1956); A.J. O'Shaughnessy, *An Empire Divided: The American Revolution and the British Caribbean* (Philadelphia, 2000).

44 Quoted in V. Harlow and F. Madden (eds.), *British Colonial Developments, 1774–1834: Select Documents* (Oxford, 1967), p. 79.

45 See, for example, William Pfaff's call for recolonization in 'Africa Could Use a Modern Version of International Control', *International Herald Tribune*, 25 May 2000.

TONY BALLANTYNE

Empire, Knowledge and Culture: From Proto-Globalization to Modern Globalization

'Knowledge' has emerged as a central problem in debates over both globalization and the study of imperialism. Analysts of globalization, especially Marshall McLuhan and Manuel Castells, have focused scholarly attention on the social and cultural transformations wrought by the new media and computer technologies central to our 'information age'.[1] Sociological discussions of knowledge and globalization, however, are often hampered by a narrow chronological framework, resulting in a frequent insistence on the unprecedented nature of contemporary change. Studies of imperialism, on the other hand, which address the theme of 'knowledge' generally pay less attention to technology and its effects, examining instead the ideological origins and uses of 'colonial knowledge'. While some of the most influential studies of knowledge construction in colonial contexts have been produced by historians, they have been overshadowed by works of a more literary sensibility informed by post-colonial theory. Such studies of 'colonial discourse' have enriched our understanding of the cultural aspects of imperialism by creating a theoretically sophisticated body of scholarship that has drawn our attention to previously neglected texts or to what seemed to be marginal in traditional readings.[2] Unfortunately, 'colonial discourse analysis' has not always embedded 'representation' in its material, social and political contexts and has frequently failed to deal with subaltern voices when they can be heard in the archives of empire.[3] Most importantly, despite Edward Said's characterization of orientalism as a 'system of circulation', post-colonial criticism has largely ignored the complex transmission of ideas and texts across space and time.[4] More generally, imperial historians and post-colonial critics alike are hesitant to deploy 'globalization' as an analytical starting point, let alone as an interpretative framework. On the few occasions it has entered the historical literature on empire, 'globalization' has been interpreted in a narrowly economistic fashion; the cultural aspects of imperial globalization remain largely unexplored.[5]

Here I attempt to navigate a course through this uneven historiographical terrain, exploring the relationship between imperial expansion, knowledge-gathering and European world-views through an examination of the British empire between the 1760s and the mid nineteenth century. At the broadest level, in bringing together the themes of empire, globalization and knowledge, this essay suggests fertile avenues for future research. It argues that globalization is a fruitful heuristic tool for historians of empire, that an historical approach to cultural globalization will allow social scientists to assess some of their claims for the unique nature of globalization in the post-colonial world, and that colonial discourse studies could be enriched by a greater sensitivity to the structures of empires and the ways in which empires acted as globalizing forces. Such an approach suggests that the many pasts of our global moment are fundamentally entwined with imperialism and that the seismic cultural and intellectual transformations enacted by colonialism are central to any understanding of globalization over the *longue durée*.

More specifically, this study explores the cultural dynamics of imperial globalization in the transition from the late Enlightenment to the modern nineteenth-century world of nation states. In this period, European empires acted as powerful agents of globalization, appropriating new lands and significant new sources of revenue, while moving people, commodities, technologies and ideas from colony to colony, as well as between the imperial centre and colonies in the periphery. These exchanges, enacted by East India Companies, missionary organizations and migrants were often beyond the control of metropolitan governments, but nevertheless resulted in a qualitative shift in the nature of European empires. Between 1760 and 1850, the various political, economic and cultural networks that comprised the British empire became markedly more extensive, while the flows of people, goods and ideas along these networks were greatly intensified.[6] This proto-globalization had far-reaching cultural effects that, in many ways, anticipated the cultural mood of post-colonial globalization. As we shall see, the late eighteenth century witnessed the emergence of an increasingly integrated Asia-Pacific region that seemed be of great importance for the future of Britain and, more generally Europe, as well as a growing perception that the world was increasingly interconnected and interdependent.

Imperial globalization was also fundamental to the seismic political and cultural reorientations that eroded the cosmopolitan intellectual traditions of the late Enlightenment. The cosmopolitanism of the 1760s was closely tied to the culture of early modern empires, which were moulded by Christianity, underpinned by slavery, fed by New World and Asian food plants and drugs, and successively reshaped by Chinoiserie, the 'Oriental Renaissance' and Europe's craze for the Pacific.[7] This culture was in tatters by the 1830s. Long before Darwin's *Origins of the Species*, ideas of biological race had begun to threaten the centrality of language and religion in ethnological analysis, while the growing strength of the nation state was dependent upon the construction of national knowledges (rather than cosmopolitan discourses), grounded in the survey, the atlas and the census.[8] It is this transition from the culture of late Enlightenment cosmopolitanism to the Victorian empire, which operated in a world transformed by the nation state, popular nationalism, industrialization and mass migration, that lies at the heart of this essay.

The 1760s as a Globalizing Decade

The disproportionate focus of both historians and post-colonial criticism on the 'new' imperialism of the Victorian period has obscured the significance of the rise of a more aggressive imperialism of the second half of the eighteenth century, which through a series of exchanges, annexations and conquests marked a pivotal moment in the 'rise of the West'. Closer attention must be paid to the shifts in the British imperial system in the three decades following the 1760s, when scientific exploration, commercial expansion and the consolidation of colonial states fashioned new bodies of knowledge and cultural networks. While many lands remained beyond British commercial influence or military power, by the 1780s British commercial factories, naval bases and missionary stations encircled the world, reaching beyond the traditional sources of British power in the Atlantic and the Mediterranean to Asia, the Pacific and the west coast of the Americas.

In a recent reconsideration of British imperial orientations, P.J. Marshall has revisited Vincent Harlow's influential identification of a 'swing to the East' in British imperial ambition in the mid 1760s, as Britain's overseas aspirations began to shift from its troubled North American colonies to Asia. While Harlow's original argument has been criticized as a misreading of the economic focus of the empire (particularly for its neglect of the continued significance of the Caribbean), Marshall rightly suggests that Harlow's formulation of 'interest and enterprise' can be interpreted in a variety of ways, not necessarily only in 'crude economic terms'.[9] Here I support Marshall's contention: the transformation and expansion of British interests (both governmental and private) in Asia and the Pacific led to a 'swing to the East', insofar as these regions took on a cultural and intellectual significance that was disproportionate to their economic contribution to empire. Exploration, surveying and commerce in these regions reshaped British understandings of the world, creating a truly global system of information-gathering and exchange that underpinned a much fuller, and increasingly theorized, picture of the world and human variety.

The most important force promoting this shift in British world-views was the emergence of the British East India Company as a territorial power in the 1760s. Ever-eager to protect and extend its sources of revenue and profit, and desperate to meet the mounting costs of an expanding military, the

Company steadily increased its territorial holdings in a long and violent process of conquest and annexation, finally removing the last major independent South Asian polity with the defeat of the Punjab army in the Second Anglo–Sikh War in 1849. Conquest in the Indian interior was accompanied by attempts to solidify the Company's influence over the broader trade networks linking South Asia to China. From the acquisition of Penang in 1786, the Company increased its influence in 'Further India' and by the time of the Anglo–Dutch Treaty of 1824 (which divided the Malay archipelago into Dutch and British spheres of influence) it had established control over the important ports of Malacca and Singapore.

Concomitant to the East India Company's expansionist drive in Asia, British naval power opened up the Pacific to trade, settlement and missionary activity. George Anson's Pacific voyage (which began in 1740 and was only saved from complete disaster by the capture of the silver-laden Acapulco galleon) and John Byron's 1764–5 circumnavigation added little to knowledge of the Pacific, but heightened British interest in the commercial possibilities and strategic significance of the region. Captain Samuel Wallis and Philip Cateret pushed through the Pacific again in 1767–8, 'discovering' Tahiti and further fuelling speculation about the existence of the mythical southern continent, *Terra Australis Incognita*.[10] Conveniently, of course, these voyages are merely seen as a prelude to Cook's three Pacific voyages, undertaken in 1768–71, 1772–5, and 1776–9, which supposedly marked the birth of an age of 'scientific exploration'. But while scientific objectives (observing the Transit of Venus on the first voyage or the pursuit of the north-west passage on the third) were given much greater prominence in Cook's instructions, commercial concerns, particularly the location, quality and availability of raw materials, continued to figure prominently in the journals kept by Cook and his crew.[11]

Producing States and Empires: Surveying

Cook's voyages, of course, were a fundamental turning point in the history of exploration and in European understanding of the world. The naturalist and ethnologist Georg Forster, who sailed on Cook's second voyage, argued that: 'What Cook has added to the mass of our knowledge is such that it will strike deep roots and will long have the most decisive influence on the activity of men.'[12] Around 450 European ships crossed the Pacific between 1521 and 1769, but the geography and the peoples of the Pacific remained largely unknown. Before Cook's second voyage, *Terra Australis Incognita* remained a geographical commonplace. Harnessing rapidly improving technology and the navigational expertise of native informants, Cook's second voyage destroyed the myth of *Terra Australis*, while the third voyage's extensive survey of Alaska dashed hopes of discovering the north-west passage. The commercial significance of cartography was particularly obvious in the north Pacific, as the publication of accounts of Cook's exploration of the Pacific north-west stimulated a British scramble for sea otter skins. Although the leading British merchants, Nathaniel Portlock and John Meares, were primarily concerned with supplying an eager market in Canton, they dedicated considerable effort to providing updated maps and charts in the published accounts of their voyages.[13]

European knowledge of Indian geography underwent a similarly abrupt shift in the 1760s; the East India Company's assumption of political authority both depended upon and facilitated the rapid extension of cartographic knowledge. British efforts shifted quickly towards mapping the interior rather than compiling maritime charts, as European knowledge of India had been previously limited to the immediate hinterlands of major political and commercial centres.[14] An up-to-date French map of 1752, for example, contained the telling observation that southern Bihar and Orissa was 'a great extent of country of which there is no particular knowledge'.[15] Accurate cartographic knowledge was of even greater value during campaigns against native states, and the Company gratefully received geographic intelligence from local merchant communities and cultural intermediaries as well as from its own military surveyors.[16]

Although surveying was increasingly important within metropolitan European contexts, it was even more important in colonial possessions; it allowed not only the mapping of the resources, political boundaries and urban centres pivotal to commercial relations and colonial authority, but also facilitated the ideological project of empire. Indispensable for the effective exploitation of resources and effective deployment of military force, maps and atlases were increasingly deployed as instruments of rule and, at an intellectual level, to order the different parts of the empire into a coherent picture of a global empire. Matthew Edney has shown that the map was a central object in the construction of India as a political and territorial unit, and that 'the *ideal* of systematic mapping' enabled administrators to 'reinforce and legitimate the conceptual image of their empire'. While topographical and cadastral surveys were structured by Mughal revenue and political districts, programmes such as the Great Trigonometrical Survey and texts like the *Atlas of India* projected an image of British India that was rational, coherent and increasingly distanced from the supposedly 'mystical' nature of Indian geographic knowledge.[17] In delineating the frontiers of India and constructing a unit of India, the region was reimagined within the emerging framework of the nation state; as Chandra Mukerji has argued, cartographic and surveying practices played a central role in the process of state definition, because they 'were also expressions of a politico-economic order that made the state seem the natural unit of geographical analysis'.[18]

The Cartographic Imagination

Cartography therefore played two important roles in imperial globalization: it facilitated the emergence of a truly global picture of the world, while at the same time helping to constitute a political order that divided the world into distinct nations and regions. Thus, in a profound sense, Britons increasingly imagined the world generally, and their empire more specifically, within a global framework shaped by a geographic consciousness fed by maps, atlases and globes. The plan of the African Association (founded in 1788 with Banks as Treasurer), for example, justified its establishment within a cartographic frame of reference, declaring 'the map of its [Africa's] interior is still but a vast extended blank'. The Association, 'strongly impressed with a conviction of the practicality and utility of . . . enlarging the fund of human knowledge', would dedicate itself to 'promoting the discovery of the interior parts of Africa'.[19]

This cartographic consciousness grew in strength as maps increasingly became an essential component of the political and cultural paraphernalia of empire. An ever-growing stream of cartographic knowledge flowed along the political and cultural networks of empire. Colonial maps featured regularly in print and politics. In the early nineteenth century a rich assortment of maps were published in the *British Parliamentary Papers*, including, for example, over one hundred maps of Australia, ranging from maps detailing the position and condition of Aboriginal communities to surveys of newly discovered goldfields. Such information was even more important in the colonies themselves, where maps played a pivotal role in commerce, the foundation of pastoralism and plantations, as well as in military campaigns against 'natives'.[20]

There can be no doubting the absolute centrality of geography in shaping British understandings of the world in this age of proto-globalization. The interweaving of the global project of cartographic knowledge and imperial ideologies was made patently clear by the time Victoria came to the throne. Any visitor to London in 1851 would have been struck by the truly global nature of empire. Aside from the Great Exhibition, the most impressive spectacle in London that year was James Wyld's 'model of the Earth'. Wyld, Member of Parliament for Bodmin, champion of technical education and a leading British cartographer, built his giant globe in London's Leicester Square to the delight of the British public; one guidebook observed that 'a more instructive object cannot be anywhere seen'.[21] This globe, measuring some fifty-six feet in diameter (the largest the world had seen), encapsulated the global aspirations of British imperialism. For, as Wyld explained in an accompanying booklet, there were no bounds to English power and it was the 'destiny' of the English 'to people the world'. Wyld railed against a 'vicious class of school-books' that perpetuated 'antiquated [geographical] divisions' or represented the world 'principally under its physical aspects': in the light of

Britain's imperial destiny, the globe itself was the only image fit to communicate the might of an empire that encircled the world.[22]

Images of Global Empire

Thus, the reorientation of imperial interest from the 1760s resulted in a significant transformation of British knowledge of the world. If European exploration, commercial expansion and conquest facilitated a fuller picture of human variation, they also enabled new broader visions of imperial destiny. Huw Bowen suggests that from the outbreak of the Seven Years' War in 1756, Britons increasingly thought of their empire in global terms and that this shift began to reshape the structure of empire: 'links were established between different parts of the imperial process; attempts were made to better facilitate the integration of Britain's overseas interests; and solutions to the problems of empire were formulated in the metropolis with a view to universal application in the wider world of empire'.[23] Political theorists and politicians, as well as men of letters, were well aware of the transformations wrought by the globalization of British power. During the Seven Years' War, the Duke of Newcastle observed that 'ministers in this country, where every part of the World affects us, in some way or another, should consider the *whole Globe*'.[24]

This sentiment would be expressed frequently over the coming decades. Most famously, Edmund Burke, in a letter congratulating William Robertson on the publication of his *History of America*, asserted that philosophers now enjoyed 'very great advantages towards the knowledge of human Nature' as:

> now the Great Map of Mankind is unrolld at once; and there is no state or Gradation of barbarism, and no mode of refinement which we have not at the same instant under our View. The very different Civility of Europe and China. The barbarism of Persia and Abyssinia. The erratick manners of Tartary, and of Arabia. The Savage State of North America, and of New Zealand.[25]

This well-known quotation neatly captures both the emergence of a cartographic consciousness (note how cultural difference is imagined through a 'Map of Mankind') and a strong awareness of the globalization of knowledge, where an observer could compare Asia, the Arab world, the Americas and the Pacific in the 'same instant'.

These transformations were not restricted to a rarefied elite. The new world of knowledge was made available through maps, books, libraries and collections of curiosities. We find, for example, an essay on 'History' in a volume of 'improving literature' observe that: 'by the amazing progress of navigation and commerce, within the last two or three centuries, all parts of the world are now connected: the most distant people are become well acquainted, who for thousands of years, never heard of one another's existence'.[26] That this book was published in Dublin reminds us that such ideas were not restricted to the metropole alone; rather they enjoyed a wide geographic reach. Protestants in late eighteenth-century Dublin could enjoy Trinity College's fine collection of Pacific material culture collected by Cook, or visit the Public Library established by Archbishop Narcissus Marsh in 1701, where a rich collection of travel narratives and histories of the Orient and the Pacific sat alongside texts and atlases on exploration and settlement in the Atlantic.[27] Even more strikingly, images of global empire abounded in valued cultural goods. The exploration of the Pacific seems to have made cartographic decorations and ornaments more fashionable. Map-screens were popular interior decorations, while globes became more specialized: some were accompanied with cards showing the 'Peoples of the world', others contained up to the minute cartographic detail derived from Cook's Pacific voyages, while others still were so small that they could be comfortably carried in a trouser pocket: the ultimate manifestation of a shrinking world![28]

Print and Exhibitions: Ordering and Circulating Knowledge

Images of empire, therefore, underwent significant changes in the eighteenth century: not only were they more common, but they also were more global in scope and were conveyed by an increasing range of media. Just as recent discussions of post-colonial globalization have exhibited considerable interest in communicative technologies, historical analyses of cultural globalization must be sensitive to the ways in which information was created and disseminated. Print was particularly important in facilitating the rapid circulation of information and intelligence from even the most distant parts of empire and stimulated a growing metropolitan interest in imperial events and the cultures of empire. A strong indication of this increased awareness is the avid middle and upper-class consumption of travel writing and accounts of 'native customs'. Paul Kaufman's study of the Bristol Library, a small private library, reveals the popularity of such texts in the late eighteenth century: the single most popular text was Hawkesworth's compilation of Pacific voyages, which was borrowed with great regularity for over a decade.[29] Even though readers in Bristol exhibited less interest in the more prosaic account of Cook's second voyage, travel narratives remained popular even as they became less entertaining and more technical: the first edition of Cook's third voyage sold out within three days.[30] Narratives of exploration and imperial adventure proliferated, as numerous unofficial journals were published, and these texts, along with the 'official' versions approved by the Admiralty, reappeared in a variety of translations, abridgements and popularizations.[31]

Interest groups intent on forwarding their visions of empire were alive to the advantages of print. From the 1790s, the press was embraced as a key instrument by the proliferating missionary organizations. For evangelicals the printing press was a central tool for the dissemination of instructional literature, and missionary reports of souls saved and the heathen awaiting the gospel were also vital fund-raising tools. In the early nineteenth century evangelical periodicals flourished, providing a metropolitan audience with lively accounts of the trials of the mission field and detailed discussions of the various communities amongst whom the missionaries worked, from the Highlands of Scotland to Tahiti, from industrializing British cities to rural Bengal. *The Methodist Magazine* and *The Evangelical Magazine* were among the most influential journals of the day, clearly eclipsing, for example, the sales figures of *The Edinburgh Review*.[32] As the evangelical book market grew, new specialized journals developed, shaping their reports from distant and exotic mission fields for the tastes of female and young readers. The title page of the influential *Church Missionary Intelligencer* clearly embodied the global purview of missionary literature, assembling a representative sample of 'native peoples', whose placid poses testified to the transformations enacted by British missionary activity throughout the empire.

The accounts of indigenous beliefs and practices common in such texts disembodied indigenous custom, as print stripped away the linguistic and social frameworks that normally shaped the transmission of knowledge. This in turn facilitated the emergence of a comparative and global understanding of culture, where accounts of Indian deities could be compared to the beliefs of ancient Greeks or Romans, or the Polynesian culture hero, Maui, compared to the Vedic god, Yama, or the boar avatar of Vishnu.[33] Similar 'decontextualization' characterized the global views of difference presented through ethnographic displays, museums and international exhibitions. The exhibitions that proliferated throughout the industrial world in the nineteenth century were guided by a 'spirit of encyclopaedism', constructing increasingly organized and precise views of commerce, technology and culture.[34] Exhibitions and displays made the world small, accessible, and digestible: a day's visit to the South Kensington museum, founded in 1857 and renamed the Victoria and Albert Museum in 1899, allowed a metropolitan audience 'to take an excursion around the world'.[35] Such displays aimed to educate Britons about their global empire, as well entertaining them with exotic curiosities and monuments to British might. Visitors to London in 1851 could sample a range of ethnographic displays in addition to the Great Exhibition. In Linwood Gallery, off Leicester Square, the tourist could visit the 'Panorama of New Zealand', 'a fine representation of these islands and their botanical productions', or view a 'Panorama of the Nile' in the Egyptian Hall, Piccadilly, take in the "moving diorama of Upper India' in the Portland gallery or, alternatively, observe the 'life and scenes' from India on display in Willis's Rooms, St James's Street.[36] These displays presented carefully structured images of the empire's native populations, making ethnological knowledge accessible and reflecting the growing popularity of empire as a theme in entertainment.

Thus, in certain contexts, the empire created fantastic spectacles, a host of objects that could be meticulously arranged by curators and entrepreneurs to meet the demands of a public curious about life in distant parts of the empire. Non-European travellers to the imperial metropoles (and increasingly, to major colonial cities as well) commented on these at length, recounting the popularity of exotica in theatres, zoos and museums, but also frequently found themselves as objects of attention, surrounded by crowds of staring onlookers.[37] Similar discomfort was also occasioned by the radical decontextualization of ethnographic objects on display: one Indian recorded his pain at seeing 'shawls without babes; musical instruments without a Hindu player; jezails and swords with sipahis and sowars; and above all hookahs without the fume of fantastic shapes'.[38]

Such ethnographic displays were heavily dependent on complex arrangements for the collection and circulation of artefacts. While the place of the museum in the definition of national identity is well established, more attention needs to be paid to the evolution of these institutions within inter-imperial and trans-national networks of exchange.[39] Exhibitions, fairs and museums have played a prominent role in the cultural aspects of a globalization firmly rooted in the colonial past. Peter Hoffenberg's recent study of imperial exhibitions has revealed the integral role of display in the creation of both national and imperial histories and identities. His sensitive analysis traces the careful organization of materials by curators to communicate ordered visions of imperial ethnology, but also emphasizes that meaning could not be fixed because visitors re-read the displays. Most importantly, Hoffenberg's examination of the development of exhibitions in Australia and India undercuts the image of the empire as a system of cultural tribute driven by the demands of an all-powerful metropole. It underlines the importance of studying various levels of knowledge creation, the need to trace flows of knowledge within the empire, and stresses the multiple positions that cities like Melbourne or Bombay, Sydney or Calcutta could occupy within the imperial system.[40]

Empire and Ethnology: From Proto-Globalization to State Ethnologies

These exhibitions were simply one component in the cultural networks of empire that multiplied and thickened between 1760 and the mid nineteenth century. How did Britons make sense of this increasingly rich and deep imperial archive?

At a fundamental level, it is important to recognize that this information explosion itself underpinned the emergence of new ethnological models that provided a framework for British interpretations of human variety. As George Stocking has shown, Pacific voyages and the work of British orientalists provided the raw material and many methodological insights for British discussions of 'civilization' before Crystal Palace.[41] Imperial expansion into Asia and the Pacific was crucial to the 'conjectural history' tradition associated with the University of Edinburgh. This tradition was not simply developed in Edinburgh itself, but was actively elaborated and refined in India, the Middle East and Southeast Asia by a generation of Scottish-educated employees of the East India Company.[42]

Concerned with the development of economic production and the development of language, the historians of the Scottish Enlightenment constructed a universal, if hierarchical, vision of history. As human diversity was, according to Dugald Stewart, the product 'merely of the different circumstances in which men are placed', all societies advanced through four stages (from hunter-gathering to commercial society) as they progressed from 'rudeness to refinement'.[43] While each of these respective stages was underpinned by different types of production, the careful comparison of languages allowed each community to be located precisely within this civilizational narrative. Thus language provided a litmus test of social advancement: John Crawfurd's *History of the Indian Archipelago*, for example, identified the Javanese as being the most advanced of the region's peoples, but argued that their development was nonetheless arrested. Crawfurd argued that the Javanese language was shallow in comparison to Indo-European languages, as it lacked the 'capacity to generalize, to make abstract or subtle distinctions'. This inadequacy fixed the Javanese as 'semi-barbarous' on the scale of civilisation.[44]

This Scottish model was influential well into the nineteenth century and ran through discussions of indigenous peoples arising out of British Parliamentary Committees in the mid 1830s.[45] Communities that engaged in trade were clearly more advanced than those that relied on subsistence agriculture alone, while agriculturalists were superior to nomadic hunter-gatherers. These beliefs had profound ramifications (no less than racial ideologies), as the literate, commercial communities of the Indian Ocean port cities and Asian religious centres were seen to be far superior to other non-literate colonized peoples. In turn Maori, skilled gardeners and enthusiastic traders, were seen to be far superior to their Australian neighbours. At a certain level, the divergent experiences of Australian Aborigines and Maori can be attributed to the prominence of Maori gardening, which led to a recognition of their title to the land and the signing of the Treaty of Waitangi, whereas the doctrine of *terra nullius* denied not only Aboriginal title, but also the very existence of indigenous communities in Australia.[46]

The work of the leading British ethnologist of the early nineteenth century, James Cowles Prichard, was influenced by this model, perhaps reflecting his medical training at the University of Edinburgh. Drawing on the work of British orientalists (many of them Edinburgh-trained), Prichard used comparative philology to establish relationships between apparently distinct peoples and to defend the accuracy of the biblical book of Genesis.[47] His study, *The*

Eastern Origin of the Celtic Nations (1831), used orientalist and celticist research to locate the Celtic peoples of Britain and Ireland within the main stream of the history of civilization. He was able to rebut those who suggested that the Celts were 'entirely distinct from the rest of mankind' by showing that ancient Welsh and its derivatives were of 'cognate origin with the Sanskrit, Greek and Latin'.[48]

Prichard's work can be seen as the final significant manifestation of a long established European ethnological tradition that used Genesis as an important interpretative framework.[49] Although an evangelical Anglican, his monogeneism was orientalized (like Sir William Jones's), in that he located the origins of civilization in Asia and subsequently rejected any rigid divisions between Asian and European history.[50] Prichard's universalism was shared by many of his fellow members of the Aborigines' Protection Society, which dedicated itself to the study of 'native customs' and the protection of 'native rights' in the face of the pressures of rapidly growing settler populations.[51] But such concerns about natives abroad and (especially in Prichard's case) Celts at home, were besieged by new intellectual currents that inscribed rigid and inflexible ethnological taxonomies. The Anglo-Saxon revival, the Teutonomania of Thomas Arnold, and the polygeneist anthropology of Robert Knox and W.F. Edwards insisted not only that the boundaries between peoples, even within Europe, were rigid but at the same time celebrated the uniqueness of the English character.[52] Mounting hostility to the Celtic peoples of Scotland, Wales and Ireland in metropolitan thought in the 1830s and early 1840s were coterminous with shifts in racial attitudes that were beginning to reshape colonial cultures and politics.[53]

An Architecture of Knowledge: Local and State Knowledges

By the mid nineteenth century, the role of ethnology itself had shifted. Ethnology was no longer primarily a domain in which human variation was discussed in order to understand the path of universal history or the development of civilization; it had also become a central adjunct to government, both in Europe and in colonial states abroad. Ethnological research allowed the population to be surveyed, through the description and quantification of various distinctive ethnic, regional, religious and occupational groups. Such knowledge was useful not only in facilitating the construction of a detailed picture of the contours of the body politic, but also because it allowed potentially rebellious or co-operative communities to be singled out. In the colonial realm, 'criminal tribes' were identified (most famously in the campaign against *thagi* – the 'ritualistic' murderers of the Indian countryside), facilitating the 'pacification' of potentially troublesome nomadic groups.[54] In a similar vein, ethnology became a crucial tool at home and abroad for military recruiters who, armed with recruiters' manuals, sought out the 'martial races' of the Scottish Highlands, rural Ireland, Nepal, Punjab or the North-West Frontier.[55] Military surveyors, military and naval surgeons, and district officers remitted reports containing a store of ethnographic material that might be potentially useful for colonial governments.[56] What united the military survey, the recruiter's manual, and revenue report as ethnographies was their concern with standardization and measurement; the attributes of any given community could be expressed through statistics, summarized in a table or plotted on a map. Ethnology had become a significant source for the bureaucrat; its cultural role was increasingly tied to the nation, whether in Europe or its colonies.

This discussion of ethnology and the rise of the state brings us to an important point: if we are to understand the construction and dissemination of knowledge we need a fuller appreciation of what we might term the 'architecture of empire', its fundamental structures, the levels at which knowledge was created, consumed and transmitted. Our starting point for such discussions (and future research) must be the development of 'local knowledges'. Just as the cunning women of Lincolnshire provided Joseph Banks with a rich vein of botanical knowledge, so were colonial ethnographers, naturalists and linguists dependent on local 'informants' and knowledge traditions.[57] Considerable headway has been made within the South Asian context as recent monographs by Brian Hatcher, C.A. Bayly and Eugene Irschick have built upon Bernard Cohn's ground-breaking work on the role of knowledge in colonial administration.[58] These studies, which have examined the evolution of colonial knowledge within a variety of specific geographic and cultural locations, have created an increasingly nuanced picture of the development of orientalism, tracing the role of indigenous learned elites in the developing East India Company state. Hatcher's social history of education in early colonial Bengal has stressed that the entrance of *pandits* (religious experts) into Company service reflected shifts in the geo-politics and economics of indigenous knowledge-production. The continued growth of Calcutta in the late eighteenth century, and the wealth generated by its bazaars, proved a powerful lure to *pandits* from smaller towns who struggled to find patronage in the wake of the famine of 1770.[59] While *pandits* from the Radh region (west of the Hughli river) were particularly prominent in the developing intellectual life of colonial Calcutta, a notable group of Shia Muslim scribes were prominent not only in British Bengal, but also in major centres of Company trade and diplomacy throughout north India. Bayly has recently traced the influence of the leading members of this elite administrative clique, arguing that they profoundly shaped Company policy and culture from 1756 through to the 1830s.[60] Bayly also notes the prominence of Muslim service families from the mid-Ganges (around Allahabad and Lucknow), who served as envoys and political informants for the Company, and Kashmiris (Muslims and Brahmins alike), who were valued experts in British service in the Delhi region.[61]

By assuming the role of patron, the East India Company was able rapidly to expand its knowledge base, not only facilitating revenue collection and conquest, but also constructing a fuller, more empirical picture of South Asian society. This qualitative change led to a marked shift in the ways in which Britons, and Europeans generally, represented India: O.P. Kejariwal has noted the elision of 'the exotic, the mysterious, the fantastic' in depictions of Indian society from the 1770s.[62] Recent research has established a very similar, if much later, shift in representation in the colonial Pacific with the increased commercialization of knowledge-production following the penetration of a vigorous market economy into previously *tapu* (forbidden) cultural domains.[63]

Perhaps most importantly, Irschick's study of agrarian society and identity in Tamil Nadu has offered a potent analytical model for the study of 'colonial knowledge'. This is a provocative analysis heavily embedded in the close empirical study of revenue records and official reports. Irschick argues that understandings of landscape and society were the product of a dynamic engagement between British administrators, local agriculturalists, and, at a later stage, Tamil nationalists. Far from being a foreign imposition created by the 'willed activity' of European invaders (*pace* Edward Said), colonial knowledge was the product of 'cultural negotiation', a 'dialogic' process whereby both British and local understandings 'altered continuously' in mutual modification.[64] While acknowledging the 'domination and exploitation' integral to a colonial regime, Irschick insists that even although this encounter was painful, it was also constructive and creative, fashioning a new body of information and understandings that were truly hybridized: 'neither "European" nor "indigenous"'.[65]

While such hybrid local knowledges were of fundamental importance in the daily administration of colonies at the level of the district or sub-district, colonial bureaucracies attempted to synthesize these various micro-knowledges into a more comprehensive, orderly and generalized body of knowledge organized at the state level. We have already alluded to this process in discussing the changing political significance of ethnology and the erosion of the cosmopolitan discourse of the Enlightenment, but we can amplify it here. The morass of materials collected by East India Company revenue assessments, for example, produced the raw material for Walter Hamilton's two-volume 1820 gazetteer of India, a work that consciously attempted to systematize British knowledge.[66] Hamilton's work was one of the earliest of many British enterprises that attempted to construct a detailed picture of British India. It dovetailed with the programme of the Great Trigonometrical Survey and was complemented by the Archaeological Survey. These early nineteenth-century ventures were extended and elaborated by the *Linguistic Gazetteer* and successive editions of the *Imperial Gazetteer*, the great bureaucratic and intellectual achievements of the Crown Raj, which also pursued the aim of reducing India to orderly blocks of empirical information which could be rendered in maps, charts and glossaries.[67] In the Pacific, the new colonial governments devoted great effort to gathering full and accurate population statistics that provided not only detailed snap-shots of the nature and extent of the indigenous population, but also accurate bench-marks for measuring depopulation.[68] Statistics, perhaps the most universal of languages by the mid nineteenth century, provided a common idiom for the projection of state power.[69]

An Architecture of Knowledge: Regionalization and Globalization

Imperial globalization created bodies of knowledge that also transcended individual states. This was particularly the case in the study of Asian and Pacific languages and religions, where we can witness an intellectual regionalization: agents of empire created intellectual networks that facilitated the extensive exchange of ethnographic data and methods across the boundaries of colonial states, cultural zones and imperial systems. As a result of this cultural and intellectual traffic, much of the ethnographic and ethnological research carried out in this region from the 1760s was explicitly comparative, often drawing its inspiration from British orientalism and Scottish conjectural history, reflecting both India's impact on the late eighteenth-century European imagination and the prominence of Scottish administrators in the East India Company's service. British analyses of the Malay peninsula and its nearby islands were framed by an Indocentric analytical gaze, as the region was seen as 'Further India' or the 'Indian archipelago', a cultural and geographic extension of India.[70] This was also the case with the region we now designate as the 'Pacific', which from an early stage was viewed by Europeans in relation to 'Asia'. Early modern cartographers tended to imagine Australia and the Pacific as extensions of Asia. Hugo Allard's chart 'India quae Orientalis dicitur' (1652), for example, represented 'New Holland' within an Asian representational framework, defining it in relation to India and populating it with elephants and coconut palms.[71] Even as exploration progressed, Australia and the central Pacific continued to be seen as part of the conceptual geography of the 'East Indies' or the 'Orient'. Many of the new maps from the 1770s through to the early nineteenth century, although full of new detail, presented images that framed Australia and New Zealand against Asia.[72] This conceptual geography was reinforced at a linguistic level by the use of the term 'Australasia' to designate Australia, New Zealand and their outlying islands: the neologism was coined by Charles de Brosses in his discussion of the structure of the Indian Ocean world in 1756 and entered the English language shortly afterwards.[73]

Europeans also interpreted the peoples of the Pacific against the backdrop of Asian ethnology. During the *Endeavour*'s extensive Pacific voyages, Banks and

Cook collected word lists that established the linguistic unity of what would become known as the Polynesian language family, agreeing that Tahiti and New Zealand were probably peopled from the coast of Asia rather than from America or the fabled Southern Continent.[74] This argument was extended by Johann Reinhold Forster, who speculated that there were two distinct Pacific races (approximating the later division between Melanesians and Polynesians) whose origins could be traced to two parent populations in the 'Indian Asiatic isles'.[75] The orientalist William Marsden gave these perceived links a solid philological basis in a 1781 paper that effectively established the deep-seated affinities that underpin the languages of the Malay peninsula, central and eastern Polynesia.[76] These early researches fashioned a basic framework for Pacific ethnology until the 1930s: despite intense debates over the precise origins of the cultures of the Pacific (which were held, variously, to be Malay, Dravidian, Aryan or tribal), leading European and settler authorities alike subscribed to diffusionist models focused on a distant Asian homeland.[77]

Viewing the geography and ethnology of the Pacific in relation to Asia echoed the realities of imperial trade and strategy, suggesting strong links between the intellectual and economic aspects of proto–globalization. The Pacific was seen as a vitally important economic frontier of Britain's Asian holdings: British interest in the Pacific was underpinned by a desire to protect and enhance its Asian trade. Various plans for the exploitation and settlement of the Pacific were sketched with the aim of augmenting Britain's position in the 'East' and extending the Company's Asian trade. James Matra, a midshipman on the *Endeavour*, elaborated a scheme for the settlement of Australia that would not only compensate for the loss of the American colonies, but also create a colony well placed to trade with east Asia and enhance British naval power in Asia.[78] Similarly, John Call, a former East India Company officer, wanted Britain to establish a base in either New Zealand or Australia to protect the 'precarious state' of the Company's trade and to offer an alternative source of naval supplies.[79] Most tellingly, Joseph Banks himself harboured an ambition 'for prosecuting and converting to national utility the discoveries of the late Captain Cook, and for establishing a regular and reciprocal system of commerce between Great Britain, the north-west coast of America, the Japanese, Kuriel, and Jesso islands, and the coast of Asia, Corea, and China'.[80] While such a coherent system of trade was never created, Banks's role as the leading exponent of the 'gospel of plant interchange', facilitated the transfer of seeds and plants through networks which spanned Asia and the Pacific and reached beyond into the Atlantic world.[81] Banks, who is increasingly recognized as one of the pivotal figures in the intellectual and political culture of the empire, played a key role in this integrative process, which drew previously disparate societies into an imperial zone of exchange where capital, commodities, human populations (and their associated biota and pathogens) circulated.[82] In this case at least, it seems that regionalization facilitated, rather than impeded, global visions of empire and imperial globalization.

An Imperial Knowledge System

At this moment, when 'trans-national' and 'history beyond the nation' are becoming key phrases within the historical profession, there is an increasing awareness amongst historians of empire that imperial knowledge structures (like flows of capital, commodities, people, animals, plants and disease) must be studied at a global level. Philip Morgan has recently stressed the importance of 'connections' which allowed the transplantation of ideas and ideologies from one part of the empire to another.[83] We have already seen in this essay one clear example of this phenomenon in the deployment of Indocentric models in the analysis of Southeast Asian and Pacific cultures. As more interest groups became involved in Britain's formal and informal empire, such exchanges were increasingly common and important. This development has been made clear in recent studies of evangelical networks: Andrew Porter, in particular, has revealed the complex exchanges that shaped British missionary theory and practice.[84] Such arguments can also be extended to the realm of imperial ideologies, as Robert Tignor's analysis of the 'Indianization' of Britain's Egyptian administration and John Cell's study of the deployment of Anglo-Indian medical theories in Africa demonstrate.[85] Perhaps the most important study of such exchanges is S.B. Cook's *Imperial Affinities*, an examination of the complex interweaving of India and Ireland within British political economy and debates over 'custom'.[86]

Cartographic knowledge was also constructed out of a complex web of circulation. From an early stage, the cartographic knowledge and experience built up by the British in India functioned as an important reference point for other imperial cartographic projects. Joseph Banks, for example, drew on the expertise of James Rennell to equip George Vancouver with the 'most detailed guide for scientific and marine exploration ever set out in the eighteenth century'.[87] But the East India Company models in India did not develop in a vacuum: they were in turn shaped by analogies and exchanges with the Irish Ordnance Survey. From the early 1830s the Ordnance Survey of Ireland served as a key reference point for the Great Trigonometrical Survey of India. George Everest, the Surveyor-General of India, established an important relationship with Thomas Frederick Colby, director general of the Ordnance Survey (1820–47), and visited the Irish survey on Colby's invitation. Everest believed that the Irish model should be transplanted to India to improve the state of British geographical knowledge and ultimately to shore up imperial authority. The other leading figure in colonial surveying in India, Thomas Best Jervis, extended these arguments, stressing that the division of labour employed in Ireland would be even more advantageous in India. The dull repetitive work at the heart of the survey would be delegated to local workers trained in a limited range of simple tasks, while the officers would be able to focus on computations and scientific issues. These links between the Ordnance Survey and the Great Trigonometrical Survey of India were further cemented by the exchange of personnel, because all engineer cadets were sent to the Ordnance Survey for training before being posted to India.[88]

In turn, Indian models and experience were important reference points for other colonial surveying ventures. East India Company models continued to have considerable longevity and influence in the Pacific: New Zealand's first Surveyor-General, John Turnbull Thomson, for example, drew upon his Company experience and his career in the Straits Settlements and Singapore.[89] Thomson, who constructed an opposition between the Malay, 'a good-humoured, respectful, unsophisticated, little copper-coloured man', and 'the rough, shaggy Maori', was a leading advocate of pastoralism and believed that the extinction of the indigenous population was a precondition for the modernization of New Zealand.[90] Surveyors like Thomson inscribed the New Zealand landscape with a new layer of European place-names, thus incorporating New Zealand into an imperial matrix of meaning with landmarks and settlements named after British naturalists (Mount Hooker or Mount Darwin); imperial heroes (Clive, Wellington, Nelson); eastern administrators (Auckland, Hastings, Lawrence) or great British victories (Plassey).[91] The British Pacific itself served as an important reference point for imperial exploration and surveying: the complexity of the cartographic cross-currents within the empire is further illustrated by the use of the marine surveying methods developed by Cook, and perfected by George Vancouver, in British surveys of the African coast between 1816 and 1826.[92]

Richard Grove has delineated equally important networks of naturalists who fashioned a global image of the empire. The vibrant intellectual circle woven together by Joseph Banks and Johann Reinhold Forster from the 1760s was central to the emergence of this global vision.[93] This group, which included Carl Linnaeus (and many of his pupils) and the young Alexander von Humboldt, formed an influential web of correspondence and patronage drawing on contacts spanning both the European and extra-European worlds.[94] What is most striking about the vision of these scholars is that their concerns with deforestation and climatic change anticipated many of the concerns that are commonly seen as characteristic of late twentieth-century globalization. Grove shows that colonial naturalists in India and Australia assembled a picture of global weather patterns with remarkable speed, after the El Niño current and Southern Oscillation led to widespread drought and famine in South Asia, Australia, southern Africa and the Caribbean in 1791. This example demonstrates the strength of imperial knowledge networks, the emergence of an interpretative consciousness that was truly global, and the innovative nature of intellectual activity in the 'colonial peripheries'.[95]

Conclusion

Richard Grove's argument is a fitting place to conclude this essay. Firstly, his reassessment of colonial science suggests that significant intellectual developments, and by extension globalization itself, can be driven by change in distant 'peripheries', not just in metropolitan centres.[96] Secondly, Grove's work encourages us to think of empires as a series of overlapping networks. One of the central contentions of this essay has been that historians must make a greater effort to understand empires as assemblages of networks, complex threads of correspondence and exchange that linked distant components together and ensured a steady, but largely overlooked, cultural traffic. While some of these networks were weak and perished quickly, there is no doubt that from the 1760s the British empire increasingly functioned as a system, albeit an often inefficient and uncertain one. Thirdly, and following from this, globalization is as much a state of mind as it is series of financial transactions or shifts in technology that can be rendered in charts and graphs. Historians and social scientists alike could gain from devoting greater attention to the cultural and intellectual aspects of globalizations, past and present. Finally, Grove's work on El Niño reminds us that many features of post-colonial globalization are far from being novel. The globalization driven by the reorientation of the British empire in the late eighteenth century gave rise to environmental anxiety, strengthened ties in the Asia-Pacific region, underpinned a sense of global interconnectedness and fed a growing concern with markers of ethnicity – all of which are issues that resonate in debates over globalization today.

Thus, the period between 1760 and 1850 is crucial for our understanding of globalization. It is in this period that we can observe the progressive undercutting of a cosmopolitan culture of archaic globalization, grounded in long-distance trade, merchant diasporas and elite consumption, by the reorientation of British imperial ambitions. The 'swing to the East' had profound ramifications both at home and abroad. In particular, the East India Company's rise to power in the 1760s transformed British involvement in Asia, initiating almost a century of violent expansion, while simultaneously energizing imperialism in the Pacific in the name of Britain's Asian interests. The militarization of Company rule in India reflected the general rise of the 'military fiscal state' in Britain and Europe, and within this context governments became increasingly concerned with the control of knowledge-production. As we have seen, it is in this period that the census, the atlas and the ethnographic report became critical tools for both the deployment of the state's coercive power and for the definition and articulation of national identities. It is important to recognize, however, that cosmopolitan culture was not simply replaced by national cultures, or still less nationalist cultures. Local and regional identities frequently co-existed with, and sometimes challenged, the nation, while trans-national communities of faith, ethnicity or (increasingly) class could transcend the nation. Thus, in the mid nineteenth century, emergent nations could not yet monopolize the allegiances of their citizens nor could they prevent the great migrations that increasingly reshaped the world's demographic profile. Moreover, even as the power of the nation state was consolidated, new, self-consciously 'modern' forms of cosmopolitanism were emerging. Richard Cobden, confident of the 'improving' power of science and England's 'armies of artisans', argued that 'free trade' would fashion a cosmopolitan world of peace and progress. In the second half of the nineteenth century re-invented forms of imperial cosmopolitanism, such as Cobdenite liberalism or the Theosophy of Madame Blavatsky, struggled against increasingly aggressive nationalist ideologies, but ultimately lost out in the bloody spectacle of World War I.[97]

Notes and References

1 Marshall McLuhan and Bruce R. Powers, *The Global Village: Transformations in World Life and Media in the Twenty-first Century* (Oxford, 1989); Manuel Castells, *The Information Age: Economy, Society and Culture*, 3 vols. (Oxford, 1999).

2 See, as a representative sample, Patrick Brantlinger, *Rule of Darkness: British Literature and Imperialism, 1830–1914* (Ithaca, 1990); Susan Meyer, *Imperialism at Home: Race and Victorian Women's Fiction* (Ithaca, 1996); Suvendrini Perera, *Reaches of Empire: The English Novel from Edgeworth to Dickens* (New York, 1991).

3 Dane Kennedy, 'Imperial History and Post-Colonial Theory', *Journal of Imperial and Commonwealth History*, 24 (1996), pp. 345–63; Benita Parry, 'Problems in Current Theories of Colonial Discourse', *Oxford Literary Review*, 9 (1987), pp. 27–58.

4 This weakness is also evident in the growing literature on American imperialism. Richard Salvatore's recent essay argues that the 'enterprise of knowledge' at the heart of the US presence in Latin America was geared towards the 'circulation' of knowledge, but provides no discussion of this. Ricardo D. Salvatore, 'The Enterprise of Knowledge: Representational Machines of Informal Empire', in Gilbert M. Joseph, Catherine C. Legrand and Ricardo D. Salvatore (eds.), *Close Encounters of Empire: Writing the Cultural History of US–Latin American Relations* (Durham, N.C., 1998), pp. 69–104.

5 See Hopkins, 'The History of Globalization – and the Globalization of History', in this volume; Jeffrey G. Williamson, 'Globalization, Convergence, and History', *Journal of Economic History*, 56 (1996), pp. 277–306; Kevin H. O'Rourke and Jeffrey G. Williamson, *Globalization and History: The Evolution of a Nineteenth-Century Atlantic World Economy* (Cambridge, Mass., 1999).

6 On 'extensity' and 'intensity' see David Held *et al.*, *Global Transformations: Politics, Economics and Culture* (Cambridge, 1999), p. 17.

7 The argument here draws upon C.A. Bayly's essay in this volume. On Enlightenment cosmopolitanism see Karen O'Brien, *Narratives of Enlightenment: Cosmopolitan History from Voltaire to Gibbon* (Cambridge, 1997). More specifically see James Walvin, *Fruits of Empire: Exotic Produce and British Taste, 1660–1800* (Basingstoke, 1997); Walter W. Davis, 'China, the Confucian Ideal, and the

European Age of Enlightenment', *Journal of the History of Ideas*, 44 (1983), pp. 523–48; Madeleine Jarry, *Chinoiserie: Chinese Influence on European Decorative Art, Seventeenth and Eighteenth Centuries* (New York, 1981); Edmund Leites, 'Confucianism in Eighteenth-Century England: Natural Morality and Social Reform', *Philosophy East and West*, 28 (1978), pp. 143–59; Raymond Schwab, *Oriental Renaissance: Europe's Rediscovery of India and the East, 1680–1880*, trans. Gene Patterson-Black and Victor Reinking (New York, 1984); P.J. Marshall and Glyndwr Williams, *The Great Map of Mankind: British Perceptions of the World in the Age of Enlightenment* (London, 1992).

8 Andrew Bank, 'Losing Faith in the Civilizing Mission: The Premature Decline of Humanitarian Liberalism at the Cape', in Rick Halpern and Martin Daunton (eds.), *Empire and Others: British Encounters With Indigenous Peoples, 1600–1850* (Philadelphia, 2000); Bronwen Douglas, 'Art as Ethnohistorical Text: Science, Representation and Indigenous Presence in Eighteenth and Nineteenth-Century Oceanic Voyages', in Diane Losche and Nicholas Thomas (eds.), *Double Vision: Art Histories and Colonial Histories in the Pacific* (Cambridge, 1999).

9 Vincent Harlow, *The Founding of the Second British Empire, 1763–93*, 2 vols. (London, 1952–64), vol. I, p. 62; P.J. Marshall, 'Britain without America – A Second Empire?' in P.J. Marshall (ed.), *Oxford History of the British Empire: The Eighteenth Century* (Oxford, 1998), p. 577. For a discussion of the continued importance of the Caribbean see Richard Drayton's essay in this volume.

10 Helen Wallis (ed.), *Carteret's Voyage Round the World*, 2 vols. (Cambridge, 1965).

11 On the interweaving of commerce and cartography in the late Enlightenment, see David N. Livingstone, *The Geographical Tradition: Episodes in the History of a Contested Enterprise* (Oxford, 1992), p. 103.

12 Cited in Michael Hoare (ed.), 'The Forsters and Cook's Second Voyage, 1771–5', in Walter Veit (ed.), *Captain Cook: Image and Impact* (Melbourne, 1972), p. 114.

13 See Nathaniel Portlock, *A Voyage Around the World*, (1793); John Meares, *Voyages Made in the Years 1788 and 1789, from China to the North West Coast of America* (1790).

14 See R.H. Phillimore, *Historical Records of the Survey of India. I: The Eighteenth Century* (Dehra Dun, 1945), pp. 1–5.

15 'Grand espace de pays dont on n'a point de connoissance particulière', Jean Baptiste Bourguinon d'Anville, *Carte de l'Inde dressé pour la Compagnie des Indes* (Paris, 1752), detail reproduced as in figure 1.1 in Matthew H. Edney, *Mapping an Empire: The Geographical Construction of British India, 1765–1843* (Chicago, 1997), p. 6.

16 C.A. Bayly, *Empire and Information: Intelligence Gathering and Social Communication in India, 1780–1870* (Cambridge, 1996), pp. 104, 119–20.

17 Matthew H. Edney, 'The Patronage of Science and the Creation of Imperial Space: The British Mapping of India, 1799–1843', *Cartographica*, 30 (1993), p. 61, and Edney, *Mapping an Empire, passim*.

18 Chandra Mukerji, *From Graven Images: Patterns of Modern Materialism* (New York, 1983), p. 128.

19 R. Hallett (ed.), *Records of the African Association, 1788–1831* (1964), pp. 44–5.

20 On the comparative significance of maps for metropolitan and colonial policy-making see Dorothy F. Prescott, 'Buried Treasure: Maps of Australia in the Nineteenth-Century Imperial and Colonial Parliamentary Papers', *The Globe*, 37 (1992), pp. 57–64.

21 Cyrus Redding, *The Stranger in London, or, Visitor's Companion to the Metropolis and*

its Environs, with an Historical and Descriptive Sketch of the Great Exhibition (1851), p. 173.

22 James Wyld, *Notes to Accompany Mr. Wyld's Model of the Earth, Leicester Square* (1851) cited in Jeremy Black, *Maps and History: Constructing Images of the Past* (New Haven, 1997), pp. 62–3.

23 H.V. Bowen, 'British Conceptions of Global Empire, 1756–83', *Journal of Imperial and Commonwealth History*, 26 (1998), p. 1.

24 Cited in ibid., p. 11.

25 Edmund Burke to William Robertson, 9 June 1777, in George H. Guttridge (ed.), *The Correspondence of Edmund Burke. Volume III: July 1774–June 1778* (Cambridge and Chicago, 1961), p. 351.

26 Hester Chapone, *Letters on the Improvement of the Mind and Miscellanies in Prose and Verse*, 2 vols. (Dublin, 1786), vol. I, p. 145.

27 Muriel McCarthy and Caroline Sherwood-Smith (eds.), *The Wisdom of the East: Marsh's Oriental Books* (Dublin, 1999). In fact this explosion of knowledge was at times difficult to assimilate into a coherent whole. In 1785 Edmund Burke complained that Britons had failed to adjust to the new world of learning he had celebrated in his earlier letter to Robertson: 'I think I can trace all the calamities of this country to the single source of our not having had steadily before our eyes a general, comprehensive, well-connected, and well-proportioned view of the whole of our dominions.' Cited in Bowen, 'British Conceptions of Global Empire', p. 21.

28 E.g., Janet Woodbury Adams, *Decorative Folding Screens in the West from 1600 to the Present Day* (London, 1982); Raymond Lister, *Old Maps and Globes: With a List of Cartographers, Engravers, Publishers and Printers Concerned with Printed Maps and Globes from c.1500 to c.1850* (London, 1979). The rage for pocket globes went back to at least the 1730s with the production of Richard Cushee's two and a half inch *New Globe of the Earth* (1731).

29 It was borrowed some 201 times between 1773 to 1784: this single volume, out of a collection of around 900 titles, constituting 1.5 per cent of the total borrowings for the period. Paul Kaufman, *Borrowings from the Bristol Library, 1773–1784: A Unique Record of Reading Vogues* (Charlottesville, 1960), pp. 39, 122.

30 Ibid., p. 32; Helen Wallis, 'Publication of Cook's Journals: Some New Sources and Assessments', *Pacific Studies*, 2 (1978), pp. 163–92; Sir Maurice Holmes, *Captain James Cook, R.N. F.R.S.: A bibliographical excursion* (London, 1952), p. 52.

31 See M.K. Beddie, *Bibliography of Captain James Cook* (Sydney, 1970).

32 R.D. Altick, *The English Common Reader: A Social History of the Mass Reading Public, 1800–1900* (Chicago, 1957), p. 392.

33 William Jones, 'On the Gods of Greece, Italy and India', *Asiatick Researches*, 1 (1792), pp. 221–75; F. Max Müller, 'Solar Myths', *Nineteenth Century*, 18 (1885), pp. 901–18.

34 Raymond Corbey, 'Ethnographic Showcases, 1870–1930', in Jan Nederveen Pieterse and Bhikhu Parekh (eds.), *The Decolonization of Imagination: Culture, Knowledge and Power* (1995), p. 59.

35 Moncure Conway, *Travels in South Kensington* (1882), pp. 21–3, cited in Tim Barringer, 'The South Kensington Museum and the Colonial Project', in Tim Barringer and Tom Flynn (eds.), *Colonialism and the Object: Empire, Material Culture and the Museum* (1998), p. 11.

36 Redding, *A Stranger in London*, pp. 173–4.

37 Timothy Mitchell, 'The World as Exhibition', *Comparative Studies in Society and History*, 31 (1989), pp. 219–22.

38 Rakhal Das Halder quoted in Ray Desmond, *The India Museum, 1801–1879* (London, 1982), p. 91.

39 On museums, the nation and globalization see Jan Nederveen Pieterse, 'Multiculturalism and Museums: Discourse about Others in the Age of Globalization', *Theory, Culture & Society*, 14 (1997), pp. 123–46; Flora Kaplan (ed.), *Museums and the Making of 'Ourselves': the Role of Objects in National Identity* (London, 1994). Unfortunately there is insufficient space here for a discussion of the complex interweaving of imperial knowledge systems. A particularly fertile avenue for future research has been suggested in Richard Drayton, 'A l'école des français: les sciences et le deuxième empire britannique (1783–1830)', *Revue Française d'Histoire D'Outre-Mer*, 86 (1999), pp. 91–118 and *idem*, *Nature's Government: Science, Imperial Britain and the 'Improvement' of the World* (New Haven, 2000).

40 Peter Hoffenberg, 'To Create a Commonwealth: Empire and Nation at English, Australian and Indian exhibitions, 1851–1914' (University of California, Berkeley, Ph.D. thesis, 1990).

41 George W. Stocking Jr., *Victorian Anthropology* (New York, 1987), pp. 9–53.

42 Jane Rendall, 'Scottish Orientalism: From Robertson to James Mill', *Historical Journal*, 25 (1982), pp. 43–69; Martha McLaren, 'Philosophical History and the Ideology of the Company State: The Historical Works of John Malcolm and Mountstuart Elphinstone', *Indo-British Review: A Journal of History*, 21 (n.d.), pp. 130–43.

43 Dugald Stewart, 'Dissertation: Exhibiting the Progress of Metaphysical, Ethical and Political Philosophy since the Revival of Letters in Europe', in *Collected Works*, ed. William Hamilton, 11 vols. (Edinburgh, 1854–60), vol. II (1854), pp. 69–70.

44 John Crawfurd, *History of the Indian Archipelago. Containing an Account of the Manners, Arts, Languages, Religions, Institutions, and Commerce of its Inhabitants*, 3 vols, (Edinburgh, 1820), vol. II, pp. 8–9, also vol. II, pp. 46–7.

45 See, for example, *Great Britain Parliamentary Papers*: 1836 (538) 7; 1837–8 (680) 21; 1838 (585) 39. Also C.A. Bayly, 'The British and Indigenous Peoples, 1760–1850: Power, Perception and Identity', in Halpern and Daunton (ed.), *Empire and Others*.

46 On these analogies see K.R. Howe, *Race Relations, Australia and New Zealand: A Comparative Survey, 1770s–1970s* (Wellington, 1977).

47 George W. Stocking Jr., 'Introduction' to James Cowles Prichard, *Researches into the Physical History of Man* (Chicago, 1973 [1813]), pp. xv–xvi, xxxix. Also Dr Thomas Hodgkin, 'Obituary of Dr. Prichard', *Journal of the Ethnological Society of London*, 2 (1850), p. 190.

48 James Cowles Prichard, *The Eastern Origin of the Celtic Nations Proved by a Comparison of their Dialects with the Sanskrit, Greek, Latin and Teutonic Languages. Forming a Supplement to the Researches into the Physical History of Mankind* (1831), pp. 42–3, 345.

49 Thomas Trautmann has recently termed this 'Mosiac ethnology' in his *Aryans and British India* (Berkeley, 1997), pp. 28–61.

50 Alun David, 'Sir William Jones, Biblical Orientalism and Indian Scholarship', *Modern Asian Studies*, 30 (1996), pp. 173–84.

51 [H.R. Fox Bourne], *The Aborigines Protection Society: Chapters in its History* (1899); Keith Sinclair, 'The Aborigines Protection Society and New Zealand: A Study in Nineteenth-Century opinion', (University of New Zealand, M.A. thesis, 1946); Stocking, *Victorian Anthropology*, pp. 240–4.

52 Hans Aarsleff, *The Study of Language in England, 1780–1860* (Princeton, 1967), pp.

182–209; Robert Young, *Colonial Desire: Hybridity in Theory, Culture and Race* (London, 1995), pp. 72–9; Gwyneth Tyson Roberts, '"Under the Hatches": English Parliamentary Commissioners' Views of the People and Language of Mid Nineteenth-Century Wales', in Bill Schwarz (ed.), *The Expansion of England: Race, Ethnicity and Cultural History* (London, 1996), pp. 171–97.

53 Andrew Bank, 'Liberals and their Enemies: Racial Ideology at the Cape of Good Hope, 1820 to 1850' (University of Cambridge, Ph.D. thesis, 1995).

54 W.H. Sleeman, *Ramaseeana, or a Vocabulary of the Peculiar Language Used by the Thugs, With an Introduction and Appendix, Descriptive of the System Pursued by that Fraternity and of the Measures Which Have Been Adopted by the Supreme Government of India for its Suppression* (Calcutta, 1836); Radhika Singha, *A Despotism of Law: Crime and Justice in Early Colonial India* (Calcutta, 1998).

55 Lionel Caplan, *Warrior Gentleman: 'Gurkhas' in the Western Imagination* (Oxford, 1995); more generally, Cynthia H. Enloe, *Ethnic Soldiers: State Security in Divided Societies* (Athens, GA., 1980).

56 Giselle Byrnes, '"The Imperfect Authority of the Eye": Shortland's Southern Journey and the Calligraphy of Colonisation', *History and Anthropology*, 8 (1994), pp. 207–35; Clive Dewey, *The Settlement Literature of the Greater Punjab: A Handbook* (New Delhi, 1991); Mark Harrison, *Climates and Constitutions: Health, Race, Environment and British Imperialism in India* (Delhi, 1999).

57 Richard Drayton, 'Knowledge and Empire', in P.J. Marshall (ed.), *Oxford History of the British Empire: The Eighteenth Century* (Oxford, 1998), pp. 231–52.

58 Bernard S. Cohn, *An Anthropologist Among the Historians and Other Essays* (Delhi, 1987); *idem, Colonialism and its Forms of Knowledge: The British in India* (Princeton, 1996).

59 Brian A. Hatcher, *Idioms of Improvement: Vidyasagar and Cultural Encounter in Bengal* (Delhi, 1996); also see S.N. Mukherjee, *Calcutta: Myths and History* (Calcutta, 1977), pp. 87–8.

60 Bayly, *Empire and Information*, p. 80.

61 Ibid., pp. 83–8.

62 O.P. Kejariwal, *The Asiatic Society of Bengal and the Discovery of India's Past 1784–1838* (Delhi, 1988), p. 25.

63 See, for example, Jenifer Curnow, 'Wiremu Maihi Te Rangikaheke: His Life and Work', *Journal of the Polynesian Society*, 94 (June 1985), pp. 97–147; M.P.J. Reilly, 'John White. Part II: Seeking the Exclusive Mohio: White and His Maori Informants', *New Zealand Journal of History*, 24 (April 1990), pp. 45–55.

64 Eugene F. Irschick, *Dialogue and History: Constructing South India, 1795–1895* (Berkeley, 1994), p. 8.

65 Ibid., p. 10.

66 Walter Hamilton, *A Geographical, Statistical, and Historical Description of Hindostan and the Adjacent Countries*, 2 vols. (1820).

67 E.g., *The Imperial Gazetteer of India. The Indian Empire*, 26 vols., (Oxford, 1907–9).

68 E.g., F.D. Fenton, *Observations on the State of the Aboriginal Inhabitants of New Zealand* (Auckland, 1859).

69 Arjun Appadurai, 'Number in the Colonial Imagination' in C.A. Breckenridge and P. van der Veer (eds.), *Orientalism and the Postcolonial Predicament* (Philadelphia, 1993), pp. 314–40; Theodore M. Porter, *The Rise of Statistical Thinking, 1820–1900* (Princeton, 1987).

70 Rendall, 'Scottish Orientalism', p. 44; B. Harrison, 'English Historians of the "Indian Archipelago": Crawfurd and St John', in D.G.E. Hall (ed.), *Historians of*

South East Asia (London, 1961), p. 245. For the 'Atlantic world' as the product of a similar process see Richard Drayton's essay in this volume.

71 Helen Wallis, 'Terra Australis, Australia and New Zealand: Voyages, Discoveries and Concepts', in Patricia McLaren-Turner (ed.), *Australian and New Zealand Studies: Papers Presented at a Colloquium at the British Library, 7–9 February 1984* (London, 1985), pp. 184–93.

72 Robert Clancy, *The Mapping of Terra Australis* (Macquarie Park, N.S.W., 1995), Maps 6.13 and 6.38–6.40, pp. 83, 100–1.

73 *Oxford English Dictionary*, vol. I, p. 569; John Callander, *Terra Australis Cognita, or, Voyages to the Terra Australis, or Southern Hemisphere, During the Sixteenth, Seventeenth and Eighteenth Centuries, Containing an Account of the Manners of the People, and the Productions of the Countries*, 3 vols. (Edinburgh, 1766–8), vol. I, p. 49.

74 Cook stated that he could not 'preswaid [sic] my self that ever they came from America and as to a Southern Continent I do not believe any such thing exists unless in a high Latitude', *The Journals of Captain James Cook on His Voyages of Discovery. Vol. I: The Voyage of the Endeavour, 1768–1771*, ed J. C. Beaglehole (Cambridge, 1968), pp. 286–8; also see Joseph Banks, *The Endeavour Journal of John Banks, 1768–1771*, ed. J. C. Beaglehole, 2 vols. (Sydney, 1962), vol. II, p. 37.

75 Johann Reinhold Forster, *Observations Made During a Voyage Round the World*, Nicholas Thomas *et al.* (eds.), (Honolulu, 1996 [1778]), pp. 187–90, here p. 190.

76 William Marsden, 'Remarks on the Sumatran Languages', *Archaelogia: or, Miscellaneous Tracts Relating to Antiquity*, 7 (1782), pp. 154–8.

77 A.J. Ballantyne, 'Imperial Networks, Ethnography and Identity in Colonial India and New Zealand' (University of Cambridge, Ph.D. thesis, 1999).

78 F.M. Bladen (ed.), *Historical Records of New South Wales*, 7 vols. (Sydney, 1892–1901), vol. II, pp. 1–6.

79 Alan Frost, *Convicts and Empire: A Naval Question, 1776–1811* (Melbourne, 1980), p. 203.

80 [John Etches], *An Authentic Statement of All the Facts Relative to Nootka Sound* (1790), p. 2.

81 Glyndwr Williams, '"The Common Center of We Discoverers": Sir Joseph Banks, Exploration and Empire in the Late Eighteenth Century', in R.E.R. Banks (ed.), *Sir Joseph Banks: a Global Perspective* (London, 1994), p. 177.

82 John Gascoigne, *Science in the Service of Empire: Joseph Banks, the British State and the Uses of Science in the Age of Revolution* (Cambridge, 1998).

83 Philip Morgan, 'Encounters Between British and Indigenous Peoples, *c*.1500–*c*.1800', in Halpern and Daunton, *Empire and Others*, pp. 56–62.

84 Andrew Porter, 'North American Experience and British Missionary Encounters in Africa and the Pacific, 1800–1850', ibid.

85 John W. Cell, 'Anglo–Indian Medical Theory and the Origins of Segregation in West Africa', *American Historical Review*, 91 (1986), pp. 307–35; Robert L. Tignor, 'The "Indianization" of the Egyptian Administration under British Rule', *American Historical Review*, 68 (1963), pp. 636–61.

86 S.B. Cook, *Imperial Affinities: Nineteenth-Century Analogies and Exchanges Between India and Ireland* (New Delhi, 1994).

87 David Mackay, *In the Wake of Cook: Exploration, Science and Empire, 1780–1801* (London, 1985), p. 100.

88 Edney, *Mapping an Empire*, pp. 276–7, 281–5.

89 John Turnbull Thomson, *An Outline of the Principles and Details connected with the*

Colonial Survey of the Province of Otago (Dunedin, 1861); *An Exposition of Processes and Results of the Survey System of Otago* (Dunedin, 1875).

90 John Turnbull Thomson, *Some Glimpses into Life in the Far East* (1864), pp. 60, 253–4; John Turnbull Thomson, *Rambles with a Philosopher or, Views at the Antipodes by an Otagoian* (Dunedin, 1867), p. 87.

91 See Malcolm McKinnon (ed.), *New Zealand Historical Atlas: Ko Papatuanuku e Takoto Nei* (Auckland, 1997), plate 33.

92 Alun C. Davies, 'Testing a New Technology: Captain George Vancouver's Survey and Navigation in Alaskan Waters, 1794', in Stephen Haycox, James K. Barnett and Caedmon A. Liburd (eds.), *Enlightenment and Exploration in the North Pacific, 1741–1805* (Seattle, 1997), p. 110.

93 Richard Grove, *Green Imperialism: Colonial Expansion, Tropical Island Edens and the Origins of Environmentalism, 1600–1860* (Cambridge, 1995), ch. 7. One powerful statement of this vision was Johann Reinhold Forster, *Observations*, pp. 97–122.

94 See Michael Dettelbach, '"A Kind of Linnaean Being": Forster and Eighteenth-Century Natural History', ibid., pp. lv–lxxiv. It is interesting to note the important literary figures and orientalists who were incorporated to varying degrees into this circle, most notably Samuel Johnson, Sir William Jones, Alexander Hamilton, Herder and Goethe.

95 Richard Grove, *Ecology, Climate and Empire: Colonialism and Global Environmental History, 1400–1940* (Cambridge, 1997), pp. 124–46.

96 For a further discussion of de-centred globalization, see the essays by Hans van de Ven, Amiria Bennison and Tim Harper in this volume.

97 A similar argument is advanced in A.G. Hopkins, 'Back to the Future: From National History to Imperial History', *Past & Present*, 164 (1999), pp. 198–243.

T.N. HARPER

Empire, Diaspora and the Languages of Globalism, 1850–1914

The universal is the local without walls.
Miguel Torga, *The Creation of the World*

At the first South Summit in Havana in April 2000, in what was perhaps the most important statement of common purpose since the Bandung conference of 1955, the leaders of the developing nations signed a manifesto on globalization and its discontents. The Havana Declaration, which went largely unreported in the North, embraced globalization as a historic opportunity for renewed collective action. Yet it also argued that, for the South, globalization was a threat to sovereignty, a device, even, for 'recolonization'. In the words of Prime Minister Mahathir of Malaysia: 'Capital is the new gunship of the rich.' Two consequences of globalization were highlighted. First, 'if money is capital for the rich', as Mahathir argued, 'labour is the capital of the poor countries'.[1] Whilst globalization removed frontiers for capital, it had erected new barriers to the flow of labour into the richer economies and the remittance of money to the poor. To Fidel Castro, modern globalization was the new apartheid.[2] A second consequence was that, while globalization opened access to information, it was a homogenizing threat to national and local cultures and languages: 'a religion that tolerates no heresy'. The Havana Declaration gave precedence to the preservation of 'diversity which is the principal wealth of human development'.[3]

Whilst these attacks by the leaders of the South on the ills wrought by globalization could serve to mask domestic failings, the Havana Declaration was a powerful statement. Unlike many similar manifestos of the time, it was informed by a clear sense of the global past: a past of slavery, conquest, underdevelopment and cultural annihilation. It was also marked by a deep scepticism about contemporary globalization's claims to present new possibilities for empowerment. It presented a perspective on globalization that rarely appears in the existing literature: the perspective of the South and of the underside of global history.

This essay charts the impact of globalization on labour migration and local cultures over the *longue durée* and explores some of the continuities between archaic, modern and post-colonial globalization. My concern here, however, lies not so much with the economic and political processes behind modern globalization. There is a danger in placing too heavy an emphasis on the global connections forged by European imperial expansion; a danger that this may generate a false Eurocentric *telos* to world history.[4] I examine instead the impact of globalization, and the possibilities it might present for writing a richer international social history of the modern period. I focus on globalization as the condition of being consciously aware of thinking and acting on a global level. Over the nineteenth and twentieth centuries this has been expressed as the idea of 'globalism', that is the ideal or pursuit of universal or world government. This essay seeks to recover some of the different layers, the different mediums and messages, of late nineteenth-century globalism.

The emerging chronology of globalization is often a narrative of the diminishing role of older patterns of movement of people and ideas after 1850, in the face of the dramatic new connections forged by European expansion. However, I begin here by suggesting that from, say, the 1850s to the 1890s, the principal expressions of globalization in the colonial world were residual and revived forms of archaic and proto-modern globalizations. I focus on two themes, diaspora and language, to examine through them ways in which the globalizations of the colonial world responded to the globalization of European empires. I then examine how, from the 1890s until the early 1920s, new diasporic public spheres were becoming more important vehicles of globalization and centres of globalist thinking. I argue that the First World War saw the tightening of the colonial and national framework, largely in response to this development. It saw the muting of many of global possibilities, and it had an enduring legacy for the globalization of our own age.

Ungoverned Globalization in the Imperial Age, c. 1850–1890

By the mid nineteenth century several different layers of globalization existed, and these layers were interdependent. First, there was the globalization of the European empires. This was an extension abroad of modern nation state-building. It was shaped by a revolution in consumption, a cluster of technological innovation, and a thrusting, cosmoplastic modernity.[5] The Europeans took into the world new structures of authority and new styles of government. They self-consciously fostered a globalist ethos of empires created not so much by a feat of arms as by a feat of imagination. These visions were underpinned by the globalization of knowledge of which the pseudo-scientific idea of 'race' was one of the most insidious legacies. Statesmen and propagandists of empire at the *fin de siècle* were enraptured by the possibilities in much the same terms as our contemporaries contemplated globalization a century later.[6] Globalization lay in visions of an integrated system of international trade and a concomitant revolution in communications: steam, print, electronic remittance of money by telegraph and telephone. The creation of an imperial penny post, for example, was underscored by a moral imperative to break down the 'walls of oblivion' within societies.[7] Global advertising, and globally marketed imperial pageants at the end of the nineteenth century had helped extend this imperial public. English (or French) was to function as a new world language. As the English historian, James Bryce, argued in 1901, it seemed as if 'a new sort of unity is being created among mankind'. He also recognized, however, that this was 'not altogether a new thing'. It was the restoration of a norm in world affairs that had been broken only by the fall of the Roman Empire: 'As Rome was the principal agent in the earlier,' he wrote, 'so had England been in the later effort.'[8] Greater Britain or Greater France were the prelude to the federation of the world. As today, globalization was applied geopolitics and it universalized the self-images of the paramount world powers.

Whilst the expansion of Europe and its settler states created a new layer of globalization, colonial conquest tore into the fabric of the old. Rich courtly cultures – Delhi and Lucknow, Mandalay and Hué – were turned inside out and their claims to universal monarchy dismissed. More insidiously, through the operation of colonial law and the expansion of Western education, existing ecumenes were placed on trial. Confronted with the categorizing imperatives of colonial administration, many communities began to recast their identities in ways that ran against the grain of the universal affiliations of their global past. The aggressive territoriality of the West was felt beyond the boundaries of formal colonial rule: there was a literal sense in which, by reforms on a European model, states such as Egypt or Siam mapped themselves into the emerging imperial order.[9] Yet, for all this, during the nineteenth century the impact of imperial globalization was felt unevenly. It was perhaps felt keenest in areas where European control was entrenched before the 1850s, as was the case in British India and Dutch Java. Yet even here, older allegiances – not least to Islamic universalism – were never wholly disavowed and were to revive in the later nineteenth century. On the new frontiers of late nineteenth-century imperial expansion, the violence of conquest, though terrible, was often short-lived. The Europeans could not permit it to last; they worked swiftly to restore patterns of trade and the productivity of labour, and this led them swiftly to seek accommodations with existing modes of globalization.

European empires were constructed on archaic foundations. They were presaged by widening interactions in the Afro-Eurasian world over the *longue durée*: its patterns of kingship and consumption, its models of universal religion, its traders and raiders.[10] In the first place, European empires were often built on old sites of royal power and attempted to usurp their claims to universalism. Just as to the Sultan of Cirebon at the beginning of the seventeenth century Batavia was a 'new Melaka', so at the outset of the nineteenth century Thomas Stamford Raffles founded Singapore as a successor state not only to Melaka but also to Majapahit. European appeals to these traditions intensified as ever greater numbers of indigenous polities were annexed or came under the mantle of 'indirect rule'. In India, the Anglo-Mughal idiom was flaunted in the Imperial Assemblage of 1876; in Egypt after 1883, the British invoked the Pharaonic past as a less intimidating, but equally legitimizing alternative to the Islamic. A vision of universal monarchy dominated the imperial pomp of the 1897 Diamond Jubilee. Much of this was invention, even whimsy, by which a Victorian adventurer might assume the mantles of Malay kingship, and a German soldier might drape an African chief in borrowed robes from the Berlin Opera House. However, it allowed Europeans to draw poetic contrasts between the colourful pageantry of African or Asian kingdoms and the harder substance of colonial power.[11] These were flattering, but blind. Princely states in India, for example, revolved around 'hidden domains' of power, and could exploit European law to advance their ritual claims; early Dutch incursions into Java provoked its royal courts into robust new formulations of Javanese style and ritual that anticipated and deflected later colonial inventions of tradition.[12] In such kingdoms, the medium was often the message. The political authority of the scribal traditions, the realm of the calligrapher, remained strong, particularly in the Islamic world. The Persian titles of Malay rulers, their invocations of lineage to Alexander and Rome, carried a resonance that the Dutch and British never adequately grasped.[13]

Much of the colonial world at the *fin de siècle* was in fact a Euro-Islamic condominium.[14] At a deeper level, earlier universal empires continued to exercise sway. A sense of the residual suzerainty of the Ottomans remained important, especially on the frontiers of the *dār al-islām*, in north Africa or Southeast Asia. The abortive extension of Ottoman sea power into the Red Sea in the sixteenth century was felt in Southeast Asia into the twentieth century in the powerful appeal of Pan-Islamism and in the consular role played by Hadhrami Arabs in The Netherlands East Indies. Indeed, the Hadhrami have emerged in the recent historical literature as a central case study of these connections, a migrant community with an impact far disproportionate to their numbers.[15] In a similar way, the late Qing state intensified its claims on the Nanyang to finance its imperial revival, which gave the overseas Chinese a new political importance within the societies in which they sojourned. Much political activity in this period was ungoverned by the Europeans, and did not take colonial rule as its central reference point. Crucially, by the 1880s, new science and knowledge did not merely diffuse from the West, but was refracted through Meiji Japan, which became a major engine of globalization in its own right. In seeking anti-colonial allies, the sultans of Riau in The Netherlands East Indies turned first to the Sultan of *Rum*, or Rome, in

Constantinople and then to Tokyo. One of the earliest Malay accounts of the 'nation', came from Malay translations of the Egyptian nationalist Mustafa Kamil's account of Meiji Japan, albeit sensitized to local needs by Islamic reformers.[16] In 1881, it was to the Meiji Emperor that the 'Cosmopolitan King' of Hawaii, Kalakana, proposed a 'Union and Federation of Asiatic Nations and Sovereigns', sealed with a marriage alliance. Mocked at the time as an 'Empire of the Calabash', this gesture too had behind it a historical tradition of pan-Pacific thinking within the kingdom and anticipated later Japanese Pan-Asianism.[17]

The very areas that were a focus of European imperial expansion in this period had, of course, always been global in their connections. Insular Southeast Asia is a classic example of this. As an axis between east Asia and the classical centres of India and the Middle East, the focus of the early modern maritime empires, the 'Sea of Melayu', had for centuries been shaped by global migrations, cultures and religions and tied together by trade and traditions of internal migration. Historians of the region have long seen its distinctiveness in its receptiveness and adaptation to new people, new things and new ideas.[18] They may in fact exaggerate the region's singularity in this regard and minimize the tensions that these accommodations generated. However, the Southeast Asian experience does indicate that colonial modernity – notwithstanding the energy with which it pressed its claims – was not a terminal trauma to states that had been committed to archaic and early modern globalization. A region such as Southeast Asia had always been porous to global influences. The chronicles of the Malay world reveal a statecraft that was based on concepts of perpetual change. A Malay ethos, and a very immediate sense of the greatness of past kingdoms, gave this a certain rootedness, which has been termed 'a developing sense of the past as a stable entity continually re-enacted in the present'. This was, of course, a central function of the courtly literature of the archipelago, in which there was little sense of 'inside' and 'outside' in this civilization. Ethnicity was a malleable concept only ever realized in specific contexts and locations. Things from outside – from China or south Asia – were as much a part of it as anything local.[19] There was therefore no sharp disjuncture between the regionalism of the *alam Melayu* and the wider world. Regionalism was a bridge to globalization.

Globalization and the Diasporic Condition

Migration, then, lies at the core of globalization in world history – the migration of funds, of people, of technology, of commodities and ideas. For both 'old' and 'new' globalization, the agents of this global sensibility were migrant groups: traders, scholars, agents, advisers. It is the study of these sojourners that is perhaps a key to writing a truly global, as opposed to 'international', or 'world' history.[20] It is, of course, impossible to generalize about the motives and character of their movements, and the level of coercion or free will that drove them. Yet, the migrant groups that were most characteristic of this kind of global outlook did often share certain important characteristics. These were, first, environmental. Often these groups originated in regions where conditions at the fringes of the desert, the forest, the hills or the sea encouraged seasonal migration. A second characteristic was that these societies were mostly to be found on the voluntary end of a spectrum of motives for migration. They possessed a degree of commercial opportunity, or entrepreneurship in knowledge, in situations where migration or sojourning was the means of realizing it. A third characteristic was in many cases a fragmented political situation, a situation of statelessness or of a weak state – fluid frontier situations in which the route to wealth and power was the accumulation of clients. There was a relative absence of the constraints on migration that were a feature of other areas where state power was stronger. Yet, by the same token, rulers, or powerful local men, occupied a pivotal role in these movements. Migration was necessary as a source of wealth, power and expertise, but it also needed to be regulated to prevent a rival accumulating the manpower or wealth to mount a challenge to a ruler's local primacy.[21] Patriarchal figures – a ruler, a chief, a holy man – were therefore an important link to the global sphere, mediating access to it internally, but also often embodying within a locality outside loyalties and connections. They occupied similar roles in very different social contexts, and were supported by the universalist discourses through which they shaped their actions.[22] This bred a sense of proximity, of universal neighbourliness, that survived into the imperial period.

The advent of colonial rule, therefore, was not merely the case of one globalization dislodging another. Old networks were not merely 'cannibalized', but re-energized by the new global connections of colonial rule. Yet, in the imperial era of the later nineteenth century, broad shifts in globalization did occur. First, old channels of migration were revitalized, and in many cases deepened with a downward spread in society. The networks of the Islamic world are one example of this. After 1850, the world was still a place where from Marrakesh to Maluku all swore on the same Qur'an. Islamic globalization, or universalism, had intensified in the seventeenth and eighteenth centuries through trade, pilgrimage and the associated growth of *tarekat* or Sufi orders. Colonial communications greatly extended these linkages. In particular, the *hajj* (pilgrimage) became a more widely attainable aspiration. The annual number of *hajis* from the Dutch East Indies rose from around 2,000 in the 1850s to 7,000 at the turn of the century, and these journeys often developed into long sojourns in Mecca or Cairo. Many *hajis* were initiated in a *tarekat*; some charismatic *ulama* were authorized to teach the techniques of the order on their return home, where they became powerful figures in their locales.[23] Connections with a Muslim world with multiple centres of authority could, of course, heighten a sense of Islam-in-the-world. Encounters with the Muslim 'other' were at least as formative as those with Europe.[24]

Secondly, the linkages between the older centres of 'archaic' globalization and new frontier economies were transformed as many regions of the globe became specialized sub-systems of the world economy. Whereas the vanguard of 'old globalization' had been skilled service elites or traders, by the later nineteenth century a series of new networks of labour migration emerged that were increasingly dominated by the unskilled.[25] Their structure and organization drew on the early modern systems of labour of the Atlantic world, chiefly in the extension of the plantation complex to the Indian Ocean and the Pacific Rim, and to Africa itself.[26] Movements both followed and reversed old crossings. They led to a reconnection of an earlier African diaspora with the continent, with the resettlement of ex-slaves in Sierra Leone, Liberia, Gambia and Kenya. They also saw, in the case of the 'Bombay Africans', the movement of Africans to new locations outside of Africa and a new influx of labour into the Caribbean, this time from Asia.[27] Many migrants within the colonial world were migrants-twice-over. Much historical writing has focused on indenture's rhetorical but often real role as 'a new system of slavery', and its relationship to the new wave of migrations from the Old World to North America and to Australasia.[28] The force of this rhetoric perhaps relates more to the earlier than to the later nineteenth-century indenture and to areas where institutions of slavery were slow to vanish. It would be wrong to see these migrations as orchestrated solely by imperial interests; in the age of indenture, the passage of those outside European systems of labour recruitment far exceeded those within and this created new pioneering communities on old models. A fresh wave of Chinese pioneers on the forest frontier of the Malay Peninsula and elsewhere worked in leagues called *kongsi*, which combined old traditions of brotherhood with economic partnership, and created a constellation of 'little republics' on the fringes of British authority.[29] The Soninke entrepreneurs in the slave trade in the Sengal river valley ironically emerged as pioneer wage labourers and sailors in migrations that had more to do with the realization of traditional aspirations – with prestige and manhood – than with the compulsions of poverty.[30]

This said, this sudden acceleration of globalization – which was founded after all on new weapons of war and means of extraction as much as trade and settlement – created a new wave of human, epidemological and ecological traumas. The disparity between the experience of the global 'winners' and 'losers' did not diminish. The world of the migrant was often one of disease and despair, suicide and sudden violence. The fresh impetus to globalization generated a dark underside: the increased traffic in arms and narcotics, in women and children. Shifts in migration patterns could also increase social differentiation within ethnic communities and tensions without: this was the period of the emergence of the classic colonial forms of the 'plural', 'dual', or 'segmented' society. As we have seen, in some parts of the world this process was already well advanced. Yet, in many of the new frontier areas, one must not overemphasize the abruptness of this shift. One might even argue that a commitment to global concerns militated against more local conflicts. Only perhaps by the inter-war period was the looser urban and agrarian pluralism in many colonial societies decisively challenged. When writers such as J.S. Furnivall and J.H. Boeke came to theorize about these societies in the 1930s, they were anatomizing something that was just coming into being. By this time, new ideas of community and 'race' were enshrined in colonial administration and law. Older, rather relative, ideas of difference were taking on a harder edge. In the later nineteenth century, new waves of settlement provided fresh constituencies for debates on globalism and, as we shall see, greatly deepened them.

By the last two decades of the nineteenth century colonial states were beginning to manage and direct these flows of people more effectively. This task was in many cases their principal *raison d'être*, the culmination of the European 'scrambles' for Africa and Asia. This is a third theme of the imperial age. Strong states have invariably been enemies to migration, where it does not serve their express ends, and by the end of the nineteenth century imperial Leviathans were growing in reach. Pioneering communities were brought under heel: the Chinese *kongsi* were reclassified as criminal 'secret societies', forest frontiers became gazetted reserves. Systems of labour recruitment and management of the plantations became more regimented. In this task, Europeans often sought the assistance of patriarchal authority, which now possessed fewer sanctions to keep young clients at home. Their shared concern in the maintenance of traditional authority helped create a proliferation of regulation: vagrancy laws and embryonic pass laws; legislation restricting access to land; and exclusionist laws restricting employment, as in the creation of Malay Reservations and 'traditional' domains in Fiji. Yet they were not always successful.[31] The settler politics of southern Africa and the Pacific colonies of settlement added a sinister edge to this process. But even where control was exercised through decisive international action, such as under the 1907–8 Gentleman's Agreement that closed emigration of Japanese labour to the United States, migrations could swiftly flow to new frontiers, in this case to the Philippines and Latin America.[32] The steel frame was closing, though not yet all-encompassing.

The emblem of both the new possibilities and new controls was the colonial city. Yet even here imperial globalization was a thin veneer on the archaic. The colonial city did not supplant the indigenous. Only rarely – at Port Sudan, Durban, Nairobi, Kenitra, Kabar – were new sites founded by the Europeans. More often colonial expansion added a new layer to earlier cities that already possessed a long reach, as in the case of the *villes nouvelles* of the Maghrib.

Moreover, local rulers – the Ottomans, the Chakris, the Meiji elite – also remodelled their urban space. Before 1896, the development of Cairo, for example, was entirely within the framework established by Khedive Ismail.[33] What the colonial connection did achieve was to accelerate the evolution of a regional reach into the global. It was only in the later period of imperial globalization that the rise of colonial centres – Saigon, Batavia, Kuala Lumpur, Rangoon, Mombasa – began to displace old seats of authority and knowledge. Nor did they acquire a monopoly of it. 'Invisible empires' emerged around the great port cities of colonial Asia, whose intellectual life and public spheres were ungoverned by European power.[34] Singapore, for example, was a British creation; the centre of imperial communications in the East. But it also revitalized much of the old ethos of movement and trade within the Malay world; it became a central locus for a number of overlapping diasporas – Chinese and Indian, Arab and Malay. These links were not merely those between places of homeland and sojourn, but intricate, crosscutting through-connections, not least of the Islamic world. In ways that were not solely bound up with its imperial role, *fin de siècle* Singapore – or for, that matter, Calcutta, Lagos or Betawi – were the prototypes of the modern global city, but in a sense that went far beyond the imaginings of their European burghers.[35]

The experience of globalism then – of thinking and acting on a global basis – has been intimately bound up with that of diaspora. Both relate to identities and how ideas are appropriated, processed and transformed as they traverse global networks. Older studies saw diasporas principally as a primordial category of belonging, linked to dispersal, longing and suffering. Here the idea of diaspora is shaped around the rise of the nation state, the crucial sense in which 'nationalism needs this story of migration, the diaspora of others, to establish the rootedness of the nation'.[36] A second, more recent, employment of the term uses the idea of diaspora to challenge bounded and static understandings of culture and society, to attack the oppressive primacy of the nation state. Diaspora in this sense has become emblematic of understandings of identity as fluid, hybrid, fragmented, and crucial to the decentred visions of post-coloniality and postmodernity.[37] The problem with this is that – focused as it is on fragments and multiple identities – it provides little for the historian to build upon.[38]

The diasporic world of the colonial city illustrates many of the problems in writing about identity in these terms. The biographies of leading personalities seem to present impossibly contradictory layers of belonging. One example from Singapore may suffice: that of the Straits Chinese leader, Lim Boon Keng (1869–1957). Lim was a *Peranakan*, a member of a community of long domicile in Southeast Asia that had intermarried with the Malay community, yet retained a very pronounced sense of its Chinese identity in its social practices. The community was vocal in its empire-loyalty and enjoyed the privilege of British citizenship. Lim was a medical doctor schooled in Britain, prominent in-colonial councils and learned societies. He was an apostate Christian, an architect of Confucian revival and a founder of the revolutionary forerunner of the Kuomintang. He wrote in Chinese, English and in Malay. One of his most singular works was entitled *The Great War from a Confucian Point of View* (1917). It was a rallying call to imperial defence and a testimony to the diffusion of languages of race *and* democracy into colonial societies. It was a powerful statement of the attraction that empire-as-globalism had for a community like the Straits Chinese. It was also a demand for recognition for his community within an empire 'whose noble example may well be the prelude to the federation of the world'.[39] One could write of Lim's work in terms of fragmented, shifting identities, as a foreshadow of what the overseas Chinese scholar Aihwa Ong has called, in a contemporary context, the 'flexible citizenship' of the Chinese in diaspora.[40] Indeed it was said of Lim: 'He could be a duck, the next day he could be a chicken'.[41] But there seems to be little that is fragmentary in Lim's approach towards his life, nor any hesitation in his loyalties; nor does the ahistorical language of ambiguous belonging show how Lim's views may have changed over time and through contacts with others. It is perhaps more helpful to adopt an approach to diaspora that emphasizes the concrete cultural bonds, the ties across distance, the networks that diaspora creates. This is not to take diaspora as a static category, in a fixed relationship to a homeland or a nation-at-large, but to adopt a *diasporic* perspective on identities, links and flows in a global context, and, above all, to examine the ways in which they interconnected with other communities.[42]

Here we run against the ever-present concern that the language of globalization is for historians merely an opportunity to re-invent the wheel. Indeed, this is partially the case. The study of diasporic networks returns us close to the 'social networks' traced by anthropologists of urbanization. These studies were often centred upon specific diasporas and specific contexts, for example that of African urbanism from the 1950s onwards.[43] Diaspora networks, too, provided many functions for their members and for colonial societies. They provided solutions to technical problems of trade and information. For centuries they had provided trust over long distances.[44] In the colonial period, they took on new functions as migrations took on a mass dimension, especially in the movement of people itself, such as in the organizing and recruiting of labour through places like Hong Kong or Madras. A wide spectrum of the mutual aid associations were spawned, and not all of them benign, from extortion and protection rackets on the frontiers of China's Nanyang, to the networks that ranged across Africa for support of the 'permanent pilgrims' in the Sudan and elsewhere.[45] Yet what I want to focus on here, and where ideas of globalization may come in useful, is not so much the functions diasporas perform for their members, but the functions that they perform for others; how they conversed with others and the ideas that emerged from this.

Learning to Talk: The Lingua Franca of Globalism

At the heart of the globalization of this period is the experience of polyglot migrant communities, dominated by small European diasporas, learning to relate to distant homelands, but also learning to talk to each other, often for the first time. Many of the layers of language and ideas that circulated in this period of globalization have been little studied; they are neither central to the literature on empire, nor to that on national awakening. But to look a little deeper at them might tell us more about the inner history of globalization, of how people lived in a global society in which others had economic dominance and cultural primacy. A civic space emerged around this kind of globalization in the colonial cities and their hinterlands in the later nineteenth century. It was to some extent shaped by colonial communications and institutions, but it was never wholly reliant on them. It was a fleeting moment, but an important and distinctive event in the history of globalization in the imperial period. By the second decade of the twentieth century this diasporic world was in decline. The reasons for this anticipate many themes of more recent, post-colonial globalization.

An opening premise of Philip Curtin's pioneering study of *Cross-Cultural Trade in World History* is that communication between diasporas has always been difficult and that this is an obstacle to the establishment of commercial trust. Yet the study of pidgins, 'jargons', creoles and lingua francas is a rich field through which to trace how what were often new communities, created by forces of globalization, surmounted this difficulty and learned to speak to each other. The study of code-switching and the translation process – through primers and dialogues, the idioms of popular literature, petitions and statements within the imperial archive – creates a fresh perspective on how communities confronted globalizing forces.[46] Pidgins, creoles and jargons can encompass the 'cant' of the low, or can be employed in the highest circles. They are 'partial' or 'parasitic' languages that perhaps extend a vernacular. They can be dismissed as vulgar, but (as in the case of the Tok Pigin of Papua New Guinea) achieve a standardized, even national form. They cross frontiers, for reasons that are often as much linked to war as to trade. They can become international and emerge as a lingua franca.[47] However, lingua francas more often arise when an existing language finds a wider role, sometimes in a reconstructed form. More rarely they can be constructed in their entirety. Sociolinguistics suggests a number of themes that might illuminate the workings of the globalization of imperial era.

A first theme is that lingua francas can exist and operate without any standardization and in many different registers. Histories of the first 'lingua franca', have gone so far as to see it as the basis of an archaic *world* language, forged when the Mediterranean was the world, spreading globally with Iberian expansion, persisting into the early nineteenth century as *petit mauresque* in pockets of North Africa. In the early eighteenth century, English traders at

Canton communicated through Portuguese Eurasian interpreters who translated the Cantonese into a Portuguese pidgin. Yet in its code-switching and its
forms, which were varied yet not arbitrary, it anticipated many later modes of
communication – Arabic, Hausa, Hindi, Swahili.[48]

The Malay world is a case in point. For centuries the lingua franca of the
region has been the Malay language. It was shaped by sojourners; its
expression was overlaid with other world languages such as Arabic and
Sanskrit. Over time, it supplanted its main competitor, Portuguese. But
Malay, or 'real Malay' as the etymologists called it, was a first language for
only a few, and many local variants competed as a definitive form. In the
colonial period most people spoke forms of pidgin or bazaar Malay, yet there
were a multitude of different kinds of these too. 'Malay' existed without a
standard, yet was clearly understood and used for communication by those
who had a better knowledge of another language. Malay was, as one scholar
has termed it, 'a slippery continuum, that is, a continuous switching between
codes and styles'. Linguistic differences were great, but not insurmountable.
One could not, perhaps, define how the system worked, yet most people
understood it, or rather one did not so much understand it as inhabit it.
Differences did not matter; somehow this heteroglossia worked to the
satisfaction of all of those involved, not least because its styles allowed it to
absorb contrary cultural streams.[49] In east Africa, the Swahili language, like the
'Swahili' themselves, was the product of centuries of trade and tradition which
linked (as did Malay) scattered and diverse communities into a common
historical experience. To this, Islam, as in the Malay world, added a
universality that transcended and enriched parochialism.[50] The range of speech
that Swahili encompassed was immense. We can glimpse this in the
extraordinary 'vocabulary of Elizabethville', a collective biography of the
houseboys: 'a vocabulary that offers thoughts on all and everything'. The
document was a product of grass-roots literacy, rooted in orality, improvised
in its spelling, written in a hybrid Shaba Swahili, laced with French
borrowings and adaptations: a masterwork of heteroglossia.[51]

This suggests a second theme. The switching of codes and styles has for
centuries been a way in which local identities met external, homogenizing
forces. Linguistics, with its bent towards the integrity of grammar systems,
and its focus on *langue* rather than *parole*, has been slow to study this. For
historians it is, perhaps, a prism through which to trace, on an intimate level,
how – in a usefully ambiguous, shifting way – communities negotiate with
authority, community or territoriality.[52] The old trading cities of west Africa
are an excellent illustration of this. In colonial Accra, for example, as with
other commercial cities in west Africa, the choice of language was very much
conditioned by the social history of its use in a community. In a plural and
pressured urban environment, people had to balance the necessity for
communication with others, with the dangers of assimilation. This meant the
use of a second language, a pidgin of lingua franca – broken English, or a

variety of Hausa – which provided a secure channel for communication which did not threaten delicately constructed ethnic boundaries. It also allowed for careful and shaded speech.[53] Again one must not idealize lingua franca and code-switching. These mediums were often employed as languages of command, with vocabularies of racial contempt. The *pataouète* of the Europeans in Algeria was a language of the towns, of a *pied noire* identity, that actually drove the early nationalists away from such linguistic experimentation, initially closer to French and later to a purer contemplation of Islamic idioms.[54] In north India, where the British adopted 'Urdu' as a language of affairs, it was rejected by Hindi writers who attacked it as a 'language of dancing girls and prostitutes', and who promoted a remodelled and highly Sanskritized Hindi language. In so doing, they turned their back on the existing linguistic mixture of everyday speech and created two distinct and largely mutually unintelligible languages.[55] Yet colonial interventions were rarely so problematic or decisive. In many parts of the world it was by utilizing varying registers, codes and styles, rather than by overcoming or surmounting them, that users of these lingua francas could begin to create new political styles.[56]

This use of language was not entirely ungoverned before the advent of a European standardizing etymology. The use of Malay, for example, was a source of conflict within the Malay world. Local studies of Malay ethos and political traditions stress that points of identity were shifting.[57] These in turn could be challenged by the emergence from within of other ways of speaking. What historians have begun to emphasize is the role of non-Malay diasporas – the *Peranakan* Chinese, Hadramaut Arabs, Javanese from the *paisir*, Eurasians – in popularizing, if not standardizing ways of speaking. This took multiple forms. There was their role in Malay publishing, which was based not only in Singapore, Betawi or Medan, but in Bombay, Istanbul, Mecca and Cairo. *Peranakan* Chinese private lending libraries appeared in Betawi and Palembang from the end of the eighteenth century, and Chinese literature reinvigorated Malay verse forms such as the *pantun* and *syair*.[58] Eurasians and *Peranakan* Chinese gave an archipelago-wide popularity to the popular music of the *kroncong*, which had its origins in the early modern global past of the Portuguese seafarers, and also to the *commedia dell'arte* of the region – the evocatively named *Stamboul*. From the 1880s and 1890s onwards, this hybrid brought, in the lingua franca, a cosmopolitan palimpsest of stories – from *Don Quixote* to *Tosca*, from *The Thousand and One Nights* to *The Mark of Zorro* – to large urban and rural audiences. In the outer islands, this often represented a first encounter with global modernity.[59] The various uses of Malay generated intense interest among colonial educators. They would respond with their own attempts to standardize the language, mostly on 'purer' lines. Emergent 'national' elites, operating at a remove from the pioneering diasporic groups, would take up their own experiments. These often, over time, converged to oust the corrupt polyphony of the bazaar forms of the language.

It is important to emphasize that ousting happened rather late in the day. Imperial communications created new channels for the spread of lingua francas, but were slow to place their stamp on them. This can be seen in the development of translation itself, a process which was central to globalization. It can be studied as part of the emergence of a system of transnational communications, a global market in translation rights, with it agents and bookfairs. It can also be studied as a 'transnational cultural field'.[60] In this sense, in contrast to the standardizing and domesticating tradition in the West, translation in the wider world could take on a more dynamic form.[61] In China, the late Qing government, through bodies such as the Jiangnan Arsenal Translation Bureau, and Christian missionaries, took initiatives in translation. Yet more important than these state projects were rather different kinds of translation genres that emerged around them. Missionary works of translation often attracted secular writers. Translation, in this context, was rarely a search for pure meaning. It was an interactive process of borrowing. Translations of works from the West were often retranslations of Japanese works; they were unauthorized and not intended to be authoritative. Translators themselves became a vocal presence in the text; the aim was often 'translating the gist' and to explicate the rest. A true prophet of globalization, Jules Verne, was one of the most popular authors of the day, and Chinese renderings were, in the Dutch East Indies, translated on into Malay.[62] At the height of colonial rule in India, translations from English into minority tongues, such as Kannada, were seen as a part of a longer tradition of 'rewriting' and were a strategy to invigorate a language tradition. Translation could be employed to highlight and preserve difference.[63] The repercussions could be revolutionary. It has been argued that it was the polyphony and heterogeneity of printed translations in Indonesia that gave Malay its power in creating new audiences that transcended the 'segmented nature' of Indonesian society; audiences where ethnic composition did not matter. The beginnings of anti-colonial struggle, it has been argued, lay not in confronting European power, but in the power of translating itself. From the practice of appropriating ideas from all over the world came a sense of the ability to drive events. In this process, as with the earlier calligraphic representations of the written word, the medium was often more important than a specific message.[64]

The utility of heteroglossia was reflected in a rather different way in the failure of alternatives. Another potential route to a lingua franca was the invention of a new global language. The late nineteenth century witnessed a rush to develop them. In one sense they were the progeny of new technologies, such as the telephone – although the compulsion of technology was often invoked as an argument after the fact. Some were *a posteriori*, like Volapük (1880), developed by a German priest with an English base and German grammar. By 1889, the 283 Volapük societies across the globe claimed a million members.[65] Other languages were *a priori*, the most outstanding example of which was Esperanto. Its prophet, Dr Ludovic Zamenhof

(1859–1917), the son of a censor of the Tsar, began work on his language at the age of fifteen. His primary motivation was spiritual. Then, as now, the early savants of new global communications were the spiritualists and the sub-cultists. Esperanto, for Zamenhof, was bound up with his non-sectarian religion, 'Homaranismo'. 'If I were not a Jew from the ghetto,' he remarked, 'the idea of unification of mankind would not have come into my head.'[66] That said, J.R.R. Tolkien took the view that, as there were no Esperanto legends, it was destined to fail.[67] 'Universal languages' were almost wholly Eurocentric in vision. Only Kenneth Searight sought to break away from the 'monotonous series of hybrid Teuto-Romantic languages' and incorporate in his Sona (1935) Arabic, Chinese and Japanese.[68] However, the quest for a strategically designed 'inter-language' persisted in the twentieth century. They were not envisaged as tools of empire: they were to serve the cause of global idealism, or even world revolution. Stalin once considered adopting Esperanto as tool of the revolution, but abandoned the idea after an unsuccessful attempt to master it. His protégé, the linguist Nicholas Marr, was a visionary who saw 'the omni-expressive, single language of the future' [as] the inevitable concomitant of a future human society without classes or nations'. Eventually, he forecast, technology would render spoken language obsolete. Yet Stalin used Marr's ideas primarily to whitewash policies of Russification, and eventually abandoned, or 'postponed', their implementation, in the face of the 'national' policy after 1950.[69] Among the 'bourgeois idealists', the attempt to fashion a new lingua franca fragmented into scholasticism and philological sectarianism.

This colourful failure helps set the imperial project in context. The promotion of English as a global lingua franca through the standardization of dictionaries and schooling has been called 'the last powerful outreach of an imperial age'. It was an important element of late nineteenth-century globalization's universalization of national 'standards'. Yet its imprint was felt quite late in the day, and the imperial project was swift to fragment and be appropriated to different ends. By 1900 there were several 'standard' Englishes; studies of them show the dexterity with which people moved through different registers of English. There was no central academy for the language, a role that the compilers of the Oxford English Dictionary undertook to fill. The growing push towards English language standardization was slow to have a global impact – 'Received Pronunciation' made little impact before the 1920s – and belonged to the end of empire.[70] The survival of English ceased to be dependent on Great Britain long before the 1930s.[71] C.K. Ogden's global 'inter-language', Basic English, was motivated by a pacifistic internationalism (as in Henry Ford's recipe for world peace: 'Make everybody speak English'). English was its basis, simply because the global demand for English made its adoption inevitable.[72] Even where a more empire-centred Anglophone consciousness was pursued with real conviction – for example, in mission schools and in the cultural politics at the end of empire – it could not complete against established local heteroglossias or emerging linguistic nationalism.[73] The colonial project would either converge with the national, or be defeated.

A Global Public Sphere, c. 1890–1920

A sense of global identity was slow to emerge from the globalization of empire. Although, in an immediate sense, the European systems did produce a degree of political integration, at a deeper level, both at home and abroad, it was perhaps the political realm that remained most resistant to the logic of globalization. Within the British empire, an estimated 150 schemes for greater imperial unity were floated in the 1870s and 1880s, and all of them failed.[74] This was perhaps unsurprising. Even for the British, globalization bred unease that, as a tool of empire, its potentialities could only be grasped by a small elite. The historian, Edward Freeman, acknowledged that 'modern science has annihilated time and space . . . that it takes no longer to get to Westminster from the most distant British colonies, than at the time of the Union of England and Scotland, it took to come from Shetland to Westminster'. Yet Freeman was deeply sceptical about the new kinds of identity that might emerge. 'There is such a thing as an idea of a nation in the mind, but . . . such an idea hardly ever answers to anything that has any actual being on earth.'[75] If, ultimately, for Britain, empire-as-globalism reinforced the nation state, it was from the American Pacific that a more utopian vision arose. In Hawaii, prominent citizens projected the islands as a 'New Geneva', 'the Hague of the World', a melting pot of East and West, and promoted a 'Pacific patriotism' through international congresses and friendship societies, tourism and exotica. Yet the tone of the experiment was elitist and racially ambiguous, and it came at a time of increasing social exclusion and 'Americanization' that provoked troubled debates on identity within the island's migrant communities.[76]

The new politics that did emerge from the *fin de siècle* empire was largely a creation of and sustained by diasporic networks. Important new research has highlighted the breadth and reach of the shared 'public sphere' of the port cities that ringed the Indian Ocean in this period.[77] This insight might be extended to encompass east Africa, the Cape and Cairo, the China seaboard, Australasia, and increasingly Japan. This public sphere perhaps reached its apogee from the 1890s to World War I. At one level, it was shaped by the imperial communications that relayed new forms of knowledge around the world. Part of it was based on the co-option of local elites into municipal and legislative councils, with their official agendas and rules of political debate. Yet what is striking about this period is the extent to which the formative political debates were conducted over vast distances, the global perspective through which people confronted change. This was a world where events far afield – be it in Egypt, Japan, the Philippines or Ireland – were a common currency for all. Ideas of political community were not imagined solely around the territorial or administrative boundaries of imperial rule, powerful though these colonial categories were. They were based on harder connections and were international in outlook. Here, old and new 'diasporic public spheres' came together through the expanded role of lingua francas and the fetish for translation. Their concerns were a long way away from those of the 'imagined communities' of modern nation statehood. In colonial Singapore, for example, the inclusive cosmopolitanism of the public sphere of the *fin de siècle* sits in striking contrast to political inwardness of the policy a century later, although both worlds operated within similar legal constraints.[78] The different layers of the global public sphere generated international congresses on matters ranging from co-operatives to women, from race to opium, and the agitation for the abolition of indentured labour.[79] This global outlook was not solely, or primarily, secular: some of its most visible moments were a World's Parliament of Religions in Chicago in 1893, the spread of Theosophy, Pan-Buddhism and Pan-Islam. While these initiatives were 'non-governmental' their vitality was paralleled by the increasing tendency of colonial governments to address problems in an international, co-operative way.

Yet this globalist ethos was not solely the preserve of the strategically positioned elite. What is striking is how deeply the networks described here reached. In Java, this era was evocatively described as *dunia bergerak*, 'a world in motion', in which new motifs, moods and movements appeared on the scene. The years from, say, the 1890s to the end of World War I, were a time of flux and experiment that occurred before the era of disciplined national parties or ideologies, in which many languages and rhetorics evolved side by side.[80] This notion might be employed more widely. Social and cultural contexts, of course, differed dramatically. Yet within these contexts, universal or global ideas – of religion, of a globally informed anti-colonialism, of the idea of politics itself – were coming to occupy a larger part of objective social reality.[81] In this way, in different locales, a wider range of predicaments was being discussed in similar terms; in adjacent locales, similar debates were being played out in similar ways, in similar language, translations or symbolism. At this point the local and the global converged. Often local communities did not need a direct external prompting to frame their actions in broader terms. Theirs was a response to a more general sense of proximity to others. This was not merely, or primarily, formed by a relation to those within an incipient 'nation', but to others far distant, and very unlike themselves.

This part of the argument is necessarily speculative, but there are ways in which the theme might be explored further. As we have already seen, globalism bred a sense of universal neighbourliness: for centuries, in Asia, Africa and the Middle East, new ideas and attitudes had been transmitted between town and country through rich traditions of inter-migration. In maritime Southeast Asia, at the village level, *ulama* and other figures often possessed – through the networks of publishers, *madrasahs* (religious schools) and Sufism – more immediate international connections than courtly elites.

They provided local leadership, but embodied wider loyalties and obligations, often in a very patriarchal way. The tension between the local and the universal lay at the centre of the local experience of Islam, and – through the Friday sermon, or debates on the translation and interpretation of texts – it was reflected in the praxis of everyday life. This tension was acute in areas such as the Malay or the Swahili world that possessed great cultural heterogeneity; societies on the frontiers of the Islamic world may have been particularly vulnerable to outsiders deemed to represent its universal authority.[82] A central link between these different worlds were diasporic networks, and it was here that heteroglossias – be they Malay, Urdu or Swahili – and code-switching styles of speaking could serve these communities well. The crisis of World War I brought to the surface the networks that had been forged across the Afro–Asian world over the preceding decades. Many of the rebellions, mutinies, and agitations of these years reflected these connections and the universal neighbourliness they had engendered.

Paradoxically, notwithstanding the power of European world systems and their 'empires of information', there were perhaps more people participating in globalization, more people consciously thinking and acting on a global basis, and from more centres, than at any time since. The *fin de siècle* was the highwater mark of long-distance migrations. It was also perhaps an era when it was very much easier to take part in these debates than later. The globalization of European imperialism was an extension of the nation state. The globalism I have tried to describe was not. The now classic account of the rise of nationalism – Benedict Anderson's *Imagined Communities* – can be taken as a master narrative of the globalization of the idea of the modern nation state – elite-driven, technological, and founded upon Western modernity.[83] The 'national' projects of the early twentieth century were formed by rather different forces, by figures who bridged the identities of the early archaic period and new global influences in equally imaginative ways. The modern nation state was achieved at a tremendous cost to other discourses.

Epilogue: 'La tyrannie du national'

Some economists have suggested that the inter-war period saw a reversal of the processes of globalization, a closing of the nineteenth century's open economy, between 1929 and 1945, with a revival only in the 1950s.[84] Others argue that, measured both in the amount of mass family migration and in the quantity of international trade and capital flows relative to GDP, the international economy was perhaps in many ways more integrated before 1914 than in the present era.[85] Seen through the perspective of politics and culture adopted in this essay, the closing of global possibilities after 1914 seems to have been very far-reaching. World War I, in many ways, marked the end of an era. During and after the war, the colonial powers moved swiftly to cut off many of the networks that had sustained the globalism of the turn of the century. The nascent public sphere they helped create was narrowed dramatically. What historians have long called 'the crisis of empire' might be better termed a crisis of globalism.

In many ways events before the war anticipated this closure: the colonial powers acted to regulate affairs beyond the framework of their own territories, often in concert with one another. This was propelled by social issues – the management of labour, disease, and the *hajj* – but it also encompassed policing and intelligence. Even international humanitarianism could be shaped by military needs and military command structures. Although the San Francisco earthquake of 1906 symbolized a global concern with disaster relief, external aid focused on social order and reconstruction, and was guided by national policy.[86] This period also saw a slow consolidation of external boundaries and the imposition of closer internal structures of authority. The war greatly accelerated this process. Amongst Europeans, it provoked new levels of hysteria over the impact of globalization, especially over links of education and pilgrimage within Islam. Unconnected events, such as the Singapore Mutiny of 1915, the Ghadr movement, the Caliphate issue, all led colonial states to crack down further on international networks.[87] Between the wars, anxiety intensified over the radicalization of overseas Chinese politics; and the perceived threats of the 'yellow peril' and Bolshevism. In Hawaii, for example, the 'spectre of alien domination' by Japanese migrants led to the reclassification of them as 'enemy aliens' and the United States military drew up contingency plans to meet the 'threat'.[88] Contemporary orientalist images of 'underground India', of the 'secret society complex' of the Chinese, echo in a sinister way present-day preoccupations with Islamicist conspiracies and 'bamboo networks'. Postal censorship allowed unprecedented investigations into local networks and business operations, and for the first time allowed surveillance of the external linkages of named individuals. The memoirs of Tan Melaka, the 'Scarlet Pimpernel' of Asia, one of the most revolutionary prophets of 'Aslia' and world government, tell of years of endless false passports and fugitive identities, a progress 'from jail to jail'.[89] Press censorship greatly narrowed the nascent public spheres of the colonial cities; new media such as the cinema were seen as a direct political challenge.

We can map this shift in the crucial field of language and translation. Again, even within pre-war systems of indirect rule, Europeans were obsessed with the formalities of communication; the political management of indirect rule demanded elaborate manipulation of status terms, inventions of linguistic tradition. The tightening hierarchies of race made the lingua francas adopted by colonial administrations ever terser languages of command. Civilizing projects played a role too in the reconfiguration of old lingua francas into modern languages. Above all, they tore them away from their heteroglossic past. The British, the French and the Dutch sought to wean 'the natives' from their own popular literature; to separate them from the scandal sheets and penny-dreadfuls that were read aloud and passed around in coffee shops and bookstalls. Indeed, this literature thrived in innuendo, salaciousness and sensationalism. The literature of the Chinese in the Indies written in Malay embodied this spirit: it was an idiom rooted in the cacophony of the port cities, a sound for which Europeans had no ear. The Dutch dismissed it; to them it was not a language of culture.[90] Translation, more generally, became a matter of state, a sphere of international co-operation and subject to its norms. Borrow-words, for example, became a political battleground. Nevertheless, it was at this point that the colonial and national projects of standardization converged.

It was at this time too that the nation state closed down the ungoverned and diasporic globalization of the later nineteenth century. External boundaries were strengthened at the same time as pressures for internal inclusion intensified. This was an era when all margins were dangerous. During the inter-war depression, flows of labour were more tightly regulated; movement was often stilled, though not reversed. The ethnic division of labour tightened. The intermediary diasporic groups came under concerted and often violent assault. Many of the globally connected elites of the port cities suffered a decline in influence. So too did many of the paternalist figures who acted as brokers between rural societies and wider attachments: they had to compete with new standardizing forces, not least the multiple agencies of the modern government. A sense of universal neighbourliness became harder to sustain. Small ethnicities were devoured by big nations. The wider forces of globalization may not have ebbed, but they proceeded in tandem with the drive to cover the globe with nation states that often presumed an ethnic and cultural homogeneity that had never existed and was against the grain of the global order of earlier eras. The goal of Islamic universalism was sacrificed to that of nation statehood. The passport emerged as an international motif of many of these changes: non-authorized movement became a crime, and a new category of human being was created – the stateless person. This revolution in identification became the property of the international system as a whole, but it needed to be reinforced by the nation state.[91] The inter-war period represented the end of *fin de siècle* globalism and the beginning of *la tyrannie du national*.[92]

Yet what is also striking is not what was lost, but what survived. These globalist currents would never be entirely extinguished, and would resurface at crucial points, especially in periods of challenge to the international order. The embracing of new media raced ahead of imperial controls on it. In the Dutch East Indies, radio became both a metaphor and a tool for the revival of a more inclusive kind of nationalism of shifting registers; the popular music of the *kroncong* became a new lingua franca, the microphone a new 'exemplary centre'.[93] In contemporary Indonesia, often taken as a miracle of integration through language standardization, the very events that promoted this also encouraged the *bahasa gadho-gadho*, the 'language salad' of code-switching.[94]

We see echoes of this elsewhere. The traders and brokers, preachers and teachers of earlier globalizations survive. Although the needs of the nation state superintended the rise of post-colonial globalization after 1950, the nation state could not escape the pressures of more trans-national forces, nor could it live without them. There had been in 1918–21, and was again in 1945–6, a sense of other global possibilities. Some observers spoke of the global shifts of 1989–93 as another such moment.[95] This was perhaps illusory. But to examine more deeply the debates of an earlier globalization, the ways in which diasporic networks mediated pivotally between trans-national, colonial and local political identities in these years, might take us a lot closer to more comparative histories of the experience of and responses to past globalization. It might also bring us a little closer to understanding some of the constraints and opportunities of the present. However, despite the evocative language of the Havana Summit, the prospects for empowerment at the outset of the present century may be less promising than at the outset of the last.

Notes and References

1 Dr Mahathir Muhamad,'Speech at the South Summit, Havana, 12 April 2000', http://www.smpke.jpm.my/pm/speeches-info.html.
2 Dr Fidel Castro Ruz, 'Speech during the Closing Session of the South Summit, 14 April, 2000', http://www.g77.org/summit/summit.htm.
3 Mahathir, 'Declaration of the South Summit', 12 April 2000.
4 A.G. Hopkins explores these issues more fully in his essay, 'The History of Globalization – and the Globalization of History?', in this volume.
5 For 'cosmoplastic' see Ronald Hyam, *Britain's Imperial Century* (2nd edn., London, 1993), p. 98.
6 This is elaborated by A.G. Hopkins in his essay, 'Globalization with and without Empires: From Bali to Labrador', in this volume.
7 Robert M. Pike, 'National Interest and Imperial Yearnings: Empire Communications and Canada's Role in Establishing the Imperial Penny Post', *Journal of Imperial and Commonwealth History*, 26 (1998), pp. 22–48.
8 James Bryce, 'The Roman Empire and the British Empire in India', in Bryce, *Studies in History and Jurisprudence* (Oxford, 1901), vol. I, pp. 1–84.
9 Timothy Mitchell, *Colonising Egypt* (Cambridge, 1988); Thongchai Winichakul, *Siam Mapped: A History of the Geobody of a Nation* (Honolulu, 1994). See also Matthew H. Edney, *Mapping an Empire: The Geographical Construction of British India, 1765–1843* (Chicago, 1997).
10 Marshall G.S. Hodgson, *Rethinking World History: Essays on Europe, Islam and World History* (Cambridge, 1993); elaborated by Jerry H. Bentley, 'Hemispheric Integration, 500–1500 CE', *Journal of World History*, 9 (1998), pp. 237–54. But see especially the essay by C.A. Bayly in this volume.
11 Terence Ranger, 'The Invention of Tradition in Colonial Africa', in Eric Hobsbawm and Terence Ranger (eds.), *The Invention of Tradition* (Cambridge, 1983), pp. 211–62, citing John Iliffe, *A Modern History of Tanganyika* (Cambridge, 1979), p. 100.

12 For example, Pamela G. Price, *Kingship and Political Practice in Colonial India* (Cambridge, 1996); John Pemberton, *On the Subject of 'Java'* (Ithaca, 1994).

13 Jane Drakard, *A Kingdom of Words: Language and Power in Sumatra* (Oxford, 1999); Brinkley Messick, *The Calligraphic State: Textual Domination and History in a Muslim Society* (Berkeley, 1993), a study of the Yemen; Anthony Milner, 'Islam and the Muslim State', in M.B. Hooker (ed.), *Islam in Southeast Asia* (Leiden, 1983), pp. 23–49.

14 Francis Robinson, 'The British Empire and the Muslim World', in Judith M. Brown and Wm. Roger Louis (eds.), *The Oxford History of the British Empire. Vol. IV: The Twentieth Century* (Oxford, 1999), pp. 398–420. See also the overview of the Islamic world by Amira Bennison in this volume.

15 Anthony Reid, 'Nineteenth-Century Pan-Islam in Indonesia and Malaysia', *Journal of Asian History*, 26 (1967), pp. 267–83; Ulrike Freitag and William G. Clarence-Smith (eds.), *Hadhrami Traders, Scholars and Statesmen in the Indian Ocean, 1750s–1960s* (Leiden, 1997).

16 Shimizu Hiroshi and Hirakawa Hitoshi, *Japan and Singapore and the World Economy: Japan's Economic Advance into Singapore, 1870–1965* (London, 1999); Barbara Watson Andaya, 'From Rum to Tokyo: The Search for Anticolonial Allies by the Rulers of Riau, 1899–1914', *Indonesia*, 24 (1977), pp. 123–56; Michael F. Laffan, 'Watan and Negri: Mustafa Kamil's "Rising Sun" in the Malay World', *Indonesia Circle*, 69 (1996), pp. 156–75.

17 Paul F. Hooper, *Elusive Destiny: The Internationalist Movement in Modern Hawaii* (Honolulu, 1980), pp. 43–64.

18 Leonard Y. Andaya, 'A History of Trade in the Sea of Melayu', *Itinerario*, 24 (2000), pp. 87–110; O.W. Wolters, 'Southeast Asia as a Southeast Asian Field of Study', *Indonesia* (1996), pp. 1–17. On a similar theme, but emphasizing the 1870–1940 period, see Jan Aart Scholte, 'Identifying Indonesia', in Michael Hitchcock and Victor T. King (eds.), *Images of Malay-Indonesian Identity* (Kuala Lumpur, 1997), pp. 21–44.

19 Adrian Vickers, 'Modernity and Being *Moderen*: An Introduction', in Vickers (ed.), *Being Modern in Bali: Image and Change* (Cornell, 1995), pp. 7–8.

20 Wang Gungwu, 'Migration and its Enemies', in Bruce Mazlish and Ralph Buultjens (eds.), *Conceptualizing Global History* (Boulder, 1993), pp. 131–51.

21 It is interesting to compare accounts of Senegal to the Malay world. See Wang Gungwu, 'Migration Patterns in History: Malaysia and the Region', *Journal of the Malaysian Branch of the Royal Asiatic Society*, 58 (1985), 43–57; François Manchuelle, *Willing Migrants: Soninke Labor Diasporas, 1848–1960* (Athens, Ohio, 1997), pp. 38–40.

22 This theme is explored by William R. Roff, 'Islamic Movements: One or Many?', in Roff (ed.), *Islam and the Political Economy of Meaning: Comparative Studies of Muslim Discourse* (London, 1987), pp. 31–52.

23 Martin van Bruinessen, 'The Origins and Development of the Sufi Order ('Tarekat)', *Studia Islamika*, 1 (1994), pp. 1–23. On the *hajj*, see the excellent unpublished study by Mary Byrne McDonnell, 'The Conduct of the *Hajj* from Malaysia and its Socio-Economic Impact on Malay Society: A Descriptive and Analytical study, 1860–1981' (Columbia University, Ph.D. thesis, 1986), especially chs. 1–2; Scholte, 'Identifying Indonesia', p. 25.

24 Dale F. Eickman and James Piscatori, 'Social Theory in the Study of Muslim Societies', in Eickman and Piscatori (eds.), *Muslim Travellers: Pilgrimage and*

Migration and the Religious Imagination (London, 1990), pp. 3–25. See also Amira Bennison's essay in this volume.

25 Christopher Baker, 'Economic Reorganisation and the Slump in South and Southeast Asia', *Comparative Studies in Society and History*, 18 (1981), pp. 325–49.

26 This process is discussed by Richard Drayton in this volume.

27 Emmanuel Akyeampong, 'Africans in the Diaspora: The Diaspora and Africa', *African Affairs*, 99 (2000), pp. 183–215; Bridget Brereton, 'The Other Crossing: Asian Migrants in the Caribbean: A Review Essay', *Journal of Caribbean History*, 28 (1994), pp. 99–122.

28 Hugh Tinker, *A New System of Slavery: The Export of Indian Labour Overseas, 1830–1920* (London, 1974); David Northrup, *Indentured Labour in the Age of Imperialism, 1834–1922* (Cambridge, 1995).

29 Wang Tai Peng, *The Origins of the Chinese Kongsi* (Petaling Jaya, 1994); Carl A. Trocki, *Opium and Empire: Chinese Society in Colonial Singapore, 1800–1910* (Ithaca, 1990).

30 Manchuelle, *Willing Migrants*, pp. 144–5.

31 On the colonial state, see James C. Scott, *The Moral Economy of the Peasant: Rebellion and Subsistence in South-east Asia* (New Haven, 1976); for the Malay Reservations, See Paul H. Kratoska, 'Rice Cultivation and the Ethnic Division of Labour in British Malaya', *Comparative Studies in Society and History*, 24 (1982), pp. 280–314.

32 Alan Takeo Mariyuma, *Imingaisha: Japanese Emigration Companies and Hawaii, 1894–1908* (Honolulu, 1985), pp. 142–56.

33 Janet Abu-Lugord, 'Tale of Two Cities: The Origins of Modern Cairo', *Comparative Studies in Society and History*, 7 (1964–5), pp. 427–57; Kenneth J. Perkins, *Port Sudan: The Evolution of a Colonial City* (Boulder, Colorado, 1993). For a general survey, see Robert Ross and G.J. Telkamp (eds.), *Colonial Cities: Essays on Urbanism in a Colonial Context* (Dordrecht, 1985), which emphasizes, erroneously, their 'newness', p. 20.

34 Susan Bayly, 'The Evolution of Colonial Cultures: Nineteenth-Century Asia', in Andrew Porter (ed.), *The Oxford History of the British Empire. Volume III: The Nineteenth Century* (Oxford, 1999), pp. 447–69.

35 T.N. Harper, 'Globalism and the Pursuit of Authenticity: The Making of a Diasporic Public Sphere in Singapore', *Sojourn*, 12 (1997), pp. 261–92.

36 Peter van der Veer, 'Introduction: The Diasporic Imagination', in van der Veer (ed.), *Nation and Migration: The Politics of Space in the South-Asian Diaspora* (Philadelphia, 1995), p. 6.

37 For example, see the statements by James Clifford, 'Diasporas', *Cultural Anthropology*, 9 (1994), pp. 302–37, and Arjun Appadurai, 'Global Ethnoscapes: Notes and Queries for a Transnational Anthropology', in Richard G. Fox (ed.), *Recapturing Anthropology: Working in the Present* (Santa Fé, 1991), pp. 191–210.

38 In writing this section I have greatly benefited from Adam Mckeown's excellent review, 'Conceptualising Chinese Diasporas, 1842–1949', *Journal of Asian Studies*, 58 (1999), pp. 306–37. See also Akyeampong, 'Africans in the Diaspora'.

39 Lim Boon Keng, *The Great War from a Confucian Point of View* (Singapore, 1917), p. 115.

40 Aihwa Ong, *Flexible Citizenship: The Cultural Logics of Transnationality* (Durham, NC, 1999).

41 Jürgen Rudolph, *Reconstructing Identities: A Social History of the Babas in Singapore* (Aldershot, 1998), pp. 379–440.

42 Mckeown, 'Conceptualizing Chinese Diasporas'.

43 See in particular, J. Clyde Mitchell (ed.), *Social Networks in Urban Situations: Analyses of Personal Relationships in Central-African Towns* (Manchester, 1969), recently deployed by Justin Willis, *Mombasa, the Swahili and the Making of the Miji Kenda* (Oxford, 1993), pp. 5–7.

44 Abner Cohen, 'Cultural Strategies in the Organization of Trading Diasporas', in Claude Meillassoux (ed.), *The Development of Indigenous Trade and Markets in West Africa* (Oxford, 1971), pp. 266–78.

45 For this last phenomenon, see C. Baura Yamba, *Permanent Pilgrims: The Role of Pilgrimage in the Lives of West-African Muslims in the Sudan* (Edinburgh, 1995).

46 There have been recent calls for the study of language as a tool of world history. However, this seems to be directed principally at charting the course of the 'linguistic imperialism' of the West, rather than the ecumene I am describing. See Frances Karttunen and Alfred W. Crosby, 'Language Death, Language Genesis and World History', *Journal of World History*, 6 (1995), pp. 157–74. For a practical discussion of sources in a colonial context, see Jeff Seigel, *Language Contact in a Plantation Environment: A Sociolinguistic History of Fiji* (Cambridge, 1987).

47 Peter Burke, 'Introduction', in Burke and Roy Porter (eds.), *Languages and Jargons: Contributions to a Social History of Language* (Cambridge, 1995), pp. 1–21.

48 Keith Whinnon, 'Lingua Franca: Historical Problems'; Albert Valdman (ed.), *Pidgin and Creole Linguistics* (Bloomington, 1977), pp. 295–310; William J. Samarin, 'Lingua Francas of the World', in Joshua A Fishman (ed.), *Readings in the Sociology of Language* (The Hague, 1968), pp. 660–72; and the exercise in linguistic archaeology by J.E. Wansbrough, *Lingua Franca and the Mediterranean* (Richmond, 1996).

49 H.M.J. Maier, 'From Heteroglossia to Polyglossia: The Creation of Malay and Dutch in the Indies', *Indonesia*, 56 (1993), pp. 37–65.

50 Willis, *Mombasa*; Wilfred Whitely, *Swahili: The Rise of a National Language* (London, 1969); Derek Nurse and Thomas Spear, *The Swahili: Reconstructing the History and Language of an African Society, 800–1500* (Pennsylvania, 1985).

51 Johnnes Fabian (ed. and trans.), *History from Below: 'The Vocabulary of Elizabethville' by André Yar. Text Translations and Interpretative Essay* (Amsterdam, 1990), preface and p. 129.

52 On the study of code-switching, see Lesley Milroy and Pieter Muysken, 'Introduction: Code-switching and Bilingualism Research', in Milroy and Muysken (eds.), *One Speaker, Two Languages: Cross-disciplinary Research on Code-switching* (Cambridge, 1995), pp. 1–14. For its historical applications, see J. Joseph Errington, *Shifting Languages: Interaction and Identity in Javanese Indonesia* (Cambridge, 1998), pp. 10, 187–91.

53 M.E. Krupp Dabaku, *Korle Meets the Sea: A Sociolinguistic History of Accra* (New York and Oxford, 1997).

54 David Prochaska, *Making Algeria French: Colonialism in Bône, 1870–1920* (Cambridge, 1990), pp. 224–32; Emanuel Sivan, 'Colonialism and Popular Culture in Algeria', *Journal of Contemporary History*, 14 (1979), pp. 21–54.

55 Christopher R. King, 'Images of Virtue and Vice: The Hindu-Urdu Controversy in Two Nineteenth-Century Hindi Plays', in Kenneth W. Jones (ed.), *Religious Controversy in British India: Dialogues in South-Asian Languages* (Albany, NY, 1992), pp. 123–48.

56 *Pace* Benedict Anderson, *Imagined Communities: Reflections on the Origins and Spread of Nationalism* (London, 1991).

57 Adrian Vickers, '"Malay Identity": Modernity, Invented Tradition, and Forms of Knowledge', *Review of Indonesian and Malaya Affairs*, 31 (1997), pp. 173–212.

58 Ian Proudfoot, *Early Malay Printed Books: A Provisional Account of Materials Published in the Singapore–Malaysia Area up to 1920, Noting Holdings in Major Public Collections* (Kuala Lumpur, 1993), Introduction; Tan Chee-Beng, 'Baba Chinese Publications in Romanized Malay', *Journal of Asian and African Studies*, 22 (1981), pp. 158–93; Claudine Salmon, *Literature in Malay by the Chinese of Indonesia: A Provisional Annotated Bibliography* (Paris, 1981), p. 16.

59 Heather Sutherland, 'Kerontjong and Komedi Stamboul: Examples of Popular Music and Theatre in Colonial Indonesia', *Jernal Sejarah*, 11 (1972/3), pp. 41–8; Vickers, *Being Modern*, pp. 19–22.

60 Johan Heilbron, 'Towards a Sociology of Translation: Book Translations as a Cultural World-System', *European Journal of Social Theory*, 2 (1999), pp. 429–44.

61 Lawrence Venuti, *The Translator's Invisibility: A History of Translation* (London, 1995), pp. 20–6.

62 David Pollard, 'Introduction', in Pollard (ed.), *Translation and Creation: Readings of Western Literature in Early Modern China, 1840–1918* (Amsterdam, 1998), pp. 5–23; Salmon, *Literature in Malay*, p. 31.

63 Vanamala Viswantha and Sherry Simon, 'Shifting Goods of Exchange: B.M. Srikantaiah and Kannada Translation', in Susan Bassnett and Harish Trivedi (eds.), *Post-colonial Translation: Theory and Practice* (London, 1999), pp. 162–81.

64 James T. Siegel, *Fetish, Recognition, Revolution* (Princeton, NJ, 1997).

65 'Volapük', *Encyclopedia Britannica* (1911),Vol. 28, p. 178.

66 E. James Lieberman, 'Esperanto and Transnational Identity: The Case of Dr Zamenhof', *International Journal of the Sociology of Language*, 20 (1979), pp. 89–107.

67 John Edwards, *Multilingualism* (London, 1995), p. 45.

68 Kenneth Searight, *Sona: An Auxiliary Neutral Language* (London, 1935), p. 12.

69 Mario Yaguello, *Lunatic Lovers of Language: Imagining Languages and their Inventors* (London, 1991), pp. 67–79; Elliot R. Goodman, 'World State and World Language', in Fishman (ed.), *Readings in the Sociology of Language*, pp. 717–36.

70 John Willinsky, *Empire of Words: The Reign of the OED* (Princeton, NJ, 1994), p. 13; *pace* Alistair Pennycook, *English and the Discourse of Colonialism* (London, 1998).

71 Tom McArthur, *The English Languages* (Cambridge, 1998), pp. 5–38.

72 C.K. Ogden, *Debabelization* (London, 1931).

73 For example, T.N. Harper, *The End of Empire and the Making of Malaya* (Cambridge, 1999), ch. 7.

74 Katherine Moore, 'The Pan-Britannic Festival', in J.A. Mangan (ed.), *Pleasure, Profit and Proselytism: British Culture and Sport at Home and Abroad, 1700–1914* (London, 1988), p. 144.

75 Edward A. Freeman, 'The Physical and Political Bases of National Unity', in Arthur Silva White (ed.), *Britannic Confederation* (London, 1892), pp. 31–56.

76 Hooper, *Elusive Destiny*, pp. 65–104. See also Eileen H. Tamara, *Americanization, Acculturation, and Ethnic Identity: The Nisei Generation in Hawaii* (Urbana and Chicago, 1994), especially pp. 53–64. For a contemporary reading of these themes, see Rob Wilson, *Reimagining the American Pacific: From South Pacific to Bamboo Ridge and Beyond* (Durham, NC, 2000).

77 For example, Ph.D. research by Mark R. Frost of the History Faculty, Cambridge.

78 Harper, 'Globalism and the Pursuit of Authenticity'.

79 One of the most comprehensive listings of these gatherings is Gabriele Schirbel,

Struckturen des Internationalismus: First Universal Races Congress, London 1911, 2 vols. (London, 1990).

80 Takashi Shiraishi, *An Age in Motion: Popular Radicalism in Java, 1912–26* (Ithaca, 1990).

81 Roff, 'Islamic Movements'; Anthony Milner, *The Invention of Politics in Colonial Malaya* (Cambridge, 1995).

82 Again this takes us into classic debates on Robert Redfield's notion of 'Great' and 'Little' traditions: Robert Redfield, *Peasant Society and Culture: An Anthropological Approach to Civilization* (Chicago, 1956), especially pp. 69–72. Explorations of the local anthropology of Islam are very suggestive in this regard; for Southeast Asia, see John R. Bowen, *Muslims Through Discourse: Religion and Ritual in Gayo Society* (Princeton, 1993); for the Swahili world, Michael Lambek, 'Certain Knowledge, Contestable Authority: Power and Practice on the Islamic Periphery', *American Ethnologist*, 17 (1990), pp. 23–40. On the sermon, see Richard T. Antoun, *Muslim Preacher in the Modern World* (Princeton, 1989); Patrick D. Gaffney, 'Authority and the Mosque in Upper Egypt: The Islamic Preacher as Image and Actor', in Roff (ed.), *Islam and the Political Economy of Meaning*, pp. 199–225.

83 See the stimulating critique by John D. Kelly, 'Time and the Global: Against the Homogeneous, Empty Communities in Contemporary Social Theory', *Development and Social Change*, 29 (1998), pp. 839–71.

84 Jeffrey G. Williamson, 'Globalization, Convergence and History', *Journal of Economic History*, 56 (1996), pp. 277–306.

85 Paul Hirst and Grahame Thompson, *Globalization in Question: The International Economy and the Possibilities of Governance* (Cambridge, 1996), pp. 18–31.

86 John F. Hutchinson, 'Disasters and the International Order: Earthquakes, Humanitarians and the Ciraolo Project', *International History Review*, 22 (2000), pp. 1–36.

87 For European reactions to Islam, see Jacob M. Landau, *The Politics of Pan-Islam: Ideology and Organization* (Oxford, 1990).

88 Gary Y. Okihiro, *Cane Fires: The Anti-Japanese Movement in Hawaii, 1865–1945* (Philadelphia, 1991).

89 Tan Melaka, *From Jail to Jail*, translated, edited and introduced by Helen Jarvis, 3 vols. (Athens, Ohio, 1990).

90 Hendrik M.J. Maier, 'Forms of Censorship in the Dutch Indies: The Marginalisation of Chinese-Malay literature', *Indonesia*, 51 (1991), pp. 67–82.

91 John Torpey, *The Invention of the Passport: Surveillance, Citizenship and the State* (Cambridge, 2000).

92 Philip Noiriel, cited in Peter Wagner, *A Sociology of Modernity: Liberty and Discipline* (London, 1994), p. 90.

93 R. Mrázek, 'Let Us Become Radio Mechanics', *Comparative Studies in Society and History*, 39 (1997), pp. 3–33.

94 Errington, *Shifting Languages*, p. 81. It has also provoked the standardization of rival tongues, see Nancy J. Smith Hefner, 'A Social History of Language in Highland East Java', *Journal of Asian Studies*, 48 (1989), pp. 257–71.

95 Jarl Simensen, 'Democracy and Globalization: Nineteen Eighty-Nine and the "Third Wave"', *Journal of World History*, 10 (1999), pp. 391–411.

HANS VAN DE VEN

The Onrush of Modern Globalization in China

A British missionary in 1908 described the changes he believed Beijing had undergone in the previous quarter of a century as follows:

> Now that I am back in the capital, one cannot help contrasting the year 1883 [when he first arrived in China] with this year. It is a new city. Government colleges and schools abound now, having replaced the old style of school house and teaching. Macadamised roads have followed the old mud ruts, the official bureaux are built on foreign models, police guard the streets, and old rush lights are being substituted by electric lights. The open sewers have been done away with, and water pipes are being laid down to convey water to the homes of the people. My first journey from Beijing to Tientsin took 10 days by boat . . . now a few hours by rail. Then the nearest telegraph office was 80 miles away, now it is at our doors, and the telephone service added. We had to travel to the port for all the silver used by us – a journey of four days – but now palatial banks adorn the city.[1]

What this missionary was describing was the effects of one episode in the history of globalization on China's capital. Banks, railways, the telegraph, the telephone and improved roads all testified to the acceleration in the 'velocity of exchanges' in China's trade with the outside world and the resulting 'time–space compression'.[2] Its effects not only were inscribed in China's urban landscape, but reached beyond, as railroads and steam vessels linked the hinterland with the great trading centres on China's coast and along the Yangtze River. In cities such as Tientsin, Shanghai, Wuhan, Mukden, Dairen and Hong Kong, very similar transformations were taking place.

A traveller who went to China for the first time in the late 1970s and returned today could have written a similar paragraph. In 1978, Deng Xiaoping instituted the policy of 'reform and opening to the outside'. First, a few Special Enterprise Zones were opened, agriculture was de-collectivized, and rural markets allowed to be re-established. 'Individual household enterprises' and 'township enterprises' began to operate as private enterprises producing for a free market, driving much of China's economic growth from the middle of the 1980s. Foreign investment was encouraged. The changes in the landscape have been phenomenal. Mao jackets have given way to business suits and in-your-face punk T-shirts. Office complexes, shopping malls, supermarkets and new apartment buildings have sprung up. Families have at least one television set, on which football, basketball, Chinese opera, and Hong Kong and Singapore soaps dominate. In the late 1980s conservatives such as Li Peng put the breaks on reform when inflation skyrocketed, the trade balance turned negative, and students began to protest. Following Deng Xiaoping's dramatic 'Tour of the South' during the Chinese New Year of 1992, the pace of economic reform and trade expansion accelerated to such an extent that Chinese wits now aver that the official ruling ideology of China, 'socialism with Chinese characteristics', should be understood as 'capitalism with Chinese characteristics', the Chinese characteristics now standing for reliance on family ties and corruption.

The challenge the historian faces is how to situate such episodes in the history of globalization. Histories making use of the concepts of imperialism and modernization have provided important insights into the first episode, while the second has been usefully constructed as the result of the collapse of communism and the victory of Anglo-Saxon capitalism. The question of why China failed to develop a modern capitalist economy, whereas European powers succeeded and built up overseas empires, continues to generate some of the best current scholarship on China, as the recent monograph by Kenneth Pomeranz demonstrates.[3]

The idea of globalization can add new dimensions to our understanding of such events. First, the focus on globalization is an opportunity to move away from constructing such events as Chinese reactions to economic and financial developments originating in Europe. While there can be no point in denying that European powers were the most active agents in pushing, even inflicting, modern globalization, nonetheless in Asia modern globalization also built on the networks and linkages that had emerged between China and Southeast Asia over many centuries, and which continued to thrive. Second, such a focus is an invitation not to think only in terms of territorial units. Both analyses of imperialism and studies aimed at answering the question of why European powers succeeded while China failed court the danger of holding to units of analysis, categories of thought, and dichotomies which emerged as a result of globalization and modernization. They stress economic issues and downplay other aspects of the history of globalization, such as military power and state finance, which were crucial to the establishment of armed trading empires. Finally, they, as well as the other approaches mentioned above, have tended to leave aside cultural issues, leaving them to historians of thought and more recently of nationalism. Yet the spread and domestication of the ideologies of globalization, both in Europe and elsewhere, as well as their impacts on life-styles should be regarded as important subjects in the study of globalization. Historical studies of globalization, as most essays in this volume suggest, are able to offer a useful new perspective on cultural issues.

This essay will focus on the first episode, the onrush of modern globalization in the late nineteenth and early twentieth centuries, and will begin by exploring the networks of social contacts, trade linkages and cultural practices that had linked China with Southeast Asia well before modern globalization took root. These linkages connected China to the larger world, making it a participant in the changes in demand and the flows of goods that made up proto-globalization. These networks remained important during the period of the onrush of modern globalization: connections with Southeast Asia and Japan and the thriving communities of overseas Chinese in these areas did not wither away but in fact expanded. Even if I am calling for a focus not on territorial units, in part to stress the complicity of many local social groups in the emergence of modern globalization, political entities were nonetheless important. I shall analyse how the Chinese state attempted, and failed, to preserve its control over revenue collection, territory and military power. Finally, in order to explore some of the cultural aspects of globalization, I shall discuss what surely is a key issue in the history of post-dynastic China, namely the difficulty of making the country cohere around a common national identity – an issue that is also discussed by Amira Bennison in this volume with respect to the Islamic world.

Toward a Multi-Centered Perspective: Archaic Mobilization during the Chinese Universal Empire

One possibility in constructing a narrative of the history of globalization is to begin with Vasco da Gama's travels, move on to the rise of European overseas empires and the plantation system, which, as Richard Drayton writes in this volume, 'put the world to work', and then discuss how European globalization was extended first to Southeast Asia and finally to China and Japan in the course of the nineteenth century. Casting the story this way ignores the linkages created between China, Southeast Asia and Japan well before the arrival of the West and the importance of these to the development of European empires, providing for instance the largest market for Spanish silver. As Joanna Waley-Cohen has pointed out, the idea that China was a closed country before the Opium Wars is an enduring myth with little basis in reality.[4] Both the Qing as well as the British nurtured it, each for their own reasons, but histories of globalization must move away from the Eurocentered-ness implicit in the 'expansion of Europe' model.

Two patterns may be distinguised in an ideal-typical way in the development of China's linkages with the South Seas areas, as the Chinese refer to Southeast Asia, and East Asia itself, especially Japan. One pattern derived from the ambitions of China's rulers, who sought to involve themselves in affairs abroad, seek recognition to their claim of universal rule, acquire the tribute that could provide lustre to their courts, adduce legitimacy to their claims, and add revenue to their treasuries. The other unofficial one was made up of merchants and traders developing trade links and building up communities of sojourners. They did so often in the wake of court-sanctioned trade and military expeditions, but then stayed on. The communities they developed and the networks they created proved enduring.

Migration from China to Southeast Asia has a long history, reaching back at least to the twelfth century. After northern China had been conquered by steppe people, the Song Dynasty moved south and established a new capital in 1127 at Hangzhou in the lower Yangtze River area. The Song built a strong navy, constructed harbours, and promoted overseas trade, linking waterborne domestic trade to overseas markets. Song junks were large: they had up to six masts and could carry up to 1,000 people. Because they followed the monsoons, sojourners stayed abroad, perhaps for a season and sometimes for years. They built up a trade in the luxury goods so desired by the Song court as well as by officials and rich merchants, who dressed in the best silk, consumed high quality rice, built beautiful gardens, and collected *objects d'art* while finding enjoyment in Song China's thriving urban leisure quarters.[5]

The dynamism of the Mongol Yuan dynasty led to the expansion of these activities in the thirteenth century. Mongol fleets, incorporating naval forces of the defeated Song, went on expeditions to Japan as well as to Java in 1293. The Japanese venture failed because of the damage caused by the kamikaze (sacred winds) storms while still at sea. The Java expedition of 20,000 men failed too, but the Chinese soldiers, pilots, seamen and shipbuilders who stayed behind may have played a role in Java's rise as a maritime power, with Chinese communities made up of the settlers and their descendants spreading through Indonesia as Java gained in power. At the same time, the Tai kingdom, which profited from the intervention of the Mongols, exchanged a series of missions with China from 1296 to 1323.

China's interactions with Southeast Asia reached its first high point in the first half of the fifteenth century. The Yongle Emperor (1403–25) declared his commitment to 'protect the weak and deter the strong' in Southeast Asia as a means of securing recognition for his claim to universal rulership. Nine Chinese imperial missions went to Champa, eight to Siam, six to Malacca, and ten to Java in the first 11 years of Yongle alone. A total of 70 missions visited Southeast Asian rulers during the first half of the fifteenth century, and 140 return missions were organized by states such as Brunei, Malacca and Ayudhya, which sought to use their Chinese contacts to gain the Ming's protection from regional challengers and of course to profit from the tribute trade. Between 1405 and 1433, Admiral Zheng He's famous fleet of 'treasure ships' reached as far as Ceylon, the Persian Gulf, and even the east African coast. For Chinese in Southeast Asia, this explosion of connections provided opportunities to make themselves indispensable to local rulers, both diplomatically and commercially. Strong Chinese commercial communities seem to have existed in Java and Sumatra in the fifteenth century.

In China, demand for products from South Seas areas, including pepper, cloves, medicine, aphrodisiacs, nutmeg and sappanwood, was considerable. In return for these products, tribute missions and Zheng He's ships carried Chinese manufactures, including textiles and handicraft products. This was also the period in which connections were forged between Southeast Asia and Japan, with Ryukyu becoming an important entrepôt. Chinese writing may have functioned as a lingua franca. Shared cultural and social practices between various Chinese settler communities may have facilitated the growth of the networks that made the intensification of trade and the extension of its reach possible.

However, the Ming's active promotion of trade and diplomatic ties with Southeast Asia ceased by 1450. China's northern neighbours had again become a serious threat. Disastrous defeats, during one of which the Emperor was taken prisoner, caused the Ming to relocate their capital from Nanjing to Beijing. All efforts went into defending the northern border. The Great Wall, as we now think of it, was built during this period.[6] In the sixteenth century, the growth of piracy and smuggling led to a ban on trade and emigration to Southeast Asia. The reach of China's trade, officially illegal, contracted to Vietnam, Siam and Champa, but did not disappear. In 1567 the ban was lifted, after people living along the south-China coast appealed against it. Both trade and migration took off once more, with many hundreds of junks sailing to the major ports of Southeast Asia.

Rapid changes in the economy of China itself intersected with equally important shifts in the larger world and led to a boom between 1570 and 1640. During the Ming, China's economy became increasingly commercialized, urban and rural handicraft industries spread, regional specialization intensified, and silver became used commonly in private trade as well as by the government.[7] Much of this commercialization was driven by developments in patterns of consumption. The rigid dress codes of the early Ming were ignored and a wide range of styles and fashions spread through the thriving cities of the Lower Yangtze and beyond. Refined rituals surrounded important life events such as birth, marriage, examination success and death. The maintenance of relations with relatives, potentially useful connections, and friends required large expenditures on banquets, theatre performances and gifts. The collection of calligraphy, paintings, books and precious objects, as well as the building of large family compounds and gardens, were important in articulating status and refinement. High-quality rice, exotic fruits, fashionable silk clothes, silver and gold housewares, rosewood furniture and gardens with rare plants marked out the prosperous elites of the late Ming, who were guided in their patterns of consumption by experts and handbooks.[8] One interesting new demand was that for ginseng from Manchuria. Its export was controlled by the Manchus and helped give them the financial resources to build up their military strength.[9]

European traders, including the Spanish, Portuguese and Dutch, arrived in Southeast Asia attracted by the spice trade. The value of silver was high in China, making risky journeys worth the effort. 20 per cent of silver bullion mined in Spanish America found its way to China via Manila. Flows of silver from elsewhere through other channels may have delivered to China an even greater amount of the world's silver production.[10] This was in part a form of arbitrage trade, as the ratio of exchange between gold and silver in China was 1:4, while in Europe it was 1:12.[11] But most important was the fact that the demand for silver bullion in China was high because of its importance to the domestic economy, where experiments with paper money had failed, and of lower production costs elsewhere.[12] Silver was also used to finance the export of silk and porcelain from China and spices from elsewhere in Asia to European markets, where the demand for these products was promoted by monopoly companies.[13]

If silver was an elite concern, the introduction of new food crops in China, such as maize, potatoes and peanuts from the Americas, was useful to all and made marginal lands productive. By the 1700s they had been widely accepted. Chinese diets changed and the demand for instance of sugar increased. Chinese merchants dominated the Asian sugar trade, transporting three times the amount of sugar as the Dutch in the seventeenth century and three times as much as the East India Company in the eighteenth century.[14] New Southeast Asian port cities emerged with sizeable Chinese communities: 4,000 to 5,000 Chinese lived in Manila; 2,000 in Patani (in Malaysia); and 3,000 in Banten (near Batavia on Java, known for its pepper). The other emerging cities of the time, including Hai On in south Vietnam and Phnom Penh, also had established overseas Chinese communities.

During the Ming-Qing transition in the middle of the seventeenth century, Chinese, fleeing from the Manchus or hoping to resist them, continued the Southeast Asian trade. Koxinga (Zheng Chenggong), claiming to fight the Manchus as a Ming loyalist, was the most famous of these influential refugees. Based in Xiamen (Amoy), he possessed a strong naval capacity and depended on a maritime network that reached to Nagasaki, Taiwan, Manila and south Vietnam. To destroy his base, the Qing ordered a ruthless clearing of the coast of Xiamen and its surrounding areas and invaded Taiwan to destroy Koxinga's position there. Activities such as those of Koxinga, and the withdrawal of European, Indian Muslim, and Japanese traders, meant that the influence of overseas Chinese in Southeast Asia did not decline during the Ming-Qing transition, but increased. In Java, the Philippines and Siam, Chinese ended up dominating internal and external trade.

These linkages became again important to China itself during the Qing's 'Prosperous Age' of the late eighteenth century. To undercut Koxinga, the Qing had imposed a ban on maritime trade in 1661, but had lifted it after he had been defeated. Many brought pressure on the Qing, arguing that the ban had cut off China from foreign supplies of silver and thereby contributed to the economic crisis of the time.[15] Again, silver from outside China, much of it now in the form of Mexican silver coins but also silver mined by Chinese in Assam, helped bring about prosperity, even if not for all.[16] China exported silk, tea, and porcelain to cater to broadening markets and a taste for things oriental in Europe. Similarly, opium consumption began to spread in China. As Zheng Yangwen has argued, during the Ming, the demand for opium, produced then in the South Seas and arriving in China as tribute, emerged first at court and among cultured elites, who saw it as a medicine and aphrodisiac and developed a refined culture of consumption around it.[17] In the first half of the eighteenth century, opium imports stood at about 200 piculs (a 'load' of about 60 kilograms) per year. By the 1770s, the total increased to 1,000 piculs per year. Between 1800 and 1820, opium imports grew to 3,000 to 4,000 piculs per year. Over the next three decades, they accelerated to 70,000 piculs per year, a level sustained between 1850 and 1890.[18] These figures suggest that important changes in demand and consumption took place in the late eighteenth and early nineteenth centuries, and that by the middle of the nineteenth century, a true mass market for opium had taken root. Opium became the mass commodity that linked India, Britain and China. It is perhaps useful to mention that, before Western medicine developed the capacity to purify it, 'proto-globalized' opium did not pack the punch that, for instance, heroin does.

The pattern of migration that accompanied these changes suggests that the interaction between various forms of globalization was complex and interdependent. The South Seas remained by far the most popular destination of sojourners.[19] In fact, the years between 1850 and 1900 formed a high point, when the numbers of sojourners going to the South Seas far outdistanced those that went to other areas. The onrush of modern globalization in the late nineteenth century was not just the story of the 'new imperialism', as the West thrust itself into China by making use of new technologies, such as steam, railroad and refrigeration, new modes of finance and banking, and new mass marketing techniques.[20] Modern globalization also built upon and even gave a new vitality to older forms of globalization. At the same time, the linkages with the global economy mattered. Following the abolition of the slave trade by European powers, Chinese migrants went to work as coolie labour on the plantations of the Caribbean. The gold rush and railroad-building projects in the USA drew many Chinese there in the second half of the nineteenth century. In the period 1901–25, sojourners went to work in the gold mines of South Africa or were hired by Britain and France during World War I to work as dock and transport workers as well as in industry.

The continued significance of established networks is suggested by the fact that most sojourners travelled through Hong Kong, Xiamen, and Shantou (Swatow), rather than through Shanghai and Tianjin.[21] Migrant networks, underpinning the world of overseas Chinese so well described by Tim Harper in this volume, depended on structures based on lineage and locality, with migrants usually following in the footsteps of kin who had earlier gone abroad. Strong connections with the home area remained in place, and many households developed a diversified labour investment portfolio: some sons worked in the fields and others became sojourning labourers away from home. In south China, with its single-lineage villages, migration was sometimes a village strategy. All males of a particular village might go abroad after training in language, bookkeeping and other skills in the village; those who stayed behind depended on remittances. Villages close by without migrant connections might have no workers abroad.[22]

The recruitment patterns of coolie labour, which in its heyday from the 1850s to the 1870s may have involved between three and seven million people, overlapped with migrant networks. Western merchants typically set up agencies, for instance in Hong Kong, Macao and Xiamen. Chinese brokers (*ketou*) relied on 'crimps', as the local labour bosses were known, who were paid per worker delivered. Crimps in turn depended on kinship networks, payment of gambling debts, deceit, the purchase of prisoners taken in the many local feuds, and outright kidnapping. The 'credit-ticketing' system financed labour migration. Migrant labourers arrived indebted for their journey. Upon arrival, this debt was transferred to employers, with lineage, native place, and secret societies ensuring that the debt was met.[23]

If one of Hong Kong's advantages was that it was free from the customary squeeze of Chinese officials, much more decisive was the fact that thousands of Chinese businesses specialized in the import–export trade (tea and Chinese curios for foreigners, and food for Chinese abroad), the sending of letters back and forth between home areas and Chinese communities abroad, and the handling of money transfers. The most 'competitive and profitable' of their activities was migration services, every aspect of which was 'commoditized'.[24] For a fee, steamer tickets, false identities, access to consuls, visas, satisfactory medical exams, citizenship certificates, proofs of kinship and smuggling opportunities were available. These businesses also provided credit.[25] As these functions suggest, Hong Kong was important not as an outpost of Empire, but because it housed the agencies that could get around the obstacles it threw up to control the movement of people and money. Lin Man-hoang has recently shown that tea merchants in Fujian took out a variety of nationalities – Japanese, French, British, and Dutch – which provided them with the protection of extraterritoriality as well as the low tariffs secured by the Unequal Treaties imposed upon China after the Opium Wars of 1839–42 and 1856–60.[26] The networks supported by these institutions and businesses have proved durable. The attention of the world was drawn to them when they sprang into action to save students fleeing China after the Tian'anmen Square incident of 1989, and later when boats carrying illegal immigrants, who had paid up to $40,000 per person, usually raised by family members already abroad, were apprehended by the US coast guard. A very recent and dramatic example occurred in 2000, when more than fifty Chinese migrants attempting to enter Britain were discovered dead in an air-tight lorry. The new wave of Chinese migration, which has taken place during the last two decades and transformed cities like Vancouver, could not have taken place without them. Hong Kong again functions as the key place making this migration possible. This fact alone suggests that the more recent phase in the globalization of China cannot just be read as the collapse of communist economic practices. Indeed, the evidence summarized here indicates that China itself was one centre in the multi-polar world of archaic and proto-modern globalization long before commentators in the Western world assigned claims of origin to themselves.

The Late Qing as the Heyday of Modern Globalization

Just when modern globalization began to take off in the West in the late eighteenth century, the prosperous days of the High Qing came to an end. If China in the eighteenth century, as in the late Ming, sustained flourishing centers of elite consumption and shared many of the processes that made up proto-globalization in Europe, modern globalization took root slowly. That type of globalization in China was arrested by a variety of factors, as some of the more recent work on China's interaction with the global economy has shown. Kenneth Pomeranz is surely right in suggesting that the complementarities between Old and New World markets were not present in the case of China's relations with Southeast Asia.[27] China's empire-building strategies were different too, focusing on central Asia to deal with the threat from the steppe. In the late eighteenth century, the White Lotus Rebellion (1796–1804) and uprisings by minorities, such as the Miao, required the transfer of unprecedented amounts of resources, both financial and otherwise, away from the coast toward the south-west.[28] Cultivation took place in small units and was not in the control of large companies that could centralize production, promote products and carry through management and technological changes.[29] Path dependency, too, was a factor. The Qing did not fear maritime trade as such, but historical experience, such as its difficulty in subduing Koxinga and coastal piracy, suggested that maritime trade linked with naval capacity was a dangerous combination, especially if armed trading organizations developed strong links with powerful groups in China itself. Hence the Qing's decision in the late eighteenth century to concentrate Western traders in Canton and restrict contact with them to merchants who were responsible to a government official. Finally, the first half of the nineteenth century was not only a period of major domestic upheavals. The inflow of silver that sustained the High Qing suddenly became a mere trickle. Accompanied by a fall in China's exports of tea and silk, and increasing silver outflows to pay for opum imports, the consequences for China's economy were grave.[30]

Modern globalization experienced its most expansive phase in China between the 1880s and World War I. The pathways had been established earlier, first by the demand in China for silver, and then by the development of mass markets for opium in China and tea in Europe, which led to the breakdown of both the East India Company's monopoly as well as the end of the Qing's canton system. After the end of the Taiping Rebellion (1850–64), foreign trade took off. Until recently it was thought that imperialism or the arrival of the West more generally in China had a negative effect on China's economy in the late Qing and early Republic by killing off the 'sprouts of capitalism', monopolizing finance and credit and destroying handicraft industries. More recent scholarship has overturned this picture. Hao Yen-p'ing argued that the introduction of new forms of money, the expansion of credit, new business practices and increased participation in world trade led to a 'commercial revolution' between the 1820s and 1880s.[31] Thomas Rawski, Loren Brandt and David Faure have argued that, contrary to popular perceptions, China's economy grew during the Republican period and that overall living standards improved, even if China remained desperately poor. Commercialization and regional specialization were spurred on by increased participation in world trade and innovations in transport and commercial and financial practices.[32]

All three scholars traced the origins of this period of growth to the late Qing, but did so in summary fashion in introductory chapters and focused on the Republican period after the 1911 Revolution itself. Yet, as Shizuya Nishimura has argued, the late Qing itself was probably the key period.[33] Between 1890 and 1910, he points out, exports grew by 4.6 per cent and imports by 3.4 per cent, while afterwards both decelerated to 1.9 per cent.[34] Data on the growth of China's international trade from 1865 to 1935 collected by China's Maritime Customs Service bears out the idea that the last two decades of the Qing formed the period of most rapid growth. However, it was not so much the fall of the Qing as the beginning of World War I that marked the end of this period of unparalleled growth in foreign trade. Moreover, as Rawski, Faure and Brandt suggested, the Chinese economy revived after the war and continued to grow until the mid 1930s, although not with the same speed as before World War I.[35]

An upsurge in international trade during the last decades of the Qing would make sense for reasons beyond the recovery after the Taiping Rebellion. First, data provided by the Maritime Customs Service are suggestive of significant changes in demand as well as supply. Beginning in the 1880s, the trade in tea and opium declined rapidly as a result of the spread of domestic opium cultivation in China, and, in the case of tea, the rise of demand for Indian tea as well as poor crops in China itself. Instead, the trade in 'sundry' products took off. Rice, raw cotton, cotton textiles, flour, tobacco products, kerosene and machinery became key import items. Rice came from Southeast Asia to the grain deficit areas of China, including the Lower Yangtze region; raw cotton was put out to households for spinning, while tobacco products and textiles met new demands for things Western.[36]

While silk continued to be a major export, the most important new development was the take-off in exports of 'muck and truck' items, such as beans, bean-cakes, cotton yarn, hides, skins, seeds, timber, bristles, straw, egg products, and minerals, including coal and iron ore.[37] As Chang Ning has argued, egg products gained importance because of the growing demand for bakery products in Britain; refrigeration and large steamships made it economically viable for China to service this demand in Britain. The same was true for chicken and meat products.[38] Industrialization in Japan created a growing demand for primary products from China there.

These products are all characteristic of modern industrialization and mass markets. In the end product, many of the original inputs had lost their shape, having been broken down into parts and then put back together into something different in a more or less industrialized process, and identified less by their place of production than by their brand names, even if that brand itself, as opposed to the ingredients of the product, was associated with a nation. The fact that the 'muck and truck' trade came to dominate is indicative itself of the fact that trade was now linked to mass markets rather than to wealthy elites requiring rare products from clearly identifiable exotic places.

An important new institution that not only recorded this trade but also helped to make it possible was the Imperial Maritime Customs Service. The Customs Service was set up by British initiative during the Taiping Rebellion in 1854 to collect the trade duties stipulated in the Treaty of Nanjing when China's *taotais* – superintendents of trade – found it difficult to do so themselves, and Western consuls, legally responsible for their countrymen because of extraterritoriality, were loath to assume the responsibility. The Customs Service developed into a large bureaucracy under Chinese control but with an international, if predominantly British, staff. It facilitated China's globalization, in good Victorian fashion, by drawing up rules applicable to goods which were to be obeyed by all regardless of status and connections and which were enforced through an efficient and centralized bureaucracy differentiated from local society. It provided the information that merchants needed to seek out commercial opportunities in its numerous and regular publications available to the public. The trade statistics published by the Imperial Maritime Customs Service also defined the goods that were traded in purely monetary terms, eliding the social and cultural contexts from which they came and thus turning them into pure commodities. It was monetary profit, rather than social or cultural capital, that mattered, or so at least the Customs Service's publications seemed to advertise. The head of the Customs Service, Robert Hart, also served as a missionary of the modern nation, 'lecturing the government from our superior standpoint', as he wrote, on how to set up the fiscal, communications, bureaucratic, and military infrastructures that were to make China into a well-governed, prosperous and civilized modern nation.[39] He accepted that this civilizing mission would lead to the eventual Chinese take-over of the institutions he nurtured so patiently but also with the faith that this was a development that would lead to prosperity and peace.

If changes in demand and institutions were important for the take-off of globalization in the last decades of the Qing, so were several other developments. A railway-building boom in the 1880s and 1890s linked agricultural areas in the hinterland to the expanding global economy, facilitating changes in the composition of China's international trade.[40] The expansion of steam-shipping, the laying of telegraph cables, and the use of refrigeration all helped to accelerate China's trade. The increase in the money supply, caused especially by the introduction of foreign currencies, had a similar effect. In 1910, 1.08 billion foreign silver dollars circulated in China; only 200 million silver dollars were minted in China itself.[41] The expansion of credit, made possible by the symbiotic relation between domestic banks (*qianzhuang*) and foreign banks, such as the Hong Kong and Shanghai Bank, which extended their presence in China during this period,[42] naturally also facilitated foreign trade, although credit remained more expensive in China than in the West.[43]

Without heavy Chinese investment and participation in Western trading and financial institutions, the expansion of foreign trade would not have been possible. Foreign enterprises often functioned like shell companies. Compradors and Chinese investors were crucial to their success.[44] Banks in Shanghai relied not only on their compradors for information on China's markets and investment but could not have operated without the commercial and financial connections of the domestic banks.[45]

The data collected by the Customs Service not only illustrate important changes in demand, but also make clear important shifts in the regional distribution of China's foreign trade. The trade between China and east and Southeast Asia after 1900 rapidly ended Western supremacy, which was overstated in the Customs data because they excluded the junk trade from south China until 1887.[46] This development resulted from rapid industrialization in Japan as well as the effects of World War I, when the Western 'global economy' declined and when Germany found it difficult to continue its trade with China. From World War I until 1935 China's Asian trade was larger than its trade with the West.

Customs data show, unsurprisingly, that Japan became China's leading trade partner in east Asia from 1890, when it surpassed India. But they also show that China's trade with the South Seas grew rapidly during the same period. Although these areas lost ground to Japan from 1900 to 1920, they quickly caught up. Between 1920 and 1930, Japan's trade with China grew by somewhat less than 50 per cent, while that of the South Seas almost trebled, and in 1935, the South Seas' trade with China was more than 20 per cent higher than Japan's.[47]

The commercialization of everything during the late nineteenth and early twentieth centuries is nicely symbolized by Sun Yatsen's practice of selling bonds among overseas Chinese to finance his revolutionary enterprises. They promised a return of 1,000 per cent after the revolution succeeded.[48] However, the revolution proved to be a disastrous investment. Sun's provisional government was bankrupted by heavy military expenditure within half a year. On the other hand, foreign financial support for his opponent, Yuan Shikai, reaped handsome rewards. Yuan, bankrolled by Western states and banks, agreed that Maritime Customs and Salt Gabelle revenues would be used first to service China's debts to Western financial institutions, and presumably (though this is much murkier) Chinese investors in those institutions. Globalization had proceeded to the point where it helped shape the outcome of political conflict.[49] The changes wrought by the onrush of modern globalization ran deep and sometimes led to surprising turns. But even Sun's practice of selling bonds to finance revolution illustrated the interaction between modern and proto-modern globalization, as many of his investors came from Southeast Asia.

Globalization, State Finance and the Military

This brings us to the effect of modern globalization on the Chinese state, which I shall examine in this section by looking at public finance and the military. What happened in the late Qing and early Republic provides a cautionary tale for those who regard contemporary global capitalism as the panacea for world poverty and other world problems. If the disintegration of the unitary Chinese empire after two millennia was largely the result of domestic disturbances and dislocations, it was also hastened by modern globalization, which not only exported European conflicts to China, and led Japan to seek its own colonies on the Asian mainland almost as a fashion accessory, but also made China a client of Western financial interests.

To understand the situation from a Chinese perspective it is necessary first of all to describe the Qing military and financial institutions. The military was made up of two separate structures. The elite Banner forces of 200,000 to 250,000 troops were heavily concentrated in Beijing, along the Great Wall, in garrisons at key strategic areas, and in provincial capitals. The Green Army of between 600,000 and 750,000 troops was dispersed in small units throughout the country. Up until 1850, regular military expenditure amounted to between 25 and 31 million *taels* (ounces) of silver. Campaign expenses, however, added considerably to these amounts. The campaign in Burma in 1767–9, for instance, cost about 13 million *taels*, the war against the Zunghars in 1771–6 between 60 and 70 million *taels*, the suppression of the White Lotus Rebellion between 150 and 200 million *taels*, and the war against the Taiping consumed even larger funds.[50]

The Qing's fiscal system was a decentralized one, with provincial treasuries being a key link. Provincial officials were responsible for tax collection in their jurisdictions, keeping up treasuries and submitting reports to Beijing, which then audited them and allocated funds. The tax revenues of the centre depended first of all on the land taxes, which brought in between 35 and 43 million *taels* annually.[51] Qing and early Republican policy aimed at controlling this tax despite its diminishing financial importance,[52] perhaps because the funds it raised were dedicated to making the 'regular' payments to the military, that is, standing costs but not incidental payments related to actual campaigns.[53] Also important to central finances were the sale of offices, bringing in 3 million in the late Qing, and merchant 'contributions', which were substantial, especially in times of crises.[54] Taxes on domestic trade and the sale of licences delivered five million *taels* annually.[55]

A substantial portion of taxation took place outside central supervision. In 1742, the Yongzheng Emperor allowed the imposition of a surtax on the land tax, which was partly remitted to Beijing and funded the 'honesty' bonuses that boosted official salaries. The bulk of this tax was retained locally and not reported to Beijing. Local officials also levied 'expenses' from local tax-payers for revenue collection, manipulated local exchange rates, and frequently made *ad hoc* levies (*tanpai*) to pay for specific projects or to deal with emergencies. In the late Qing, it has been estimated, two thirds of revenue collection took place 'informally'.

The creation of the Imperial Maritime Customs Service improved central revenues at first. The Service centralized the taxation of foreign trade and placed its revenues, rising from 5 million Treasury *taels* in 1861 to 35 million in 1910, at the disposal of Beijing. After the indemnities incurred during the Arrow War were paid off in 1866, revenues from this source helped pay for the upkeep of Banner and Green Standard forces; Zuo Zongtang's campaign to recover the Northwest between 1868 and 1873; the creation of arsenals and ship-building facilities in Shanghai, Fuzhou, Tianjin and Wuhan; the improvement of coastal and river defences, the latter especially important along the Yangtze; the upkeep of some of the semi-private armies that had emerged during the Taiping Rebellion; the creation of new armies; and lastly the acquisition of modern naval vessels.[56] Without the Customs revenue, the survival of the Qing until the 1911 Revolution would have been much more problematic.

Another new source of revenue, the *lijin* or transport taxes, was originally created during the crisis of the Taiping Rebellion. Local elites, under supervision of provincial officials, began to collect the tax on a variety of commodities to meet the cost of raising militia. Originally intended as a temporary measure, the tax proved useful and was not abolished after the Rebellion. As Susan Mann has shown, the idea that this was a local tax over which Beijing had no control is not entirely correct. By the end of the Qing, Beijing's share of the tax amounted to between 17 and 20 million *taels* annually and official approval was necessary for provinces to retain 'their' portion of the *lijin*, which in the case of Guangdong, for example, ranged between 30 and 80 per cent.[57] Even if this suggests that Beijing had more say about *lijin* disbursements than has been thought, it remains true, as Mann acknowledged, that 'much of the tax . . . was pocketed by functionaries and officials beginning at the sub-county level'.[58] According to Mann, estimates of this amount 'range as high as 40 per cent of the actual quotas reported to Beijing'.[59] Moreover, *lijin* revenues retained in the provinces declined only after the Sino–Japanese War of 1894–5 and the Boxer Uprising of 1900, when provinces were ordered to release *lijin* revenues to pay for the indemnities imposed upon China. The central government did not benefit from this semi-centralization of *lijin* revenues.[60]

The indemnities imposed on China were huge. The Japanese indemnity of 1895 amounted to 231 million *taels* and the Boxer indemnity to 450 million *taels* at a time when annual central revenue was around 80 million *taels* per year. Indemnity payments required one fourth of central revenue. Both the financing of the wars during the late Qing and the Japanese indemnity had forced the Qing to borrow heavily from British-dominated banks, such as the Shanghai and Hong Kong Banking Corporation, as well as banking consortiums with non-British banks in whose organization the British often assumed a key role. Such borrowing continued during subsequent crises, including the 1911 Revolution, when Yuan Shikai secured a £25 million re-organization loan from an international banking consortium that was put together with the help of the British Foreign Office.

The impact on China's state finance was serious. From the last decade of the Qing, between one third to one half of all central revenue was spent on servicing foreign debt.[61] From the Boxer Rebellion, indemnity payments and foreign debt service had first call on Customs revenues. From the 1911 Revolution, the Imperial Maritime Customs Service deposited the revenue that it collected in the Shanghai and Hong Kong Bank. Only the surplus was passed on to Beijing. After the 1911 Revolution, the International Banking Consortium agreed to the re-organization loan on condition that a new bureaucracy, much like the Maritime Customs Service, would be set up to administer the Salt Gabelle. The revenues it collected served as security for the new loans.

Financial shortages made the pursuit of military strengthening as well as other reforms difficult. After the Boxer Rebellion, the court in Beijing approved proposals for the creation of a German-style army of 36 divisions, something that until then it had resisted, despite the advice of Robert Hart and the German military adviser, von Hanneken, because it feared that such a force might be difficult to control and might end up in the hands of either a regional or central group seeking its overthrow, as indeed happened.[62]

Financial shortages, as well as the arms embargo imposed on China after the Boxer War, made it impossible to establish more than two divisions before the Russo–Japanese War of 1904–5, which was fought on Chinese territory. From then until the 1911 Revolution, the army expanded to eight full divisions and some 20 brigades. However, the upkeep of one division cost 1.5 to 2 million *taels*. Central revenues were not sufficient for the 25 to 36 million *taels* that the whole army required. As with indemnity payments, provinces were asked to make contributions. Most provinces, themselves facing shortages, were not able to meet the quotas they had been assigned and resisted to a greater or lesser degree. Tensions thus created contributed greatly to worsening central–provincial relations, which came to the fore during the 1911 Revolution. The dangerous expedient of stationing divisions in provinces and making provincial governments responsible for their upkeep helped create the basis of military fragmentation that characterized warlordism.[63] Efforts to reform the tax system and develop new sources of revenue failed. New sources of revenue never delivered more than 20 per cent of central revenue during the early Republic of Yuan Shikai. Throughout the Republican period, Customs revenue, the Salt Gabelle and borrowing continued to be the most important sources of central revenue. Debt service consumed 30 per cent of total revenue through most of this period.[64]

China's experience stands in clear contrast with Britain. In Britain the creation of excise and customs bureaucracies between 1688 and 1783 enabled the British state to tax capitalist agriculture and commerce, and to use these revenues to finance the National Debt, created in 1694. These measures were crucial in enabling Britain to build up its naval and military power. As Inspector General of the Maritime Customs Service, Robert Hart was influenced by the British model to a considerable degree and strove to bring about something similar in China, but did not succeed. The contrast with Japan in the late nineteenth century is also clear. During the Meiji Restoration, closely fought battles between the centre and regional powers led to the military ascendancy of the first. Central strength made radical land reform possible. In the 1870s, in a huge bureaucratic effort, all land was registered, regional differences in tax rates eliminated, and all assessments converted into payments based on productive capacity. These reforms restructured state–society relations, and ensured a steady, if diminishing, source of revenue to the central state. Because of its strength, the state was also able to centralize its fiscal bureaucracy and halt payments to special interest groups. In 1878, it ceased to pay stipends to the *samurai*, which until then consumed about a third of revenues. In contrast, Yuan Shikai failed in his attempt to register land and reform the land tax in 1915, when he turned to the Japanese model after foreign sources of borrowing dried up during World War I.[65] Nor was the Qing able to end payments to useless military groups, including the Banners and the Green Army. Some of these payments continued even after the 1911 Revolution.

Why China was unable to make the transition to a modern fiscal and military apparatus is a complicated question, requiring an examination of both long-term and short-term developments, and hence is well beyond the scope of this essay. However, I have brought up this issue in part to add a historical example to contemporary concerns about the impact of the global financial capitalism on poor states. I have also done so to stress the connection between weak state finances, military fragmentation and the brutalization of the public order. In China, in a context where the state lacked the resources to develop a strong military and keep control over it, let alone to fund a police force, the availability of cheap firearms produced by modern industries, as well as the enormous profits to be earned from mass markets in illegal but highly popular drugs, helped bring about warlordism and widespread banditry. Very similar conditions pertain in parts of Africa and the former Soviet Union today.

Modern globalization and nationalism

Ideas, of course, do not necessarily follow trade routes. Nonetheless, the period of the onrush of modern globalization in the late Qing and afterwards also saw the importation into China of its core ideologies and categories of thought. Yen Fu translated Western political thought and Lin Shu Western literature. Periodicals sprang up both in China and abroad, among communities of overseas Chinese in the South Seas and Japan, which reported on Western affairs and discussed the West and China in the new categories of politics, economics, society, culture, race and nation. Schools provided education into the ways of modern nationalism, if only for an elite few. The Maritime Customs Service promoted British systems of revenue collection, public borrowing, accounting and governance. Advertisements taught Western ways of consumption. Clubs, theatres, racecourses, bars, church organizations like the YMCA, and charities like the Red Cross provided new models of leisure and benevolent behaviour. As the culture of global capitalism spread, the Chinese began to nationalize it.

It is true that the contemporary Chinese state has assumed many of the features of the Western nation state.[66] It claims supreme authority in a clearly bounded territory, seeks to exclude other political entities from exerting power within China, and claims international legal sovereignty, denying it to other representatives of China, such as Taiwan. It issues passports to its citizens; its border controls check the passports of those who want to enter, and the Aids certificates of those who want to stay long term. There is a constitution which defines the rights of China's citizens and a National People's Congress formally elected by universal suffrage. It is not the Son of Heaven who is sovereign because of his exclusive contact with Heaven, but the Chinese people, defined in terms of ethnicity, descent, culture and geography. Time is no longer marked by reference to monarchs and dynasties, and, at least in dominant discourses, history is no longer portrayed as a fall from grace in ancient times into an imperfect present, but the emergence of a modern nation respected in the contemporary world.

And yet, even if radical proponents of 'smashing the Confucian shop' and radical Westernization have tended to dominate respected elite discourse from the 1920s until the 1970s, and if both the Nationalists and the Communists mobilized state power to discipline Chinese society and transform it into a modern nation, believing that they knew the future and the rest of China had to be instructed in it,[67] it is also true that both before this period and afterwards, important voices called for incorporating older philosophical and religious traditions in new conceptualizations of Chinese identities and the Chinese polity. Moreover, neither succeeded in developing the vision and institutions of a modern nation around which China could be made to cohere.

Let me first turn to the continuing echoes of the past, so clearly pointed out by Philip Kuhn recently.[68] In the middle of the nineteenth century, Wei Yuan, the noted Confucian statecraft thinker who rebelled against the tradition of moral speculation and insisted on careful evidence-based research into concrete public policy problems, called for a greater interest in Western affairs and the adoption of Western military methods. Responding to the crises of rebellion, corruption, political timidity and foreign threats, he did not accept that rule by the masses or the political enfranchisement of local communities could strengthen China's state. Instead, he continued to defend authoritarian government, which, he believed, should use its armies, tax collectors and courts with extreme toughness if the situation required, a view clearly shared by Taiping suppressors such as Zeng Guofan, who flattened Nanjing after dislodging the Taiping rebels from their capital. At the same time, Wei Yuan sought to reinvigorate the state by insisting that the Qing should permit policies to be discussed broadly, not just within the bureaucracy, but outside it, by those qualified to do so by virtue of their education and knowledge. He called on literati to abandon their distaste for practical affairs and again venture into pragmatic policy discussions, as of course he himself did. Wei would have had little problem with 'market socialism': he was perfectly comfortable with private businessmen running even government monopolies because they could do so efficiently, but strong government would need to protect the public good. He also would have understood the problems that China's leadership faces today, as it tries to develop ways to open up the political system in the wake of the disasters of the Great Leap Forward and the Cultural Revolution – which, it is believed, were made possible by the timidity of intellectuals and officials in failing to stand up to Mao Zedong – while at the same time preventing local interest groups, corrupt officials, and sects like the Falun Gong from undermining the socio-political order.

Kang Youwei is a more complex case. Following China's defeat in the Sino-Japanese War of 1894–5, Kang Youwei called for the adoption of Western representative institutions, the eradication of Manchu privileges, a clean-out of the bureaucracy, the inclusion of Western subjects into China's educational system, and much more vigorous resistance to outside aggressors. But he also proposed to make Confucianism into a national religion as expressing China's essential cultural identity and as a source of strength that could never be conquered by force of arms. According to Kang, cultural solidarity was needed precisely in a time of governmental breakdown and foreign aggression. He argued too that Confucianism had brought democracy, equality, freedom and the law to China two millennia before the Enlightenment and the French Revolution did so in Europe. Kang proposed that the Qing calendar should be replaced, arguing that Confucius's year of birth should be taken as year 1. Before the fall of the Qing, he supported the Qing Emperor, saw himself as a sage, called for moral reinvigoration, and sought a renewal of the bonds that should tie Emperor and subject together. Afterwards, he continued to believe in Confucian moral bonds and sets of personal obligations as a basis for the construction of a socio-political order that derived from China's past. Kang was willing to nationalize Confucianism, a step he regarded as being a regrettable necessity, and to articulate a new Chinese identity based on an essentialized version of it, arguing that this was the will of the people and the only way to save China.[69] At the same time, the past remained relevant for the present, as Chinese identities became construed in terms of loyalties less to a state than to a culture.

When the Qing did abolish the examination system and introduced a system of universal education, Western subjects such as science and mathematics were brought into the official curriculum. But the Confucian classics had to be studied too, because they contained the ingredients that made China unique. Following the 1911 Revolution, radical reformers such as Cai Yuanpei, who became Minister of Education, tried to do away with such trappings of the 'feudal and backward' past. He was opposed by a 'Confucianism movement' led by Kang Youwei and many others. As this movement gained support amongst some intellectuals but also officials and the military, the government of Yuan Shikai, at first reluctantly but then with an increasing and fateful stubbornness, tried to associate itself with it. This attempt at nationalizing Chinese culture ran foul of the criticism of the iconoclastic Westernizers of the May Fourth Movement who wanted to 'smash the Confucian shop'. This was important to its demise, but so were the humiliating imposition of Japan's 21 Demands during World War I and Yuan Shikai's attempt to make himself emperor, which went against his oath made at the time of his assumption of the presidency of the Republic. His elevation also required him to make his new status stick on the battlefield, which he failed to do.[70] The May Fourth vision of redemption through totalistic modernization then became dominant; later, the Communists tried to turn it into their foundation myth.[71]

Yet, the victory of the May Fourth Movement was not as complete as earlier historians of Chinese thought imagined. If conservative critical voices always remained present,[72] the issues of what precisely the modern nation was and what agency would seek its realization in China gave rise to a series of culture wars that tore China's educated elites apart and remained a core issue between Nationalists and Communists. From this perspective, the New Life Movement promoted by the Nationalists in the 1930s should not be read as a retrograde Nationalist effort to combine elements of Confucianism and fascism,[73] but as an attempt to evolve a new vision that combined Kang Youwei's call for the protection of China's cultural traditions, especially Confucianism, with the May Fourth's calls for democracy, modernity and science.[74]

The Nationalists set up a great many committees which went to work on such tasks as defining who could serve as China's culture heroes. Confucius came out as the greatest of them all. However, despite the argument put by Kang Youwei, Confucius was defined, in an attempt to modernize and Westernize him, not as religious but as a secular thinker, equal to Aristotle and Plato in the West. Other committees examined local religious cults in order to determine which had the sanction of ancient texts and therefore could be tolerated even in the age of secular modernity, because they expressed an authentic cultural essence, and which were perversions, created by cynics to hoodwink the Chinese people. Such committees also worked on reshaping China's calendar. In the end, a calendar was adopted based on the solar system. 1912 became year 1 as then the Republic was founded (and this remains the practice in Taiwan), but it also incorporated the lunar calendar. Holidays marked in the calendar commemorated dates and figures of the Nationalist revolution, but auspicious days and select traditional Chinese festivals were incorporated as well.[75] It was in fact Western merchants who had pioneered this kind of calendar to advertise their products, as Leo Ou-fan Lee has shown.[76] Rather than indicating the arrival of modern conceptions of linear time, as he believed, they are interesting for their attempt at articulating a vision of time which was Western and modern, but also incorporated a re-imagined Chinese past expressing a supposed Chinese identity, partly derived from the Nationalist revolution but also from the past. Modern time is linear and forward looking, but also multi-layered, combining the frictions and noise of the present with reflections on certain epochs and episodes of the past, as James Joyce showed in *Ulysses*.

The New Life Movement failed, of course, as would the Communist attempt to make a new culture stick during the Cultural Revolution, which attacked both the Chinese past as well as bourgeois modernity. Both the feudal past, including Confucius, and 'capitalist roaders' – those in the party of whom it was asserted that they were seeking the restoration of capitalism – were subjected to relentless attacks carried out by mass movements and in 'struggle sessions'. Instead, the Cultural Revolution tried to fix a highly militarized and romanticized revolutionary moment as an all-absorbing and eternal present. It was deeply paranoid, about the enemy within, but also about vestiges in the present of anything of the past or of bourgeois modernity.

China is a large and populous country, with a long history, a myriad of local traditions, and plenty of resources in local society to make local collective action possible. To orient these to the nation, however, proved difficult, both during the late empire as well as in the twentieth century. Qing officials sought to make distinctions between heterodox and orthodox cultural practices, suppressing the first and endorsing the latter, in the process often provoking rebellion. In the same way, during the twentieth century successive states defined groups in society as feudal, superstitious, exploitative, deviant, or certain individuals as 'evil gentry and local bullies', and sought to transform or suppress them as they were held to be obstacles to the emergence of a new disciplined, modern nation. One must of course resist temptations to romanticize such groups, as this was an age of much banditry and violence. However, not all were destructive or became so only when marginalized, and some 'local bullies' were probably energetic upstarts whose greatest fault was to have provoked local resentments.[77] China failed to evolve the structures and practices capable of orienting such groups to the nation – ranging from a calendar, national festivals and holidays, sports meetings, anniversaries and the opening of parliament to national hierarchies of church organizations, national professional bodies, representative institutions, and religious organizations. Here the fear that local interest groups might invade the public realm and that it was officialdom's task to protect the public may have played a role. That fear is echoed in China now by those, including not just the Communists themselves but also eminent intellectuals, who claim that the Party must protect the public order and that democracy could not yet be made to work in China because nasty local elements would exploit their local connections and wealth to corrupt state and party cadres to the great harm of the local populace. The popular press is full of stories of good cadres and the police protecting the public by breaking up conspiracies of such elements.

Conclusion

The analysis above has been an attempt at contextualizing a distinct period in the history of globalization in China, first of all by contrasting it to earlier forms of globalization and by discussing how such forms continued to echo through in later periods. The expansion and intensification of trade is of course a core issue, and I have discussed at some length the decades before World War I in order to rehabilitate this period, which was characterized by important changes in demand and consumption, as well as in financial institutions, communications structures, government and technology. I have also discussed the impact of the export of European rivalries, military power and financial interests, especially for China's military and financial health. Finally, I have touched on attempts to localize and nationalize globalization, suggesting that past political and cultural concerns remained relevant in the discourse of twentieth-century Chinese nationalism, but also pointing out that efforts to create a disciplined moral–cultural community around a single national identity have proved difficult.

This broad approach to the issue of globalization may help in situating the current phase of globalization. Maoism was an attempt to make manifest a Chinese form of communist globalization, or, as the Chinese Communists put it, 'socialism with Chinese characteristics'. Maoism failed to become a new civilization, like Stalinism in the Soviet Union, despite initial broad support, especially among a young generation of state and party cadres and at least some parts of the peasantry, because communist globalization did not deliver the goods, as capitalist countries in Asia so clearly demonstrated. People did not only want to be fed (which they were not during the Great Leap Forward), but also wanted attractive clothes, TVs, refrigerators, habitable homes and opportunities for tourism, entertainment and dining out.[78] Communist globalization failed also because the practices and structures Maoism offered for social and public intercourse were straightjackets. Many Chinese turned away in horror from the coercive aspects of this programme, which was also undermined from within, for instance by families squatting in work units.

As China opened up to the outside world after Deng Xiaoping seized power in 1978, the connections forged during earlier periods of globalization again became relevant. If contact with overseas Chinese had often been impossible in the first decades of the People's Republic, Deng encouraged it. Overseas Chinese, some of whom had their property returned or were offered payment of damages, went back to invest in their home areas. China's current economic growth is made possible not just by globalized capital seeking out opportunities around the globe, but also by the revitalization of networks of overseas Chinese that stretch back for many centuries. These connections are readily visible in popular culture, with music, films and religious traditions such as the Mazu Cult being not national in scope, but crossing political divides and binding together communities in China and Southeast Asia.

In the more moderate times that came after Mao Zedong's death, the relaxation of cultural controls immediately led to a resurgence of family life, popular religion, Buddhism, local festivals and regional ties. Temples have been rebuilt and processions of various kinds again take place. In Taiwan, a highly industrialized and democratic country, the spread of neighbourhood temples, thriving Buddhist monasteries, and the huge Mazu Cult continues to confound all those who believed that modernity would lead to the gradual withering away of superstition and tradition. In the same way that contemporary globalization has been accompanied by the resurgence of ethnic identities, practices and life-styles in many areas of the world, in China regional and religious practices have also revived, and are acceptable because they are taken to express a distinct Chinese cultural essence. One of the first acts of Chen Shuibian, the new president of Taiwan, was to visit a famous Buddhist master to solicit his advice on how best to rule Taiwan and overcome the tensions which his election had brought. Neo-Confucianism has equally made a comeback.

In China, the Buddhist Falun Gong sect, whose leader, Li Hongzhi, dresses in smart Western suits and uses the Internet to spread his message, has brought a new twist. Even a decade ago, it still was Western bourgeois influences which provoked vilifying rhetoric in Beijing; now Chinese authorities draw from the deep pools of invective in Chinese political rhetoric to demonize something with clear connections to the Chinese past, but also with distinctly contemporary practices and with a global reach. Their condemnation makes use of the same vocabularies and arguments as their dynastic predecessors employed when they attacked sects which, they argued, threatened the moral bonds of the established social order, including family ties as well as sanctioned political hierarchies. The charge goes deeper of course: the Falun Gong is depicted as denying the ethno–cultural identities and the social and moral bonds which the state sees as its task to uphold and which it regards as crucial to maintain order. Like Taiwanese who make a claim for Taiwanese exclusiveness, members of the Falun Gong are depicted in China's controlled media as heinous criminals because they fail to admit to being, in the words of Frederic Wakeman, '"just" Chinese'.[79] The idea and ideal of unity remains tenacious: even if Chinese states are not universal, and Chinese may reside in different countries, the essential identity of all Chinese must be marked by loyalty to just one Chinese culture of which only one political entity can be the true representative. It is this that makes Beijing's problems with Taiwanese nationalism so difficult to resolve.

It is difficult to foresee how all this will end. It is clear that China has never been a closed country, and that the past was never an 'iron house', as Lu Hsun, the May Fourth author whose iconic status remains intact, charged. If globalization brought Westernization, even of the past, it also was a process in which past concerns remained alive, and were incorporated in new Chinese understanding of modernity. Yet, the problem of re-imagining a new Chinese identity and constructing a polity for China remains as difficult as during the twentieth century, and continues to possess considerable potential for taking destructive and violent turns.

Notes and References

1 Rees, 'Report for 1908', London Missionary Society Archives, School of Oriental and African Studies, London: Reports, North China, 1908, Box 6, folder 1.
2 David Smith *et al.*, Introduction, in Smith *et al.* (eds.), *States and Sovereignty in the Global Economy* (London, 1999), p. 4.
3 Kenneth Pomeranz, *The Great Divergence* (Princeton, 2000).
4 Joanna Waley-Cohen, *The Sextants of Beijing* (New York, 2000).
5 Shiba Yoshinobu, *Commerce and Society in Sung China* (Michigan, 1970), pp. 126–40, 202–7.

6 Arthur Waldron, *The Great Wall of China* (Cambridge, 1992), pp. 72–90 and Frederick Mote, 'The Tumu Incident of 1449', in Frank Kierman and John Fairbank (eds.), *China's Ways in Warfare* (Cambridge, Mass., 1974), pp. 243–72.

7 On Ming commerce, see Timothy Brook, *The Confusions of Pleasure: Commerce and Culture in Ming China* (Berkeley, 1998); on silver, see Richard von Glahn, *Fountain of Fortune: Monetary Policy in China, 1000–1700* (Berkeley, 1996) and Frederic Wakeman, *The Great Enterprise*, vol. I (Berkeley, 1985), pp. 1–9.

8 Brook, *The Confusions of Pleasure*, pp. 190–223. See also Craig Clunas, *Superfluous Things* (Cambridge, 1991).

9 Nicola di Cosmo, 'The Manchus in Three Keys', unpublished lecture, Faculty of Oriental Studies, Cambridge University, 29 November 2000.

10 Wakeman, *Great Enterprise*, I, pp. 1–9.

11 Ibid., I, p. 3, n. 5.

12 von Glahn, *Fountain of Fortune*, p. 257.

13 Pomeranz, 'Two Worlds of Trade, Two Worlds of Empire', in Smith *et al.* (eds.), *States and Sovereignty*, p. 89.

14 Mazundar, *Sugar and Society in China* (Cambridge, Mass., 1998), p. 95, 111, 113.

15 Von Glahn, *Fountain of Fortune*, pp. 215–25.

16 Philip Kuhn, *Soulstealers* (Cambridge, Mass, 1990), pp. 37–41.

17 Zheng Yangwen, 'The Social Life of Opium', Ph.D. thesis, Cambridge University, 2001.

18 Lin Man-hoang, 'World Recession, Indian Opium, and China's Opium War', in K.S. Mathew (ed.), *Mariners, Merchants, and Oceans: Studies in Maritime History* (India, 1995), pp. 387–9.

19 Lynn Pan, *Encyclopaedia of Overseas Chinese* (Richmond, Surrey, 1999), p. 62.

20 Hao Yen-p'ing, *The Commercial Revolution in Nineteenth-Century China: The Rise of Sino–Western Mercantile Capitalism* (Berkeley, 1986), pp. 64–111, 138–63; Thomas Rawski, *Economic Growth in Pre-War China* (Berkeley, 1989), pp. 81–148; Sherman Cochran, *Big Business in China, 1890–1930* (Cambridge, Mass., 1980), pp. 10–53; David Faure, *The Rural Economy of Pre-Liberation China* (Oxford, 1989), pp. 22–40; Jennifer Ning Chang, 'Sino–British Relations During 1910–30: A Case Study of British Business in Hankow', Ph.D. thesis, Cambridge University, 1995.

21 Adam McKeown, 'Conceptualising China's Diasporas, 1842–1979', *Journal of Asian Studies*, 58 (1999), p. 315.

22 Lynn Pan, *Encyclopaedia*, p. 61, McKeown, 'Diasporas', pp. 315–17.

23 McKeown, 'Diasporas', pp. 315–16.

24 Ibid., p. 320.

25 Ibid., pp. 319–20.

26 Lin Man-hoang, 'Overseas Chinese Merchants and Multiple Nationality: A Means for Reducing Risk', *Modern Asian Studies* (forthcoming).

27 Pomeranz, *The Great Divergence*, pp. 264–97.

28 Chen Feng, *Qingdai Junfei Yanjiu* [A Study of Military Expenditures during the Qing Dynasty] (Wuhan, 1992), pp. 260–78.

29 Mazunder, *Sugar*, p. 189.

30 Lin Man-hoang, 'World Recession', pp. 402–5; W.E. Cheong, *Mandarins and Merchants* (Richmond, Surrey, 1979), pp. 27–43; Kuhn, *Soulstealers*, p. 38.

31 Hao Yen-p'ing, *Commercial Revolution*.

32 See n. 11. For an argument about 'involution' rather than productivity growth in China's economy, see Philip Huang, *The Peasant Economy and Social Change*

(Stanford, 1985). Marie-Claire Bergere, *The Golden Age of the Chinese Bourgeoisie* (Cambridge, 1989) also focused on the Republican period.

33 Shizuya Nishimura, 'The Development of a Commercial Metropolis: Trade and Banks in Shanghai, 1870–1914', p. 5 (Manuscript article).

34 Nishimura, 'Commercial Metropolis', p. 5.

35 Hsiao Lianglin, *China's Foreign Trade Statistics, 1864–1949* (Cambridge, Mass., 1974), pp. 138–64.

36 Ibid., pp. 27–70.

37 Ibid., pp. 70–124.

38 Chang, *British Business in Hankow*, pp. 146–75.

39 'The Peking Legations: A National Uprising and International Episode', in 'Manuscripts of Robert Hart', The Second Historical Archives, Nanjing, file 679(9)/8794. Manuscript and proof of an article published in London following the Boxer Uprising.

40 Li Zhancai, *Zhongguo Tielu Shi* [History of Chinese Railroads] (Shantou, 1994), pp. 62–142.

41 Hao, *Commercial Revolution*, p. 66.

42 Frank H.H. King, *The History of the Hong Kong Bank and Shanghai Banking Corporation* (Cambridge, 1987), vol. II, pp. 503–23; Rawsky, *Economic Growth*, pp. 125–45.

43 For reasons that remain unclear, although Faure, *Rural Economy*, pp. 79–84, suggests that general poverty and hence a lack of collateral explains the high cost of credit. A lack of competition among lenders and the relative depreciation of silver in relation to gold were probably also factors.

44 See King, *The Hong Kong and Shanghai Bank*, vol. I, for the history of the Hong Kong and Shanghai Banking Corporation, and pp. 503–23 for the role of compradores and *qianzhuang*.

45 Hao, *Commercial Revolution*, pp. 72–111; Nishimura, 'Commercial Metropolis', pp. 6–10.

46 Hsiao, *Trade Statistics*, pp. 138–64.

47 Ibid.

48 'Foreign Ministry to Ministers in Britain and the Netherlands', 6 June 1907, in Archives of the Historical Commission of the KMT, Taipei, file 711/6.12. The message mentions that Sun Yatsen was selling several million Military Notes (*junwu piao*).

49 See Hans van de Ven, 'Military and Financial Reform in the Late Qing and Early Republic', in Lin Man-hoang (ed.), *Caizheng yu Jindai Lishi* [Finance and Modern History] (Taipei, 1999), pp. 65–75.

50 Chen, *Qing Military Expenditures*, pp. 20–2, 31–9, 87–101, 245–75.

51 Albert Feuerwerker, 'Economic Trends in the Late Ch'ing Empire', in Denis Twitchett and John Fairbank (eds.), *The Cambridge History of China* (Cambridge, 1980), vol. XI, p. 61.

52 Philip Kuhn, 'Local Taxation and Finance in Republican China', in Susan Mann Jones (ed.), *Select Papers from the Center for Far Eastern Studies: Number 3* (Chicago, 1979), p. 116.

53 See Chen, *Qing Military Expenditures*, p. 202.

54 Ibid., pp. 201–2, 288–345; Wang Yeh-chien, *Land Taxation in Imperial China* (Cambridge, Mass., 1973), p. 9; Zhao Erxun, *Qing Shi Gao* [Draft History of the Qing] (Taipei, 1986), vol. V, p. 3619.

55 For the growth of tax liturgies, see Susan Mann, *Local Merchants and the Chinese Bureaucracy*, pp. 175–89.

56 Tang Xianglong, *Zhongguo Jindai Haiguan Shuishou Fenpei Tongji* [Statistics on Revenue Collection and Disbursements of the Modern Maritime Customs Service] (Beijing, 1992), pp. 14–43.

57 Mann, *Local Merchants*, pp. 103–5. To regard provincial expenditures on 'military affairs' funded by *lijin* revenues as part of central finances, as Mann does, accords with the presentation in the accounts, but not necessarily with reality.

58 Ibid., p. 103.

59 Ibid. For *lijin* collection on salt and actual control by Beijing, see S.A.M. Adshead, *The Modernisation of the Salt Administration* (Cambridge, Mass., 1970), p. 25.

60 Tang, *Maritime Customs*, pp. 32–3; Zhu Shoupeng, *Guangxu Chao Donghua lu* [The Donghua Gate Record for the Guangxu Reign Period] (Beijing, 1958), vol. III, pp. 4725ff; Mann, *Local Merchants*, p. 107.

61 Van de Ven, 'Military and Financial Reform', p. 78.

62 Robert Hart, 'The Peking Legations'; van de Ven, 'Financial and Military Reform', pp. 49–53.

63 Van de Ven, 'Financial and Military Reform', pp. 53–7, 75–93.

64 Hans van de Ven, 'Public Finance and the Rise of Warlordism', in *Modern Asian Studies*, 30 (1996), p. 832.

65 Arthur Young, *The Presidency of Yuan Shih-kai* (Ann Arbor, 1977), p. 189.

66 Prasenjit Duara, *Rescuing History from the Nation* (Chicago, 1995), pp. 17–82; Roger Thompson, *China's Local Councils in the Age of Constitutional Reform* (Cambridge, Mass., 1995), pp. 3–20.

67 John Fitzgerald, *Awakening China: Politics, Culture, and Class in the Nationalist Revolution* (Stanford, 1996), pp. 1–66.

68 Philip Kuhn, 'Ideas behind China's Modern Nation-state', *Harvard Journal of Asian Studies*, 5 (1995), pp. 295–337.

69 Luke Kwong, *A Mosaic of the Hundred Days* (Cambridge, Mass., 1984); for examples of Kang's writings, see Tang Zhijun (ed.), *Kang Youwei Zhenglun Ji* [Collected Political Writings of Kang Youwei] (Beijing, 1981), pp. 112–23, 201–11. For documents on the Confucianism movement, collected during the Cultural Revolution, see Republican History Group of the Institute of Modern History of the Chinese Academy of Sciences, *Zhongguo Jindai Zun Kong Niliu Shishi Jinian* [Chronology of the Countercurrent to Revere Confucius in Modern China] (Beijing, 1974), pp. 16–69.

70 On Yuan's demise, see Hou Yijie, *Yuan Shikai Quanzhuan* [A Complete Biography of Yuan Shikai] (Beijing, 1994), pp. 449–509 and van de Ven, 'Military and Financial Reform', pp. 79–93.

71 On the May Fourth movement, see Chow Tse-tsung, *The May Fourth Movement* (Stanford, 1960), and Lin Yunsheng, *The Crisis of Chinese Consciousness* (Madison, 1979).

72 Charlotte Furth (ed.), *The Limits of Change* (Cambridge, Mass., 1976).

73 See Frederic Wakeman, 'A Revisionist View of the Nanjing Decade: Confucian Fascism', *China Quarterly*, 150 (1997), pp. 395–432. On the New Life movement, see also William Kirby, *Germany and Republican China* (Stanford, 1984), pp. 176–85, and Arif Dirlik, 'The Ideological Foundations of the New Life Movement', *Journal of Asian Studies*, 34 (1975), pp. 945–94.

74 Relevant documents and speeches can be found in Second Historical Archives of China (ed.), *Zhonghua Minguo Shi Dang'an Ziliao Huibian* [Compendium of

Archival Sources for Republican History] (Shanghai, 1994), vol. I:1 (Culture), pp. 490–580.

75 Ibid., pp. 490–515.

76 Leo Ou-fan Lee, 'The Cultural Construction of Modernity in Urban Shanghai: Some Preliminary Explorations', in Yeh Wen-hsin (ed.), *Becoming Chinese: Passages to Modernity and Beyond* (Berkeley, 2000), pp. 53–5.

77 John Fitzgerald, '"Local Bullies" and the Republican State', unpublished lecture, Fourth International Conference on the History of Republican China, Nanjing, 22–4 September 2000.

78 Deborah Davis (ed.), *The Consumer Revolution in Urban China* (Berkeley, 2000).

79 Frederic Wakeman, 'Hanjian (Traitor): Collaboration and Retribution in Wartime Shanghai', in Yeh Wen-hsin (ed.), *Becoming Chinese*, p. 325.

JOHN LONSDALE

Globalization, Ethnicity and Democracy: A View from 'the Hopeless Continent'[1]

New York et Paris sont des banlieues de Dakar![2]
Xa kunje siye sikhumbule amaswi ka Horatius[3]

This chapter questions the popular wisdom which holds that Africa's troubles are caused by 'tribalism'. Commentators see this as a psychic derangement, symptom of the failure of 'tradition' to embrace 'modernity'. Today's modernity is 'globalization', a process that is said to give international finance the puckish power to put a girdle of capital about the earth in forty minutes, before leviathan states can swim a league. What then can Africa's supposedly ancient tribes, far less agile than states, do but retreat into themselves before this competitive challenge? Africa, *The Economist* recently conceded, was not alone in its tribalisms; Yugoslav succession wars and the Irish 'troubles' were proof of that. Like Africa, too, North Korea suffered from destructive dictatorship; and corruption flourished not only in Africa but all over the world. Nonetheless, Africa seemed to be alone in enduring all three political pathologies at once. This was not due to any racial defect, the paper assured us, but to the peculiarities of the continent's history.

In the past, *The Economist* began, Africans had lived in small communities. Bitter experience in mastering a volatile climate and unusually poor soils taught them a hardy conservatism. The Atlantic demand for labour that accompanied Europe's first global expansion had then set these communities at each others' throats, under slave-catching warlords. Western colonialism, later, proceeded to undermine African self-confidence. Worse still, in the middle of the twentieth century, departing white rulers had bequeathed unreformed, authoritarian, power to tiny successor elites. Their new states lacked the long histories of nation-building and external war that had, at great cost, provoked the rise of critically patriotic politics in Europe. African regimes had, therefore, to rule by 'manipulating tribal affiliation', for want of consent. History condemned them to manage two-faced states.[4] These had to appear to meet Western expectations of public probity but their real business was private gratification. Their administrative shells were for outer show. Within, 'hidden networks' of kin and clients manufactured the trust that all states need but Africa's lacked. Until a more civic trust created a public opinion alert to the abuses of power, *The Economist* concluded, Africa would never escape its crises and 'the whole world might just give up on the entire continent'.[5]

The Economist's diagnosis was unusual both in its historical depth and in its linkage of the local and the global. The popular wisdom is normally too much coloured by the continent's present crises. Their day-to-dayness and local specificity distort judgement. Africa's familiar face makes its behaviour seem all the more delinquent. Thanks to the instant connotations of a branded world, from our sofas Africans look to be the same as we Westerners – normal as we are, global models of respectability. The same corporate icons of allure stare at us on television, whether from perfumed malls or flyblown markets, from Atlanta to Zanzibar. The African ordeals that are beamed from our screens, however, seem to be horrifically different, quite 'other' to recent Western experience – or to that comfortable part of the Atlantic world that lies north of the river Drava and west of the Bug. Nike shirts clothe corpses by Rwandan roadsides; Adidas bags hold machetes or AK-47s. These common-place global commodities seem grotesquely out of context in their blood and dirt. They are out of place in another sense, too. They will often have been acquired not as new items, over a shop counter, but as the disposable cast-offs of Western charity. Globalization can take highly unequal forms. The media images themselves, moreover, are like Janus; they face two ways. In west Africa's forests, rebel boy-soldiers in Sierra Leone take courage from Alvin Toffler's message in *Future Shock* that the electronic revolution may allow the Third World to overleap the Western geography of industrialization. In generator-powered video parlours, they show the Rambo film *First Blood* as a training manual. From the Hollywood image of war's mental trauma they draw their own, very different, conclusion – that youthful energy can revive a political culture corrupted by its elders.[6] It is with such counter-intuitive, postmodern, insight that historical wisdom can begin.

The key to subverting the popular perspective is a sense of history different from that of *The Economist*. There is nothing original in my view; it is widely shared by students of Africa. It rests on two premises. First, ethnicity is common to humanity, even modern humanity; it is not a peculiarly African pathology, a dysfunctional relic from the past. Secondly, Africa's hardy communities have long been open to the world, if by means more particular than the borderless markets that are too readily associated with 'globalization'.[7] Africans are like the rest of us, shaped by both external and internal relations.[8] They are not unusually disturbed by the threat of cultural cosmopolitanism, however much they suffer the inequalities of international trade. The 'tribalization' of ethnicity, modern though it may be, does not come from closure of the antique mind. I will discuss ethnicity first, before turning to Africa's place in world history. For brevity's sake I treat ethnic identity as no historian should – as an ideal type, innocent of state connections, and in the 'ethnographic present', not in a properly contingent, historical, past tense.

Our ethnicity makes us all human, often without our having to think about it. Patriotic ethnicity is not the same as the aggressive political tribalism of the popular imagination. Nor does a self-conscious identity necessarily stem from a 'highly charged romantic nationalism', resistant to modern, urban, anonymity.[9] Ethnicity is more mundane. It has been, and still is, a universal cradle of civility. Disciplined socialization is common to humankind. It is also particular. It imparts, and celebrates, the gendered duties peculiar to locality and occupation. Ethnic cultures have developed to honour the specialized skills that are required to civilize a local nature, to make a decent subsistence from the raw material of a particular ecology; they teach the reciprocities expected between neighbours, whether kin or strangers.[10] Ethnicity has throughout history produced moral beings, socially alert to their local 'moral economy' of rights and obligations between 'ourselves' and 'others'. Civic entitlements to the resources of subsistence – negotiated between the genders, generations and classes – have always been hard earned.

Ethnic cultures have in consequence always been argued from within. People dispute the rules and rewards of industrious behaviour with those to whom they stand closest.[11] Identities are created and re-created in debate on proper conduct. Rough cast by a mode of subsistence, their civic courtesies are polished by reasoned talk. Because they keep changing, ethnic groups keep telling old stories; they develop terrifying folklores to deter disobedience or discord. Trying to instil household discipline by re-telling myths of origin, elders often liken their ethnic community to a family tree, a 'tribal' lineage – what the social scientist would call a primordial group. But this is patriarchal polemic, a search for security. No social group has been that comfortable, or so permanent, least of all in 'archaic' Africa, with its ease of movement.[12] Identities are not what they seem in the elders' tales, 'stable points of reference which were like that in the past, are now and ever shall be, still points in a turning world'.[13] They cannot be; they are too demanding, too unequal, and therefore too quarrelsome. Their local codes of honour censoriously differentiate degrees of success in what in the past were never private lives. As Jomo Kenyatta, first President of Kenya, in his earlier guise of London-trained anthropologist, wrote of his own Kikuyu people, 'a man is judged by his household . . . A good leader begins in his own homestead.'[14] Nobody listened to a man who '[gave] counsel in other people's homes while his own [was] going to ruin'.[15]

Ethnic groups have always been in flux within and without, in relation to ethnic 'others', whether in Africa or elsewhere. Their inner and outer faces are not easily separated. Women marry in, and teach their children a broadly regional rather than a narrowly ethnic outlook.[16] Big men aim to marry out as much as within, an advantage of polygyny; few small societies lack a wider web of dynastic alliance. External trade, appropriation of the ritual wisdom and ceremony of strangers, the patronage or enslavement of destitute immigrants – all these are commonplace. All carry the seeds of changing allegiance. No group, now or in the past, has been shut off from a commerce of people, goods, and ideas. Folklore was cosmopolitan long before pop music. All African peoples have evolved rules of exchange with 'others' possessing different skills and products. Even tributary submissions have been interpreted as diplomatic *coups* from below, bargains struck with overmighty neighbours for the supply of peace and justice.[17] Internal African power has often been an imported good.[18] Europeans see alien, deracinated, power as the dark side of globalization. Africans have long negotiated with external powers and rendered them to varying degrees locally accountable, whether in pre-colonial or colonial times or in our own day.[19]

Ethnicity, to repeat, is not necessarily a political constituency. People who litigate in the same language, know the same stories, share in or squabble over the daily round, the common task, or compete for the costly honour of sponsoring the same festivals, rarely constitute a team, in competition with other groups so formed. Different identities breed co-operation more often than conflict. If that were not so humanity would long ago have left the world a smoking ruin. This essay examines both the universal ethnicity of daily life and its contingent mobilization, in order to seize opportunity or avert danger. The politics of African ethnicity has a long and varied history, governed by changing relations of power internal and external to the continent. 'Tribal conflict', the apparent problem of the present day, did not dominate the African past. It is not inevitable that it should blast the future. It is best understood, to turn to my second premise, as the product of a peculiarly modern and undecided struggle – in Africa at least – between two competing modes of keeping the gate of profit and power between locality and the wider world.

The contestants for global contact have been local communities on the one hand and their over-arching, multi-ethnic, states on the other. Multi-ethnicity has been the mark of civilized states throughout history, those whose vigour has attracted immigrants. The one exceptional place and period was Europe, in its 'modern', nation-building era, between 1792 and 1945.[20] Here, by the mid twentieth century, the imagined and then socially engineered monoglot community of the nation state appeared to have driven out other, less clearly bounded, political entities. Leagues of city ports, ethnic diasporas, imagined international class solidarities, real international (thus alien) royal dynasties, the little vernacularisms of peasant custom – all had succumbed to the coal-fired industry, schooled print culture, and urban labour markets of nation states. This nation-building conquest of Europe was an anomaly in world history but became the modern norm. With its attendant overseas empires, it defined the modern era of globalization.[21]

The chief tool of nationalizing European states was the standardization of ceremony and language from out of regional vernaculars. Their cultural building-sites were schoolroom and parade ground. For peasant conscripts from the provinces the best reason for learning the national language at school was to be able to jump to the bark of a sergeant-major.[22] Africa was different. Europe's overseas imperialism was culturally feeble compared with nation-building at home. In Africa's long half-century of colonial rule there was little education, still less military conscription. Few bashed a regimental square. Tiny colonial armies were recruited from often marginal peoples deemed to be 'martial tribes'. Their lingua franca of command was some local vernacular, not the European tongue that became the language of state.[23] It was not the least malign of Europe's legacies to the African imagination that nationalists nonetheless strove to emulate the cultural conformities of Europe's monoglot nationhoods. Careless of their different state histories, they could not envisage any other polity that might promote Africa globally and maintain internal peace.[24] But independent Africa's aspirations to universal primary education and national youth services did not outlast the global decline in primary produce markets in the 1970s; its armies remain small, their hierarchies of rank often matching the economic rankings of region.

This want of classroom and parade-ground nationalism is the most obvious reason why Africa lacks nation states. There has been still less of the 'military-fiscalism' that in Europe stimulated capital formation, which in turn provoked and funded the engineering of national cultures.[25] Yet in Africa, everywhere save in post-revolutionary Ethiopia and post-apartheid South Africa, the formal pursuit of the alternative, that is, a multi-cultural nation, is seen as a defeat. Elsewhere, ethnic difference remains an undercover rather than open distributor of the costs and benefits of power. Conflicts of identity are not subject to the statutory compromises between multiple, layered, loyalties that some African historians are putting forward as a renewed basis of civility.[26] Some Western political theorists are raising similar questions about their own societies. They ask if Western nation states, hitherto the tacit African model, damage rather than protect individual civil rights by an insistence that citizens be subject to the cultural conformity of the melting pot.[27] Post-colonial globalization raises multi-ethnic issues for Western publics that may make them readier to understand the African experience for what it is – a competition not in nostalgic security but for modern opportunity. This comparative reflection provides my organizing theme.

This essay sets out to show that the history of African ethnicity in its wider setting is far from a strange exotic. To the contrary, it bears a similarity, in miniature, to the international history of the European nation state. One can discern a crude periodization common to both. First, and for centuries, they shared an 'archaic' cosmopolitanism. The modern African schooling in ethnicity then paralleled that of European nationalism, if a century later. Now, in the post-colonial world, tensions between ethnicity and state citizenship in Africa match those between nationhood and 'ever closer union' in Europe. Popular wisdom thus errs in thinking that modern Africans are 'reverting to tribalism'. It is a distinctively modern consciousness. It encourages a more singular selfhood than Africans, like Europeans, knew in earlier times.

The parallelism proposed between African ethnicity and European nationality comes from placing the continent more firmly within global history than it has been in the past. It used to be said that desert sands and the poor load-bearing capacity of the camel, the rocky cataracts strewn across the navigability of Africa's rivers, and the tsetse fly – winged death to draught oxen – had together cut Africa off from the Eurasian Old World. While there is some truth in this claim, there is also much to be said for seeing African history within world history rather than as a thing apart.[28]

The four-part chronology of globalization deployed in earlier chapters will more or less serve for Africa.[29] Two cautions are in order. First, Africa is a large and diverse continent. Its regions have had contrasting economic and political histories, and varied global connections.[30] Secondly, as this book has demonstrated with respect to other parts of the world, it is all the more true of Africa, even today, that its global commercial and ideological connections have filtered through specific networks, such as ethnic diasporas, chartered companies, Islamic brotherhoods, cartels, Christian churches and armed mafias. The impersonal markets suggested by the term 'globalization' are a fiction with respect to Africa.[31]

Generalizing, again, in a way no historian should consider decent, each of the four eras we have earlier identified was marked by changing forms of conflict between small communities and large polities for the control of international trade, both within the continent and beyond. In summary, Africa's part in 'archaic' globalization's cosmopolitanism lasted longer than elsewhere in the world, until the nineteenth century – but only in its furthest interior. Around Africa's coasts local rulers had tried to to take greater control of overseas commerce since the seventeenth century, in what one could call 'reactive proto-globalizations'. In that century the recently conquered Ottoman provinces of north Africa prospered again in the Mediterranean trades, after half a millennium of decline, and west African kingdoms expanded, the better to control the Atlantic slave trade. The Dutch also settled the Cape, to secure the route to the Indies. During the nineteenth century other Africans attempted to join in this proto-globalization, largely by military modernization without benefit of nation-building. Their limited successes and more spectacular failures helped to stimulate the European conquests that brought the century to its close. This 'modern globalization' of nation-state imperialism now synchronized the continental chronology of Africa's state-managed place in the world. As suggested, however, colonial state-building was but a poor shadow of the cultural coercions practised in Europe. That is one important reason why, in the era of 'post-colonial globalization' since 1960 – and especially of 'post-Cold War globalization' since 1989[32] – some African states, perhaps quasi-states, have fallen into civil war or, as in Somalia, into statelessness, unable to police the many links forged between the local and international trades in credit, guns and skill.

The periodization of African ethnicity is entangled with that of its competitor, the state. In archaic global times large African states were few and, as now, projected little power.[33] Ethnicities were fluid and porous, not 'tribal'. Their customs were cosmopolitan, jostling on open frontiers, much like eighteenth-century Europe's high cultures.[34] African trading diasporas could span half a continent.[35] 'Proto-global' self-strengthening thereafter had limited effects on political culture; some of these initiatives, however, tried to combine rearmament with world religion. In the modern global period African ethnicities learned self-consciousness, emulating nineteenth-century European nationhoods. They acquired print histories; their boundaries hardened; they became cockpits of internal class conflict, disputed within new public spheres. Conversely, they also became external, 'tribal', competitors in wider markets for jobs, land and power. Their co-operative experience of anti-colonial nationalism often enhanced a nervous awareness of ethnic difference and disadvantage. In post-colonial times the suppression of tribal competition was the chief rationale of the one-party state. Some now-tribalized ethnic groups and their over-arching states have today reached stalemate in the struggle for global opportunity. The more the outer world, in the shape of oil companies or mafia networks, funds these conflicts, to acquire access to oil, diamonds or strategic minerals, the bloodier and more inconclusive they tend to be. This fragmentation of linkages, all too common in Africa now as in the past, constitutes a narrow, malign, decivilizing form of globalization.[36]

Two observations may conclude this introduction. The first is simple. Civil war is not typical of Africa; Africans are not by nature more brutal than others. The second is more complex, but just as equivocally hopeful. It is that there is a useful comparison to be made between the politics of the European Union and that of individual African states. The EU comprises nation states, African states comprise ethnic minorities. Europe's states are not yet reconciled to sharing, or losing, their supposed sovereignty. Many African minorities, similarly, see themselves as frustrated nationalities. The EU differs from much of Africa in the studied civility of its political practice, disciplined by Europe's own violent past. Some European politicians nonetheless fear an 'African' future for their own countries, in which mafia capitalism allies with ethno-regional nationalism.[37] Conversely, as among the nations of Europe, so too among Africa's minorities, one can find passionate protagonists for a larger citizenship that could both attract, and discipline, the cross-border intercon- nectedness promised by post-colonial globalism.

Africa and Archaic Globalization

Africa is the cradle of humankind.[38] Africans were among the first to take to the drudgery of agriculture and the discipline of herding, in place of the freedoms of hunting and gathering.[39] North Africa was Rome's breadbasket, western Africa the largest supplier of labour to the Islamic and Atlantic worlds in early modern times. Until the twentieth century, however, and perhaps even today, after a half-century of the fastest population growth the world has ever seen, the continent's history has been governed by the scarcity of people. African populations – checked by 'poor soils, fickle rainfall, abundant insects and unique prevalence of disease' – expanded more slowly than their emigrant cousins overseas. Underpopulation is fundamental to understanding Africa's relations with the rest of the world and the history of its own communities.[40]

Sparse populations are mobile. They can vote with their feet. They make state power difficult to build. States can, and could, demand little of their subjects in blood, toil or treasure. The subjection of strangers, or slaves, often made better political and economic sense. Before the twentieth century African towns were rare, found only where water supply and rich soils combined to impart a scarcity value to productive land.[41] Yet towns often represented clusters of commercial self-interest rather than crucibles of power.[42] Outside the Nile valley, walled towns were confined to the open savannahs of western Africa, an area well suited to cavalry warfare and slave production. Eastern Africa's town walls, by contrast, were better at keeping out 'dogs and wild pigs than any serious invaders'[43] – evidence of a habit of peace. Without power it was hard to accumulate capital. Wage labour was rare. Even in the west African interior, where a proto-industrial textile industry emerged, independent craft production was the norm. Some large merchants 'put out' their work but that was exceptional.[44] Elsewhere, capital was thinly spread in inefficient modes of transport, and in attracting followers. In an empty continent, the best investment was 'wealth in people', not property.[45] In this characteristic archaic Africa was not alone.

The principled pluralism of the medieval European frontier states of Lithuania and Hungary, for instance, was very similar. Admonitions, falsely attributed to the eleventh-century St Stephen, advised Hungary's kings that immigrants with different languages, customs and weapons would 'adorn the kingdom and glorify the court and discourage the pride of foreigners. For a kingdom of one language and one custom [was] weak and fragile.' In a world of movement it paid to attract the mobile. Two centuries later the Lithuanian grand dukes saw strength in permitting women to be Christians while men continued in paganism, and in exploiting Orthodox and Catholic scribal skills while consulting pagan prophets.[46] African leaders also sought wealth in a diversity of dependants. They exchanged clients, often by marriage, in order 'to surround themselves with a variety of kin and affines who could produce the entire range of foods, crafts, clothing, wood, and skins they desired without having to seek the materials themselves outside the primary communities *they thus created*.'[47] The African genius, in which, as will be seen, there lurked great danger, lay in assembling human, not material, capital. There was little concentration of production, little incentive to intensify agriculture with an elaborate toolkit. Agrarian systems minimized risk rather than maximized returns. All these factors – and the lack of an ocean-going shipbuilding capacity – meant that Africans were unable to take market initiatives in archaic globalization. Power, difficult to accumulate at home, could scarcely be projected abroad. Africa's most elaborate external trade network, before the coming of the Atlantic trades, linked west Africa to the Islamic world of the Mediterranean and west Asia. Basing themselves on the regional trades in salt, labour, grain, iron and weaponry, textiles and leather goods, its merchants used Arabic weights and measures and Islamic commercial paper. They rarely kept accounts and employed few agents in foreign parts.[48] This dependence did not mean that Africans were not important to archaic globalism. In one respect they were disastrously so.

West African, and to a lesser extent, Zimbabwean, gold exports were a vital lubricant of the archaic globalization of trade in late medieval and early modern times. But gold production remained small in scale, with few workings underground. The political power it generated through trade was magnificent in its trappings but militarily fragile.[49] Beyond the goldfields and Saharan trade routes Africans gained no market sway over the global commerce that their gold facilitated.

It was the same with labour exports. The first African slave was shipped to Atlantic islands – not yet across the ocean to the New World – in 1451. In the previous eight hundred years perhaps four million enslaved Africans, most of them women, had been taken north and east to the Mediterranean and Islamic worlds. African men served as slave soldiers as far away as Muslim India. The largely male Atlantic trade did not last as long as the Islamic trade, but far outstripped it in annual volume, especially in the eighteenth century. Up to twelve million Africans were carried westwards to the Americas. That was almost as large a total as the less knowable numbers taken overland to the north and, by Arab *dhows*, to the east.

The importance of African labour to Europe's Atlantic economy is the subject of much dispute.[50] The nature of the internal African slaveries which this labour export trade first tapped and then encouraged is even more tragically contentious. But it does seem, first, that underpopulation made it difficult for African rulers to exploit their free peasantries. Slave-catching was a rational alternative – as for rulers in much of the archaic world. Secondly, internal slave trades were needed to turn war-captives, keen to escape, into workers, too far removed to walk home. Existing inequalities and enmities within weaker African societies were also increasingly transformed into legal pretexts to offer dissidents and delinquents to the trade. Finally, to return the argument to underpopulation, the imported manufactures exchanged for slaves were cheaper than the local craft products with which chiefs had previously enlarged their wealth in people. West Africa, in particular, became a mosaic of predatory states and marginal peoples, not all of whom succeeded in hiding from the fatal lure of commercial collaboration beneath the political camouflage of statelessness.[51] This regional differentiation fostered ethnic consciousness. It was also the basis of an equally patchwork proto-globalization.

Much of Africa was but indirectly connected to archaic global networks of trade and knowledge. Regional exchanges flourished, all the same. Histories of trade, language-use, colonization and religion make that plain. Trade networks existed everywhere, fostering non-ethnic diplomacy. The entrepreneurship of the Kerebe islanders of Lake Victoria Nyanza, as reconstructed for the early nineteenth century, must be sufficient illustration. Kerebe exported grain from their well-watered fields south-west, along the lakeshore. In return they imported iron hoes. They then re-exported worn-out hoes to the north-east, as scrap iron for spear makers. Middlemen in canoes bought the scrap with packets of sun-dried salt. This waterborne commerce stretched up to three hundred miles, and linked with other networks.[52] More generally, eastern Africa's uphill farmers invested their grain incomes by buying shares in plainsmen's cattle, while the latter reinsured against livestock crashes, through drought or disease, by marrying farmers' daughters.[53] Africa may have been empty. It was not idle; its sparse populations were not isolated. Historical linguistics are the best proof of their cosmopolitanism. Loan-words, borrowed between language groups, speak of how outsiders' crops, tools, and animals 'became part of the "we", not of the "them"', through flexible fictions of kinship, as well as by subordination.[54]

Archaic Africa's peoples exploited commercial complementarities. They also competed on numberless frontiers of colonizing opportunity. They fought not so much for land, of which there was plenty, as for authority, of which there was little. 'Latecomers' claimed rights by conquest or by their more civilized agriculture. They also reached accommodations with 'firstcomers' who might be despised as hunters, but nonetheless 'knew the land'. Constitutions of co-existence often balanced ritual and political powers.[55] Local ethnicity was a referee of contract rather than a cause of conflict. This was especially true of immigrant communities who received fresh migrants themselves. But so did they all. The history of indigenous Igbo religion, in eastern Nigeria, is one example that will have to stand for many. Their earth-cult – and it was not theirs alone – made fresh immigration safe over the centuries precisely by braving the ritual abominations that were accepted as the price of change. In the end the earth priests even tamed the abomination of British rule.[56] Africans developed traditions of political thought about the brokerage between cosmopolitan and local power, without benefit of literacy and world religion.

Reactive Proto-Globalization in Africa

Few African attempts to control the local profits of European proto-globalization by means of their own political enlargement lasted very long. Some fell apart. The more successful ones aroused the fears of white traders on Africa's coasts, or of settlers in south Africa and Algeria. On either score they were soon supplanted by European colonialism. African efforts at state-strengthening were comparatively weak examples of military fiscalism. The most effective examples, not always technically the most advanced, nurtured a popular culture that could, for a time, bear the weight of political enlargement. The kingdom of Asante was one of these, the Zulu another.

Proto-globalization came to Africa around 1680, not long after the Treaty of Westphalia,[57] when the Golden Stool is said to have fallen from the sky, to endow the first king of Asante, Osei Tutu, with what in local terms was a universal kingship. More vital for the new state's stability was its code of honour. Derived from the clan labour needed to hack a civilization out of the forest, this combined the pursuit of valour, wealth and public service in the new Asante state for more than a century. It was not until the late nineteenth century that extravagant royal violence, a growing mercantile self-interest, and the declining profitability of war combined to divide the loyalties of Asante's chiefs.[58] The degree to which Asante was almost a *nation* state, with the power to attract and absorb strangeness, is shown in the embodiment of one of her generals, Kwame Boakye. His corporeal humours, hot for war and cool for manhood, were enhanced by charms sewn on his war coat, of distant savannah provenance, both Muslim and animist. Popular belief in 'the supernatural resources of the . . . "other"' was thus 'domesticated to Asante use'.[59]

In black south Africa it was not until over a century after the Golden Stool's descent that Shaka Zulu brought reactive proto-globalization to the southern shores of the Indian Ocean. One of many leaders whose competition for the ivory-export trade had been sharpened by drought, he won the battle of Mhlatuze River in 1818, three years after Waterloo, and with it the power to smother, or disperse, local disputes. Shaka, famously, was a warrior, but the ideological framework of his Zulu empire was more convincingly matrimonial and dynastic than military. As in other transitions, the enlargement of power rested on former habits of management.[60] Unlike Asante, for instance, the Zulu never solved the old habit of princely rivalry. Despite the Zulu preference for the continued use of spears, both they and the Asante could be said to have made a better match, if scarcely a perfect one, between new political culture and greater military power than the more spectacular would-be modernizers of north Africa, from the Atlantic to the Nile.[61]

Like Asante, Zulu became a nation through war, but a deeply divided one, and perhaps not conscious of its nationhood until Christianized intellectuals later reconstructed local history after the onset of colonial rule. Sub-Saharan Africa's two most impressive examples of proto-globalization had the benefit of both pre-colonial literacy and world religion. The rise of the early nineteenth-century *jihad* states in the western Sudan was in part provoked by the general crisis into which Napoleon's landing in Egypt, in 1798, had plunged the Islamic world.[62] There was greater provocation on the spot, in clerical competition on Islam's frontier and in tension between Islamic commerce and local dynastic war. For us the most interesting question about the *jihads* is the identity of their Fulani leaders. Colonial scholars later saw them as a tribe of natural aristocrats, with light skins and thin noses – like district commissioners – and their *jihads*, therefore, as wars of tribal conquest. Fulani may well have agreed with this interpretation, but only in retrospect. 'The Fulani', like others, were a recently imagined community.[63] Fulani-speaking pastoralists and clergy had lived in dispersed, only tenuously connected, communities across the western Sudan long before the *jihads*. Their learned members had a vernacular literacy, rare in Africa or in Islam; conversely, it was an identity that ambitious Muslims of whatever origin could learn. The *jihads* were led as much by a clerisy with global connections as by a locally rooted 'tribe'. But the winners became a coherent tribe in hindsight, after they had won their holy wars – and become Africa's largest slave-masters. Their scholars invented unifying genealogies of descent from the centre of the Muslim world, appropriate to those whose victories proved them to be God's instruments. Europeans later took these invented traditions of global origin to be a real 'tribal history'.[64] Ethnicities could thus be born of cosmopolitan scholarship, universal religion and holy war – as well as from a local ecological mastery. Multi-ethnic African nations could similarly combine elements of global and local culture.

Ethiopians say that theirs is the oldest Christianity in the world, conceived long before the Christian era in King Solomon's bedchamber as he lay with the Queen of Sheba. Court chronicles claim that their son, Menelik I, then removed the Ark of the Covenant to Africa, to save it from Israel's wars. A medieval emperor, Lalibela, later incised a replica city of Jerusalem into the Ethiopian plateau.[65] Ethiopians cherished their links with the centre of world history partly for reasons of state, surrounded as they were by Muslims, also claimants to a global role. But universal religion also shaped local culture. While there was much that was 'African' in Menelik II's heroic preservation of his wealth in people through the famine that afflicted Ethiopia in the 1890s, his court's charity was also Christian. His imperial famine relief was arguably as vital as a generous supply of Italian guns to Ethiopia's 'proto-global' victory over the Italians at Adwa in 1896.[66] Ethiopians were keenly comparative historians. Their chroniclers put Ethiopia into world history; the lives of their saints outdid the miracles of Scripture. Fulani clerics were equally well versed in Islamic world history. When the British occupied their capital, Sokoto, in 1903, the chief minister pondered the rival claims of faith and survival. He concluded that a diplomatic submission of the tongue was lawful; it was clearly not a traitor's heart. Two considerations comforted him. From what he knew of their rule elsewhere, Europeans seemed to respect Islam. Even had they not done so, a repentant patience under infidel conquest would surely be rewarded. World history offered that hope. More than six centuries earlier, had not the faithful of Baghdad survived to flourish again, after the Mongols sacked the Abbasid capital in 1258?[67]

Modern Globalization: African Ethnicities and Colonial Rule

Colonial conquest sharpened the competition between states and local communities to keep the gate of Africa's global business. Colonial states had the advantage of force, law, bureaucratic knowledge, and access to credit. Communities learned, by contrast, a subversive social energy and trust, while also exploiting state power. Africans whose ethnic or linguistic name had been one of a number of identifiers learned to think of themselves as members of a particular tribe.[68] Their formerly overlapping identities – linguistic, clannish, occupational, religious, or clients of a patron's 'house' – all became focused on, or folded into, one primary category, defined by its territory, its codified 'customary' law, and its standardized print language. Modern Africans acquired a valuable self-knowledge and, often, self-confidence, in this new, 'tribalized', ethnicity. It could provide a firm base from which to explore the world. Some set off officially, with a state bursary for overseas education in their pocket. More set off on their own, smugglers of contraband ideas and goods, first as seekers after unfettered Islamic or Western enlightenment, later as entrepreneurs of the untaxed 'informal' or 'second' economy.

Learning ethnicity was a two-way process, from without and within. Colonial officials, proud products of the new national cultures that fired up Europe's modern globalization, thought their own 'race' was rational, scientifically adept, above all self-controlled, able to hold power in trust over others. Africans, they believed, lacked these qualities and needed tutelage, especially in self-discipline.[69] Insofar as Africans were thought to have governed themselves responsibly, they had done so in tribes, like the Europeans of long ago, before the Romans came. Against such racial, and restrictive, knowledge, African subjects constructed their own ideologies, and histories, of self-esteem. Their politics of identity was one not of difference but of equipoise. This was not a purely intellectual exercise, although our sources are the writings of African scholars, products of Qur'anic or mission schools. Nor were these alienated intellectuals; to the contrary, they feared that 'their people' might think them so. In some parts of Africa the most quoted biblical parable was that of the Prodigal Son (Luke 15). Excluded by whites, African Christians were careful to maintain domestic relations with their unlettered kin.[70] By recourse to comparative history they also showed that ethnic culture must be renewed in Christian literacy. Africans could not otherwise overcome their colonial fate and join the modern world on their own account. In Iliffe's pithy summary, 'Europeans believed Africans belonged to tribes; Africans built tribes to belong to.'[71] This section sketches in that state-and-society dialectic, by considering European policies, African experience and, finally, African thought.[72]

Historians have come round from a view that Africans had their ethnic identities 'invented' for them by others, like a straitjacket, to an acceptance that tribal community was also 'imagined' from below, as an enlargement of social scale.[73] But the colonial imagination clearly mattered. However feeble by contrast with that of nineteenth-century Europe, colonial state-building, like state-building anywhere, needed above all to fix responsibility for collective obedience to command.[74] White officials needed law and order, revenue, labour for public works, expanded markets for imported goods. They had to find local agents, 'chiefs', round whom to map lines of authority, to prevent 'their' people from playing truant. For colonial rulers, 'tribe' was, above all – as for the Romans – a tributary device. Fluid identity was death to tax returns. However, if chiefs were to be held to account, they had to be helped to exercise the control that Africa seemed to lack. Colonial states were, above all, alliances of masculine power, white and black. Law codes supportive of male authority curbed the liberties that the colonial *pax* and markets in labour and foodstuffs so unnervingly offered young men, wives or ex-slaves. Elders readily agreed that 'custom' demanded a revival – in fact, an authoritarian reinterpretation – of generational and gendered disciplines.[75]

This tribe-formation in the service of colonial states could be called a de-globalization of Africa.[76] But it was not easily done; and ethnicity was also an identity of comparison, of global perspective. Tribal courts, tribal treasuries, minute-taking councils, it is true, all developed in due course, to tie up identity in red tape. White employers similarly demanded identity cards, with name, chief and tribe, to tag and trace absent workers. They also simplified a too-complex Africa with stereotypes, by marking some 'tribes' as sisal cutters, others as clerks, and so on, just as governments thought that some were better at soldiering. All these limitations of possibility were tried. But there was another side to tribe-making. Missionaries spent devoted years, in company with expert African advisers, not only in standardizing a local language to be fit for God's universal Word, but in arguing out its orthography.[77] Words became drilled, even if young men were not often conscripted, but words – and this is the point – can float free. It was the same with colonial agriculture. Seeds got drilled too, as agricultural officers and marketing men, often in alliance with African commercial ambition, determined that some districts were promising for cotton, others for cocoa, and so on. 'Cotton' and 'cocoa' or 'peanut tribes' emerged accordingly, often with a producers' co-operative society. The green-fingered ethnicity of local ecology was acquiring clerks who recorded global export sales. Colonial state-building, weak though it was by comparison with Europe, is not to be dismissed.[78] It enclosed Africans; it also offered new institutions of access to the world. The contradictory possibilities were perhaps best appreciated by the Fulani. Their fate under the anti-clerical French and monarchical British could scarcely be more different. In Guinea the French, for a time, tried 'to bring ... 1789 to the Futa Jallon' by overturning Fulani rule. Further inland, Fulani identity almost disappeared; it seemed wiser to call oneself Bambara, of the local soil, without the taint of cosmopolitan and militant Islam. In northern Nigeria, on the other hand, the British treated Fulani as 'natural rulers'. They were allowed to lord it locally, in the name of Indirect Rule. Their leaders also became Knights of the British Empire, and their commoners, by the 1970s, the most numerous of Mecca's pilgrims from all the countries in the world, apart from Saudi Arabia.[79]

Tribe also became the object of a passionate African imagination. How far this colonial identity hardened pre-existing, more expansive, collectivities, how often entirely new social constructions emerged to cope with the new ecology of power, is difficult to say. Cases differed. Chroniclers have endowed their tribes with a retrospective primordial 'essence' – just as Fulani scholars did nearly two centuries ago, or most elders long before that. Fortuitously, drought and disease during the period of disruptive colonial conquest had induced an uncharacteristic fear of strangers in some areas.[80] Colonial political economy both increased these perceptions of difference from 'others', and at the same time focused anxious debate on what made people 'ourselves'. In many areas colonial rule, for the first time, gave some Africans a non-contractual power over people different from themselves, as policemen, tax-collectors, works foremen, pay-clerks, and so on. Migrant labour to mines, estates and towns brought many into contact with other Africans whose language they found strange. To defend themselves *en route* to work, to find a job and housing on arrival, migrants often enlarged their concepts of kin to include any whose language they shared, however dialectically differentiated. Modern tribes or nationalities are often larger than old ethnicities.[81]

This was a moment in African history very similar to that highlighted by the social historians of nineteenth-century Europe, when peasants became the urban workers and petty functionaries of increasingly industrial and bureau-cratic states. At this conjuncture – famously portrayed by Ernest Gellner – central European, 'Ruritanian', peasants who migrated to the polyglot towns of their 'Megalomanian' empire, could suddenly awake to their Ruritanian identity, indeed nationhood, a community unimaginable to them in their village homes.[82] So too could twentieth-century Africans. Each European colony was its own Habsburg Megalomania. Each contained different possibilities of self-conscious ethnicity. As in Ruritania a century earlier, Africans too were obliged to rethink their social relations, thanks to a process one can only call class formation.[83] Social differentiation originated within African agrarian societies, within the rural capitalisms so characteristic of modern globalization. Their inequalities were reinforced by schooling for only a minority and, for the still more fortunate few, access to colonial power. These emergent African classes received no direct encouragement, however, from colonial states. Trade unions were legalized late in the day, educated and entrepreneurial Africans were mistrusted too, as much by bank managers as by officials. Without statutory class entitlements to property or protection, the only material base of belonging lay in one's tribal 'reserve'. Yet this was the very cockpit in which antagonistic classes were forming as population grew, land values rose with export crop growth, and the rights of poorer households were left undefended by their men, away in wage-employment elsewhere. The household income of the powerful – increasingly produced by the casual labour of poorer neighbours' wives, on expropriated lineage land – could be invested in the professions. At the bottom of the kin-connected heap, the poor clung on to what they could as their insurance against social extinction in a rightless proletariat. Africans increasingly argued their claims against those closest to them, those with most power to do them harm, in a 'language of class' that drew on local histories of disputed entitlement.[84] The search for a new moral economy that did not tear localities apart was the modern stimulus to ethnic patriotism, or moral ethnicity, debated in the many small public spheres of vernacular press and local council. The multi-ethnic territory of the colony had no such intimate memory, or forum, and thus no urgent sense of the gendered, moral, threat that class-formation levied against responsible manhood, womanhood, and the reciprocities of neighbourhood, however unequal they may always have been.

Out of such experience came political thought, bolstered by comparative history. The most widely available vernacular history was in the Bible, Europe's and now Africa's 'primary text book'. The Children of Israel provided 'the original model of the nation'.[85] Scriptural reference became as frequent as indigenous proverbs in African political texts, and the Exodus the most common image of struggle.[86] The disjunction between vernacular Scripture and European languages of government denied to Africa the imaginative connection between community and power that energized the critical civil societies of state-building Europe.[87] But vernacular thought was not restricted to the locality, far from it. All cultural nationalists are comparativists, setting up their own history to be the equal of others', especially that of their alien rulers. Africans were fascinated by French and British history not because they lacked self-confidence in their own but because these were the universal measures of prowess to which their own histories must aspire. To recite the 'Lays of Ancient Rome' was no act of cultural cringe but of global aspiration. There were instructive examples around the world of what befell those who lacked such broad awareness. In 1907 the Zulu newspaper *Ilanga lase Natal* pointed to the destruction of 'whole peoples who have attempted to remain "as they were"'. Where now were the Maoris, or 'the black men of Australia? . . . the Red Indians of North America?' All had resisted 'the wonderful thing which the white man calls civilization'. And how could the Zulu join 'this grand march of civilization?' By founding their own local industries.[88] The Zulu journalist of a century ago had seen the destruction wrought by globalization and its perhaps illusory remedy.

Here was a local patriotism conceived within a global 'grand march', similar to that imagined by Iberian and Latin American elites in an earlier, thought to be Christian, global age.[89] Ethnic global ambitions are easily enough traced, through the ever-extending trees of tribal genealogy that were constructed, as 'Fulani' scholars had done after their Holy Wars. In 1910 for instance, the remembrancers of Uyombe chiefdom, in what is now Zambia, claimed that their ancestors had come from across Lake Malawi, quite close by. By 1930 this history had acquired a civilizing, Christian, gloss: the founders had proved their superiority over the locals by bringing iron axes and weapons; they were known as 'the makers of wondrous things', independently of the British to whom their descendants now owed their rule. When, thirty years later still, the chief was in competition with nationalists from elsewhere in Zambia, he claimed descent from much further afield, from the famously Christian kingdom of Buganda, which was even then bidding for sovereignty within the wider entity of Uganda. By the 1990s, long after independence, Uyombe had taken to celebrating an annual founder's day – and he originated now from Ghana, a nation senior to Zambia in its attainment of sovereign self-rule. There is nothing unique in this story of a globally conscious local patriotism investing itself with ever more ambitious traditions that 'anticipate a future saturated with projects of an indisputable modernity'. It is found all over Muslim and Christian Africa. The Kikuyu were not the only ones to conclude, once the Bible allowed them to compare their dietary taboos, that they must be one of the lost tribes of Israel.[90] By contrast, not many believed that the new state of Ghana, formerly the Gold Coast, had much connection with the medieval kingdom of Ghana, hundreds of miles to its north.

The African president who thought most deeply on how history could teach political culture, Julius Nyerere, thought both locally and globally, rather than nationally. He dug back to 'traditional society', to 'tribal society' – the two were to him synonymous – and at the same time translated into Swahili *Julius Caesar* and *The Merchant of Venice*, among world literature's finest evocations of the temptations of autocratic rule and tribal prejudice. There was at the time no 'Tanzanian' history in the middle for him to consult.[91] His neighbour, Jomo Kenyatta, had a similarly splayed cast of thought. Like other 'Kenyan' nationalists of his generation, he placed trust in the Labour government in Westminster, among whom he had friends, but felt that responsibility for the future lay mainly with one's own people, by now one's tribe. Reform of ethnic morals was to him a precondition of international sovereignty. 'De-tribalization' could not build a Kenyan nation. In his view cultural change presaged moral anarchy rather than a wider citizenship. Faithfulness to inherited culture was what taught 'a man . . . his mental and moral values and makes him feel it is worth his while to work and fight for liberty'.[92] As first president of Kenya, accordingly, Kenyatta countenanced no *Kulturkampf* against ethnicity. To the contrary, his public statements suggest that he believed – to adapt Richard Aldington – that '[ethnic] patriotism was a lively sense of a collective responsibility', while '[territorial, or Kenyan] nationalism was a silly cock crowing on [other people's] dunghills'.[93] Africa entered the post-colonial age with most of its principled fragmentations, all of them outward-looking, still intact.

Post-Colonial Globalization

Samora Machel of Mozambique, leader of a tougher nationalism than Kenyatta chose to command, had an entirely different political imagination. For Machel, ethnicity was inward-looking. For that reason, he argued, 'for the nation to live, the tribe must die'.[94] This was the common justification for creating one-party states after independence. African leaders proclaimed them to be the only means to control the excessive, ethnically based, competition for the global goods of modernity – education, health and the eradication of poverty. Restricted democracy, they said, would enable Africans to save for future development. Competitive democracy, which tried to satisfy demands stoked by both popular aspiration and demographic multiplication, could lead only to penury.[95] Yet one-party rule, unrestrained by the moral check of shared political community, had the same result. It proved to be a mask of oppression, ethnocracy, and kleptocracy – 'the politics of the belly' – in the first post-colonial age, before the fall of the Berlin Wall, *avant la chute du mur*.[96] This was a protected time for dictators, who strove to close the gates of perception of the wider world and its comparative political systems. So long as they were obedient to their global patrons, the Cold War's superpowers, and kept the local peace, they could rule much as they chose, with no questions asked by the so-called 'international community'.

Today the question is whether, in the second post-colonial era, with end of the Cold War and, with it, the loss of Africa's strategic significance, the continent's governance will change yet again. Dictatorship is no longer so easily tolerated as a dam against the global tide of comparative ideas. In the early 1990s many African countries held national debates on how to win a 'second independence'. It was hoped that their 'civil societies' – professional associations, the churches, the press, trade unions, and so on, but not, it should be noted, ethnicities – would enforce democratic cultures of political accountability and freedom of thought. Not so much is heard of those hopes now, although trade unions are at the core of Zimbabwe's courageous opposition. The 'problem of tribalism', moreover, seems to have returned, and in blood. Ethnic cleansing in Kenya, civil war almost everywhere there are diamonds or oil, and, most horribly, ethnocide in Rwanda, seem to be proof enough.

Nonetheless, tribal chauvinism is not fate but conjuncture. It is the product of very particular alliances and conflicts between the holders of state power and the champions of ethno-regional interests. Ethnicity is universal, as also is resentment of tribal inequality. But civil war is rare. High politics rather than popular sentiment determines the local course of the politics of identity. Hutu did not kill their Tutsi neighbours out of hatred alone, although that had become deep-rooted over many years. They did so because they were ordered to turn on their neighbours by state officials, at a paranoid moment when 'the Tutsi' had become embodied in a tribal army of invasion. Where officials were brave enough to honour their local history of inter-ethnic co-operation, and did not authorize murder, no killing occurred.[97] Elsewhere, too, it seems that moral ethnic thought may protect local understandings against the divisive urgings of the state. All Africa's 'tribes', hardened containers of identity though they may seem to have become, have their diasporas to consider, on the land or in the employment of others, and dependent therefore on the goodwill of strangers. Many African societies are showing a renewed interest in chiefship, a link between locality and the state that may have better prospects for popular control and peace, because it is more historically rooted than any party branch in the old compromises of the mobile frontier.[98]

All Africans can recall, even against their leaders' wishes, subsistence norms in which cross-ethnic exchange and marriage were once a condition of survival. Two examples must suffice, from west and east Africa, respectively. In Mali, on the upper Niger, it was only when the state drew back from attempted mediation through manipulation that agriculturalists and transhumant pastoralists, two different peoples, could negotiate in the mid-1990s a settlement over access to land that was seasonally valuable to both.[99] In Kenya, similarly, the trans-ethnicity of the pre-colonial past shows periodic signs of refusal to be co-opted into the political tribalism of state intrigue. The moral ethnicity of self-help that acknowledges the subsistence entitlement of others can, it appears, imagine Kenya as a community of communities, at times of crisis even a nation. Intimations of citizenship encouraged all to donate blood to all after the bombing of the American embassy in Nairobi and, more recently, to engage in the collective voluntary effort of famine relief on behalf of the country's ordinarily despised nomadic northerners. The fund was organized by the aptly named newspaper, *The Daily Nation*. Contributors made it a condition that the state should have nothing to do with it. In such briefly co-operative trans-ethnicity one may perhaps discern the seeds of a new democratic politics.[100]

It is not tribalism so much as the despairing, or desperado, effects of poverty on rulers and ruled alike, that is the problem with Africa. Africans are not afraid of globalization's culture. What hurts is its deeply politicized economics. Northern farmers are protected against peasants in the South; they enjoy subsidies that are in total larger than the gross income of all of Sub-Saharan Africa. Few established Northern banks and public companies have much interest in Africa, deterred by the weakness of African states. Many new

Northern entrepreneurs who seek to profit from Africa do not open the continent to a free world market so much as negotiate exclusive concessions, whether to drill for oil, or trade arms in exchange for diamonds. The poverty of African states makes it hard to resist such temptations to a fragmented criminalization. But the continent is not without hope. Its youthful peoples are full of energy. On their own internal frontiers of colonization they have for centuries known and mastered cosmopolitan culture. They are entirely at home in Paris or New York. What too many of the best-qualified lack, those who have heard of brave Horatius, is the incentive, and freedom, to apply their energies in Dakar.

Notes and References

1 This contentious title is taken from *The Economist* (London), 13 May 2000. John Iliffe, Jackie Klopp, Mottie Tamarkin and Wilson Wanene have been kind enough to comment on a draft but bear no responsibility for this final version.

2 Professor Mamadou Diouf, of Senegal and Ann Arbor, Michigan, as heard at the UNESCO conference on 'Histoire et perception des frontières en Afrique du Illè au XXè siècles', held at Bamako, Mali, 15–19 March 1999.

3 'When it is like this we remember the words of Horatius,' as a Pan-Africanist Congress convict on South Africa's Robben Island called out, in Xhosa, to his leader, Robert Sobukwe. Horatius's words, as imagined by Thomas Macaulay – 'And how can man die better Than facing fearful odds, For the ashes of his fathers, And the temples of his Gods?' – were popular at PAC funerals, see Benjamin Pogrund, *How can Man Die Better . . . Sobukwe and Apartheid* (London, 1990), pp. 190–1.

4 Formally analysed in Robert H. Jackson, *Quasi-States: Sovereignty, International Relations and the Third World* (Cambridge, 1990).

5 'The Heart of the Matter', *The Economist*, 13 May 2000, pp. 23–5; quotation from the Editorial, 'Hopeless Africa', p. 17.

6 Paul Richards, *Fighting for the Rain Forest: War, Youth and Resources in Sierra Leone* (Oxford and Portsmouth, NH, 1996), pp. 52–9.

7 Different types of globalization are discussed by A.G. Hopkins and C.A. Bayly in their essays in this book; and see the cautionary analysis in Frederick Cooper, 'What is the Concept of Globalization Good for? An African Historian's Perspective', *African Affairs*, 100 (2001), pp. 189–213.

8 For a vigorous statement, see Jean-François Bayart, 'Africa in the World: A History of Extraversion', *African Affairs*, 99 (2000), pp. 217–67.

9 A.D. Smith, *The Ethnic Revival in the Modern World* (Cambridge, 1981), p. xii.

10 Steve Feierman, *The Shambaa Kingdom: A History* (Madison, 1974), pp. 17–22; *idem, Peasant Intellectuals: Anthropology and History in Tanzania* (Madison, 1990), ch. 3; John Iliffe, *A Modern History of Tanganyika* (Cambridge, 1979), pp. 9–11. Agrarian ethnicity could almost, not quite, bridge the gulf between white farmers and black tenants in South Africa; see Charles van Onselen, *The Seed is Mine; The Life of Kas Maine, a South African Sharecropper, 1894–1985* (Cape Town, 1996).

11 James C. Scott, *Domination and the Arts of Resistance* (New Haven, 1990).

12 Jan Vansina, *Paths in the Rainforests: Toward a History of Political Tradition in Equatorial Africa* (Madison, 1990), pp. 78–9.

13 Stuart Hall, 'The Local and the Global: Globalization and Ethnicity', in A.D. King (ed.), *Culture, Globalization and the World System* (Basingstoke, 1991), p. 22.

14 Jomo Kenyatta, *Facing Mount Kenya* (London, 1938), pp. 76, 175.

15 H.M. Gichuiri, quoted in John Lonsdale, 'The Moral Economy of Mau Mau', in Bruce Berman and Lonsdale, *Unhappy Valley: Conflict in Kenya and Africa* (London, 1992), p. 321.

16 David William Cohen and E.S. Atieno Odhiambo, *Siaya: The Historical Anthropology of an African Landscape* (London, 1989), pp. 92–5.

17 Classically, in Aidan Southall, *Alur Society: A Study in Processes and Types of Domination* (Nairobi and New York, 1954), pp. 181–263.

18 Luc de Heusch, *The Drunken King, or, the Origin of the State* (Bloomington, 1982).

19 John Lonsdale, 'Political Accountability in African History', in Patrick Chabal (ed.), *Political Domination in Africa: Reflections on the Limits of Power* (Cambridge, 1986), ch. 7. On the other hand, Bayart, 'Africa in the World', sees extraversion as a means to evade internal accountability.

20 William H. McNeil, *Polyethnicity and National Unity in World History* (Toronto, 1986).

21 These themes are discussed further in A.G. Hopkins and C.A. Bayly's essays in this volume.

22 The classic study remains Eugen Weber, *Peasants into Frenchmen: The Modernization of Rural France, 1870–1914* (London, 1977).

23 Timothy H. Parsons, *The African Rank-and-File: Social Implications of Colonial Military Service in the King's African Rifles, 1902–1964* (Portsmouth, NH, 1999), ch. 3; Robin Luckham, *The Nigerian Military: A Sociological Analysis of Authority and Revolt, 1960–67* (Cambridge, 1971), p. 183; Myron Echenberg, *Colonial Conscripts: The Tirailleurs Sénégalais in French West Africa, 1857–1960* (Portsmouth, NH, 1991), p. 115.

24 Jean-François Bayart, *L'état au Cameroun* (Paris, 1979); for a different view, see Basil Davidson, *The Black Man's Burden: Africa and the Curse of the Nation State* (London, 1992).

25 John Brewer, *The Sinews of Power: War, Money and the English State, 1688–1783* (London, 1989); Lawrence Stone (ed.), *An Imperial State at War: Britain from 1689 to 1815* (London, 1994).

26 J.F. Ade Ajayi, 'The National Question in Nigeria and Historical Perspective' (1992), in Toyin Falola (ed.), *Tradition and Change in Africa: The Essays of J.F. Ade Ajayi* (Trenton, NJ, 2000), ch. 15.

27 Charles Taylor et al., *Multiculturalism and 'The Politics of Recognition'* (Princeton, 1992); Andrea Baumeister, *Liberalism and the 'Politics of Difference'* (Edinburgh, 2000).

28 See three recent, outstanding, histories of the continent: Roland Oliver, *The African Experience* (London, 1991); John Iliffe, *Africans: The History of a Continent* (Cambridge, 1995); John Reader, *Africa: A Biography of the Continent* (Harmondsworth, 1998).

29 As discussed particularly in A.G. Hopkins and C.A. Bayly's essays in this volume.

30 Frederick Cooper, 'Africa and the World Economy', *African Studies Review*, 24 (1981), p. 22.

31 Cooper, 'What is the Concept of Globalization Good for?'

32 Jonathan Hyslop, 'Introduction' to *idem* (ed.), *African Democracy in the Era of Globalisation* (Johannesburg, 1999).

33 Jeffrey Herbst, *States and Power in Africa: Comparative Lessons in Authority and Control* (Princeton, 2000).

34 Jean-Loup Amselle, *Logiques Métisses: Anthropologie de l'identité en Afrique et ailleurs* (Paris 1990); Roy Porter, *The Enlightenment* (London, 2001).

35 See T.N. Harper's essay in this volume.

36 Christopher Clapham, *Africa and the International System: The Politics of State Survival* (Cambridge, 1996), ch. 9; Jean-François Bayart *et al.*, *The Criminalization of the State in Africa* (Oxford, 1999); Patrick Chabal and Jean-Pascal Daloz, *Africa Works: Disorder as Political Instrument* (Oxford, 1999); Cooper, 'What is the Concept of Globalization Good for?'

37 Jacques Attali, 'La fin d'une France', *L'Express* (Paris), 27 July 2000.

38 For recent evidence, see Daniel Lieberman, 'Another Face in our Family Tree', and Maeve G. Leakey *et al.*, 'New Hominin Genus for Eastern Africa Shows Diverse Middle Pliocene Lineages', *Nature,* 410 (22 March 2001), pp. 419–20, 433–40.

39 Oliver, *Experience*, ch. 3; Iliffe, *Africans*, pp. 12–17; Reader, *Africa*, chs. 16 and 17.

40 A.G. Hopkins, *An Economic History of West Africa* (London, 1973), pp. 14–27. Underpopulation is the organizing theme of Iliffe's *Africans*; the quote is from p. 1. For the intercontinental comparisons see also Reader, *Africa*, pp. 3–4.

41 Graham Connah, *African Civilizations: Precolonial Cities and States in Tropical Africa: An Archaeological Perspective* (Cambridge, 1987), pp. 230–1.

42 Roderick J. McIntosh, 'Clustered Cities of the Middle Niger', in David M. Anderson and Richard Rathbone (eds.), *Africa's Urban Past* (Oxford, 2000), ch. 1.

43 Jim Allen, quoted by Graham Connah, 'African City Walls: A Neglected Source?', in Anderson and Rathbone, *Africa's Urban Past*, p. 43.

44 John Iliffe, *The Emergence of African Capitalism* (Basingstoke, 1983), pp. 6–13.

45 Jane Guyer, 'Wealth in People, Wealth in Things'; Jane Guyer and Samuel Eno Belinga, 'Wealth in People as Wealth in Knowledge: Accumulation and Composition in Equatorial Africa', *Journal of African History*, 36 (1995), pp. 83–90, 91–120.

46 Nora Berend, *At the Gates of Christendom: Jews, Muslims and 'Pagans' in Medieval Hungary*, c. *1100–1300* (Cambridge, 2001), ch. 2; S.C. Rowell, *Lithuania Ascending: A Pagan Empire within East-Central Europe 1295–1345* (Cambridge, 1994), chs. 5 and 10.

47 Joseph C. Miller, *Way of Death: Merchant Capitalism and the Angolan Slave Trade*, c. *1730–1830* (London, 1988), p. 49; emphasis added.

48 Iliffe, *African Capitalism*, pp. 5–6; Ralph Austen, *African Economic History* (London, 1987), pp. 40–4.

49 Hopkins, *Economic History of West Africa*, p. 82; Austen, *African Economic History*, pp. 37–44; Iliffe, *Africans*, pp. 51–2.

50 Recently summarized in David Eltis, *Economic Growth and the Ending of the Transatlantic Slave Trade* (New York, 1987); and Barbara Solow (ed.), *Slavery and the Rise of the Atlantic System* (Cambridge, 1991). See also Richard Drayton's essay in this volume.

51 Of a vast literature essentials include: Jack Goody, *Technology, Tradition and the State in Africa* (London, 1971); Paul E. Lovejoy, *Transformations in Slavery: A History of Slavery in Africa* (Cambridge, 1983); Austen, *African Economic History*, chs. 2–4; Miller, *Way of Death*, chs. 2–4 for goods and people; Patrick Manning, *Slavery and African Life* (Cambridge, 1990); Oliver, *African Experience*, ch. 10; Iliffe, *Africans*, ch. 7; Reader, *Africa*, chs. 28 and 37; Martin Klein, *Slavery and*

Colonial Rule in French West Africa (Cambridge, 1998), ch. 1; *idem*, 'The Slave Trade and Decentralized Societies', *Journal of African History*, 42 (2001), pp. 49–65.

52 Gerald W. Hartwig, *The Art of Survival in East Africa: The Kerebe and Long-Distance Trade, 1800–1895* (New York, 1976), pp. 106–8.

53 R.D. Waller, 'Ecology, Migration, and Expansion in East Africa', *African Affairs*, 84 (1985), pp. 347–70; Charles Ambler, *Kenyan Communities in the Age of Imperialism* (New Haven, 1988).

54 Vansina, *Paths*; Christopher Ehret, *Southern Nilotic History* (Evanston, IL, 1971); David L. Schoenbrun, *A Green Place, A Good Place: Agrarian Change, Gender, and Social Identity in the Great Lakes Region to the Fifteenth Century* (Portsmouth, NH, 1998), p. 86.

55 Igor Kopytoff (ed.), *The African Frontier: The Reproduction of Traditional African Societies* (Bloomington, 1987), especially Kopytoff's Introduction.

56 Ike Achebe, 'Religion and Politics in Igboland from the Eighteenth Century to 1930: Earth, God and Power', unpublished manuscript, 2001.

57 See A.G. Hopkins, 'The History of Globalization', above.

58 From another large literature essentials include: Ivor Wilks, *Asante in the Nineteenth Century: The Structure and Evolution of a Political Order* (Cambridge, 1975); *idem*, *Forests of Gold* (Athens, OH, 1993); Kwame Arhin, 'Rank and Class among the Asante and Fante', *Africa*, 53 (1983), pp. 2–22; T.C. McCaskie, 'Accumulation, Wealth and Belief in Asante', *Africa*, 53 (1983), pp. 23–43; McCaskie, *State and Society in Precolonial Asante* (Cambridge, 1994), ch. 1, 5 and 6; Gareth Austin, '"No Elders were Present": Commoners and Private Ownership in Asante 1807–96', *Journal of African History*, 37 (1996), pp. 1–30; A.G. Hopkins, 'Asante and the Victorians: Transition and Partition on the Gold Coast', in Roy Bridges (ed.), *Imperialism, Decolonisation and African History: Essays in Honour of John Hargreaves* (London, 2000), pp. 25–64.

59 T.C. McCaskie, 'The Consuming Passions of Kwame Boakye: Agency and Identity in Asante History', *Journal of African Cultural Studies*, 13 (2000), pp. 43–62.

60 David Hedges, 'Trade and Politics in Southern Mozambique and Zululand in the Eighteenth and Early Nineteenth Centuries', University of London, Ph.D. thesis (1978), ch. 3; Adam Kuper, 'The "House" and Zulu Political Structure in the Nineteenth Century', *Journal of African History*, 34 (1993), pp. 469–87.

61 For these and other proto-globalizers – not his term – see Iliffe, *Africans*, ch. 8.

62 See Amira Bennison's essay in this volume.

63 Benedict Anderson, *Imagined Communities: Reflections on the Origin and Spread of Nationalism* (London and New York, 1983) has much influenced historians of African ethnicity – as distinct from nationhood.

64 David Robinson, *The Holy War of Umar Tal* (Oxford, 1985), chs. 2 and 9; Amselle, *Logiques Métisses*, pp. 71–9 for earlier (counter-) constructions of Fulani (Peul).

65 Tadesse Tamrat, *Church and State in Ethiopia, 1270–1527* (Oxford, 1972); Steven Kaplan, *The Monastic Holy Man and the Christianization of Early Solomonic Ethiopia* (Wiesbaden, 1984).

66 John Iliffe, *The African Poor: A History* (Cambridge, 1987), ch. 2; Richard Pankhurst and Douglas H. Johnston, 'The Great Drought and Famine of 1888–92 in Northeast Africa', in Douglas Johnson and David Anderson (eds.), *The Ecology of Survival: Case Studies from Northeast African History* (London, 1988), ch. 2.

67 R.A. Adeleye, 'The Dilemma of the Wazir', *Journal of the Historical Society of Nigeria*, 4 (1968), pp. 306–11.

68 More has been written on African identities under colonialism than for any other period; this section is yet more terrifyingly impressionistic than the rest of the essay. Two excellent surveys are Carola Lentz, '"Tribalism" and Ethnicity in Africa: A Review of Four Decades of Anglophone Research', *Cahiers de Sciences Humaines*, 31 (1995), pp. 303–28; and Bruce Berman, 'Ethnicity, Patronage and the African State: The Politics of Uncivil Nationalism', *African Affairs*, 97 (1998), pp. 305–41.

69 Ann Stoler and Frederick Cooper, 'Between Metropole and Colony', in Cooper and Stoler (eds.), *Tensions of Empire: Colonial Cultures in a Bourgeois World* (Berkeley and Los Angeles, 1997), pp. 1–56; Robert Hudson, 'The British Origins of South African Segregation', Cambridge, Ph.D. thesis (2000).

70 John Lonsdale, '"Listen while I Read": Orality, Literacy, and Christianity in the Young Kenyatta's Making of the Kikuyu', in Louise de la Gorgendière *et al.*, (eds.), *Ethnicity in Africa: Roots, Meanings and Implications* (Edinburgh, 1996), pp. 17–53.

71 John Iliffe, *A Modern History of Tanganyika* (Cambridge, 1979), p. 324.

72 For a recent study of this dialectic, see Carola Lentz, 'Colonial Constructions and African Initiatives: The History of Ethnicity in Northwestern Ghana', *Ethnos*, 65 (2000), pp. 107–36.

73 See Terence Ranger's exemplary conversion, from 'The Invention of Tradition in Colonial Africa', in Eric Hobsbawm and Ranger (eds.), *The Invention of Tradition* (Cambridge, 1983), ch. 6, to Terence Ranger, 'The Invention of Tradition Revisited: The Case of Colonial Africa', in Ranger and Olufemi Vaughan (eds.), *Legitimacy and the State in Twentieth Century Africa* (Oxford, 1993), ch. 2.

74 For contrasting studies of British West and East Africa: Anne Phillips, *The Enigma of Colonialism: British Policy in West Africa* (London, 1989); Bruce Berman, *Control and Crisis in Colonial Kenya: The Dialectic of Domination* (London, 1990), especially chs. 3 and 5. Crawford Young, *The African Colonial State in Comparative Perspective* (New Haven, 1994) appears to attribute too much power to colonialism.

75 Martin Chanock, *Law, Custom and Social Order: The Colonial Experience in Malawi and Zambia* (Cambridge, 1995); Sally F. Moore, *Social Facts and Fabrications: 'Customary' Law on Kilimanjaro, 1800–1980* (Cambridge, 1986); Diana Jeater, *Marriage, Perversion and Power: The Construction of Moral Discourse in Southern Rhodesia, 1894–1930* (Oxford, 1993); in the global imperial context: Rosalind O'Hanlon, 'Gender in the British Empire', in Judith M. Brown and Wm. Roger Louis (eds.), *The Oxford History of the British Empire, Vol IV: The Twentieth Century* (Oxford, 1999), ch. 16.

76 Cooper, 'What is the Concept of Globalization Good for?', p. 206.

77 For a Kenyan example, see John K. Karanja, *Founding an African Faith: Kikuyu Anglican Christianity, 1900–1945* (Nairobi, 1999), ch. 5; Derek Peterson, 'Writing Gikuyu: Christian Literacy and Ethnic Debate in North Central Kenya, 1908–1952', University of Minnesota, Ph.D. thesis (2000), ch. 6.

78 D.K. Fieldhouse, *The West and the Third World* (Oxford, 1999), ch. 6.

79 Christopher Harrison, *France and Islam in West Africa, 1860–1960* (Cambridge, 1988), p. 73; Amselle, *Logiques Métisses*, p. 79; Francis Robinson, *Atlas of the Islamic World since 1500* (Oxford, 1982), pp. 194–5.

80 Ambler, *Kenyan Communities*, ch. 6–7.

81 The emergence of 'super-tribes' was best studied by the 'Manchester School' of the social anthropology of the Copperbelt after World War II; for which see Richard Werbner, 'South-Central Africa: The Manchester School and After', in Richard

Fardon (ed.), *Localizing Strategies: Regional Traditions of Ethnographic Writing* (Washington, DC, 1990), pp. 152–81.

82 Ernest Gellner, *Nations and Nationalism* (Oxford, 1983), pp. 58–62.

83 Here I generalize from my case study, 'Moral Economy of Mau Mau'; simplified in John Lonsdale, 'Moral Ethnicity, Ethnic Nationalism, and Political Tribalism: The Case of the Kikuyu', in Peter Meyns (ed.), *Staat und Gesellschaft in Afrika: Erosions- und Reformprozesse* (Hamburg, 1996), pp. 93–106.

84 For the recent historiography of English 'languages of class' and 'the politics of place', see Jon Lawrence, *Speaking for the People: Party, Language and Popular Politics in England, 1867–1914* (Cambridge, 1998), Part I – a reference I owe to Max Jones.

85 Adrian Hastings, *The Construction of Nationhood: Ethnicity, Religion and Nationalism* (Cambridge, 1997), pp. 3–4.

86 More generally, see Michael Walzer, *Exodus and Revolution* (New York, 1985).

87 Except in Tanzania, where the missionary adoption of the 'Muslim' lingua franca Swahili for Bible translation, and later in the Mass, may have helped create an unusually strong national identity, see Hastings, *Construction*, p. 165.

88 Quoted in Paul la Hausse de Lalouvière, *Restless Identities: Signatures of Nationalism, Zulu Ethnicity and History* (Pietermaritzburg, 2000), p. 13.

89 David Brading, 'Patriotism and the Nation in Colonial Spanish America', in Luis Roniger and Mario Sznajder (eds.), *Constructing Collective Identities and Shaping Public Spheres: Latin American Paths* (Brighton, 1998), ch. 2.

90 George C. Bond, 'Historical Fragments and Social Constructions in Northern Zambia: A Personal Journey', *Journal of African Cultural Studies*, 13 (2000), pp. 76–93; Kenyatta, *Facing Mount Kenya*, p. 275. 'Indisputable modernity' from Mamadou Diouf, 'The Senegalese Murid Trade Diaspora and the Making of a Vernacular Cosmopolitanism', *Public Culture*, 12 (2000), p. 684.

91 Julius K. Nyerere, 'Ujamaa, – The Basis of African Socialism' (1962), in *idem*, *Freedom and Unity* (London, 1967), pp. 162–71.

92 Kenyatta, *Facing Mount Kenya*, pp. 251, 317. I treat Kenyatta at greater length in 'Kenyatta, God, and the Modern World', in George Deutsch et al. (eds.), *African Modernities* (Oxford, forthcoming).

93 Aldington quoted in letter to editor, *Financial Times*, 22 July 2000. For the Kenya context, see John Lonsdale, 'KAU's Cultures: Imaginations of Community and Constructions of Leadership in Kenya after the Second World War', *Journal of African Cultural Studies*, 13 (2000), pp. 107–24.

94 Quoted in Mahmood Mamdani, *Citizen and Subject: Contemporary Africa and the Legacy of Late Colonialism* (Princeton, 1996), p. 135.

95 Iliffe, *Africans*, ch. 11.

96 Jean-François Bayart, *The State in Africa: The Politics of the Belly* ([Paris, 1989] London, 1993).

97 John Janzen, 'Historical Consciousness and a *prise de conscience* in Genocidal Rwanda', *Journal of African Cultural Studies*, 13 (2000), pp. 153–68.

98 Richard Rathbone, *Nkrumah and the Chiefs: The Politics of Chieftaincy in Ghana, 1951–60* (Oxford, 2000).

99 Kare Lode, *Synthèse du processus des recontres intercommunitaires du Nord du Mali* (Stavanger, 1996); Robin-Edward Poulton and Ibrahim ag Youssouf, *A Peace of Timbuktu: Democratic Governance, Development and African Peacemaking* (New York, 1998).

100 Generally, see Mordechai Tamarkin, 'Culture and Politics in Africa: Legitimizing

Ethnicity, Rehabilitating the Postcolonial State', *Nationalism and Ethnic Politics*, 2 (1996), pp. 360–80. For Kenya, see Jacqueline Klopp, 'Electoral Despotism in Kenya: Land, Patronage, and Resistance in the Multi-Party Context', McGill University, Ph.D. thesis (2000) – to whom I also owe much helpful discussion of recent Kenyan politics.

A.G. HOPKINS

Globalization with and without Empires: From Bali to Labrador

Connections between Bali and Labrador do not come readily to mind, so it is not surprising to learn that the two have never been joined together for purposes of historical enquiry. Profound differences of geography, economy, society and politics appear to violate, comprehensively, the rule that like should be compared with like. Even their juxtaposition on this occasion is to a degree fortuitous. The choice of Bali arose from a visit to the famous art gallery at Ubud, and from the realization on the return journey that none of the exhibited paintings, which cover a range of styles and subjects, depicted the Dutch, who had ruled the island as part of The Netherlands East Indies during the first half of the twentieth century.[1] Why had powerful, alien masters been given a thick undercoat of paint by indigenous and expatriate artists alike, and why was Bali represented almost exclusively by paintings of tropical landscapes in both 'primitive' and modern naturalist styles, even during the colonial period? As these questions were being formulated, others presented themselves, coincidentally, following the appearance of Survival's compelling report on the fate of the Innu in Canada.[2] In the 1990s the Innu were on the point of extinction: they had been overwhelmed by Western forces, not in the distant past but in the post-colonial era and by policies promoted by the modern nation state they inhabited. How and why had this happened?[3]

Separate answers could well be, and indeed have been, given to these questions. Juxtaposing the two cases, however, suggests that the experiences of the Balinese and the Innu, though very different, can nevertheless be placed in the broad context of the history of globalization. Specifically, both were affected by what we have termed here modern globalization in its imperial guise, though to different degrees and with very different consequences; similarly, both felt the imprint of post-colonial globalization, though again to varying depths and with divergent outcomes.[4] The exposition that follows is an exercise in historical counterpoint: it might also be thought of as being the intellectual equivalent of the slogan 'think global – act local'. Common elements are contained in the main theme; diversity of place and differences of time are represented by variations in the particularities of the two cases.

Colonial Expansion and the Conquest of Klungkung, 1908

On the morning of 28 April 1908, four companies of the Netherlands Indies Army began the march from their coastal base to the capital of Klungkung, the paramount realm on the island of Bali.[5] We know that it was hot and humid because it always is: in Bali, situated – as the travel brochures might put it – a stone's throw from the Equator, even the mosquitoes sweat. We may guess that the mood of the troops was grim: the Dutch had not forgotten their failure, in the face of resolute resistance, to subdue Klunkung in 1849, and they had received intelligence that Klungkung's king had resolved on a fight to the death – referred to by the Balinese as *puputan* or 'finishing'. Moreover, spies had reported that the capital and surrounding villages were heavily fortified. However, the troops reached Klungkung in the afternoon without encountering opposition or indeed without seeing anyone at all. It was only when they rolled their field guns into place opposite the royal residence that a cluster of men and boys emerged dressed entirely in ceremonial white and brandishing lances and daggers. Without pausing, they charged the Dutch troops but were killed or wounded by volleys from repeater rifles and howitzers before they could make contact. They were immediately replaced by other white-clad figures, including women – many resplendent in gold and jewels and leading or carrying children. They, too, were felled but were in turn replaced until nearly two hundred Balinese lay dead or wounded. It was then that the king and his remaining nobles appeared, repeated the charge, this time across the bodies of their compatriots, and were also brought down – as was the kingdom itself.

The suicide of Klungkung's king and his immediate followers was a poignant and tragic statement of helplessness in the face of forces that could neither be diverted nor controlled. Denpasar, an independent and much larger town to the south, had already fallen to Dutch troops in 1906, when over 3,000 Balinese had been killed in a suicidal confrontation that foreshadowed the equally one-sided contest at Klungkung two years later.[6] The history of these episodes can be looked at from several different angles: much could be written, for example, about the nature of political authority in Bali's fractious kingdoms, about the ritual significance of official suicides, and about indigenous perceptions of the foreign presence.[7] For present purposes, however, the events of 1908 can be seen as completing the subjugation of Bali and signalling the start of a new phase in its history as a component of The Netherlands East Indies. From the perspective of this volume, they marked

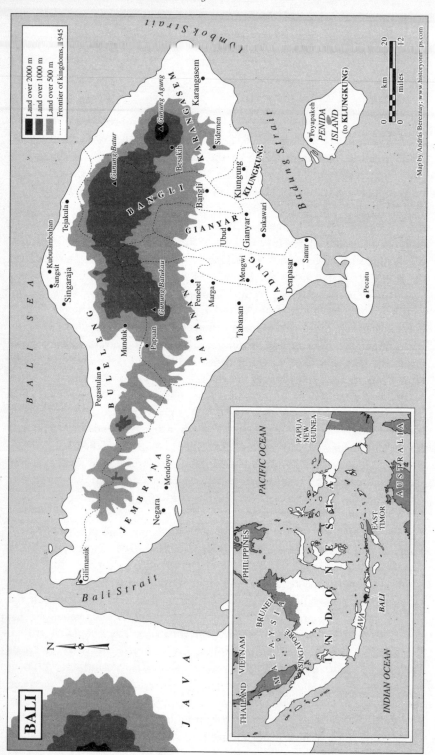

the triumph of the form of modern globalization propelled by Dutch imperialism.

In 1815 the Dutch began the task of modernizing their newly liberated state, which had been invaded by France in 1794–5, turned briefly into a republic, a commonwealth and a kingdom, and annexed by Napoleon in 1810 before regaining its independence in 1813. The peace settlement united the northern and southern segments of the Netherlands and restored the country's possessions in the East Indies with the aim of building a strong and friendly buffer state in north-west Europe – an aim echoed in the peace settlement that followed World War II.[8] Nation-building under William I (1815–40) and his successors involved an ambitious programme of political consolidation and economic development. The political strategy suffered a major setback in 1830, when the southern territories seceded to form a new state: Belgium. The scheme for a consolidated Netherlands was a piece of imposed diplomatic cartography that never stood much chance of success. However, the residual element, The Netherlands, transformed itself in the course of the nineteenth century into a stable nation state. This process was greatly assisted by a dual strategy of development that linked the economy with the Ruhr to the east and to the wider world through the great ports of Amsterdam and Rotterdam to the west.[9]

The restoration of the East Indies was seen by Dutch policy-makers to be a key element in building a stable polity in The Netherlands.[10] Raffles, who had devised his own agenda for promoting British interests in Southeast Asia, might fume at lost opportunities. Observers closer to home realized the compelling need for strong and friendly states across the Channel, since the French, though down, could never quite be counted out. Accordingly, in 1824 Britain acknowledged the claim of the Dutch to territories south of the Straits of Singapore – essentially Sumatra and Java but also points to the east that had still to be determined. The British guarantee boosted Dutch colonial enterprise: The Netherlands Trading Society was formed, also in 1824, to promote commercial links that had been cut by the French wars; in 1830 a new Governor-General, Johannes van den Boosch, introduced the Cultivation (or Culture) System, which gave local villages responsibility for producing fixed proportions of the required export crops.[11] These innovations were followed by a sizeable growth of agricultural exports, first indigo and sugar, then coffee, tea and tobacco, and by a return trade in manufactured goods, both very largely financed and transported by Amsterdam and Rotterdam with additional investment and political support from The Hague. In 1870 the Cultivation System was replaced by what became known as the Liberal Policy, which opened up state-led development to private interests and encouraged the rapid expansion of capital flows to fund new expatriate-run estates (producing rubber and copra) and mining activities that generated exports of tin and petroleum.

Colonial development made a significant contribution to nation-building at home.[12] Trade and investment tied key interest groups in Amsterdam, Rotterdam and The Hague into the new state. The value of exports from The Netherlands East Indies grew about tenfold between 1870 and 1930, drawing successively on rubber, copra, tin and palm oil, and shifting, as the period advanced, from Java to Sumatra. Taxes derived from colonial trade stabilized government finances and were a key element in settling the nation's balance of payments, in the same way as surpluses on trade with India helped Britain to meet her deficits elsewhere. According to one estimate, almost one third of Dutch state income between 1850 and 1870 stemmed, directly and indirectly, from The Netherlands East Indies.[13] Furthermore, the extension of colonial rule and the development of plantations in the late nineteenth century created a group of officials, settlers and managers who were committed to the maintenance of empire.[14] This growing colonial interest was well placed to promote its activities in the press and through the influence of the Liberal Party, which favoured free trade and the privatization of colonial enterprise. By the time Klungkung fell in 1908, the Dutch had come to believe that the empire was vital to their position as 'first among the middle powers of Europe'.

From the Dutch perspective, the subordination of Klungkung was the culmination of the efforts begun in 1824 to reoccupy their possessions in the East Indies.[15] The economic development of the region required the extension of political control, which in turn provoked resistance. War with Java between 1825 and 1830 pointed the way to hostilities that continued in different parts of the region throughout the century. Military expeditions to north Bali in 1846 and 1848 met fierce resistance and were repulsed; a further invasion, in 1849, achieved limited success in some parts of the island but was driven out of Klungkung. If, in the event, some of Bali's rulers were obliged to acknowledge the suzerainty of The Netherlands, in practice they were left to govern themselves. It was not until the late nineteenth century that the Dutch made further moves, this time determined and ultimately successful, to consolidate their hold on Indonesia. A long campaign in Aceh, begun in 1873, led to its incorporation in 1908. The kingdoms of Bulelang and Jembrana in north Bali were annexed in 1882; the island of Lombok was taken in 1894.[16] These and other advances coincided with the new wave of investment that accompanied the adoption of the Liberal Policy after 1870. They were also prompted by the fear that, at a time when the great powers were competing for the remaining 'unclaimed' parts of the world, The Netherlands might be out-manoeuvred by larger rivals unless her own title was fully staked and properly registered.

How did this invasion of peripheral forces look from its centre, the volcanic Mount Agung, the highest point on the island and considered by Balinese to be 'the navel of the world'? As we have just seen, the Balinese kingdoms resisted Dutch encroachments in the nineteenth century. When resistance became futile, they acknowledged, in the most dramatic way possible, that their world had come to an end. Yet those who died in Denpasar and Klungkung could not have foreseen that their traditions were shortly to be refurbished and made the basis of colonial rule. As The Netherlands fits the pattern of modern globalization and its imperial annex outlined earlier,[17] so the Balinese experience illustrates how colonial states were made or reconfigured in the aftermath of conquest. The case of Bali, in contrast to the fate of the Innu, also shows how local identities could be reinforced as well as dismembered: in the twentieth century, the Balinese became more like themselves than they had ever been.

In the nineteenth century the Balinese, like the Innu, had been very largely bypassed by the accelerating forces of international and imperial expansion. Theirs was a small island at the edge of much larger and more valuable territories. When the Dutch relaunched their empire in the East Indies in the 1820s, they first concentrated on Java; when the next wave of expansion came, after 1870, Sumatra came to the fore. The Balinese kingdoms were left, more or less, to run their own affairs. The shock of conquest, when it came, was therefore more acute than it would have been had annexation been preceded by a period of creeping imperialism. On the other hand, when the first Dutch administrators looked over their new possession, they concluded that it was a prime candidate for conservation precisely because it had not been sullied by foreign influences. They then set about re-erecting the structures they had just torn down.

A mixture of reasons lay behind this decision.[18] The Liberal Policy implemented after 1870 had brought disruption as well as development. Colonial excesses caused a reaction in The Netherlands that found expression in a programme of reform known as the Ethical Policy, which was adopted officially in 1901. As the World Bank shifted in the 1990s from 'getting prices right' to 'bringing the state back in', so the Dutch government amended its liberal policies at the start of the century to enable the colonial authorities to play a greater role in the development process, notably by promoting education and welfare services. In this way, the policy validated a new version of the civilizing mission: the duty to protect indigenous peoples authorized interference and even annexation and justified the removal of rulers who failed to meet the test of civilization. In the event, the Ethical Policy was more impressive on paper than on the ground.[19] Nevertheless, Bali, being a late acquisition, gained a measure of protection from the new policy, which took a more benign view of indigenous social structures. Practical considerations pointed in the same direction. As the Dutch made the transition from conquest to management, they created a demand for local agents to assist the colonial administration. From the 1920s, the Dutch version of indirect rule, like its British and French counterparts, began by restoring displaced ruling groups; officials then spent the greater part of the colonial period devising means of sustaining them. A further calculation suggested that local rulers could be useful allies in the face of militant Islamic movements, whose presence (imagined as well as real) terrified officials throughout the colonial world from the late nineteenth century onwards. The same argument was applied when nationalism made its appearance: if 'culture' remained strong, 'politics' – so it was thought – would remain weak.[20] Similarly, 'crass materialism' was to be held at bay: Bali, unlike Java and Sumatra, never became a site for expatriate plantations or factories.

Underlying these arguments in favour of preservation was the belief that Bali was distinctive, if not unique, because of the survival there of ancient Hindu cultural traditions.[21] Hindu beliefs had spread to much of Java by the seventh century before being overlaid or replaced by Islam, a process that was more or less complete by the sixteenth century. At that point, Bali became an island of refuge for Hindu nobles and priests who had a motive for escaping from eastern Java and the means of doing so. Thereafter, the small kingdoms they took over or established on the island acquired an Indian imprint, though, as is the way with what has been termed 'glocalization', the recipients adapted and blended imported influences to suit local needs.

European visitors had long been aware of Bali's semi-Indianized culture and forms of government. Under the influence of the orientalism sponsored by the Enlightenment, they also accorded it importance and respect. The Dutch, following the course set by Raffles and others early in the nineteenth century, saw their task not simply as one of preserving what they found but of paring away recent accretions to reveal the alleged purity of the original. The restoration and elevation of Bali's rajas after 1908 was followed by a raft of supporting measures during the next thirty years:[22] legal enactments hardened the definition of caste; ancient Balinese texts were assembled to provide a supposedly authentic basis for customary law; *corveé* labour was revived on the convenient justification that it was in accord with distant traditions; educational policy promoted Balinese instead of Malay; action was taken to foster the production and adoption of traditional dress; the education of young upper-class girls was designed to preserve tradition and to encourage them to instil it into the peasantry.[23] In 1932, the Dutch celebrated their success in reinstating antiquity by opening a large museum in Denpasar displaying Balinese customs and crafts. By then, Balinese music and dance had begun to make the transition from sacred rites to art forms, and the first major hotel on the island had already been open for four years.[24]

Bali became 'the last island paradise' because the Dutch presented it as such.[25] This is what the first Western anthropologists and artists – headed by Walter Spiess – found when they arrived in Bali in the 1920s.[26] They were entranced to discover authenticity and simplicity in a world so recently turned upside down in Europe by war; they were inspired to embellish and publicize the image and thus to put the island on the global map. Scholars for long followed suit. To study Bali was to study a fertile island inhabited by a peaceful, artistic people living in social harmony. Contrary indications were ignored or explained away as aberrations. In being endowed with tradition, however, Bali was denied even colonial forms of modernization[27] while continuing to experience, as we now know, considerable conflict and hardship.[28] The kingdoms annexed by the Dutch had long been rent by internal rivalries: social harmony was not a priority of Bali's slave-trading rulers in the pre-colonial era. In reinstating and creating 'ancient' customs, the Dutch contributed to these tensions by generating dissent among castes and nobles, and disaffection among those who felt excluded from the structure of opportunities put in place by colonial rule. An alternative history of colonial Bali would now be obliged to emphasize the poverty, disease and unrest that characterized Dutch rule, and the ways in which hardship increased during the 1930s and became even heavier under the Japanese occupation between 1942 and 1945.[29]

But myth continued to mask reality. The Dutch themselves became convinced of their own propaganda: they believed that they could reoccupy their colonial possessions after 1945 and complete their colonial mission.[30] The awakening and the retreat were equally sudden. However, the myth of the island paradise endured. The massive outbreak of violence that occurred in 1965 and caused the deaths of some 80,000 people (five per cent of Bali's population) puzzled even experienced observers, who attributed it to 'a touch of madness . . . on these weird and lovely islands' perhaps brought on by the religious fervour that had inspired mass suicide in 1908.[31] In reality, the eruption can be explained fully only by understanding the interaction between Bali's indigenous politics and social structure and the form of imperial globalization projected by the Dutch, who endowed the island with more traditions than it possessed and then tried to freeze them in a rapidly changing world.[32]

There is, however, one last twist to the story. By an amazing quirk of historical fate, the wholly backward-looking policies promoted by the Dutch have enabled Bali to spring fully armed into the twenty-first century. Having bypassed both significant export-crop development and manufacturing during the colonial era, the island has leapt in one bound from agriculture to tourism, one of the major activities in the new globalized economy.[33] Tourism is now easily the largest industry on the island (apart from agriculture): in 1988 it attracted about one and a half million foreign visitors to the island, which had a total of three million inhabitants. Bali's name has become its fame; its trademark, the 'last island paradise', is known throughout the world. It is a place where celebrities go to escape the burdens of success, but where the roads are well made and sufficiently spacious to allow the *paparazzi* to follow. The final irony is that the Dutch have now been edited out of the story they did so much to initiate: the former colonial rulers have been excised because they have no part to play in Bali's preferred account of its past. Their greatest legacy may have been to have enabled myth to become reality, thereby making themselves redundant.

The Last Frontier and the Crisis of the Innu, 1993

The second event takes us from the tropics to the tundra, and from the age of great European empires to the present. One day in February 1992, six children aged 12–14 burned to death in a house fire in the Innu settlement of Davis Inlet (known to the Innu as Utshimassits) on the coast of Labrador.[34] This was a tragic event but not, so it was thought at the time, one to arouse concern beyond the community itself. However, almost one year later, six of their friends barricaded themselves in an unheated shack in temperatures of −40C degrees and tried to commit suicide by sniffing petrol from plastic bags. Fortunately, an Innu policeman discovered them in time: they all survived and subsequently were able to speak of the extreme depression they felt at the approaching anniversary of the death of their friends, and of their conviction that the ghost of a young Innu was telling them to end their lives. With great presence of mind, the policeman had managed to video the scene as the children were removed to safety. The tape was shown on television. The whole of Canada was shocked by pictures of the children fighting the attempts to rescue them and pleading to be left alone so that they could die.[35] At this point, journalists and television crews descended on Davis Inlet and put the spotlight on the small community. It emerged that the 500 or so Innu in the tiny settlement were living in conditions that resembled a refugee camp in one of the least favoured parts of the underdeveloped world. They were without running water or mains drainage; infant mortality rates were exceptionally high; the life expectation of adults was exceptionally low. Almost one third of the adults in the community had tried to kill themselves; the suicide rate was the highest in the world and 13 times that for Canadians as a whole. 80 to 85 per cent of the residents aged over 15 were alcoholics.

As we shall see, these suicides, like those at Klungkung 85 years before, were tragic statements of the abandonment of hope in the face of alien forces that could be neither diverted nor controlled. As the events at Klungkung completed the subjugation of the kingdom, so the deaths at Davis Inlet marked the last stand of the Innu and the prelude, so it seemed, to their final extinction. Yet the episodes occurred in very different contexts. The events of 1908 signalled the advance of a form of imperial globalization; those of 1993 occurred in the post-colonial era, within a nation state, and without external interference. Globalization was strongly implicated in both cases, but in the 1990s it was of a type that was sufficiently new and powerful to be capable of pushing the frontier of change towards and eventually over the remote and scattered population of north Labrador. However, to explain the fate of the Innu exclusively in terms of recent developments is to miss an important element of causation: their relative isolation, the shock they felt as the immensity of the forces bearing down on them was revealed, and their response in abandoning hope, all need deeper probing; so, too, do the policies that brought these developments together. Accordingly, we must start by looking at the history of the Innu's involvement with the wider world.

As the Dutch sought to reconstruct their much-battered state after 1815, so the British set out to win a definitive peace that would provide a permanent safeguard for their world-wide interests.[36] This strategy was driven by a complex of interests and involved far-reaching reforms at home and the further extension of Britain's presence abroad. On the home front, political and social reforms signalled the shift from Old Corruption to New Probity: the franchise was extended, the monarchy was renovated, and the English gentleman was re-educated to serve the new liberal state. The key international development, the adoption of free trade, promoted British manufactured exports and a rising volume of primary commodities, and provided extensive opportunities for British capital. As the century advanced, the pound sterling became the master currency of world trade, and income from overseas investment played an increasing role in settling Britain's balance of payments and, indirectly, in upholding the political system. In these ways, the British adjusted to the potentially destabilizing forces of population growth, industrialization and urbanization while avoiding political upheaval. In the process, they developed a more defined sense of national unity and a concept of Britishness that overlaid class and regional divisions.

Nation-building at home was closely connected to the spread of Britain's global influence overseas. Free trade and empire created opportunities that incorporated key interest groups (not least in Scotland) into the state and generated mass employment in the new industrial centres, thus helping to reconcile the potentially hostile forces of capital and labour. A Christian, liberal ideology spanned the social classes at home and provided a justification for expansion abroad. The application of universal principles was a duty that had the advantage of producing a scattering of like-minded allies throughout the world. What became known as the civilizing mission entailed refashioning others, where possible, in Britain's own image. Since conversions of this kind needed to be anchored in appropriate institutions, Britain became involved in social engineering on a global scale – offering constitutions, reforming property rights, training elites and erecting whole new states. The scale and scope of this endeavour were such that it can be referred to, without exaggeration, as the world's first development plan; nothing comparable was attempted until the United States launched its own global programme after 1945.[37]

Where indigenous populations predominated, universal principles had to be adapted to take account of existing and often entrenched institutions and customs.[38] Co-operative elites could be created or reshaped and sometimes fully converted to British values and the British way of life. But the task of transforming whole societies proved to be insuperable. In any case, it became clear that there were advantages to maintaining and sometimes reinforcing what were later termed 'traditional societies'. In these circumstances, the

NEWFOUNDLAND PROVINCE

Map by András Bereznay; www.historyonmaps.com

imperial style of globalization created colonial states out of existing ethnic groups or established smaller polities. What the Dutch did in Bali, the British did on a much larger scale in India and Africa.

Elsewhere, however, scattered populations and open lands invited a different solution.[39] In the Americas, Australia and New Zealand, territory was first claimed and then populated by white settlers. The series of migrations that took place in the nineteenth century provide one of the best examples of the globalization of the time. These movements took Europeans in vast numbers to all corners of the world, especially after 1850, when better transport facilities and improved information became available. The results included colonies of settlement that were designed to complement the mother country. They were expected to supply agricultural products and to import British manufactures and to use the wealth so gained to reproduce the social and political institutions of the home country. In short, they were to be carbon copies of the original, places where solid gentry and yeomen values would flourish, where loyalty to the crown would be unwavering, and where imitation would be accompanied by deference. The reality was rather different. 'Glocalization' operated to produce institutions that were adapted, to some extent, to the environment, and the aspirations of the settlers found expression in nationalist claims that sometimes conflicted with British interests. The results, nevertheless, remained gratifying. The copies may have been faint but they could still be recognized. Greater Britain, as the settler colonies were often called, remained tied to the British economy until well into the twentieth century. Their respect for the monarchy remained undiminished, their loyalty was demonstrated during two world wars, and their well-practised deference in cultural affairs (known in Australia as 'cultural cringe') survived, for a time, the demise of empire in the 1960s.

Canada's development was therefore an extension overseas of Britain's own economic and nation-building endeavours. The civilizing mission was an important part of settler ideology from the early nineteenth century, but it was borrowed from the master plan devised in Britain. The maxim joining 'the Bible and the plough' was as prominent on the prairies as it was in the tropics. The aim was to produce God-fearing farmers who would sustain themselves and make the country self-supporting too. The ideal was that of assimilation rather than of association. Admittedly, the federal constitution that was eventually adopted was a formal departure from the unitary system favoured in Britain.[40] Nevertheless, the predominantly British settlers who began to fill up Canada's vast spaces from the 1850s were clear that their model of life and values was the one that deserved to be spread, and needed to be spread, if the new country was to gain coherence. When stiffened by the racist ideas that came to the fore at the close of the nineteenth century, the model acquired an element of assertiveness that was further reinforced by the evident weakness and seemingly backward condition of Canada's indigenous people.

Assimilationist theories found their clearest expression in policies devised to deal with 'native peoples'.[41] As early as the 1830s, there were determined attempts to concentrate indigenous hunters and gatherers in reservations and to convert them to settled agriculture and Christianity.[42] This endeavour required the colonial authorities to define ethnicity and to classify local peoples.[43] In 1857 the Gradual Civilization Act set down the conditions under which 'Indian' status could be exchanged for full citizenship. When Canada became a Dominion in 1867, jurisdiction over Indians and their land was assigned to the Federal Government, which adopted a more assertive attitude towards Indian resistance. In 1884 the first of a series of Indian Acts was passed, partly in response to pressure from a coalition of missionary interests. The aim was to destroy tribal and clan systems by controlling the movements of nomadic peoples, curbing traditional customs, and redefining the role of women in particular.[44] The goal of total assimilation remained unaltered and unbending until the late twentieth century. In 1945, the year the Dutch reaffirmed their policy of conserving traditional Bali, the Canadian government endorsed its established policy of assimilation.[45] The only concession, in a world suddenly peopled by liberation movements, was that, henceforth, there would be more persuasion and less coercion.

How, then did the British state, at one remove, impinge upon the Innu, formerly known as the Montagnais-Naskapi Indians?[46] The Innu are nomadic hunters (mainly of caribou and fish) who at one time ranged from the northern shores of the Gulf of St Lawrence to the grasslands and tundra of the Labrador plateau that reaches up to the Arctic circle.[47] Their location ensured that they were one of the first indigenous people to come into contact with European explorers and traders who made their way up the St Lawrence River in the sixteenth century.[48] Population estimates for this period are little more than careful guesses, but one calculation suggests that in 1500 the Montagnais-Naskapi numbered about 4,000 and were divided into 25 to 30 bands. They were, then, a relatively small group who at that time patrolled a large area. Territorial boundaries were not closely defined; political authority was decentralized. Rights of use, however, were clearly established, and disputed claims over access were a source of occasional conflict with neighbouring peoples, especially the Inuit in the north-west and the Iroquois to the south. There are several other imponderables about the history of the Innu between the sixteenth and the nineteenth centuries. It is certain that they were involved in the fur trade from the outset and had long-standing connections with the Hudson's Bay Company; it is less clear how the trade affected their political economy. Export growth may have promoted individualism and enhanced the position of men in particular. It brought imports of guns and metal goods, but also transmitted disease and probably reduced the size of the population.[49] Given the fragmentary state of the information currently available, it is hard to know precisely what the consequences of these early contacts were. At present, however, it appears that the Innu avoided a major disaster to their way of life and were able to incorporate external demands without seriously disrupting their established hunting and gathering activities.[50]

When Canada's sparsely populated lands began to fill up from the 1850s, indigenous peoples were either overrun, where they got in the way, or were displaced and marginalized. Numbers everywhere dropped dramatically, partly through warfare but mainly through the spread of European diseases, such as measles and smallpox. It might be thought that the Innu, being so close to the point of entry into Canada, were the first to suffer. However, this was not the case. The fur frontier receded in the nineteenth century. The Grand Trunk and other railways ran westwards to open up the plains for wheat production, and it was there (and further west still in British Columbia, where there was competition for mineral rights) that the main confrontations took place. The extension of the settler frontier brought conflict with the Cree and Blackfoot in the 1860s, and instances of serious resistance on the Red River in 1869 and in Saskatchewan in 1885.[51] By this time, moreover, the Innu had already begun to move northwards in response to encroachments from the Iroquois, their more powerful southern neighbours.[52] As a result, the Innu were largely bypassed by the development of Canada's imperial economy between 1850 and 1950. Very few incoming settlers chose to venture into such harsh and unpromising territory, where the arctic winter lasted eight months and there was no prospect of agricultural development; no troops trekked in their direction. Like the Balinese, the Innu survived colonial rule,[53] but through neglect rather than through paternal protection.

The 'age of irrelevance', as it has been called, ended for the Innu in the 1950s, when they became caught up in developments that affected other indigenous peoples in northern Canada.[54] A new frontier, spearheaded by trans-national corporations rather than by hardy settlers, was opened up in hitherto remote and often impenetrable areas. The old agricultural economy had already fostered the growth of manufacturing in Canada's major southern towns. The newer economy was made possible by technical advances in prospecting techniques and in mineral extraction, by improved engineering skills and by a further revolution in communications based on radio, motor vehicles and aeroplanes. Oil was discovered in Alberta in 1947; uranium was found in Saskatchewan shortly afterwards. Schemes for generating hydro-electric power followed as the potential of the northern rivers occupied by the Inuit, Cree and others was revealed. Economic prospects were partnered by political ambitions. When Newfoundland joined the Canadian Confederation in 1949, bringing Labrador with it, the Innu, like other indigenous peoples of northern Canada, were subjected to a reinvigorated programme of nation-building. Ottawa's claims to sovereignty, founded on the doctrine of *terra nullius*, assumed that the state possessed rights over all land within its borders. Policies of assimilation were given a new impetus. As the Director of Northern

Labrador Affairs put it in 1955: 'One fact seems clear – civilization is on the northward march, and for the Eskimo and the Indian there is no escape . . . The only course now open, for there can be no turning back, is to fit him as soon as may be to take his full place as a citizen in our society.'[55]

The Innu were hit simultaneously by strikes from all directions.[56] The search for new sources of energy led to the development of the Churchill Falls hydro-electric plant in 1972. Currently there are plans to enlarge the complex to meet the demand for electricity in the United States. In this respect, the Innu are right up to date: the new scheme is the product of the North-American Free Trade Association, a regional grouping that is both an expression of, and a response to, the forces of contemporary, post-colonial globalization. The search for minerals resulted in the discovery of the world's largest nickel deposits in Innu territory in 1994; a scheme to drive the Trans-Labrador Highway into the heart of Nitassinan was announced in 1997. An aerial bombardment added to the land-based assault: since 1979 the Innu have been subjected to heavy concentrations of low-level flying for military training from Goose Bay. The revived 'civilizing mission', promoted vigorously by missionaries and officials, attempted to convert, educate and settle the Innu.[57] By turning the Innu into wage-labourers, the government hoped to prevent them from becoming 'loafers whose only aim is to extract more and more handouts' from the state.[58]

The consequences have been devastating. Land has been appropriated without consultation. The Innu economy, which depends on access to natural resources and on maintaining a careful ecological balance over a very wide area, has come under severe pressure. Hunting grounds have been degraded; fish stocks have been reduced; birth and burial sites have been destroyed. Economic disruption has damaged the Innu sense of being, which is derived from the relationship between people and nature; lacking economic and spiritual support, the social structure has fallen apart. When, belatedly, the destruction was noticed, government responded by redoubling its effort to apply policies of assimilation that had been tried and found wanting for more than a century.[59] In a final effort to turn the Innu into good Canadians, the government grouped them into 20 settlements. This experiment, like its predecessors, failed. New schools marginalized the Innu language and separated young Innu from a way of life that conformed to the rhythm of the seasons rather than to the calendar of the school term. The settlement at Davis Inlet, founded in 1967, turned out to be a disaster that ended in the events of 1993.

However, the story of the Innu is not yet over. History has played a trick on Canadians as it did on the Dutch in Bali, though it is one of a different kind. Canada's nation-building enterprise has always tended to look outwards, notwithstanding the insular presence of Quebec. Britain was the first point of reference: to begin with, it was a model to be copied; later it served to define difference. The United States became in turn a threat and an ally, and in both capacities helped to shape the idea of Canadian nationality. This external orientation meant that Canada was ill-prepared to respond to an unexpected attack from the rear, which came in the form of claims made by indigenous peoples. The Innu, like the Inuit and other First Nations in Canada, are now fighting back in the courts, through peaceful protest, and via the media to reclaim their land rights and to secure their own homeland.[60] The courts have now recognized the concept of aboriginal title; pressure for self-government is growing. The Innu Nation, originally intended to be a device for perpetuating a form of indirect rule by Canada, has become an powerful advocate of the Innu cause.[61]

Ideologically, the tables have been turned. White Canadians who defined themselves against British colonialism in the nineteenth century now find themselves accused of being the true colonizers of the land and the real exploiters of its original inhabitants. The assimilationist policies pursued so resolutely since the 1830s, being now so visibly out of joint with the times, have been replaced by vaguer notions, such as participation.[62] In Canada, as in New Zealand and to some extent in Australia too, established concepts of nationality have been called into question by the claims of First Nations. Modern globalization helped to define the nation state; post-colonial globalization has blurred its identity.

Conclusion

It is easy to suppose that the Balinese and the Innu have more that sets them apart than draws them together, and, furthermore, that they are unrepresentative of the history of the regions of which each forms only a tiny part. Generalizations about The Netherlands East Indies are derived from developments in Sumatra and Java; Bali, long at the margin of larger events, was deliberately cordoned off by the Dutch. Generalizations about Canada depend almost exclusively on the development of the frontier from the St Lawrence to British Columbia and on the history of white settlement. The Innu, to the north, were not so much fenced off as left behind. Only the most recent studies recognize their name and their existence.

Yet the Balinese and the Innu both have places in the wider world, and not just as exceptions or oddities. They fit into two phases of globalization, modern and post-colonial, and they illustrate the different strategies deployed in each stage to integrate or to manage the evolving international order. Modern globalization, as defined here,[63] was bound up with the creation of a global economy based on exports of industrial manufactures and imports of primary commodities, the promotion of nation states in Europe, and the formation of new states overseas. Under this regime, integration took place either by harnessing indigenous societies, as occurred in The Netherlands East Indies, or through the agency of white settlers, as in the case of Canada.

The colonial states that were called into being by this process employed two managerial strategies: association and assimilation. Where indigenous peoples were numerous, well organized and in control of valuable and accessible resources, as they were in Indonesia, they were drawn into the colonial world of export-crop production, whether as farmers or as wage-earners, but were not subjected to intensive policies of assimilation. However, not every locality fitted this template at all points. As colonial rulers became aware of the difficulties of promoting export crops and of the political costs involved, they were more inclined to concentrate on established or promising regions and to conserve those that appeared to have more problems than potential. In The Netherlands East Indies, the two great producers of exports, Java and Sumatra, served the needs of the time. Bali, a small, outlying island, provided an excellent case for indirect rule and colonial conservation – a place where mini-states were built or restored to promote stability rather than development.

Where white settlers predominated, as they did in Canada, they either overran the indigenous inhabitants or pushed them to one side, principally to secure land to develop agricultural exports. The residue of the indigenous population was then subjected to policies of assimilation (though in the course of time the experiment often led to the creation of reservations overseen by an ideology of paternal neglect). However, there were limits to the penetrative power of even steamships, railways and motor vehicles. The Innu were bypassed during this period because their wintry and forbidding land had no part to play in the era of modern globalization.

The positions of both societies changed dramatically in the second half of the twentieth century in ways that can be fully understood only by placing them in the context of the new forces represented by post-colonial globalization. We can now see that colonial rule inadvertently prepared Bali to become an exemplar, unrivalled in the tropics, of one of the most striking features of the new, post-colonial economy: tourism. Thus positioned, the Balinese, long the victims of colonial neglect, became not just passive recipients of post-colonial globalization but its active proponents. In terms of economic integration, Bali's boundaries have not merely become porous: they have been dismantled. As foreign influences and a large foreign presence fill their land, the Balinese, like others exposed to contemporary globalization, have been obliged to rethink the relationship between their image and their identity.[64] They also face new political dilemmas. While the Cold War lasted, the old colonial boundaries were maintained, not least in Indonesia. More recently, however, the strains of converting a colonial state to a nation state have begun to express themselves, in Indonesia as elsewhere, in separatism and violence. Meanwhile, tourism has increased Bali's wealth and political leverage. The Balinese may now have the strength, if they choose to exert it, to achieve greater autonomy – providing such a move does not disturb the tourist trade. In the post-colonial world, globalization may well create conditions that allow separatism to develop; it may also provide reasons to prevent them from being realized.

Post-colonial globalization has affected the Innu to an even greater extent because it has threatened their very existence. With hindsight, it is clear that the Innu were fortunate to have been neglected for so long. Many other First Nations in the newly designated settler state of Canada were rolled on and over in the nineteenth century as the frontier advanced. It was not until the second half of the twentieth century that innovative engineering and allied skills, combined with changing industrial and consumer demands, provided the means and the incentive for trans-national corporations to open the final, northern frontier. The Innu, having been neither entrenched through policies of preservation nor assimilated, were no match for the weighty forces that then imposed themselves. Their group suicides, like those of the Balinese, were final acts of protest as well as of despair.[65]

The confrontation occurred at a moment when Canada was making determined efforts to deepen and widen its own nation state. In associating itself with the economic development of northern Labrador, the Canadian government also determined to assimilate the Innu and make them into good Canadians. Yet today, in the post-colonial era, Canada finds itself assailed from both supra-national and infra-national forces. The trans-national corporations that moved the frontier northwards have other allegiances; the North-American Free Trade Agreement has greatly increased the flow of influences from the United States. The once isolated peoples of the north, from Inuit to Innu, now claim rights of land and sovereignty. Canada no longer propels globalization in the same way as it did in the days of empire, when it acted either as a proxy for Britain or as a sub-imperialist force in its own right; Canadians, like Balinese, have been obliged to rethink their identity and the meaning of nationality in the twenty-first century.

The story of the Balinese and the Innu continues. At present, the view from Mount Agung is more inviting than that from Davis Inlet. The Balinese, notwithstanding their problems, are in a better position to manage globalization; the Innu remain its victims. But the sub-empire is striking back. The fact that the fate of the Innu attracted world-wide attention, to the huge embarrassment of the Canadian government, is itself testimony to the power of the international media and to the emergence of a global civil conscience. In Innu cosmology *manitou* represents a pervasive world force that individuals can learn to turn to their advantage. Several generations of Innu must have concluded that they had lost the skill or had it withdrawn. Yet the Innu policeman who used a video camera to record the attempted suicides at Davis Inlet may have given a signal that the art of *manitou* has not been entirely lost, and that some at least of the new power is in the hands of the people.

Notes and References

1 Formally from 1908 to 1949, when The Netherlands East Indies achieved independence as Indonesia. Bali joined Indonesia in 1950. The formal presence goes back to treaties made with some of the island's polities in the mid-nineteenth century, and the informal (if also intermittent) presence to the sixteenth century.

2 Survival, *Canada's Tibet: The Killing of the Innu* (London, 1999), written by Çolin Samson, James Wilson and Jonathan Mazower. Survival 'stands for their right [of tribal peoples] to decide their own future and helps them protect their lives, lands and human rights'. The organization can be contacted via www.survival.org.uk, and survival@gn.apc.org. One purpose of this essay is to help, in a small way, to raise consciousness among historians about an issue that falls at least partly within their own area of expertise.

3 It is appropriate, given the theme of this book, that the sources used include the web sites of the two communities: http://www.innu.ca/ contains a mass of material not readily obtained elsewhere; http://www.baliwww.com/bali/klungkung1.htm is far less valuable; on the other hand, the published secondary material dealing with Klungkung is extensive, whereas that on the Innu is very limited. Problems of interpreting Bali's rich sources are discussed by Adrian Vickers, 'Balinese Texts and Historiography', *History and Theory*, 29 (1990), pp. 158–789.

4 The definition of these terms is discussed in my essay 'The History of Globalization – and the Globalization of History' in this volume.

5 There are several accounts of this episode and not all agree on the details. The most comprehensive recent treatment is Margaret J. Wiener's excellent study, *Visible and Invisible Realms: Power, Magic and Colonial Conquest in Bali* (Chicago, 1995), chs. 7–9.

6 The episode is commemorated in Puputan Square in Denpasar, which is now a tourist attraction. A full account of the event, accompanied by numerous photographs, is Ide Anak Agung Gde Agung, *Bali in the Ninteenth Century*, (Jakarta, 1991), ch. VI.

7 See Weiner, *Visible and Invisible Realms*; and J.F. Guermonprez, 'Dual Sovereignty in Nineteenth-Century Bali', *History and Anthropology*, 4 (1989), pp. 189–207. A scholarly and accessible introduction in a literature over-populated by travel books is Angela Hobart, Urs Ramseyer and Albert Leeman, *The Peoples of Bali* (Oxford, 1996).

8 Castlereagh's strategy, which included a scheme to marry Princess Charlotte to the Dutch heir apparent, Prince William, is discussed by John C. Hogan, 'Great Britain and the Netherlands, 1813–1814: A Failed Policy of Empire-Building', Consortium on Revolutionary Europe,1750–1850, *Proceedings*, 20 (1990), pp. 769–79.

9 The early stages of economic development are dealt with by Richard T. Griffiths, *Industrial Retardation in the Netherlands, 1830–1850* (The Hague, 1979). On Indonesia see Anne Booth, *The Indonesian Economy in the Nineteenth and Twentieth Centuries* (London, 1998). A recent guide to the historiography of overseas expansion is H.L. Wesseling, 'Overseas History in the Netherlands after the Second World War', *Itinerario*, 18 (1999), pp. 97–115.

10 The most important recent restatement of Dutch colonial policy is Maarten Kuitenbrouwer, *The Netherlands and the Rise of Modern Capitalism: Colonies and Foreign Policy, 1870–1902* (Oxford, 1991). The journal *Itinerario* is an indispensable source for studying the history of The Netherlands East Indies, though it also covers all aspects of European overseas expansion. Most scholarly energy has been

concentrated, understandably, on Java and Sumatra; studies of Bali have shown a marked bias towards anthropology and indigenous history, often in combination.

11 Roughly one sixth of cultivated land was to be devoted to export crops; financial sanctions were imposed on villages that failed to meet their allotted quotas.

12 This is now a controversial subject. The standard view, represented principally by Henk Wesseling, that Dutch imperialism was a feeble force that bore little relationship to developments in The Netherlands, has been challenged by Maarten Kuitenbrouwer, who argues that overseas expansion was a dynamic interest that both expressed and reinforced Dutch capitalism. See Henk Wesseling, 'The Giant that was a Dwarf, or the Strange History of Dutch Imperialism', *Journal of Imperial and Commonwealth History*, 16 (1988), pp. 58–70; *idem*, 'British and Dutch Imperialism: A Comparison', *Itinerario*, 13 (1989), pp. 61–76; Kuitenbrouwer, *The Netherlands and the Rise of Modern Capitalism*; *idem*, 'Capitalism and Imperialism: Britain and The Netherlands,' *Itinerario*, 18 (1994), pp. 105–16; Maarten Kuitenbrouwer and Huibert Schijf, 'The Dutch Colonial Business Elite at the Turn of the Century' *Itinerario*, 22 (1998), pp. 61–86.

13 And 19 per cent between 1831 and 1850. See Angus Maddison, 'Dutch Income in and from Indonesia, 1700–1938', in Angus Maddison and Ge Prince (eds.), *Economic Growth in Indonesia, 1822–1940* (Dordrecht, 1989), p. 19.

14 Frances Gouda, *Dutch Culture Overseas: Colonial Practice in the Netherlands Indies, 1900–1942* (Amsterdam, 1995).

15 Alfons van der Kraan, *Bali at War: A History of the Dutch–Balinese Conflict of 1846–49* (Victoria, Australia, 1995); Wiener, *Visible and Invisible Realms*, ch. 6.

16 Alfons van der Krann, *Lombok: Conquest, Colonization, and Underdevelopment, 1870–1940* (Singapore, 1980).

17 See my essay 'The History of Globalization – and the Globalization of History' in this volume.

18 Joost Cote, 'Colonising Central Sulawesi: The "Ethical Policy" and Imperialist Expansion', *Itinerario*, 20 (1996), pp. 87–107; Geoffrey Robinson, *The Dark Side of Paradise: Political Violence in Bali* (Ithaca, 1995), pp. 24–32; Raechelle Rubinstein, 'Allegiance and Alliance: the Banjar War of 1868', in Adrian Vickers (ed.), *Being Modern in Bali* (New Haven, 1996), pp. 53–5; Wiener, *Visible and Invisible Realms*, pp. 89–90, 223–4, 233–4, 251, 256–8, 331–2.

19 The debate, which cannot be entered into here, centres on whether Liberal and Ethical policies were as neatly defined as their names suggest, the differences between pronouncements and practice, and regional variations in applying policies to the far-flung territories that made up The Netherlands East Indies.

20 The argument is convincingly demonstrated in Robinson's outstanding study, *The Dark Side of Paradise*, ch. 2; the quotation is on p. 6. Manifestations of popular nationalism appeared elsewhere in The Netherlands East Indies in the 1920s. In modifying the Ethical Policy to reintroduce indirect rule to Bali, the Dutch were trying to 'get their retaliation in first' – before nationalism could spread to the 'island paradise'.

21 For an introduction and further references see Hobart, Ramseyer, and Leeman, *The Peoples of Bali*, especially pp. 40, 67–8, 76–84, 105, 207–8.

22 Robinson, *Dark Side of Paradise*, ch. 2; Guarmonprez, 'Dual Sovereignty', explores the limits to the power of status of Bali's 'kings' in the nineteenth century.

23 Frances Gouda, 'Teaching Indonesian Girls in Java and Bali, 1900–1942', *Women's History Review*, 4 (1995), pp. 25–62.

24 Michel Picard, 'Dance and Drama in Bali: The Making of an Indonesian Art

Form', in Vickers, *Being Modern in Bali*, pp. 115–57; Tilman Seebass, 'Change in Balinese Musical Life: "Kebiar" in the 1920s and 1930s', ibid. pp. 74–5.

25 On the longevity of the mythology, see James A. Boon, *The Anthropological Romance of Bali, 1597–1972* (Cambridge, 1977), and Adrian Vickers (ed.), *Travelling to Bali: Four Hundred Years of Journeys* (Kuala Lumpur, 1994). For the latest evidence of its durability see Antony Thorncroft, who writes of Bali's 'way of life that has remained more or less unchanged for centuries'. *Financial Times*, 17 February, 2001, p. xix.

26 Henk Schulte Nordholt, 'The Making of Traditional Bali: Colonial Ethnography and Bureaucratic Reproduction', *History and Anthropology*, 8 (1994), pp. 89–127.

27 Mark Poffenberger and Mary Zurbuchen, 'The Economics of Village Bali: Three Perspectives', *Economic Development and Cultural Change*, 29 (1981), pp. 91–103, analyse wet-rice agriculture, labour exchange groups and mechanisms for equalizing incomes.

28 Robinson, *The Dark Side of Paradise*, is convincing on this subject, which is one of the main themes of his book. See also Weiner's valuable account, *Visible and Invisible Realms*, chs. 3–8.

29 O. Goswami, 'The Depression: Its Effects on India and Indonesia', *Itinerario*, 10 (1986), pp. 163–76. Bali was affected, despite its limited involvement in export-crop production, mainly through tax increases.

30 Gouda, *Dutch Culture Overseas*, provides an excellent account of this theme. On the delayed transition from conservative to development policies see Maarten Kuitenbrouwer, 'The Never Ending Debt of Honour: The Dutch in the Post-Colonial World', *Itinerario*, 20 (1996), pp. 20–42.

31 Robinson, *Dark Side of the Landscape*, p. 278, and pp. 1–4, ch. 11.

32 This is not, of course, to deny the importance of the immediate causes, which lay in the military coup of 1965 that brought Suharto to power and instigated a purge of communist and other opposition groups in Indonesia. The limits of this explanation are dealt with persuasively by Robinson, *Dark Side of the Landscape*, ch. 11. An interesting case study is R.A.F. Paul Webb, 'The Sickle and the Cross: Christians and Communists in Bali, Flores, Sumba and Timor, 1965–67', *Journal of Southeast Asian Studies*, 17 (1986), pp. 94–112.

33 It will be apparent that the main point of my argument is to establish the link between colonial rule, invented traditions and globalization. It is not my purpose here to engage with the arguments about whether tourism is beneficial or harmful. A thoughtful perspective on contemporary issues is Raechelle Rubinstein and Linda H. Connor (eds.), *Staying Local in the Global Village: Bali in the Twentieth Century* (Honolulu, 1999).

34 The principal source for this paragraph is Survival, *Canada's Tibet*, pp. 6–7. The Innu should not be confused with the Inuit – formerly known as Eskimo.

35 In 1999 the Human Rights Committee of the United Nations condemned Canada for 'extinguishing' the rights of aboriginal peoples: Survival, *Canada's Tibet*, p. 5.

36 P.J. Cain and A.G. Hopkins, *British Imperialism, 1688–2000* (London, 2001), ch. 2; also n. 39 below.

37 A.G. Hopkins, 'The "New International Economic Order" in the Nineteenth Century: Britain's First Development Plan for Africa', in R.C.C. Law (ed.), *From Slave Trade to Legitimate Commerce* (Cambridge, 1995), ch. 10.

38 The state building, conserving and destroying functions of nineteenth-century imperialism are discussed in A.G. Hopkins, 'Back to the Future: From National History to Imperial History', *Past and Present*, 164 (1999), pp. 198–243.

39 See the case studies in Cain and Hopkins, *British Imperialism*, chs. 8, 9, 23, 24.

40 But circumstances were of course very different. Among other considerations, Britain had to reach an accommodation with French *colons*. The authority on confederation is Ged Martin, *Britain and the Origins of the Canadian Confederation, 1837–67* (London, 1995); but see also Peter Burroughs, 'State Formation and the Imperial Factor in Nineteenth-Century Canada', *Journal of Imperial and Commonwealth History*, 24 (1996), pp. 118–31.

41 See J.R. Miller, *Skyscrapers Hide the Heavens: A History of Indian–White Relations in Canada* (Toronto, 1989); and Edward J. Hedican, *Applied Anthropology in Canada: Understanding Aboriginal Issues* (Toronto, 1995).

42 The role of the missionaries is not a glorious one. Aside from promoting policies that attacked the social structure of the Innu, there is a long history of abuse of various kinds. See Survival, *Canada's Tibet*, pp. 20–1. Adrian Tanner, Robin McGrath and Carol Brice Bennett, '"Spirituality" among the Inuit and Innu of Labrador', http://www.innu.ca/tanner1.html (1998), discuss the role of Moravian and Roman Catholic missionaries and the relationship between Christian beliefs and Innu spirituality.

43 On the examples that follow see Miller, *Skyscrapers Hide the Heavens*, pp. 92–7, 108–14, 152–3, ch. 8.

44 Eleanor Burke Leacock, 'Montagnais Women and the Jesuit Program for Colonization', in Mona Etienne and Eleanor Burke Leacock (eds.), *Women and Colonization: Anthropological Perspectives* (New York, 1980), pp. 25–42.

45 Miller, *Skyscrapers Hide the Heavens*, p. 221.

46 The Montagnais ('mountaineers') occupy the northern shores of the Gulf of St Lawrence; the Naskapi (an Indian name meaning, interestingly, 'rude' or 'uncivilized') live further north on the Labrador plateau.

47 The Innu attracted very little scholarly attention before the 1990s. The best guide to recent research is found on their web site, which devotes a good deal of space to Innu history: establishing their antiquity and claims to sovereignty are vital to their case for gaining control over resources in their hunting grounds. The pioneering work is by Georg Henrikson, *Hunters in the Barrens: The Naskapi on the Edge of the White Man's World* (St John's, 1973), and Eleanor Burke Leacock cited in notes 44 and 48.

48 The early history remains very sketchy: see Eleanor Burke Leacock, 'The Montagnais-Naskapi of the Labrador Peninsular', in R. Bruce Morrison and C. Roderick Wilson (eds.), *Native Peoples: The Canadian Experience* (Toronto, 1995), pp. 150–80.

49 On this subject see Russell Thornton, *American Indian Holocaust and Survival: A Population History since 1492* (London, 1987).

50 For some additional comments on this theme, see Marie Wadden and Douglas McIntrye, *Nitassinan: The Innu Struggle to Reclaim their Homeland* (Toronto, 1991), pp. 31–3.

51 Miller, *Skyscrapers Hide the Heavens*, pp. 168–71.

52 Leacock, 'The Montagnais-Naskapi'.

53 Their numbers may have increased slightly in the twentieth century: in the 1990s there were about 16,000 Innu in about 20 settlements: 'The Innu: an Introduction', http://www.innu.ca/innuintro.html (n.d. but *c.* 1999).

54 Miller, *Skyscrapers Hide the Heavens*, pp. 249–51. The patronizing phrase is cited by Miller but not, of course, endorsed by him.

55 Walter Rockwood, quoted in Survival, *Canada's Tibet*, p. 16.

56 For further details, see ibid., pp. 30–2.

57 Donald M. McRae, *Report on the Complaints of the Innu of Labrador to the Canadian Human Rights Commission* (Faculty of Law, University of Ottawa, 1993), provides details of the policy of 'sedentarization'.

58 Walter Rockwood in 1956, quoted in Survival, *Canada's Tibet*, p. 16. It is interesting to note that the Portuguese called the coast 'Labrador' – the 'source of labour' – in the fifteenth century, while searching for slaves.

59 Notwithstanding the fact that the principle of multiculturalism was incorporated into Canada's constitution in 1982: Miller, *Skyscrapers Hide the Heavens*, p. 275.

60 See, for example, the effective presentation by Daniel Ashini, Vice-President, Innu Nation, 'Culture and Contact', St. John's, Newfoundland, 1997, in http://www.innu.ca/cabot3.htm; and the powerful 'Appeal for Justice for the Innu of Labrador', http://www.innu.ca/appeal 112K.html (2000).

61 'The Innu Nation', http://www.innu.ca/the-innu.html (2000). This is not to say that it is problem-free: Survival, *Canada's Tibet*, pp. 28–9.

62 As French colonial policy shifted from 'assimilation' to 'association'.

63 Readers are again referred to my essay 'The History of Globalization – and the Globalization of History' in this volume.

64 Rubinstein and Connor, *Staying Local in the Global Village*.

65 'Suicide is the ultimate denunciation of the absence of choice for an individual or a community'. Jean-Charles Pietacho, Innu representative, quoted in Survival, *Canada's Tibet*, p. 25.

DAVID REYNOLDS

American Globalism: Mass, Motion and the Multiplier Effect

In February 1941 Henry R. Luce, the owner of *Time* and *Life* magazines, published what became a celebrated essay entitled 'The American Century'. In it he claimed that humanity constituted 'for the first time in history one world, fundamentally indivisible'. Luce also insisted that the twentieth century would and should be 'the American Century', defined by the country's wealth, power and values in four fundamental respects. Only the United States, said Luce, could determine whether 'a system of free economic enterprise' would prevail globally. He also argued that America must act as the main source and trainer of skilled labour. Third, it was the country's duty to be 'the Good Samaritan of the entire world', feeding the hungry and helping the destitute. Above all, Luce argued, the United States should serve not merely as a 'sanctuary' for 'the ideals of Freedom and Justice' in an era of war but also 'the powerhouse' from which those ideals 'spread throughout the world'.[1]

Sixty years on, many Americans would probably say that Luce's agenda has been amply realized. The twentieth century seems indeed to have been the American century. Having 'won' the Cold War and watched the collapse of the Soviet Union, having witnessed the collapse of communism across Eastern Europe and its slow but apparently inexorable metamorphosis within 'Red China', the United States was left as the sole superpower. America was also the centre of the Internet revolution and the internationalization of financial markets. Its consumer values of 'fast music, fast computers and fast food' were apparently carrying all before them, 'pressing nations into one homogeneous theme park, one McWorld'.[2] The most celebrated exponent of American triumphalism, Francis Fukuyama, argued that the 'unabashed victory of economic and political liberalism' in the Cold War signalled 'the end point of mankind's ideological evolution and the universalization of Western liberal democracy as the final form of human government'. In terms of meaningful change, he argued, humanity had reached 'the end of history'.[3] For Fukuyama, globalization was eschatology: not only had America conquered the world, it had also stopped time.

Globalization became a cult concept of the 1990s. Pundits filled up the column inches; academics generated weighty tomes. Their work is discussed in the introductory essay to this volume,[4] but two points should be made briefly here. First, much of the literature was written by economists, sociologists and political scientists interested in the present and the future. If they looked back, it was rarely beyond World War II. A longer historical perspective is therefore appropriate. Second, although a good deal of this work was written by Americans and came close to equating globalization with Americanization, it did not show much interest in the pre-history of the process within the United States itself. America's 'rise to globalism'[5] – its aspiration to and achievement of worldwide influence – was the essential precondition of contemporary globalization. This process needs further analysis.

It is a fundamental aim of this volume to locate contemporary globalization in broader and longer contexts, by showing the globalizing patterns of other societies and earlier epochs. To do that is an essential antidote to the residual dogmas of American exceptionalism – the idea that the United States is both *exempt* from the general patterns of historical development and also *exemplary* in that its structures and values were superior to those of other nations.[6] But we also need to relate America's own globalism to the earlier history of the integration and development of the United States. That is my aim in the first part of this essay where I shall argue that twentieth-century US globalism was, in significant respects, an extension of nineteenth-century national integration which, in turn, was connected to earlier patterns of globalization. I shall then ask why and how the United States turned outward in the twentieth century, noting the ways in which globalism served to reinforce national integration. Having thus 'historicized' American globalism by relating it to international and national developments, I nevertheless go on to suggest that twentieth-century American globalism *was* historically distinctive, not so much because of some intrinsic American virtues but because of its interaction with the historical novelty of modern mass technologies. Finally, I shall briefly address the issue of globalism as imperialism – by alluding to the reciprocity of the global and the local ('glocalization') and to the mutability of America's own identity in this so-called 'American century'.

In such a short essay, of course, I can only be suggestive – delineating some approaches rather than documenting a case. Both text and notes are necessarily lean. But I hope to counter the tendency of writing on globalization to highlight the purely economic aspects, by giving as much emphasis to political framework and social context, and also to stress that the mutuality of the national and the international has been a leitmotif of American history.

The Integration of the Union

The roots of American globalism can be found in the way that the country was integrated and developed during its colonial and early national periods. The United States was a product of an earlier phase of 'proto-globalization', namely the Atlantic world of the seventeenth and eighteenth centuries – that intricate web of migration, trade and intellectual exchange, embracing Europe, Africa and the Americas, which has in recent decades been the subject of intense scholarly scrutiny.[7] The original European presence in North America took the form of colonies of settlement, not clientage. Here was an important contrast with the imposition of Britain's empire in India. Native Americans were gradually driven westward as white settlement spread down the length of the eastern seaboard and into the hinterland. In this respect British America was analogous to later white settler colonies with persecuted indigenous minorities, such as those that formed Australia and New Zealand.

Yet there were some very important differences. The American colonies were also the product of another central dynamic of the Atlantic economy: the slave trade. Although the import of African slaves into the United States was banned in 1808, it continued illegally. Moreover, the fertility of black slaves, the lucrative internal slave trade, and the booming world demand for slave-cultivated cotton all ensured that slavery continued to flourish in the South long after it had been abolished in the North. The South's 'peculiar institution' became the focal symbol for rival national identities and the slavery question briefly split the Union in 1861–5. Even after Southern secession was defeated, blacks remained second-class citizens and, right to the present, they have been much less easily integrated into the mainstream of American life than other ethnic groups.

In a further contrast with the Australasian settler colonies, the Americans won total independence from the mother country at a very early date (the war of 1776–83). This struggle engendered an ideology of moral separateness from Europe – republic versus monarchy, liberty against empire, the New World in antithesis to the Old. Consequently, subsequent American expansion was ambiguous, when seen within the intellectual framework of this book. In one sense, it was an indirect continuation of the European globalization from which it had been spawned. Yet its intense anti-imperialist ideology also meant that American expansion was the first phase of 'post-colonial globalization', in which global influence has been achieved without formal empire. The theologian and social commentator, Reinhold Niebuhr, remarked in 1931: 'We are the first empire of the world to establish our sway without legions. Our legions are dollars.'[8]

This was still a long way in the future, however, as the new republic struggled for survival. The United States was the creation of individual colonies/states, which came together for limited purposes, notably military security and economic advancement. The national government was therefore left deliberately weak. These principles were enshrined in the federal character of the 1789 constitution, which sought to protect the rights of states and localities. The centrifugal nature of US politics was reinforced by the country's subsequent democratization. Although the franchise was determined by each state, by the 1830s most states in the Union were democracies in the sense of white adult male suffrage. Democratic localism loosely connected within a federal system – this was the distinctive nature of the American polity. American-style federalism, for all its faults, proved essential for holding together a country that soon engrossed a continent. This continent-wide base has, in turn, been the necessary precondition for American globalism.

Continental hegemony was by no means inevitable, however. The United States was already a precociously large country in 1776 – stretching some 1,500 miles down the Atlantic seaboard and several hundred miles into the interior. Subsequent purchases or annexations from France, Spain and Britain, together with wars against Mexico and near-extermination of native Indians, spread its domain across to the Pacific by 1850. In area the United States equalled the distance from the Pyrenees to the Urals and from Sweden to the Sahara. But self-governing republics were traditionally small. James Madison, in the fourteenth *Federalist*, wrote famously in 1787 of the audacious 'experiment of an extended republic'.[9] Most European observers assumed that the experiment would fail, especially given the lack of a centralized, sovereign government. As historian Gordon Wood has observed, to someone steeped in British legal thought 'the explicit retention of legal sovereignty in the people was preposterous'. In the 1830s, Hegel spoke of the 'North American Federation' as lacking a 'real State' and a 'real Government'.[10]

From this perspective, the growing rift between the 'slave states' and the 'free states' and the collapse of the second-party system in the 1850s seemed hardly surprising. Many European observers believed they were watching the inevitable breakup of an over-large and unstable polity. The secession of the 'Confederate States of America' in 1861 came as little surprise. W.E. Gladstone, no friend of slavery, spoke for many of his countrymen in October 1862, after the South's success at the battle of Antietam, when he claimed that the leaders of the Confederacy 'had made a nation'. Gladstone added that 'it is for the general interests of Nations that no State should swell to the dimensions of a Continent'.[11]

The outcome of the 'War between the States' was therefore of momentous historical importance. Had the South secured its independence, the future history of north America and the world would probably have taken a very different course. The Mason–Dixon line might have become the equivalent of the inter-war Rhineland divide between France and Germany or of Cold War Korea's 38th Parallel. Instead the North forced the Confederacy back within the Union. The cost was appalling: 620,000 dead. This was double America's combat deaths in World War II and equal to the combined total in all America's foreign wars from Independence up to Korea. Truly the Civil War was America's Great War.

Its results were clear-cut. The South was marginalized from national life for almost a century, its 'peculiar institution' of slavery metamorphosed into quasi-serfdom for blacks until after World War II – but secession was never again a remote possibility. In this absolutely fundamental respect, the history of the United States differs from that of almost every large polity in modern history, from Canada to India, from Nigeria to the Soviet Union. In their cases, internal unity was problematic; in the United States it was axiomatic. Significantly, the Civil War was the crucible of a new American nationalism, epitomized in Lincoln's preference for 'the nation' rather than 'the Union'. This was reflected more generally by growing use of 'the United States' as a singular rather than plural noun – 'the United States is', instead of 'the United States are'.[12]

Economics followed politics. Once the Union was secured, its economic integration and development proceeded apace in the last third of the nineteenth century. The United States was now reaping the benefits of a continent-wide polity with a common currency, no internal tariffs and a single-gauge railroad network. These are too often taken for granted. But they were distinctive and vital. On the other hand, the development of the United States was still intertwined with European globalization, which in the nineteenth century was characterized by an increasingly open world economy and by free and large migrations of labour.[13] Economically, America's reliance on British industrial exports lasted until the Civil War; dependence on British capital was a feature of the whole nineteenth century. And the United States could not have industrialized so quickly but for the vast influx of European labour, totalling 25 million people between 1860 and 1914. This, coupled with the high American birthrate, enabled the country to more than triple its population from 31 million to 100 million. Though economically beneficial, the tide of immigration was socially divisive, since the later waves came from many parts of southern and eastern Europe, unlike the predominantly British, Irish and German majorities of earlier decades. Their ethnic and religious differences from older immigrants were a source of acute cultural tension and political division around the turn of the century, with issues such as prohibition a litmus test. At times it seemed debatable whether the economic integration of the United States could be contained within the established political and social frameworks.

By 1900, the base for twentieth-century American globalism had been established in a continent-wide country with a flexible political system, a distinctive ideology and an integrated industrial economy. In 1913 the United States accounted for nearly a third of world manufacturing output. Yet the 'nationalization' of this large, widespread and diverse population could not be taken for granted. Sectional, ethnic and racial divisions remained intense. If nations are 'imagined communities', America is truly a prodigy of imagination, lacking as it does a shared ethnicity, a compact territory and a politically dominant religion. Elsewhere, these commonalities have served as catalysts of national identity. 'Only in a country where it is so unclear what is American do people worry so much about the threat of things "un-American",' observes historian Michael Kammen.[14] Even more than most nations, therefore, the national self has been defined in antithesis to the foreign 'Other'. For colonial Americans, what mattered was that they were not Indians or Blacks (unlike other European settlers, British Americans had strict laws against miscegenation). Independent Americans defined themselves as not British. Citizens of the Union declared themselves as 'free men' not subjects of the 'slave power'. Antithesis to the Other would matter as much in the twentieth century.[15]

So globalism depended on prior integration; but globalism also served to strengthen nationalism. In the twentieth century, the bid to Americanize the world was, in similar vein, interwoven with the effort to Americanize Americans.

Global Expansion

Around 1900, the world was peripheral to the prosperity of the United States. Unlike Britain, an island nation that lived on imports, America was largely self-sufficient and only about five per cent of the GDP came from foreign trade. Its late nineteenth-century growth stemmed largely from the expansion of the internal market. Why, then, the turn outward?

In part, New Left historians argued, because the market was saturated or at least perceived to be so. According to William Appleman Williams, during the depression of the mid 1890s Americans came to believe that the era of westward expansion across the continent was largely over and that 'continued expansion in the form of overseas economic (and even territorial) empire provided the best, if not the only, way to sustain their freedom and prosperity'.[16] Clearly market forces *were* a part of the argument. By 1927, for instance, there was one automobile for every five Americans; in France and Britain the proportion was one to 44, in Germany almost one to 200.[17] Exports or overseas production therefore made economic sense. But economic imperatives were only a part of the story. In any case, America's overseas empire was miniscule by comparison with that of the Europeans. There was a brief flurry of empire-building during the 1890s (which resulted in such hostages to fortune as Hawaii and the Philippines – with fateful consequences in December 1941). For the most part, however, American imperialism was informal rather than formal – a web of trade and investment, bases and alliances that spread out from the Western Hemisphere during the course of the twentieth century. Just as the earlier internal development of the United States owed much to the impact of European globalization, so America's global outreach has depended in critical respects on the decline of the Europeans as world powers.

In such a short essay, a few examples of this point must suffice. Financially, World War I was of special importance. In 1913 the United States had been a net international debtor to the tune of $3.7 billion; by 1919 it was a net creditor to the tune of almost exactly the same amount. During the war the British had liquidated the bulk of their American assets and had also become dependent on American war loans, which were financing about one-third of their war effort by 1917. Hitherto American banks and investors had concentrated almost entirely on the domestic market. As a result of Allied loans, financial houses such as J.P. Morgan developed new engagement and expertise in Europe and Latin America. This continued in the 1920s when US capital became essential for the financial stabilization of Germany and France.

On the other hand, there was nothing inexorable about this expansionist trajectory. The 1930s constituted a marked reversal of globalizing trends,[18] not least because the United States cut back on capital investment and led the charge toward higher tariffs and currency blocs. The domestic foundations of its globalism, never firm, had come close to collapse. Regulation of the stock market was scanty and national monetary institutions were primitive. There was no central bank and the Federal Reserve system, established just before World War I, was ineffectual. The stock market collapse in 1929 and the ensuing liquidity crisis prompted a run on US domestic banks, most of them unit rather than branch operations that therefore lacked the reserves to sustain themselves. Thousands of banks collapsed over the next few years and by 1933 investment was only two-thirds of its 1929 figure in real terms. A quarter of the workforce was unemployed (compared with three to five per cent for most of the 1920s). In 1931 some Africans in the French colony of the Cameroons clubbed together and sent the city of New York $3.77. It was, they said, for 'the starving' – a minute but richly ironic example of reverse global capital flows.[19]

The Depression dragged on through the 1930s. Unemployment was still 17 per cent in 1939. Recovery did not start until Allied war orders began in 1940 and America joined the belligerents in 1941. Far more than the conflict of 1914–18, World War II was America's opportunity. The defeat of continental Europe in 1940 and then the collapse of European colonial rule in Asia in 1941–2 were decisive moments in world history. Victory over the Axis powers would depend in large measure on the non-Europeans. The war ended with the United States and the Soviet Union facing each other across a ravaged Germany and the Americans in pre-eminent occupation of Japan. The United States produced half the world's manufactures and controlled half its gold and convertible currency reserves. Over the next decade it expanded further to fill the vacuums created by the contraction of European power. As the French pulled out of Indo-China in the 1950s, so the Americans moved in. After the British abandoned the Persian Gulf in the late 1960s, the Americans built up the Shah of Iran as their proxy. When Portugal finally relinquished its African empire in the mid 1970s, the United States became the major international player in southern Africa. Europe's recessional was America's moment.

But 'push' mattered as much as 'pull'. American globalization was fuelled by a new globalist ideology. The world crisis of 1940–1 had a profound effect on the outlook of US policy-makers.[20] Although 'isolationists' still advocated a largely self-sufficient Western Hemisphere, able to provide its basic needs and defy external powers, this no longer seemed a compelling argument. For one thing, internationalists argued, it would require a radical transformation of the US economy, both to re-orient trade and production and also to sustain the fiscal burden of a 'garrison state'. Internationalists such as Franklin Roosevelt also insisted that the new era of airpower overruled the old ocean barriers, requiring military bases and friendly powers thousands of miles from the United States. For those two reasons, it was deemed essential that in future the United States did not allow key economic and political regions of the world, such as western Europe and Japan, to fall under the control or influence of hostile states.

There was also an ideological element to the new internationalism, though Roosevelt and his disciples often packaged it in 'realist' terms (mindful of the fate of Woodrow Wilson's crusade 'to make the world safe for democracy' in 1917–19). They shared the Wilsonian sense of mission to reshape the world in America's politico-economic image. Enthusiasts for liberal, capitalist democracy had been on the defensive throughout the Depression; fascism and communism seemed the waves of the future. But the domestic boom and international triumph of the war years gave Americans a new sense of purpose and mission. As Harry Hopkins, Roosevelt's closest aide observed in 1945:

> I have often been asked what interests we have in Poland, Greece, Iran, or Korea. Well I think we have the most important business in the world – and indeed, the only business worthy of our traditions. And that is this – to do everything within our diplomatic power to foster and encourage democratic government throughout the world . . . We believe our dynamic democracy is the best in the world.[21]

In the 1940s the concept of 'totalitarianism' provided a new tool for defining foreign policy and sharpening national identity. First applied to the Axis powers in World War II, it was carried over into the Cold War when a new 'Other', the Soviet Union, was seen as threatening American interests abroad and subverting American values at home. National Security Council paper NSC-68, one of the defining documents of US Cold War policy, applied the 1850s language of slavery versus freedom to the 'shrinking world' of 1950 which lived under the shadow of the atomic bomb. The Soviet Union, the paper argued, was 'animated by a new fanatic faith, antithetical to our own' and sought 'to impose its absolute authority over the rest of the world'. There was 'a basic conflict between the idea of freedom under a government of laws, and the idea of slavery under the grim oligarchy of the Kremlin'. The 'implacable purpose of the slave state to eliminate the challenge of freedom has placed the two great powers at opposite poles'.[22]

During the Cold War anti-communism replaced anti-imperialism as a basic imperative of American foreign policy. Sometimes that meant trying to prop up European empires about which they had deep reservations, such as the French in Indo-China until 1954 or the British in the Persian Gulf until the 1970s. It has even been argued that the British Empire was effectively an Anglo–American condominium after 1945.[23] Sometimes the gospel of anti-communism seemed little more than a fig-leaf for the imposition of American military and economic influence, as in South Vietnam, the Philippines or Iran. In the process, the United States was supporting unsavoury dictators such as Diem, Marcos or the Shah. But even if these men were 'bastards', at least they were '*our* bastards'. US policy-makers justified the compromise with the principle of national liberty by arguing, as Eisenhower did in 1953, that 'world communism is taking advantage of that spirit of nationalism to cause dissension in the free world'.[24]

In the Cold-War era anti-communism also came to define American life and culture. In the 1950s conservatives used it to rein in New Deal liberalism, cow racial protestors and curtail the new power of labour unions. The Federal Government loyalty programme of 1947–57 investigated 13.5 million people (20 per cent of the workforce, of whom nearly two thirds were defence contractors from the private sector).[25] After a Depression decade in which the United States lurched leftward, the Cold War helped stabilize the country in a new conformity.

Cold War globalism promoted national integration in other ways. The militarization of the West (arms industries in California, testing ranges in the deserts of Utah and New Mexico) advanced its economic development and helped shift the country's centre of gravity. The high-tech military establishment required by the Cold War was the main reason for the expansion of the US government bureaucracy and the enlargement of the federal budget (four-fifths of which was going to defence-related activities by the early 1950s). The military–industrial complex of World War II and the Cold War was largely responsible for the consolidation of corporate capitalism during the 1940s. The imperatives of national security were the main reason for Eisenhower's decision to initiate the Interstate highway system in the mid 1950s. And so on.

Nineteenth-century national integration laid the base for twentieth-century globalization, and globalization in turn reinforced national integration.[26] In the nineteenth century European expansion helped promote American integration; in the twentieth century Europe's retreat was a spur to America's expansion. Such are the dialectics of international history.

The Multiplier Effect

Within the confines of a brief essay, I have tried so far to suggest that American globalism should be contextualized. But that does not mean it should be relativized too far. The global impact of the United States, particularly in the second half of the twentieth century, was out of all proportion to its share of the world's population (less than five per cent today; around seven per cent when Henry Luce wrote his 1941 essay). Compared with other imperial powers, international ideologies or economic networks in past ages, the modern United States has displayed an exceptional reach. Why was this?

Much of the explanation for the extent and intensity of American globalism lies in the distinctiveness of modern technologies and the pre-eminence of the United States in exploiting them. My shorthands for this process are mass, motion and the multiplier effect. Mass has two referents. One is the truism that the twentieth century is in various ways 'the age of the masses', especially in democratic politics, consumer economies and popular culture.[27] The other referent is the 'mass' of the United States itself as a very large and very prosperous state that also enjoyed, in the twentieth century, remarkable stability. America's mass was the crucible of 'massification'. And that mass was mobilized internationally through the multiplier effect of modern technology. This has enabled America to ratchet up its power, wealth and cultural influence to a historically unprecedented degree. Let me look briefly at some facets of what, in my terms, might be called America's mass mobilization.

First, mass destruction. It is a truism that modern firepower has transformed war. One-to-one combat is cost-ineffective in time and manpower – the era of sword against sword. Gunpowder enabled a few to kill many, but this still took time. In terms of mass firepower the first modern wars are conventionally regarded as the American Civil War of 1861–5 and the Great War of 1914–18. The nuclear age inaugurated far greater destructive power, first through the atomic bomb of 1945 and then through much more devastating thermonuclear weapons developed in the 1950s. Winston Churchill observed after the US H-bomb test in 1953 that humanity was 'now as far from the age of the atomic bomb as the atomic bomb itself from the bow and arrow'.[28]

But the revolution in delivery systems mattered as much as the revolution in firepower. Although airpower heightened America's sense of vulnerability, it also encouraged an enlarged definition of security. As Franklin Roosevelt put it in 1942, instead of burying its head in the sand like an ostrich, the American eagle must henceforth be able to 'fly high and strike hard' from secure perches in the United States and far beyond.[29] The era of intercontinental missiles, whose harbinger was the Soviet Sputnik launch in 1957, was another quantum leap in the globalization of mass destruction. It brought Washington and Moscow, hitherto protected from mortal threats by wide oceans or vast terrain, within thirty minutes of large-scale devastation. The vulnerabilities of the missile age were dramatized by the superpower confrontation over Cuba in 1962. This was a genuinely world crisis, from which few parts of the globe would have escaped unscathed if nuclear war had broken out.

Taken together, modern firepower and delivery systems gave possessor states a historically unprecedented global reach. When the American political scientist William T.R. Fox coined the term 'superpower' in 1944, to connote a new ranking of states (superior to 'great powers' or even 'world powers'), he defined it as a country with 'great power plus great mobility of power'.[30] Unquestionably, in the age of mass destruction, the United States had both. Despite recurrent bouts of paranoia, it stayed ahead of the Soviets in the Cold War arms race, both quantitatively and qualitatively.

The United States also dominated the emerging era of global mass consumption. Consumer societies have been dated back well before the twentieth century but American consumerism since the 1920s has been distinctive. The production and marketing of a variety of household goods helped move the majority of Americans beyond subsistence. Immediately after World War II, consumerism remained an American domain – in the late 1950s Americans accounted for three-quarters of all household appliances manufactured in the world and for two-thirds of its 75 million television sets.[31] After the 1950s, however, consumer durables spread to western Europe and beyond as part of the culture of consumption. That took on a life of its own, independent of the United States and far beyond its shores, but America was its pioneer and exemplar.

The culture of consumption also facilitated the consumption of culture. The United States was exporting not just American goods but also American values, propagated by two related means. One was the prevalence of the English language. In the 1990s about a quarter of the world's population was fluent or competent in English.[32] (This, of course, built on the linguistic imperialism of the British empire, for instance in India.) A second, and related, mechanism was the international appeal of the English-language cinema, in which the United States was dominant for most of the century. The base for this lay in Hollywood's vast and protected domestic market, which gave it the economic edge over all competitors.[33]

Mass destruction, mass consumption and mass culture were all made possible by techniques of mass production. These were developed in the United States in the early twentieth century and then emulated abroad. The catchwords of the 1920s were Fordism and Taylorism, connoting the assembly line and rationalized management, which foreigners often simply called 'Americanism' or 'Americanization'. These techniques were the vogue in Europe in the 1920s; even the Soviet Union was captivated. 'We need Marxism plus Americanism,' declared Nikolai Bukharin, the Bolshevik theorist, in 1923. The following year Stalin himself told party workers that 'the combination of Russian revolutionary sweep and American efficiency is the essence of Leninism'.[34] 'Americanism' became the synonym for modernization, used to critique the attitudes and practices of peasant agriculture and craft industry as part of Stalin's Great Leap Forward.

Europe's passion for Americanism waned in Depression, when the

American Dream turned into nightmare. But the hiatus was only temporary. To wage World War II the United States developed a sophisticated system of centralized mass production based on a limited number of standardized, interchangeable parts. Both the Soviets and the British followed suit, building on precedents from the inter-war period, and this system of war production proved more effective than German or Japanese craft traditions. Economic historian Mark Harrison has noted how the war of 1941–5 established this as the Soviet norm. The gradual sclerosis of the Soviet economy in the post-war period was not simply because of the rooted denial of the market; it was also the result of this entrenched commitment to methods of mass production derived from inter-war America.[35] 'We will bury you,' crowed Khrushchev, after the Soviets had beaten the Americans into space.[36] Instead Fordism eventually buried the Soviet Union and its clients. Whereas the United States was able to transcend the Western economic crisis of the 1970s and shift to post-Fordist production methods, the Soviet bloc never did: its advanced technology was mostly pirated from the West, especially the United States and West Germany. Charles Maier's comment about East Germany in the 1980s was applicable to the Soviet bloc as whole – it was in 'a race between computers and collapse'.[37] Collapse came first.

The transcendence of mass production was achieved through mass communications. Again the United States was in the vanguard – moving on from the tele-technologies of the late nineteenth century (telegraph and telephone) that had opened up the continent and also exploiting the economies of scale made possible by America's unique mass market. The key technologies of post-industrial society were telecommunications and computing. Their origins lay in new hardware developed in bulk in the United States in the 1950s and 1960s, such as satellites, semiconductors and mainframe computers. In each case, the Federal Government played a decisive role in their research and development, impelled by the challenges of the Cold War.

But these technologies would not have had such revolutionary effect if they had remained in the military domain: the information revolution depended on a mass market. In computing the turning point was the development of the personal computer in the 1980s. (In January 1983 the PC won *Time* magazine's 'Man of the Year' award – the first time in fifty-five years that a non-human had been chosen.) In telecommunications the turning point was the enforced break-up of AT&T in 1984, which fragmented its quasi-monopoly of phone systems and equipment in the United States. This set a precedent for Britain, Japan and much of the world in the ensuing decade. Deregulation breached a historic pattern whereby post, telephone and telecommunications (PTT) services had been under the tight control of the state (or, in the US case, a monopoly closely linked to the government) on the principle that information is power and states must retain a monopoly of power. New technologies and deregulated markets made possible the IT revolution that has been central to the recent phase of globalization, especially the fusion of financial markets.[38]

Once again technological innovation multiplied by national integration generated mass mobilization.

Mobilization, Opposition and Modification

My main aims in this essay have been to locate US globalism in historical perspective and to hint at an explanation for its extraordinary reach. But the world was not a blank slate for Americans to write on. Mobilization provoked opposition: that is a familiar, though important, point. More interesting are the ways in which America's international impact varied according to national circumstances – the global modified by the local.

In the arena of power, the Vietnam War is a classic example of what has been called the impotence of omnipotence. Despite committing 500,000 troops, sustaining 50,000 deaths and dropping a larger tonnage of bombs than it did in the whole of World War II, the United States could not avert a communist takeover of South Vietnam. Some of its impotence was self-induced (the domestic backlash against US involvement), some of it a consequence of Cold-War confrontation (the desire to avoid direct conflict with the Russians and the Chinese). Nevertheless, the outcome of that war was a reminder that the size of a country's GDP or the magnitude of its nuclear arsenal did not automatically determine international outcomes.

More generally, recent scholarship has criticized a simple view of coercive American power. Historians of European imperialism have been at pains to explore the interaction of colonizers and colonized; so, too, have historians of the American empire. If the American Cold-War alliance system was a manifestation of informal empire, as the New Left claimed, then it was also 'empire by invitation', to quote the aphorism popularized by the Norwegian historian Geir Lundestad.[39] Key sectors of western-European political opinion sought and then shaped American involvement in structures such as the European Recovery Plan and the North Atlantic alliance. Their aim, encapsulated in the words of a wartime British diplomat, was to 'make use of American power for purposes which we regard as good'.[40] How far they succeeded is a separate question: the general point is that America's alliances were not one-way streets.

The export of America's consumer culture also encountered strenuous resistance. Post-war France was notorious for its cultural anti-Americanism, seen for instance in its vehement rearguard action against the importation of Coca-Cola in the 1950s. One peeved US Congressman responded that drinking Coke would give the French exactly what they had needed ever since World War II – 'a good belch'. Despite succumbing to Coke, many Frenchmen remained culturally dyspeptic. Do we want to become like America, 'a civilization of bathtubs and Frigidaires?' asked the poet Louis Aragon. Judging by the consumer boom of the 1960s, most Frenchmen did.[41]

resistance was not always successful, the story was often one of reciprocity: 'empire by invitation' in the cultural field as well. As Reinhold Wagnleitner has argued in the case of post-war Austria, so-called 'Coca-Colonization' was often a form of 'self-colonization', in which local political and cultural elites exploited American influences for their own reformist ends.[42]

Cultural penetration also entailed local modification. Consider the fast-food giant, McDonald's, which, by the mid 1990s, was serving over thirty million customers a day in more than one hundred countries. This would seem the epitome of global Americanization, based on Fordist principles of mass production. Against that, however, one might set some fascinating recent studies of how McDonald's local franchisees have subtly adapted its uniformity to their Asian cultures – slowing down the fast-food factory to tea-house tempo or featuring Little Emperor birthday parties for the one-child families of Deng Xiaoping's China.[43] An instance of 'glocalization' at work?

In similar vein, the United States did not impose a simple economic model on the world. The prevalence of ideas to the contrary, especially in the United States, is a tribute to Cold-War self-indoctrination (the slogans of 'capitalism versus communism') and to the sterility of much academic economics, which divorces wealth-creation from its political and cultural contexts.[44] It was not until the paranoia of the late 1980s about the looming 'Pacific Century' that this point came home to many Americans. A succession of books and articles explored the distinctiveness of the Japanese economy, based on principles of social solidarity in the firm and competitive polyopoly within key industries that are at odds with basic American practice. Profound contrasts were also apparent at the management level. Toyota's global success in the 1970s and 1980s, for instance, rested on a fundamental critique of existing US mass-production methods.[45]

In any case, America's own political economy is a far cry from the 'system of free economic enterprise' celebrated by Henry Luce. By 1947 the two hundred largest industrial companies in the United States accounted for 30 per cent of value added in manufacturing and 47 per cent of corporate assets. Twenty years later that last figure had risen to over 60 per cent.[46] Industrial concentration partly reflected the economics of the mass market. But big government also helped foster big business, pre-eminently through defence orders. What turned IBM, for instance, from typewriters and punched-card machines to electronic computers in the 1950s were huge government contracts such as the SAGE air defence network and the guidance system for the B-52 bomber. In the words of its president, Thomas J. Watson, Jr.: 'It was the Cold War that helped IBM make itself the king of the computer business.'[47] To take another example, the development of the American West would have been impossible but for sustained intervention and subsidies from the Federal Government. Encouraged by generous land grants in the nineteenth century, pioneers pushed across the Plains and over the Rockies. In the twentieth century massive infrastructure projects (especially dams) made possible intensive settlement. Much of California would still be uninhabitable if Uncle Sam had not, quite literally, watered the West.[48]

In various ways, therefore, it is simplistic to imply that the world is being Americanized. Moreover, as in earlier epochs of US history, America's own identity is not fixed: the international is also still being used to define the national. In the 'unipolar' era of the 1990s, some pundits discerned new threats to replace that of Soviet-directed communism. Near the top of the list was a supposed monolith called militant Islam. Samuel Huntington enlarged this anxiety into a general argument that 'the fault lines between civilizations will be the battlelines of the future'.[49] On closer examination, however, many of the most ruinous recent wars have occurred *within* rather than *between* his putative civilizations (Vietnam–Cambodia, Iran–Iraq or Hutu–Tutsi). As John Gray has remarked, Huntington's vision 'tells us more about contemporary American anxieties than it does about the late modern world'.[50]

The real threat for Huntington appears to be 'the divisive siren calls of multiculturalism' at home, which challenge the country's survival as 'a coherent society'. Multiculturalism for Huntington means 'a country not belonging to any civilization and lacking a cultural core'. Instead he insists that the United States must be re-Americanized, to save itself and the world. 'The futures of the United States and the West depend upon Americans reaffirming their commitment to Western civilization' and to 'the American Creed' of 'liberty, democracy, individualism' and associated principles.[51] The West versus the rest, America as the bastion of civilization against barbarism – this typology of bipolar absolutes should now be familiar. In the twenty-first century, as in previous eras of American history, the definitions of Self and Other will be closely intertwined.

The American Century?

What, then, should we make of Henry Luce's assertions about the American Century? As this book makes clear, Americans did not invent globalization, nor did they simply stamp the modern world in their own image. In critical respects twentieth-century American globalism represented the continuation of national integration in the nineteenth century, which in turn owed much to an earlier, European phase of globalization. In both centuries, globalization was a way to accentuate the 'nationalization' of a vast, pluralist country. Moreover, the New Left model of informal American imperialism should be tempered by closer analysis of the dialectics of resistance and of modification around the world.

But historians should be alert to change as much as to continuity. We should not relativize the 'American Century' out of existence. When all is said and done, I have argued that American-led globalization has been historically distinct. This is because of the unusual bulk and coherence of the United

States as a very large yet functionally effective polity and economy and because that mass was mobilized globally through the unprecedentedly large multiplier effect of modern technologies. The twentieth century was neither the end of history nor the beginning of globalization. But it was conspicuously American.

Notes and References

1 Henry R. Luce, 'The American Century', *Life*, 17 February 1941, pp. 61–5.
2 Benjamin R. Barber, *Jihad vs. McWorld: How Globalism and Tribalism are Reshaping the World* (New York, 1996), p. 4.
3 Francis Fukuyama, 'The End of History?', *The National Interest* (Summer 1989), pp. 3–18, quoting from pp. 3 and 4.
4 A useful guide to the literature is provided by David Held, Anthony McGrew, David Goldblatt and Jonathan Perraton, *Global Transformations* (Oxford, 1999). For my own comments, see David Reynolds, *One World Divisible: A Global History since 1945* (New York, 2000), especially pp. 650–7.
5 The title of a bestselling history of US foreign policy since 1938 by Stephen Ambrose, whose first edition appeared in 1971.
6 Jack P. Greene, *The Intellectual Construction of America: Exceptionalism and Identity from 1492 to 1800* (Chapel Hill, 1993), p. 201. On the concept, see Daniel T. Rodgers, 'Exceptionalism', in Anthony Molho and Gordon S. Wood (eds.), *Imagined Histories: American Historians Interpret Their Past* (Princeton, 1998), pp. 21–40. More generally see Ian Tyrrell, 'American Exceptionalism in an Age of International History', *American Historical Review*, 96 (1991), pp. 1031–55, and the essays in Byron E. Shafer (ed.), *Is America Different? A New Look at American Exceptionalism* (Oxford, 1991).
7 For instance, D.W. Meinig, *The Shaping of Atlantic America: A Geographical Perspective on 500 Years of History. Vol. I: Atlantic America, 1492–1800* (New Haven, 1986); Peggy Liss, *Atlantic Empires: The Network of Trade and Revolution, 1713–1826* (Baltimore, 1983); Nicholas Canny and Anthony Pagden (eds.), *Colonial Identity in the Atlantic World, 1500–1800* (Princeton, 1987).
8 Reinhold Niebuhr, 'Awkward Imperialists', *Atlantic Monthly*, 145 (May 1930), p. 670.
9 Max Beloff (ed.), *The Federalist* (2nd edn., Oxford, 1987), pp. 65–6.
10 Gordon S. Wood, *The Creation of the American Republic, 1776–1787* (New York, 1969), pp. 382–3; Georg Wilhelm Friedrich Hegel, *The Philosophy of History*, trans. J. Sibree (New York, 1956), pp. 85–6.
11 Speech of 7 October 1862, quoted in D.P. Crook, *The North, the South, and the Powers, 1861–1865* (New York, 1974), pp. 227–8, 230.
12 James M. McPherson, *Battle Cry of Freedom: The Civil War Era* (New York, 1990), pp. 4–7.
13 See Kevin O'Rourke and Jeffrey G. Williamson, *Globalization and History: The Evolution of a Nineteenth-Century Atlantic World Economy* (Cambridge, Mass., 1999).
14 Michael Kammen, *People of Paradox: An Inquiry Concerning the Origins of American Civilization* (New York, 1973), p. 4.
15 See the argument of David Campbell, *Writing Security: United States Foreign Policy and the Politics of Identity* (Manchester, 1992).

16 William Appleman Williams, *The Tragedy of American Diplomacy* (2nd edn., New York, 1962), p. 21.

17 Jean-Pierre Bardou *et al.*, *The Automobile Revolution: The Impact of an Industry*, trans. James M. Laux (Chapel Hill, 1982), p. 112.

18 As noted by Jeffrey G. Williamson, 'Globalization, Convergence, and History', *Journal of Economic History*, 56 (1996), pp. 277–306.

19 William E. Leuchtenburg, *Franklin D. Roosevelt and the New Deal, 1932–1940* (New York, 1963), p. 28.

20 For what follows see David Reynolds, *From Munich to Pearl Harbor: Roosevelt's America and the Origins of the Second World War* (Chicago, 2001).

21 Quoted in Thomas G. Paterson, *On Every Front: The Making and Unmaking of the Cold War* (2nd edn., New York, 1992), p. 100.

22 Quotations from NSC-68, 14 April 1950, in Thomas H. Etzold and John Lewis Gaddis (eds.), *Containment: Documents on American Policy and Strategy, 1945–1950* (New York, 1978), respectively pp. 390, 385, 387.

23 Wm. Roger Louis and Ronald Robinson, 'The Imperialism of Decolonization', *Journal of Imperial and Commonwealth History*, 22 (1994), pp. 462–511.

24 Quoted in William Stivers, 'Eisenhower and the Middle East', in Richard A. Melanson and David Meyers (eds.), *Reevaluating Eisenhower: American Foreign Policy in the Fifties* (Urbana, Ill., 1989), p. 203.

25 Campbell, *Writing Security*, p. 172.

26 In this particular case, it would seem, globalization strengthened rather than weakened a nation state.

27 See M.D. Biddiss, *The Age of the Masses: Ideas and Society in Europe since 1870* (Hassocks, Sussex, 1977), p. 14.

28 John Colville, *The Fringes of Power: Downing Street Diaries, 1939–1955* (London, 1985), p. 676.

29 Quoted in David Reynolds, 'Power and Superpower: The Impact of Two World Wars on America's International Role', in Warren F. Kimball (ed.), *America: Unbound: World War II and the Making of a Superpower* (New York, 1992), p. 24.

30 William T.R. Fox, *The Superpowers* (New York, 1944), p. 21.

31 See Reynolds, *One World Divisible*, p. 159.

32 David Crystal, *English as a Global Language* (Cambridge, 1997), pp. 4–5.

33 A theme of Tino Balio (ed.), *The American Film Industry* (Madison, Wisconsin, 1976).

34 Hans Rogger, '*Amerikanizm* and the Economic Development of Russia', *Comparative Studies in Society and History*, 23 (1981), pp. 384–5.

35 Mark Harrison, *The Economics of World War II: Six Great Powers in International Comparison* (Cambridge, 1996), pp. 39–40, 295, 297.

36 See Michael R. Beschloss, *Mayday: Eisenhower, Khrushchev and the U-2 Affair* (New York, 1986), p. 195.

37 Charles S. Maier, *Dissolution: The Crisis of Communism and the End of East Germany* (Princeton, 1997), p. 73.

38 For this argument see Reynolds, *One World Divisible*, pp. 495–519.

39 Geir Lundestad, 'Empire by Invitation? The United States and Western Europe, 1945–1952', *Journal of Peace Research*, 23 (1986), pp. 1–23.

40 Quoted in David Reynolds, 'Rethinking Anglo-American Relations', *International Affairs*, 65 (Winter 1988/9), p. 96.

41 Quotations from Richard F. Kuisel, *Seducing the French: The Dilemma of Americanization* (Berkeley, 1993), pp. 63 and 38 respectively.

42 Reinhold Wagnleitner, *Coca-Colonization and the Cold War: The Cultural Mission of the United States in Austria after the Second World War* (Chapel Hill, 1994), e.g. p. 2.

43 See James L. Watson (ed.), *Golden Arches East: McDonald's in East Asia* (Stanford, 1997).

44 As argued, for instance, by Charles Hampden-Turner and Alfons Trompenaars, *The Seven Cultures of Capitalism* (New York, 1993).

45 Michael A. Cusamano, *The Japanese Automobile Industry: Technology and Management at Nissan and Toyota* (Cambridge, Mass., 1985). See, more generally, Reynolds, *One World Divisible*, ch. 12.

46 Alfred D. Chandler, Jr., *The Visible Hand: The Managerial Revolution in American Business* (Cambridge, Mass., 1977), pp. 482–3.

47 Thomas J. Watson, Jr., and Richard Petre, *Father and Son, & Co.: My Life at IBM and Beyond* (London, 1990), p. 230.

48 See Clyde Milner II, Carol A. O'Connor and Martha A. Sandweiss (eds.), *The Oxford History of the American West* (New York, 1994), especially pp. 452–60, 482–97.

49 Samuel P. Huntington, 'The Clash of Civilizations?' *Foreign Affairs*, 72/3 (Summer 1993), p. 22.

50 John Gray, 'Global Utopias and Clashing Civilizations: Misunderstanding the Present', *International Affairs*, 74 (1998), p. 157.

51 Samuel P. Huntington, *The Clash of Civilizations and the Remaking of World Order* (New York, 1996), pp. 305–7.

Notes on Contributors

Tony Ballantyne was a research student at Wolfson College, Cambridge, and is currently Assistant Professor of Transnational/International History at the University of Illinois, Urbana-Champaign. His research focuses upon cultural and intellectual networks in the British empire in the long nineteenth century and he has published on the religion, race and language on the South Asian and New Zealand frontiers.

C.A. Bayly is Vere Harmsworth Professor of Imperial and Naval History at the University of Cambridge and a Fellow of St. Catharine's College. He has published widely on Indian history, most recently *Empire and Information* (1997), and also on broader issues of imperial history, for example, *Imperial Meridian* (1989).

Amira K. Bennison is a Lecturer in Middle Eastern and Islamic Studies in the Faculty of Oriental Studies at the University of Cambridge. She specializes in the history of the Middle East and north Africa from 1750 and has published several articles on nineteenth-century Moroccan political culture. She is the author of a forthcoming book, *Jihad and its Interpretations in Pre-Colonial Morocco*.

Dr Richard Drayton is University Lecturer in Imperial and extra-European History at Cambridge and Fellow and Director of Studies in History at Corpus Christi College. He is the author of *Nature's Government: Science, Imperial Britain, and the 'Improvement' of the World* (2000).

Dr T.N. Harper is University Lecturer in History at Cambridge University and Fellow and Director of Studies in History at Magdalene College. He is the author of *The End of Empire and the Making of Malaya* (1999).

John Lonsdale is Reader in African History at the University of Cambridge and a Fellow of Trinity College. He was President of the African Studies

Association of the United Kingdom from 1999 to 2001. He is co-author of *Unhappy Valley: Conflict in Kenya and Africa* (1999).

David Reynolds is Reader in International History at the University of Cambridge and a Fellow of Christ's College. He has also held visiting appointments at Harvard University and Nihon University, Tokyo. He is the author or editor of eight books, the most recent of which are *One World Divisible: A Global History since 1945* (2000) and *From Munich to Pearl Harbor: Roosevelt's America and the Origins of the Second World War* (2001).

Hans van de Ven is University Lecturer in Modern Chinese History at Cambridge University and a Fellow of St. Catharine's College. He has published *From Friend to Comrade* (1991), on the early history of the Chinese Communist Party, and edited a volume of essays, *Warfare in Chinese History* (2000), on military history. He is currently completing a study of the Nationalist military of Chiang Kaishek during the Republican Period.

Index